nakaba suzuki presents

18

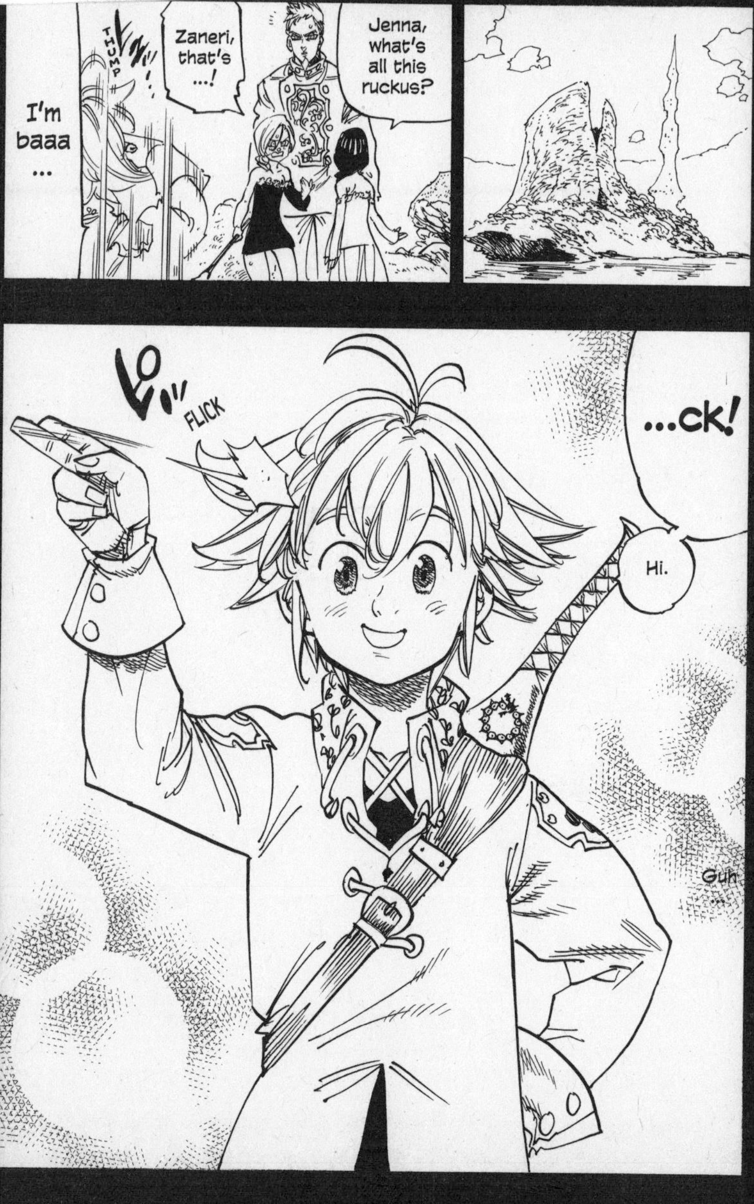
Jenna, what's all this ruckus?
Zaneri, that's ...!
THUMP
I'm baaa ...
...ck!
FLICK
Hi.
Guh ...

# CONTENTS

BOAR HAT
The Seven Deadly Sins

# Chapter 136 - Spreading Fear

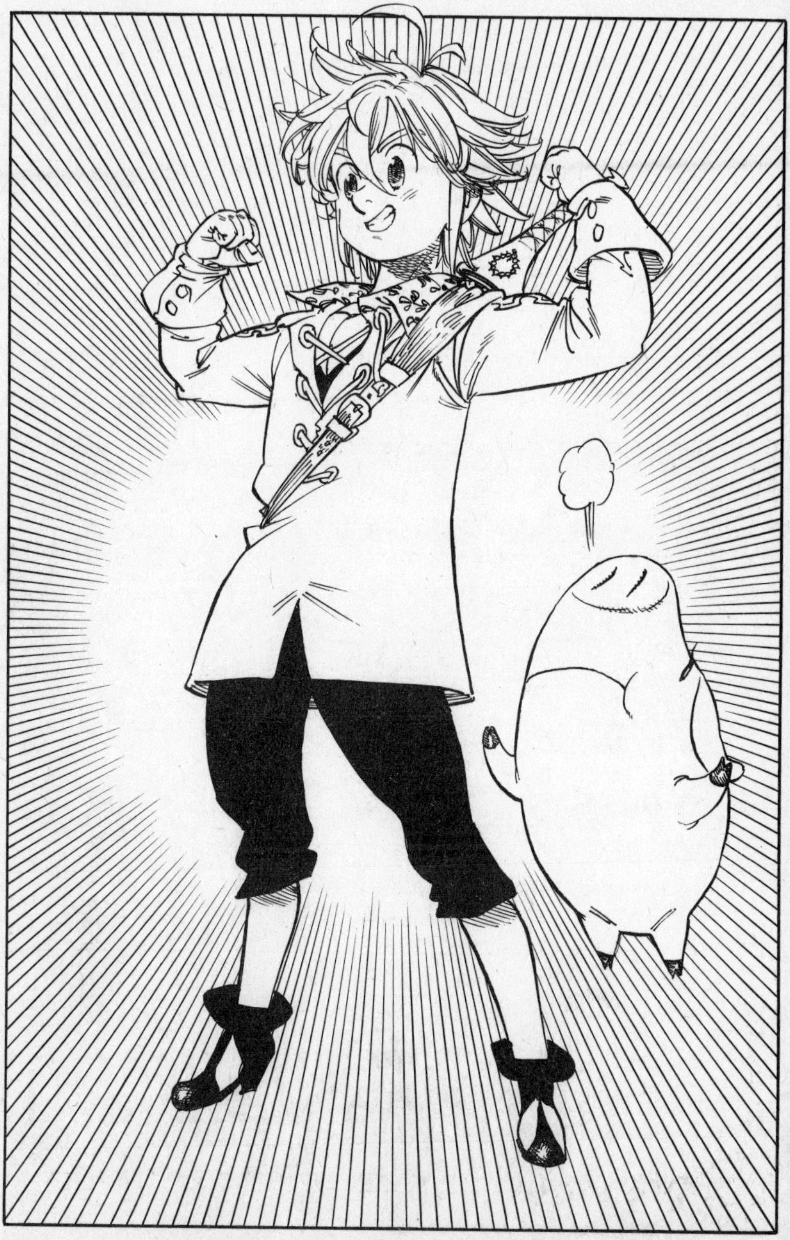

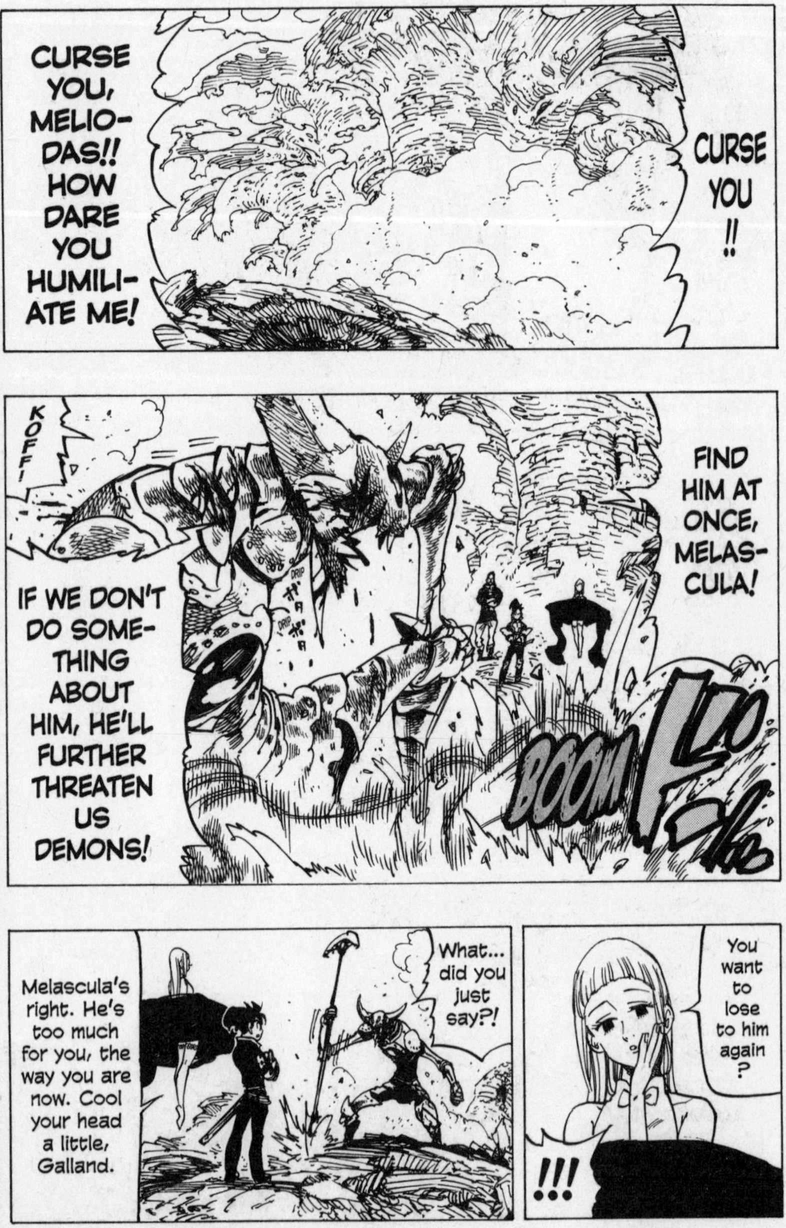
CURSE YOU !!
CURSE YOU, MELIODAS!! HOW DARE YOU HUMILIATE ME!
KOFF!
FIND HIM AT ONCE, MELASCULA!
DRIP
DRIP
IF WE DON'T DO SOMETHING ABOUT HIM, HE'LL FURTHER THREATEN US DEMONS!
BOOM
You want to lose to him again?
!!!
What... did you just say?!
Melascula's right. He's too much for you, the way you are now. Cool your head a little, Galland.

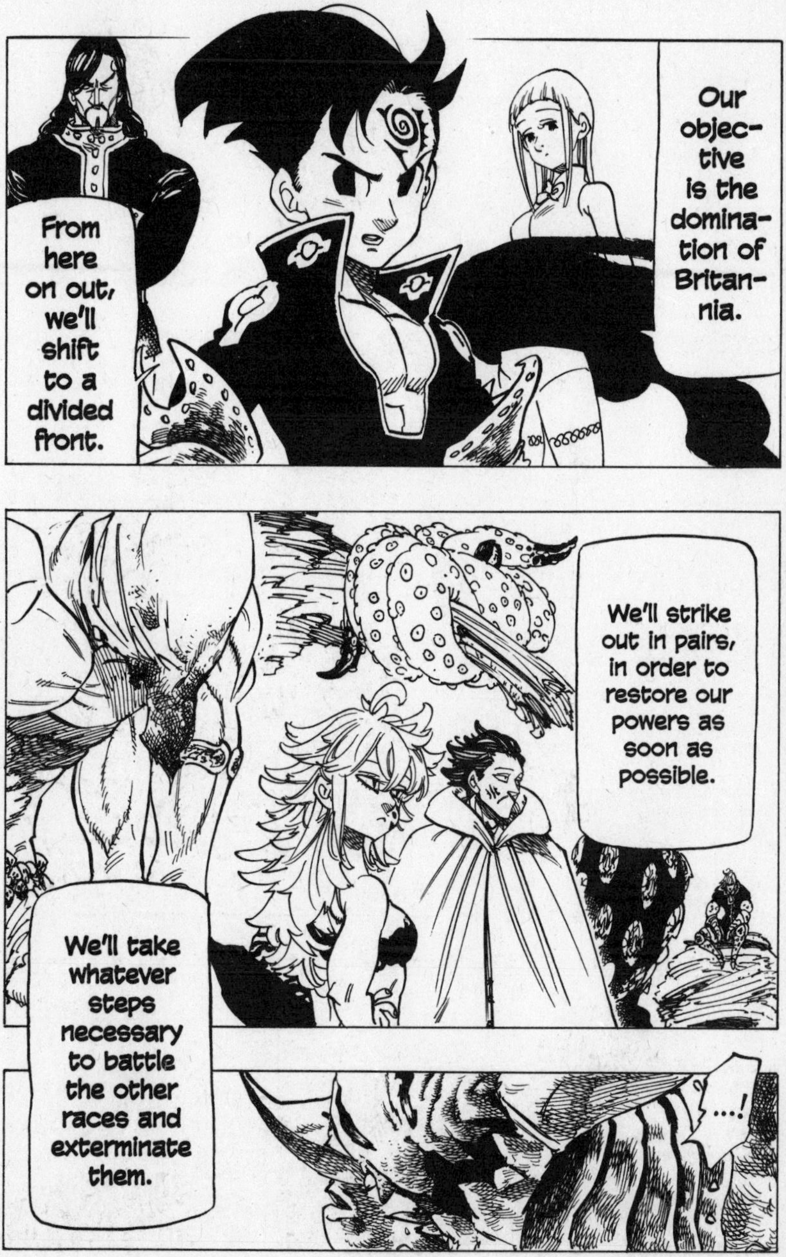
Our objective is the domination of Britannia.
From here on out, we'll shift to a divided front.
We'll strike out in pairs, in order to restore our powers as soon as possible.
We'll take whatever steps necessary to battle the other races and exterminate them.
....!

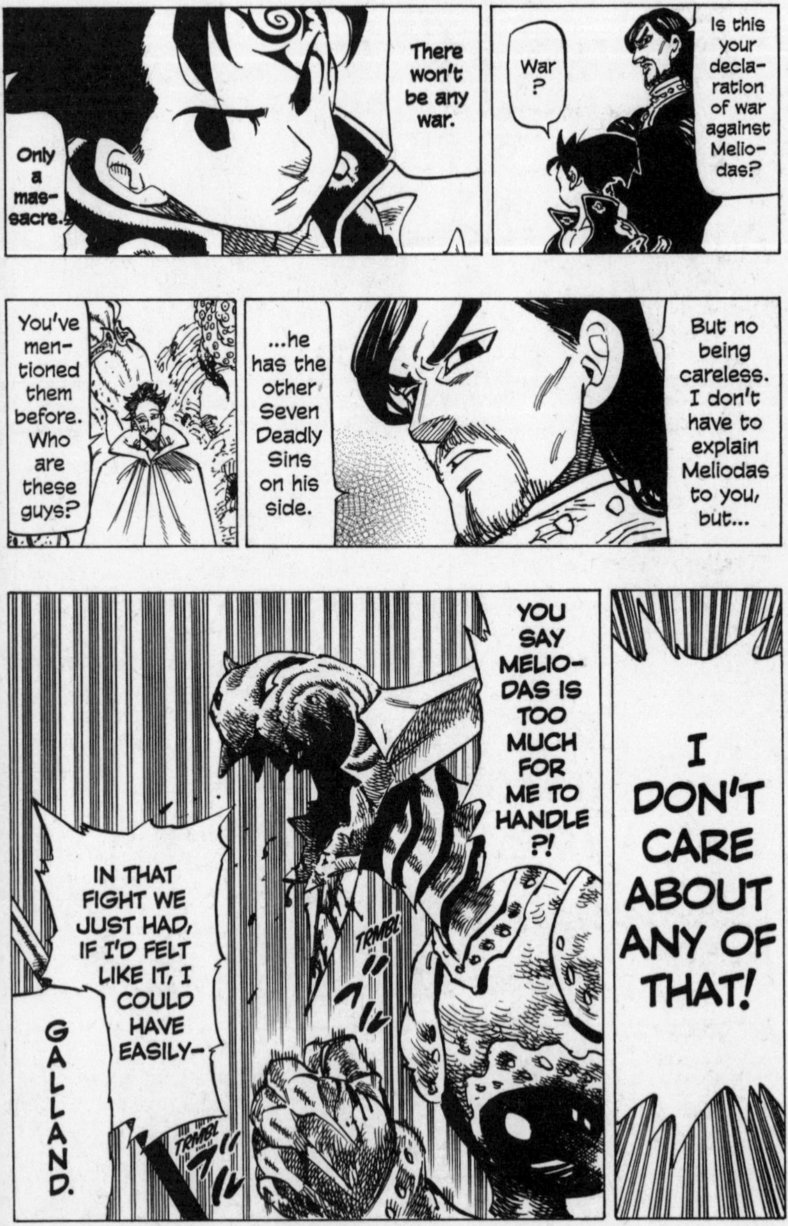
Is this your declaration of war against Meliodas?
War?
There won't be any war.
Only a massacre...
But no being careless. I don't have to explain Meliodas to you, but...
...he has the other Seven Deadly Sins on his side.
You've mentioned them before. Who are these guys?
I DON'T CARE ABOUT ANY OF THAT!
YOU SAY MELIODAS IS TOO MUCH FOR ME TO HANDLE?!
TRMBL
IN THAT FIGHT WE JUST HAD, IF I'D FELT LIKE IT, I COULD HAVE EASILY—
GALLAND.
TRMBL

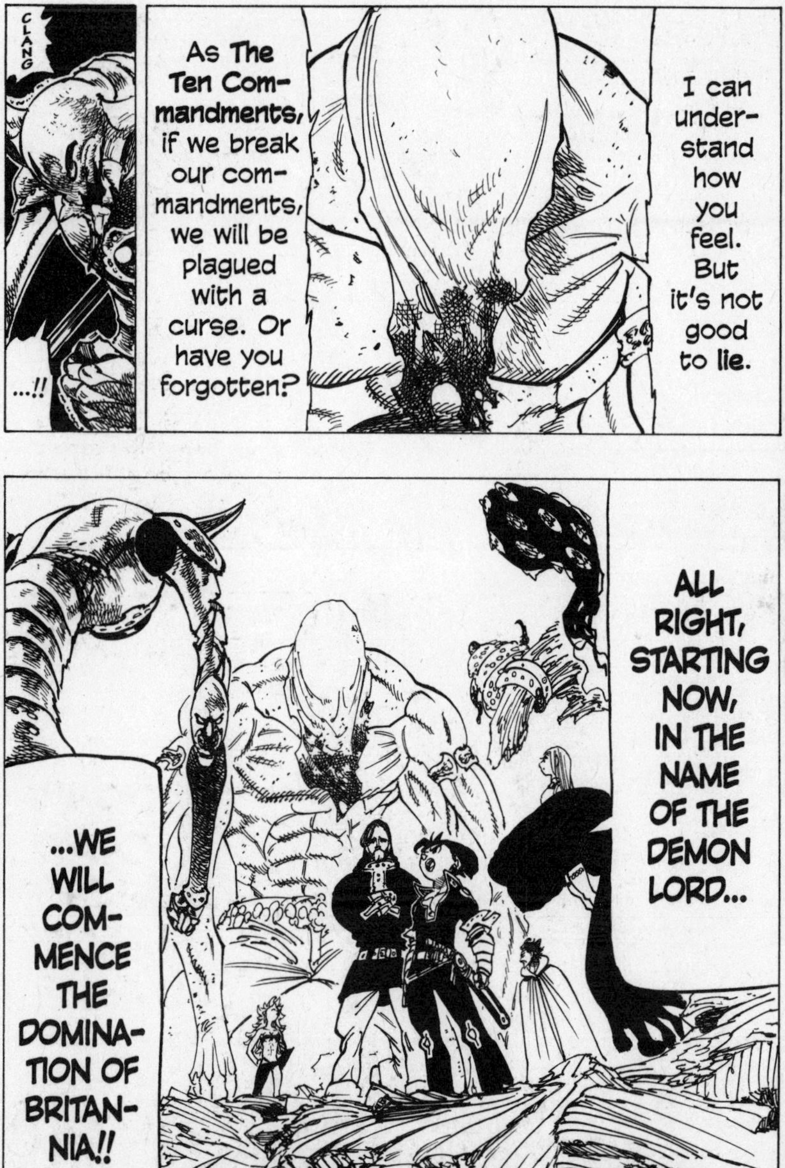

I can understand how you feel. But it's not good to lie.
As The Ten Commandments, if we break our commandments, we will be plagued with a curse. Or have you forgotten?
CLANG
...!!
ALL RIGHT, STARTING NOW, IN THE NAME OF THE DEMON LORD...
...WE WILL COMMENCE THE DOMINATION OF BRITANNIA!!

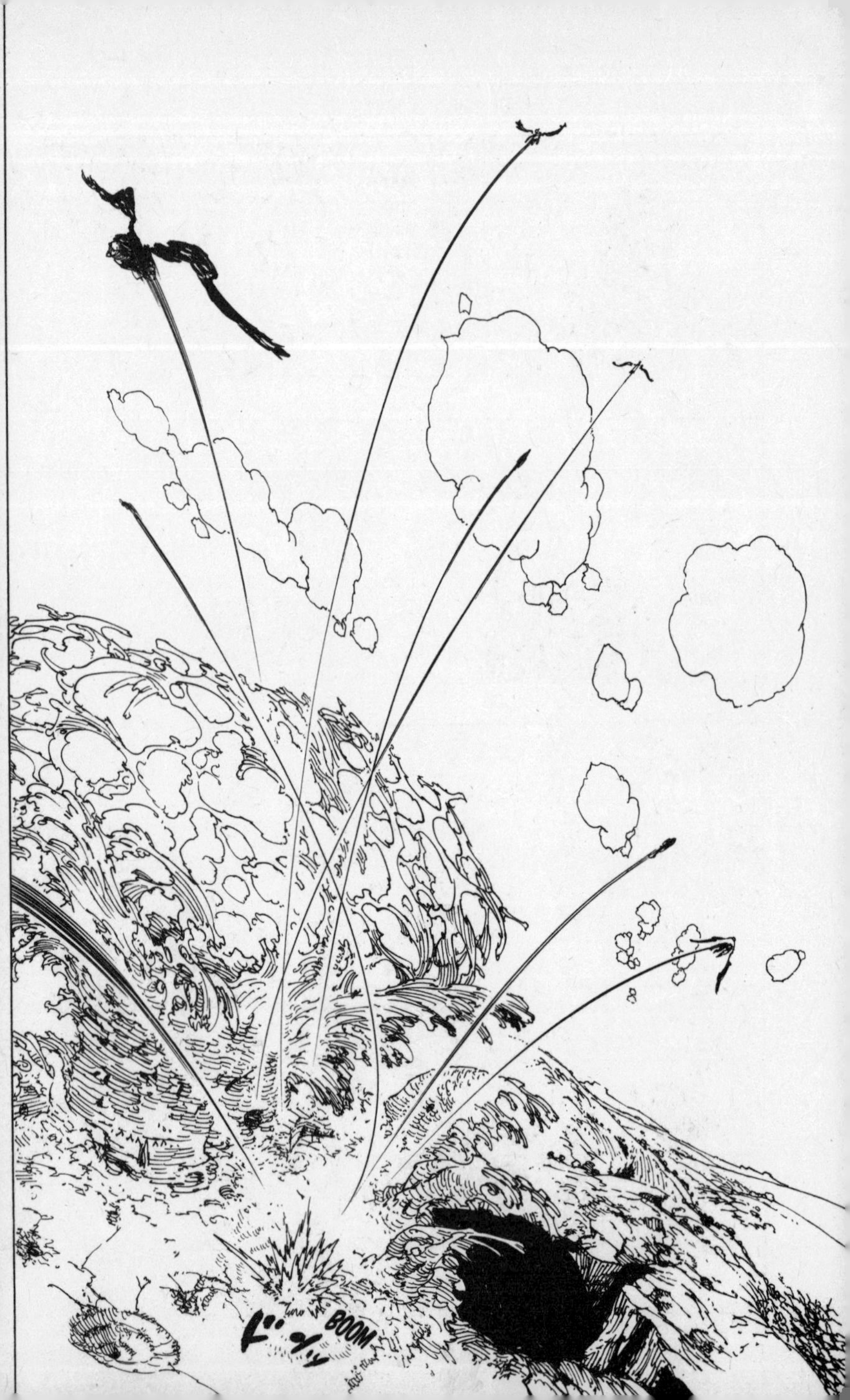
BOOM

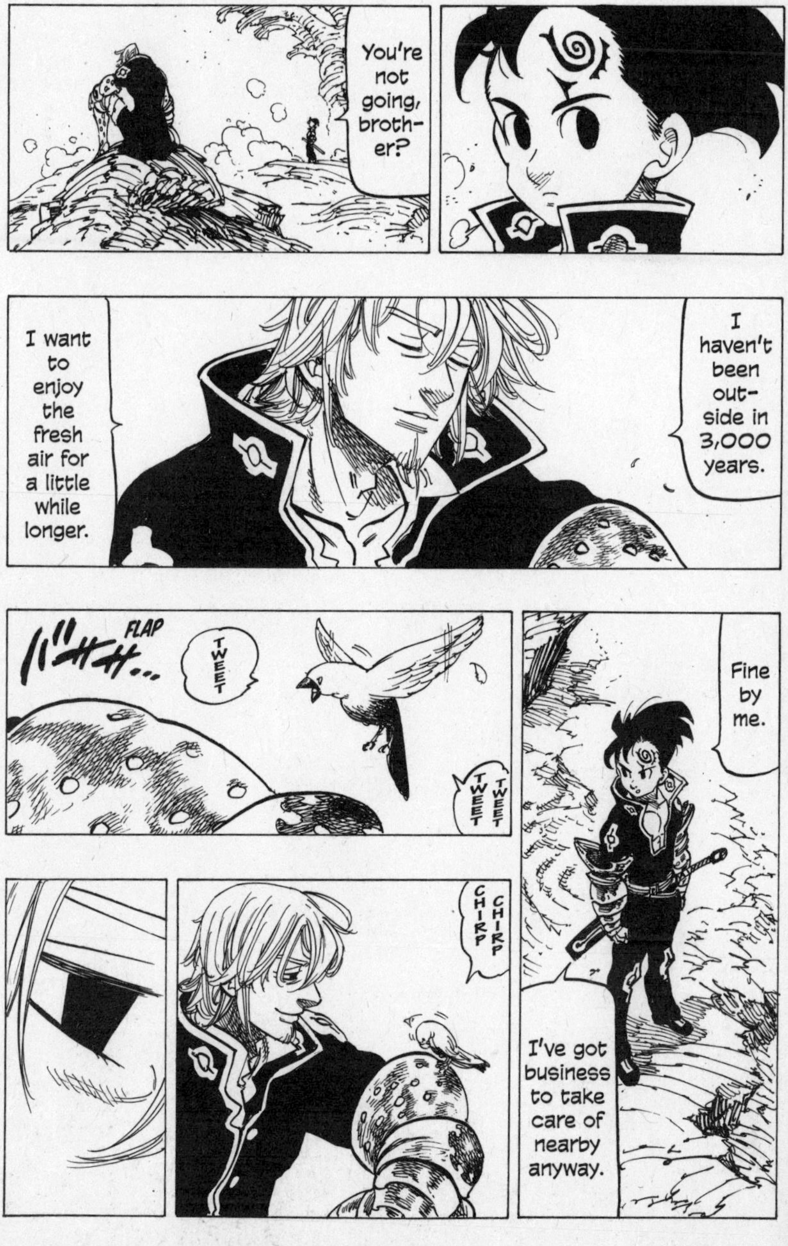
You're not going, brother?
I haven't been outside in 3,000 years.
I want to enjoy the fresh air for a little while longer.
Fine by me.
I've got business to take care of nearby anyway.
バサササ...
FLAP
TWEET
TWEET TWEET
CHIRP CHIRP

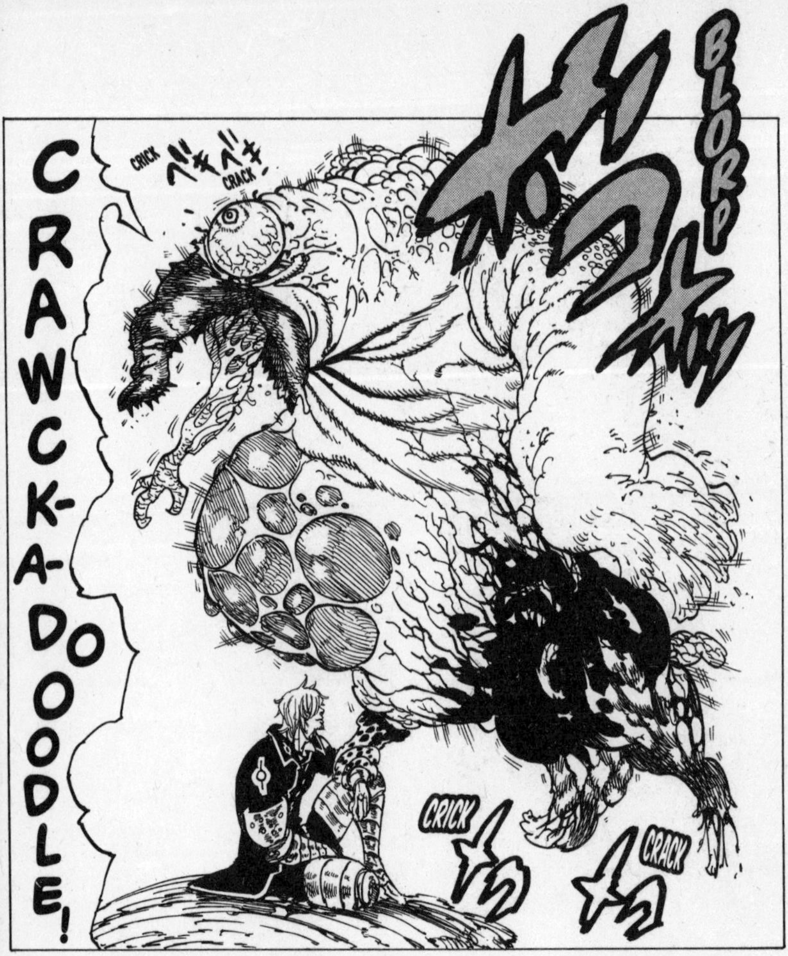
BLORP
CRICK
CRACK
CRAWCK-A-DOOODLE!
CRICK
CRACK
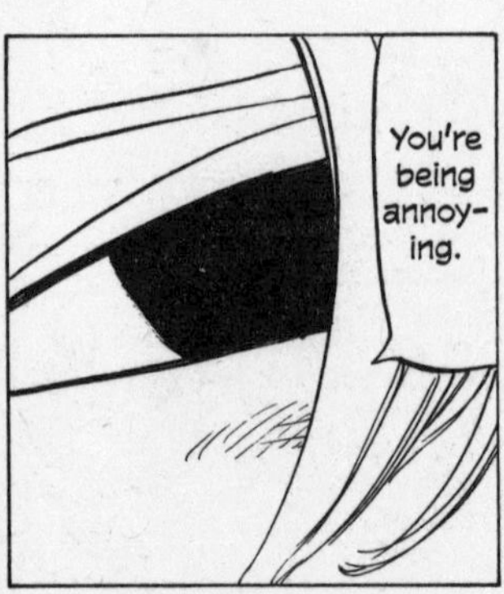
You're being annoy-ing.
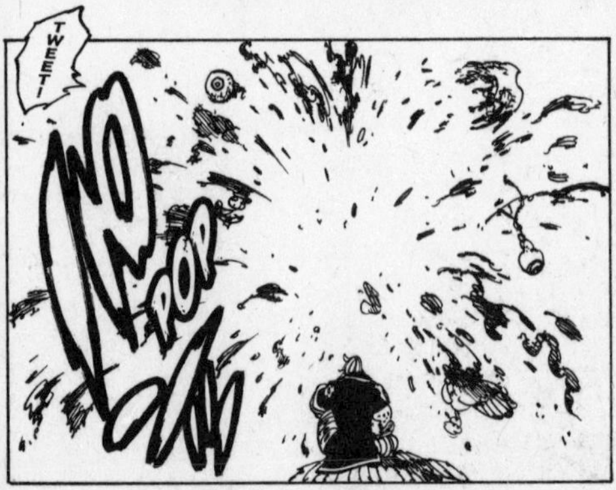
TWEET!
POP

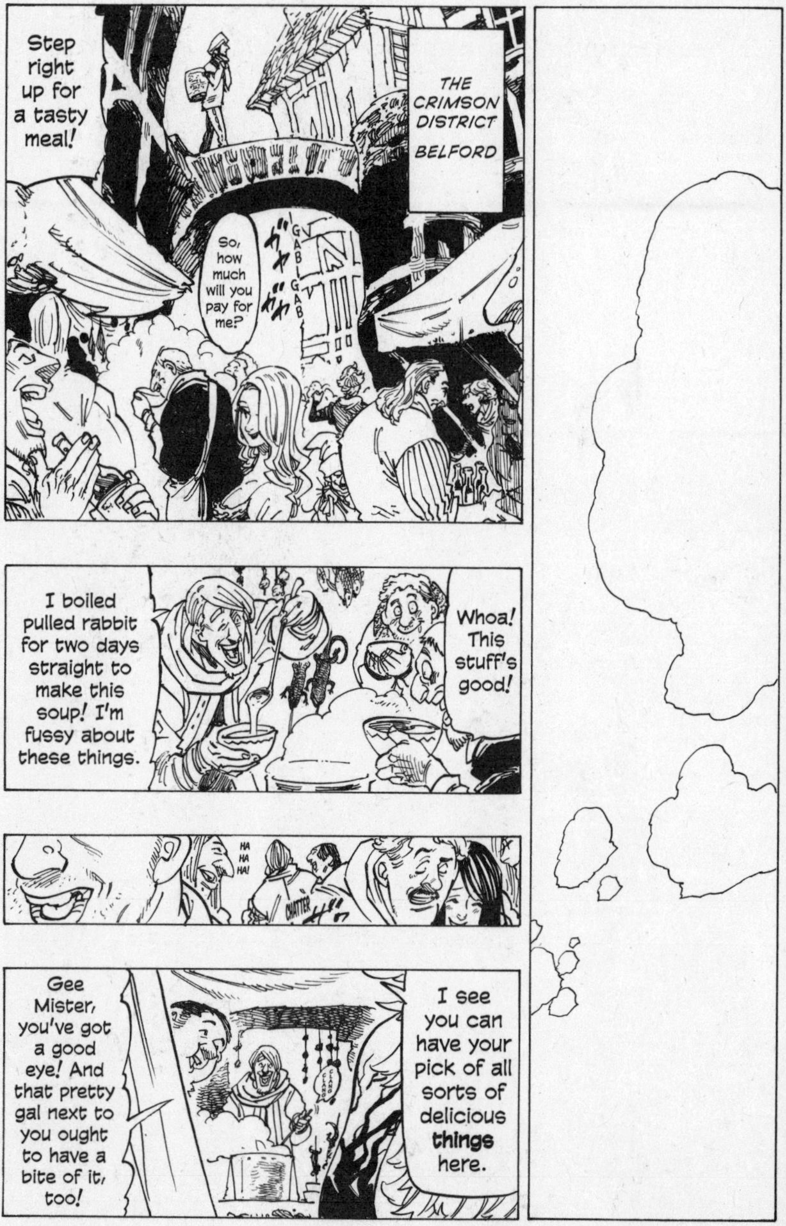
THE CRIMSON DISTRICT BELFORD
Step right up for a tasty meal!
So, how much will you pay for me?
GABL GAB
Whoa! This stuff's good!
I boiled pulled rabbit for two days straight to make this soup! I'm fussy about these things.
HA HA HA!
CHATTER
I see you can have your pick of all sorts of delicious **things** here.
Gee Mister, you've got a good eye! And that pretty gal next to you ought to have a bite of it, too!

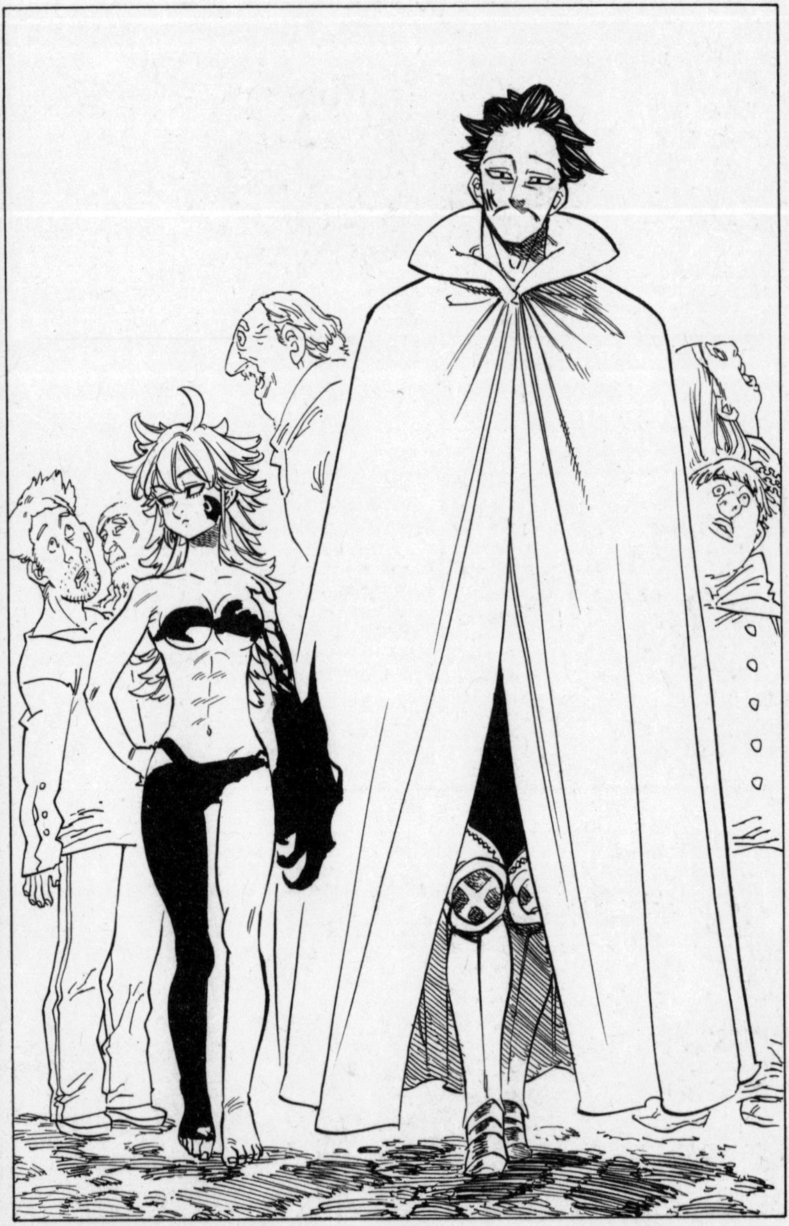

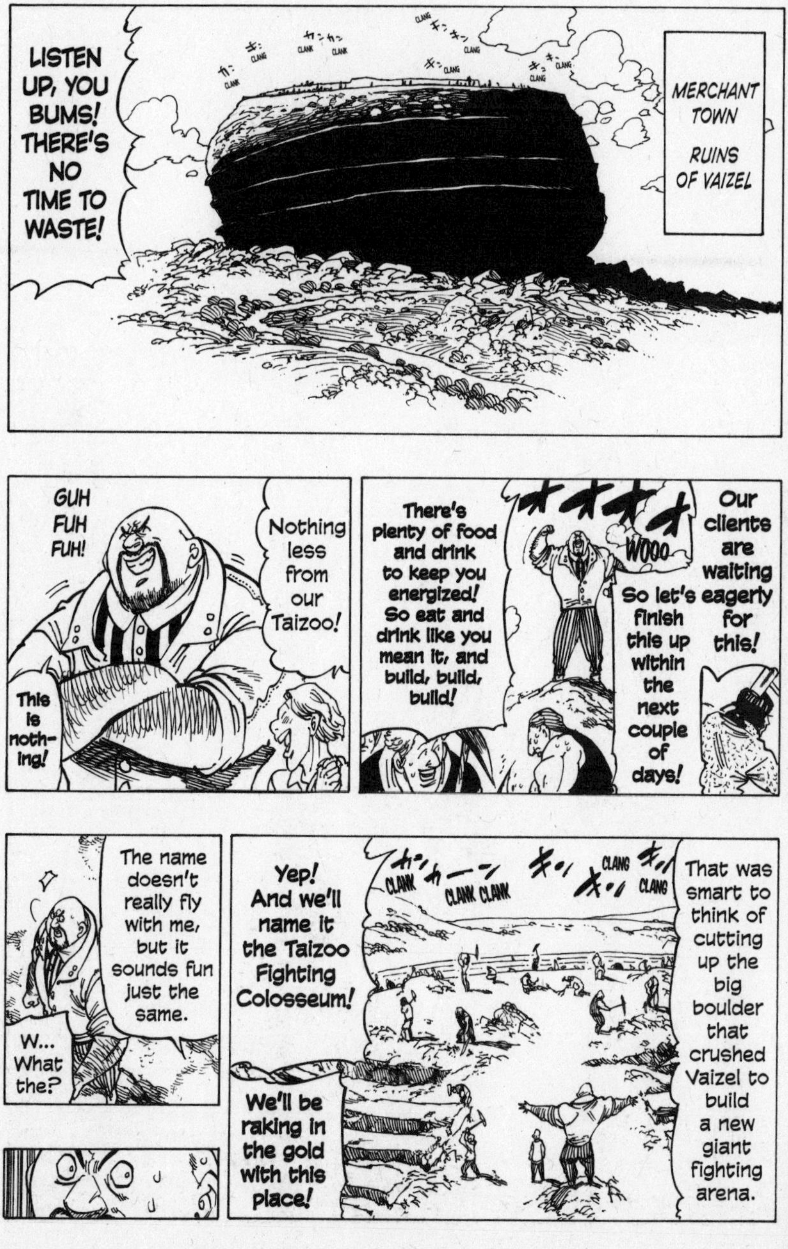
MERCHANT TOWN
RUINS OF VAIZEL
CLANG
CLANG
CLANG
CLANG
CLANK
CLANK
CLANG
CLANK
LISTEN UP, YOU BUMS! THERE'S NO TIME TO WASTE!
Our clients are waiting eagerly for this!
WOOO
So let's finish this up within the next couple of days!
There's plenty of food and drink to keep you energized! So eat and drink like you mean it, and build, build, build!
Nothing less from our Taizoo!
GUH FUH FUH!
This is nothing!
That was smart to think of cutting up the big boulder that crushed Vaizel to build a new giant fighting arena.
CLANG
CLANG
CLANK CLANK
CLANK
Yep! And we'll name it the Taizoo Fighting Colosseum!
We'll be raking in the gold with this place!
The name doesn't really fly with me, but it sounds fun just the same.
W... What the?

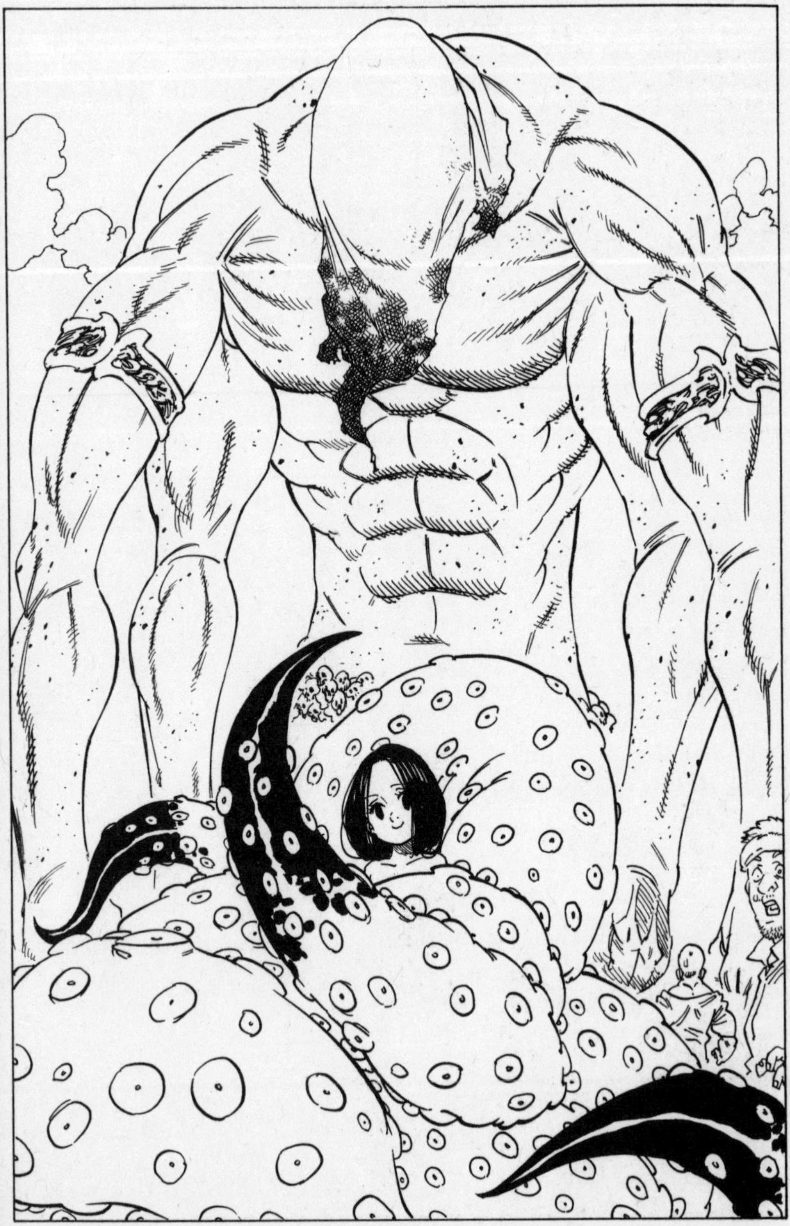

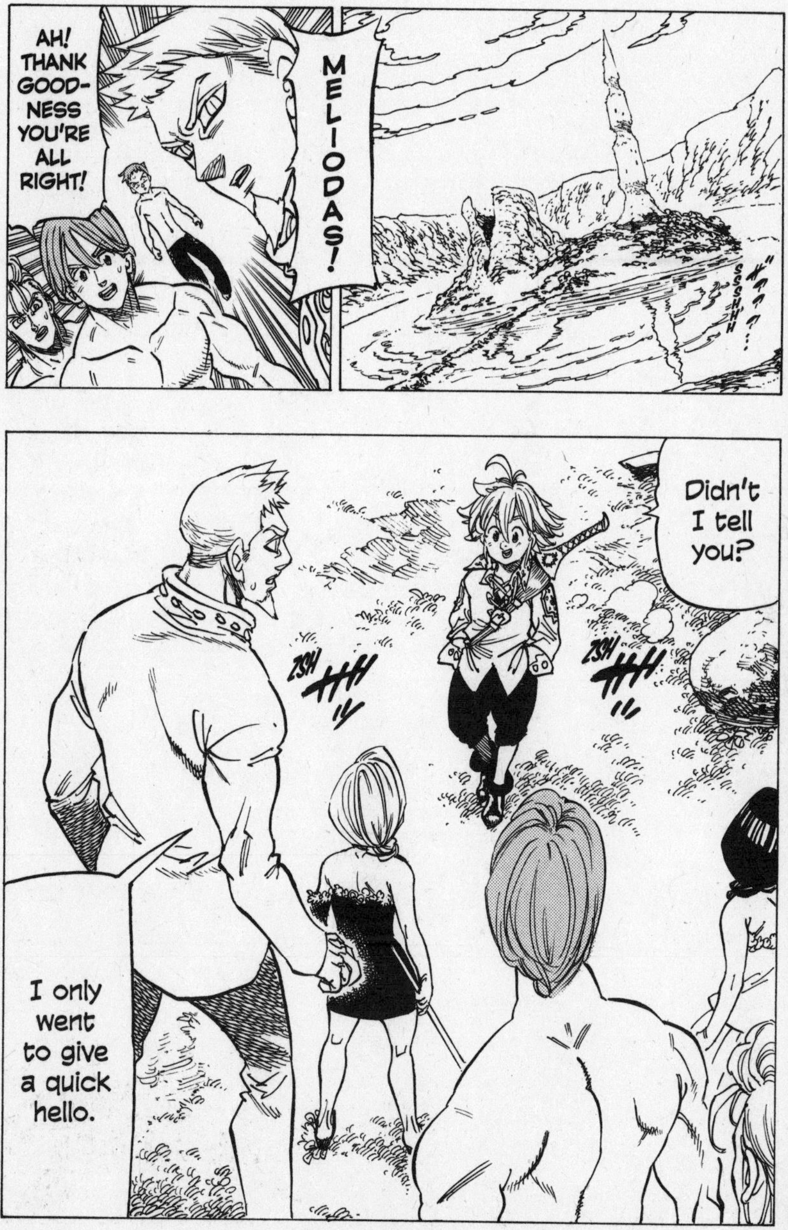
SSSHHH
MELIODAS!
AH! THANK GOODNESS YOU'RE ALL RIGHT!
Didn't I tell you?
ZSHHH
ZSHHH
I only went to give a quick hello.

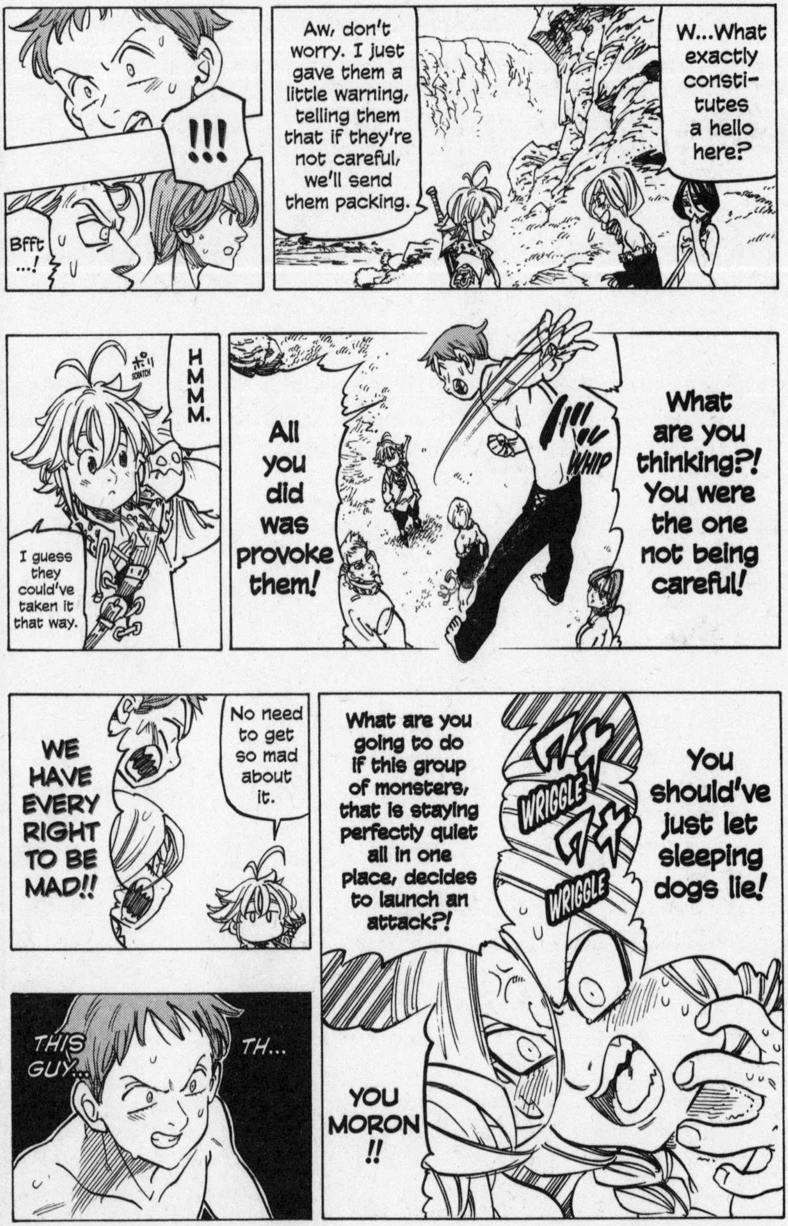
W...What exactly constitutes a hello here?
Aw, don't worry. I just gave them a little warning, telling them that if they're not careful, we'll send them packing.
!!!
Bfft ...!
What are you thinking?! You were the one not being careful!
WHIP
All you did was provoke them!
HMMM.
ポリ SCRATCH
I guess they could've taken it that way.
You should've just let sleeping dogs lie!
ウネ WRIGGLE ウネ WRIGGLE
What are you going to do if this group of monsters, that is staying perfectly quiet all in one place, decides to launch an attack?!
YOU MORON !!
No need to get so mad about it.
WE HAVE EVERY RIGHT TO BE MAD!!
TH...
THIS GUY...

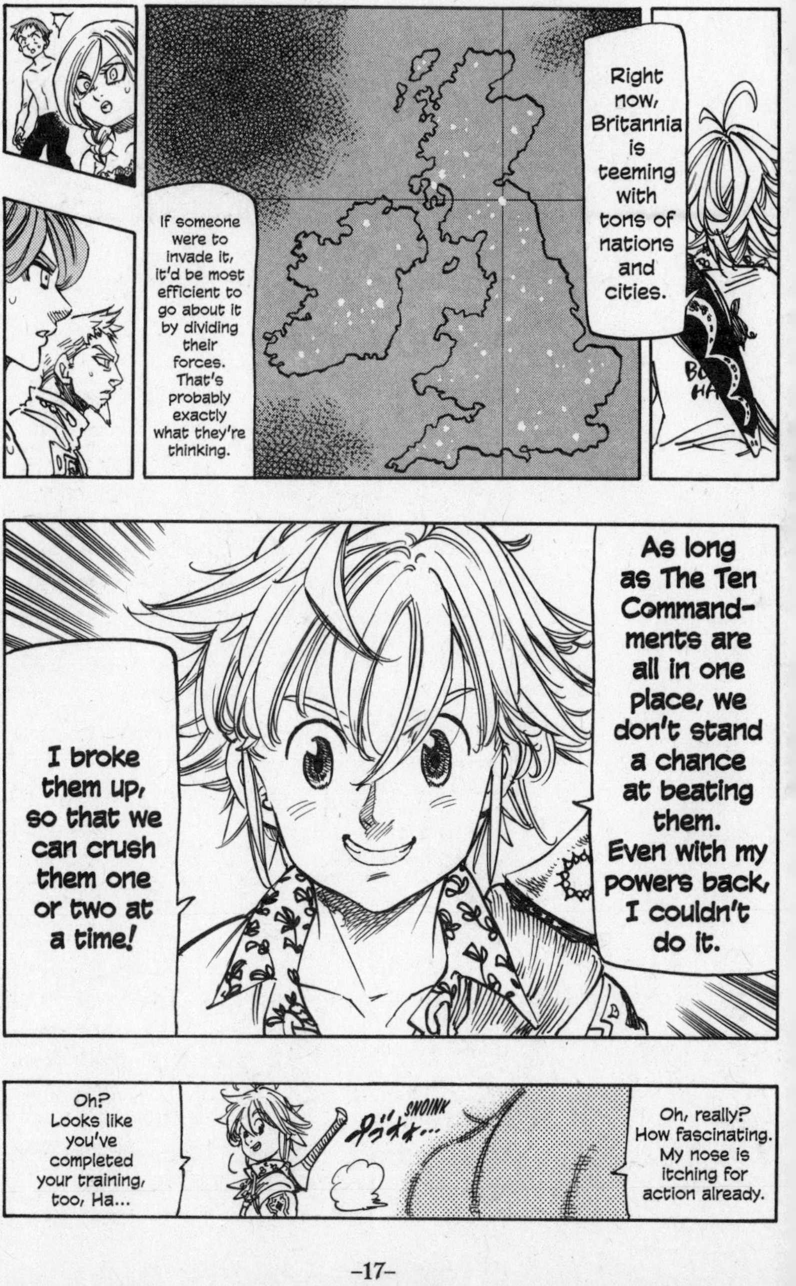
Right now, Britannia is teeming with tons of nations and cities.
If someone were to invade it, it'd be most efficient to go about it by dividing their forces. That's probably exactly what they're thinking.
As long as The Ten Command-ments are all in one place, we don't stand a chance at beating them. Even with my powers back, I couldn't do it.
I broke them up, so that we can crush them one or two at a time!
Oh, really? How fascinating. My nose is itching for action already.
SNOINK
Oh? Looks like you've completed your training, too, Ha...

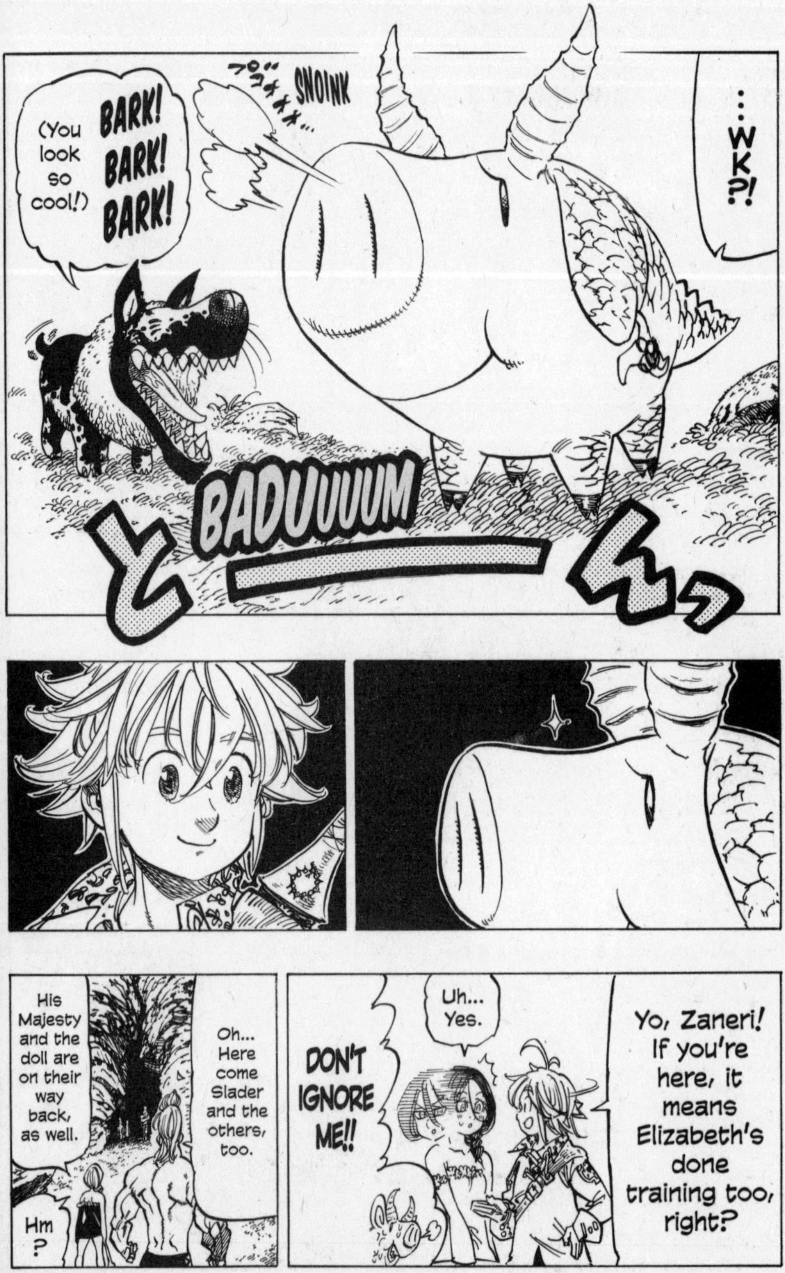
...WK?!
SNOINK
BARK! BARK! BARK!
(You look so cool!)
BADUUUUM
Yo, Zaneri! If you're here, it means Elizabeth's done training too, right?
Uh... Yes.
DON'T IGNORE ME!!
Oh... Here come Slader and the others, too.
His Majesty and the doll are on their way back, as well.
Hm?

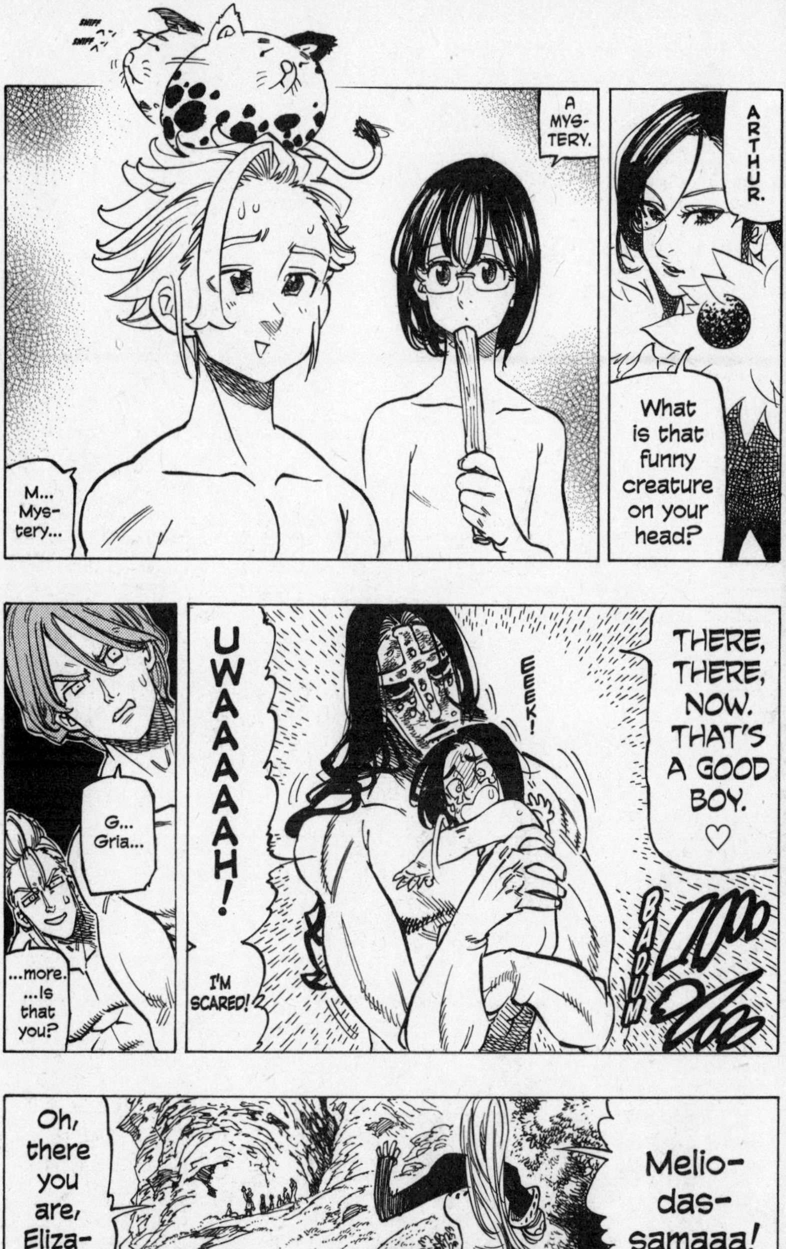
ARTHUR.
What is that funny creature on your head?
A MYSTERY.
SNIFF SNIFF
M... Mystery...
THERE, THERE, NOW. THAT'S A GOOD BOY. ♡
BADUM
EEEK!
UWAAAAAAH!
I'M SCARED!
G... Gria...
...more. ...Is that you?
Melio-das-samaaa!
Oh, there you are, Elizabeth!

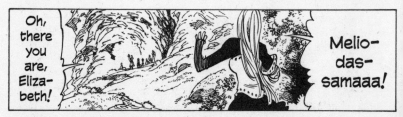

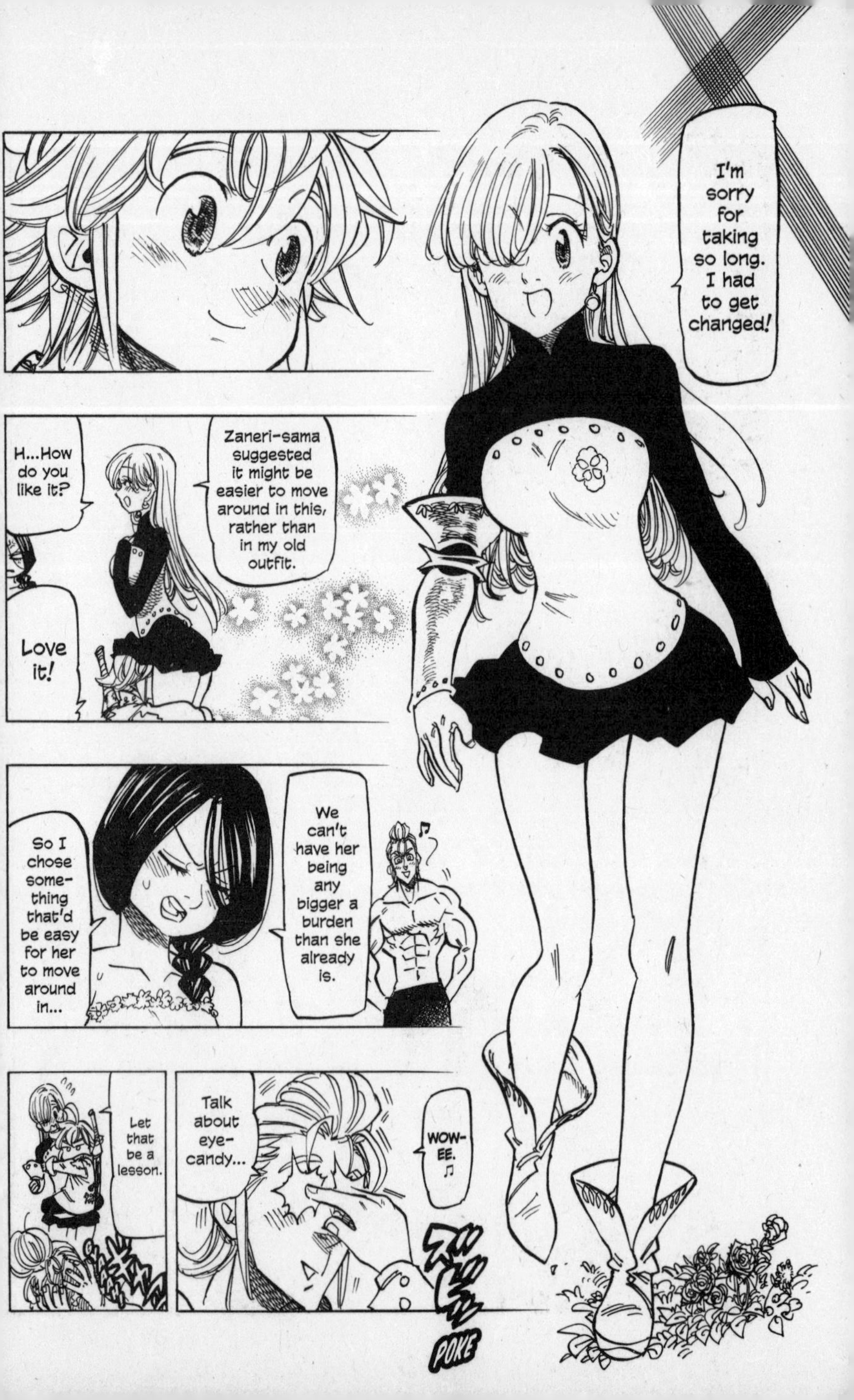
I'm sorry for taking so long. I had to get changed!
Zaneri-sama suggested it might be easier to move around in this, rather than in my old outfit.
H...How do you like it?
Love it!
We can't have her being any bigger a burden than she already is.
So I chose some-thing that'd be easy for her to move around in...
WOW-EE. ♫
Talk about eye-candy...
POKE
Let that be a lesson.

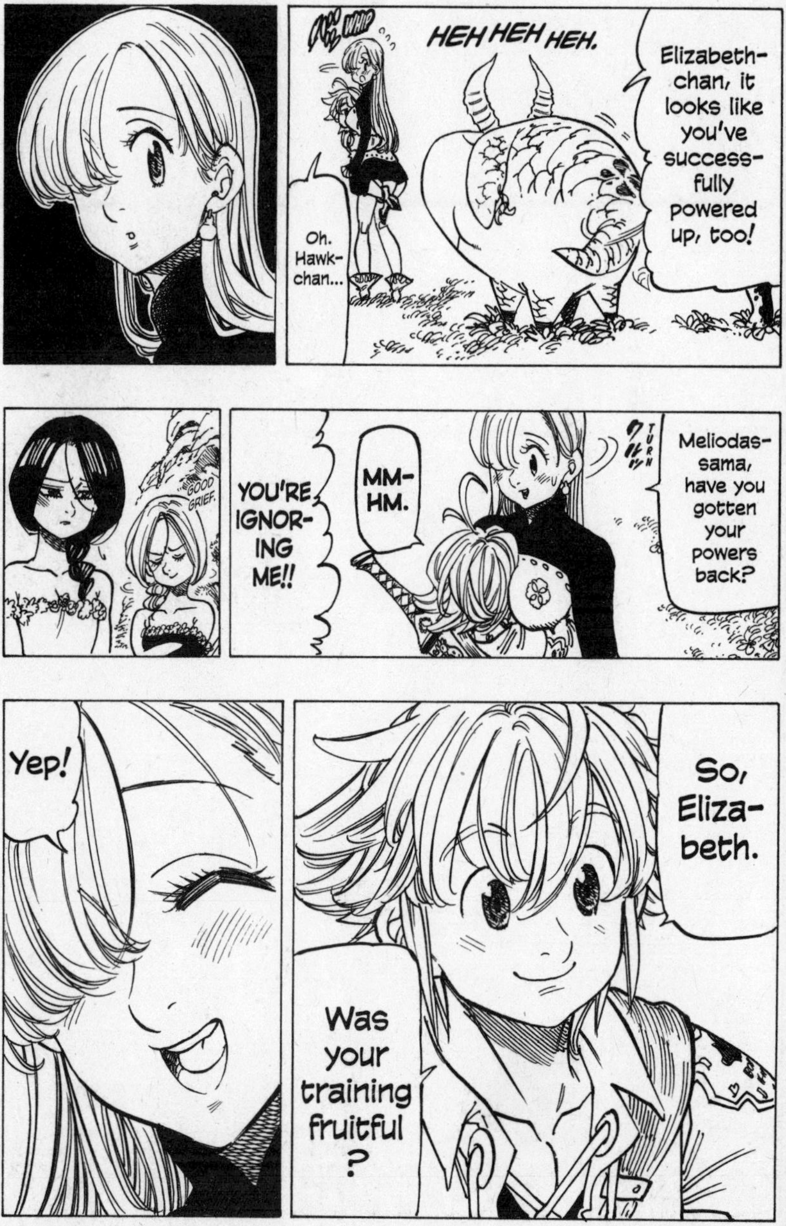
HEH HEH HEH.
Elizabeth-chan, it looks like you've successfully powered up, too!
WHIP
Oh. Hawk-chan...
TURN
Meliodas-sama, have you gotten your powers back?
MM-HM.
YOU'RE IGNORING ME!!
GOOD GRIEF.
So, Elizabeth.
Was your training fruitful?
Yep!

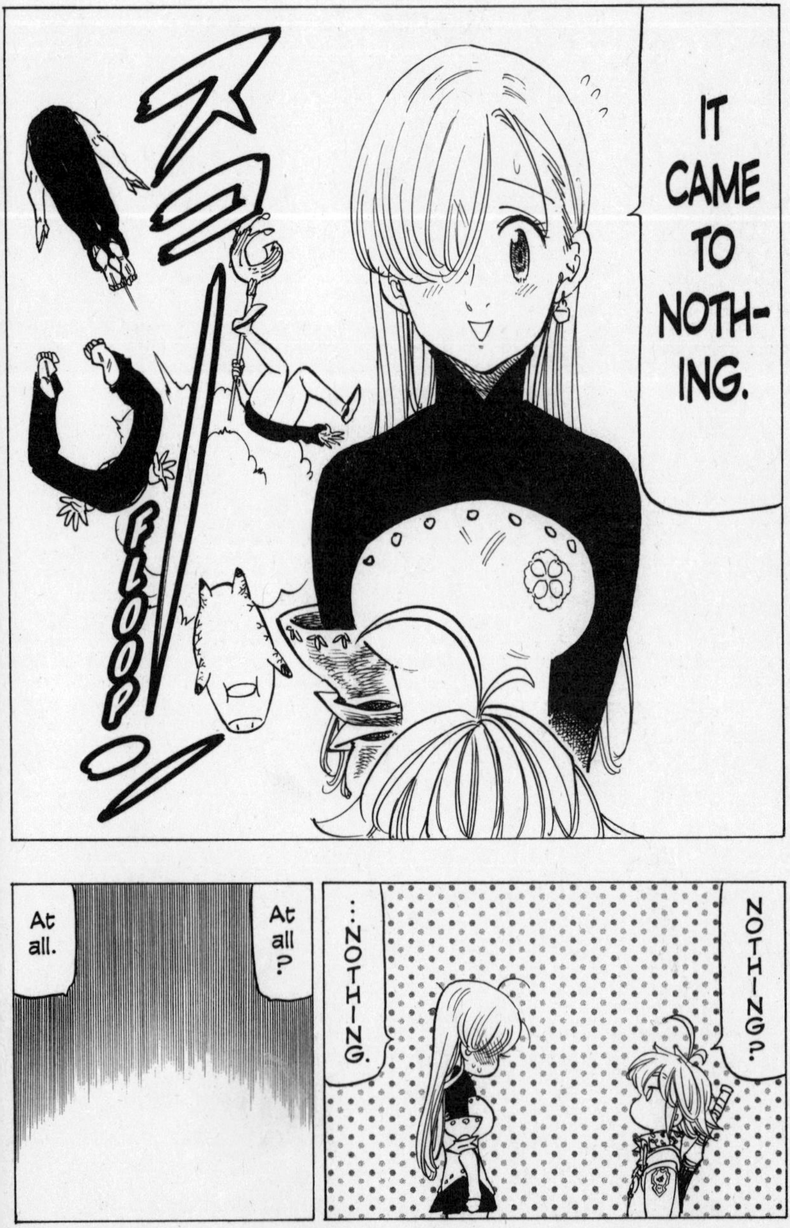
IT CAME TO NOTH-ING.
FLOOP
NOTHING?
...NOTHING.
At all?
At all.

# Chapter 137 - Between You & Me

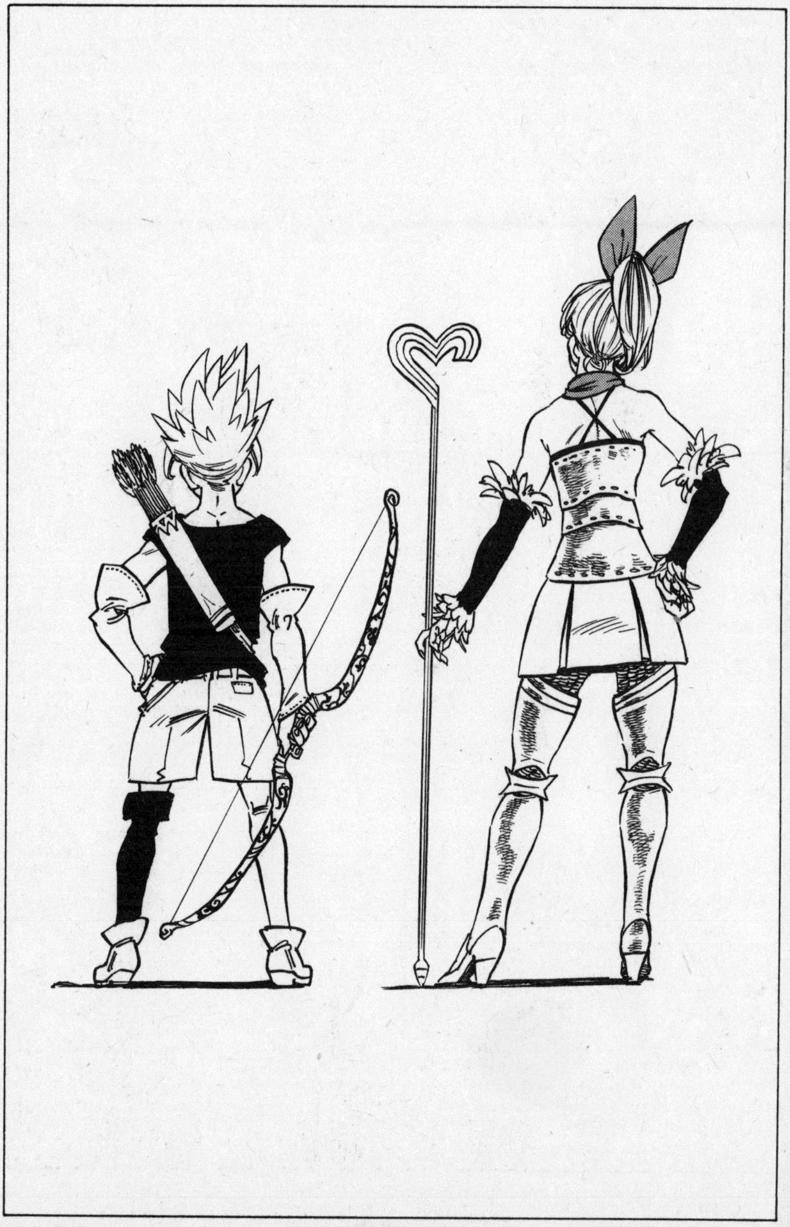

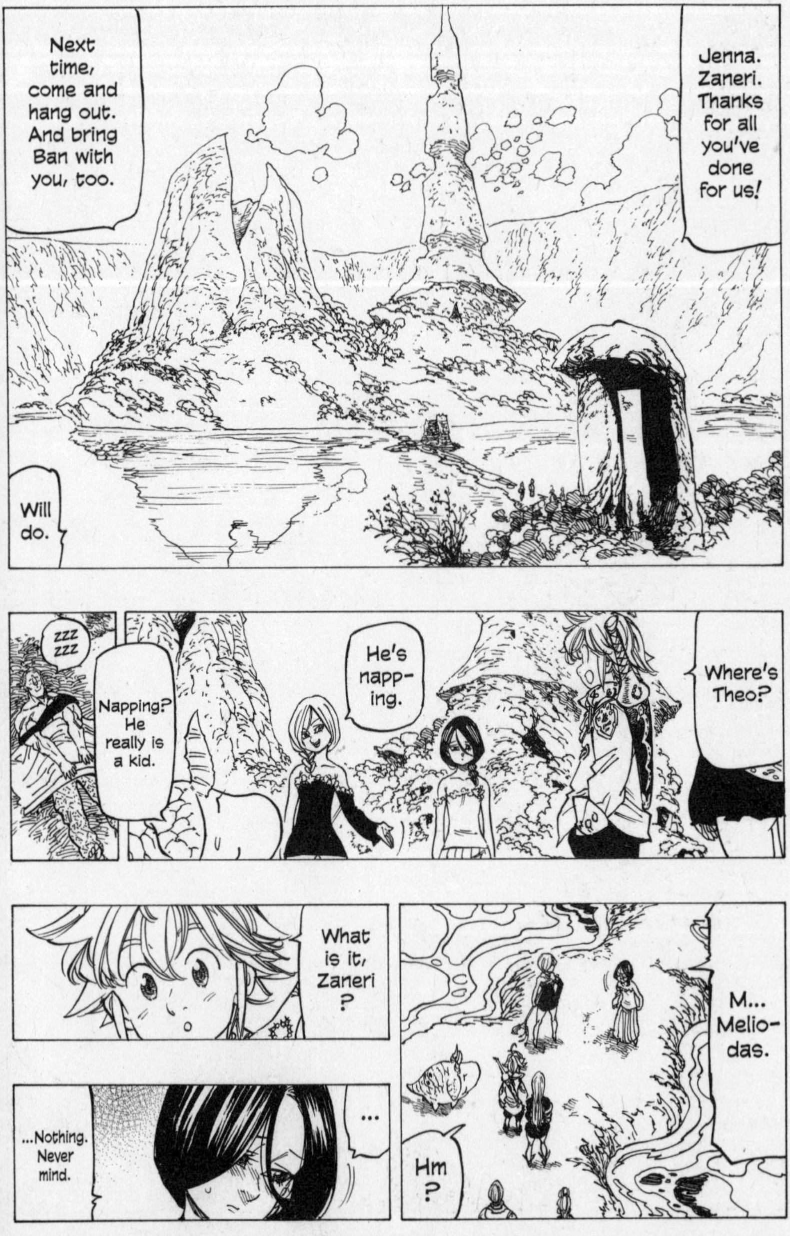
Jenna. Zaneri. Thanks for all you've done for us!
Next time, come and hang out. And bring Ban with you, too.
Will do.
Where's Theo?
He's napp-ing.
Napping? He really is a kid.
zzz zzz
M... Melio-das.
Hm?
What is it, Zaneri?
...
...Nothing. Never mind.

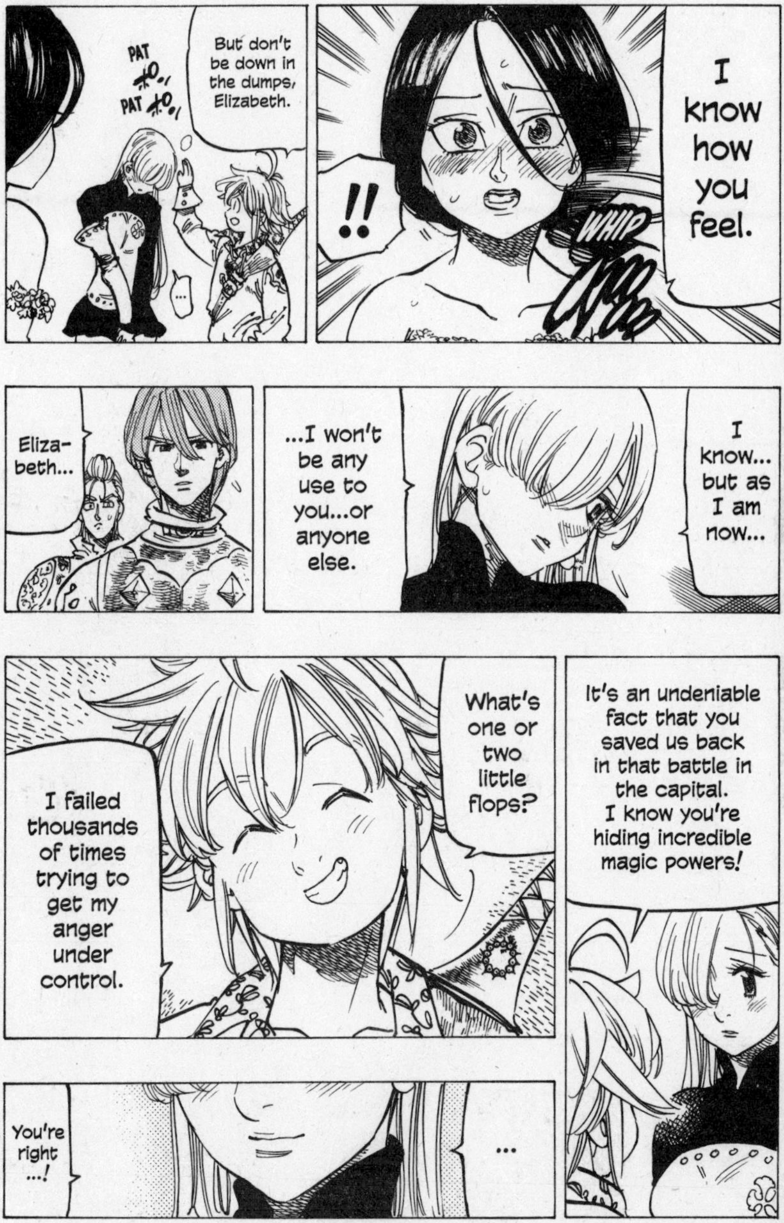

I know how you feel.
!!
WHIP
But don't be down in the dumps, Elizabeth.
PAT
PAT
...
I know... but as I am now...
...I won't be any use to you...or anyone else.
Eliza-beth...
It's an undeniable fact that you saved us back in that battle in the capital. I know you're hiding incredible magic powers!
What's one or two little flops?
I failed thousands of times trying to get my anger under control.
...
You're right ...!

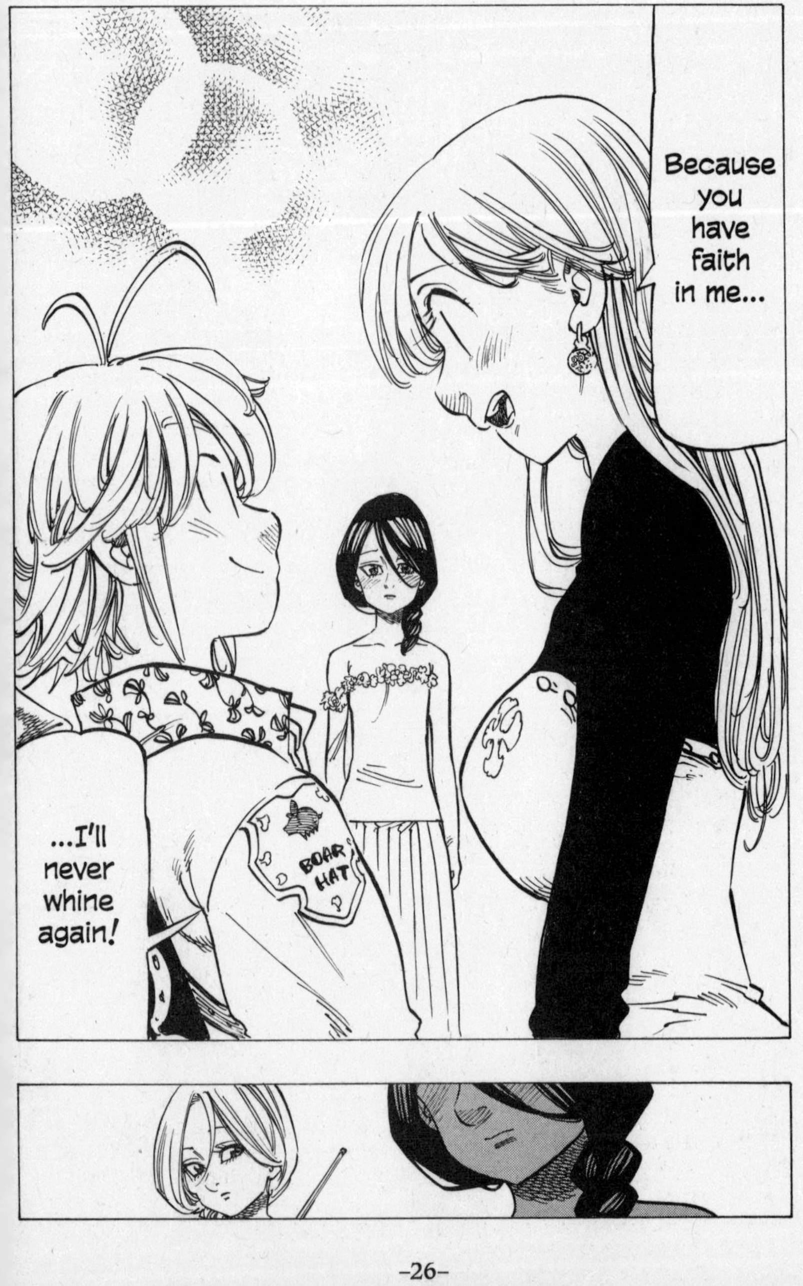
Because you have faith in me...
BOAR HAT
...I'll never whine again!

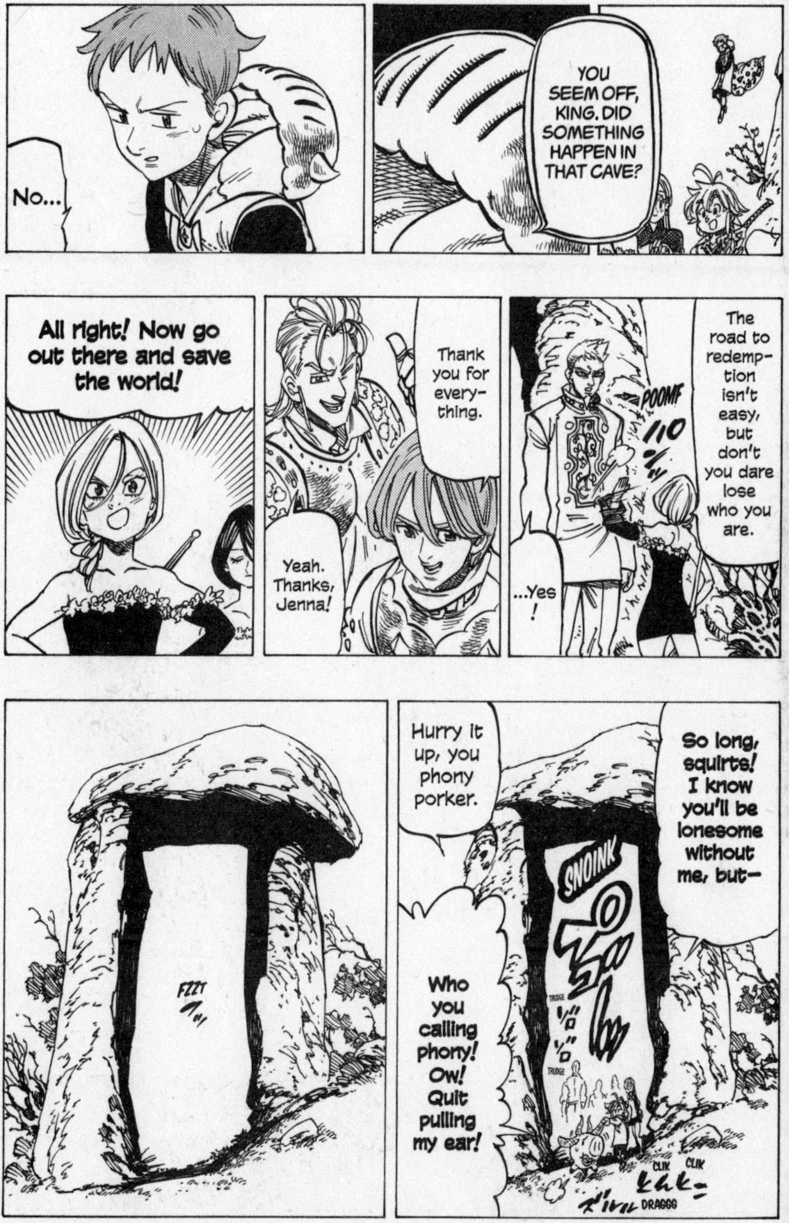
YOU SEEM OFF, KING. DID SOMETHING HAPPEN IN THAT CAVE?
No...
The road to redemption isn't easy, but don't you dare lose who you are.
POOMF
...Yes!
Thank you for everything.
Yeah. Thanks, Jenna!
All right! Now go out there and save the world!
So long, squirts! I know you'll be lonesome without me, but—
Hurry it up, you phony porker.
SNOINK
Who you calling phony! Ow! Quit pulling my ear!
TRUDGE
TRUDGE
CLIK
CLIK
DRAGGG
FZZT

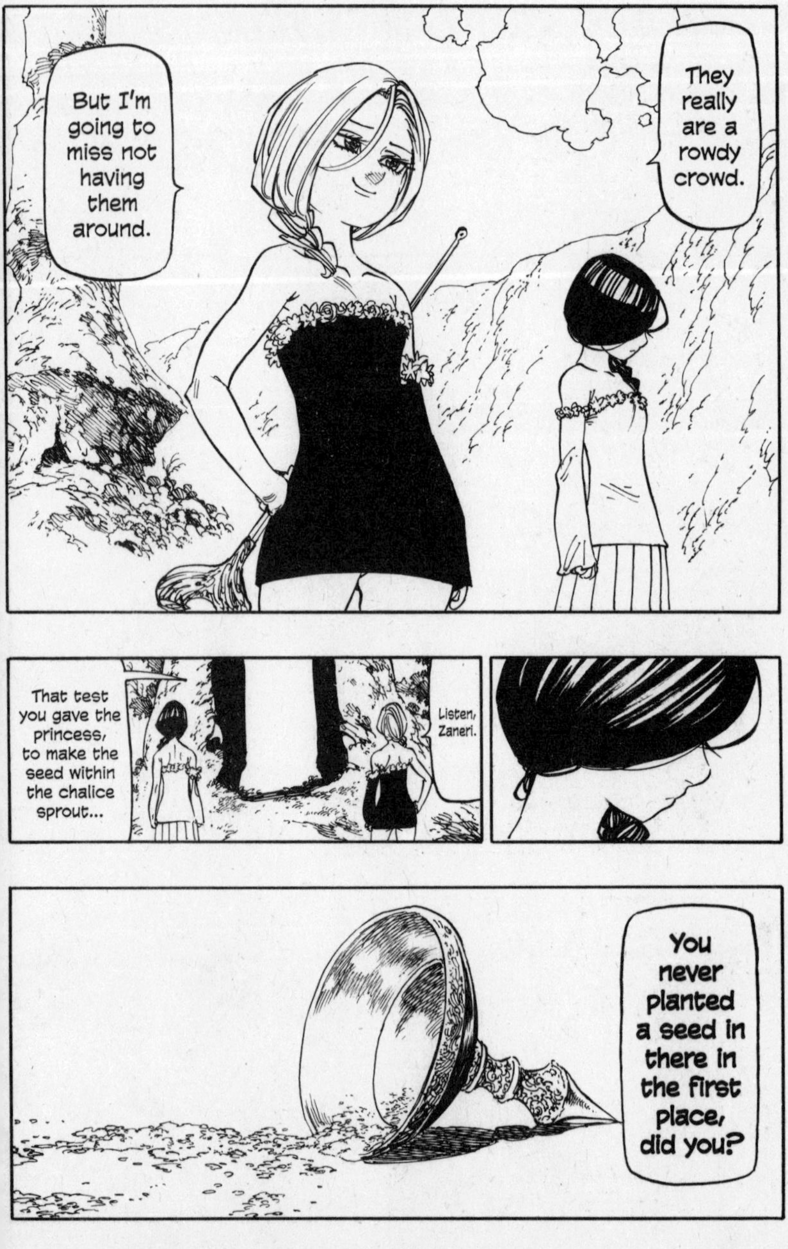
They really are a rowdy crowd.
But I'm going to miss not having them around.
Listen, Zaneri.
That test you gave the princess, to make the seed within the chalice sprout...
You never planted a seed in there in the first place, did you?

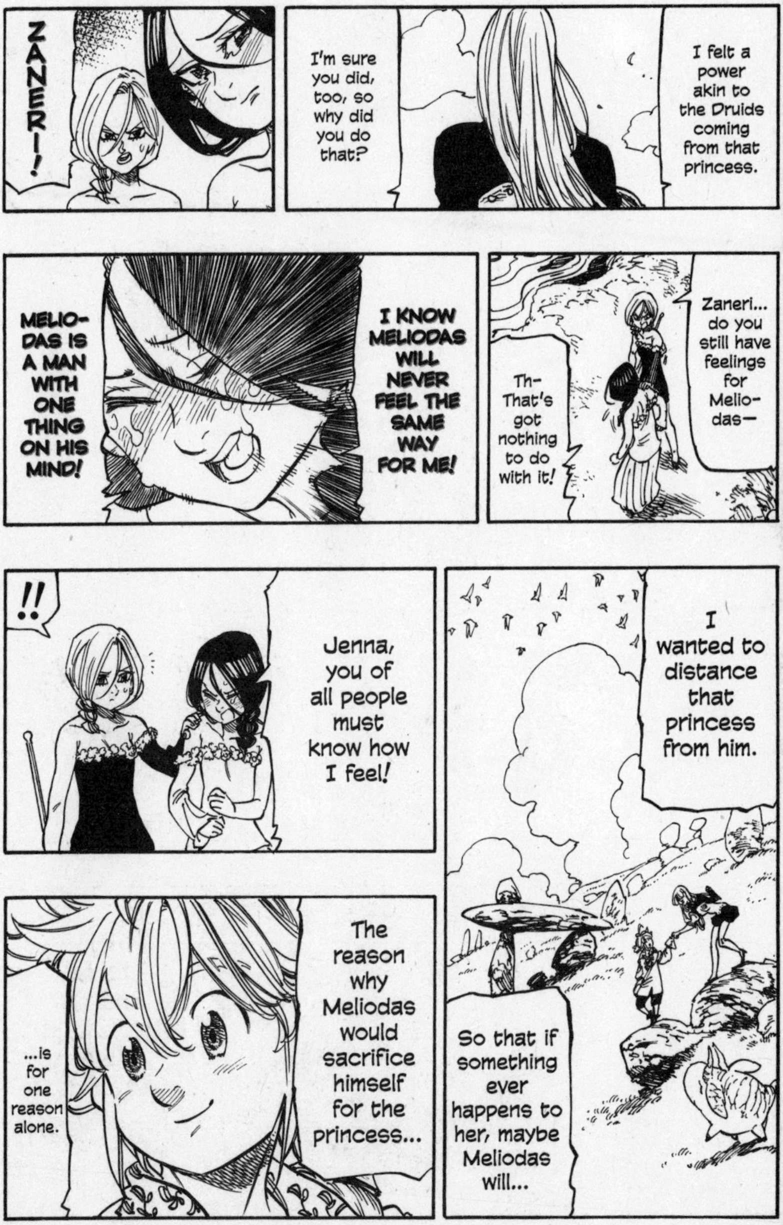
I felt a power akin to the Druids coming from that princess.
I'm sure you did, too, so why did you do that?
ZANERI!
Zaneri... do you still have feelings for Melio-das—
Th-That's got nothing to do with it!
I KNOW MELIODAS WILL NEVER FEEL THE SAME WAY FOR ME!
MELIO-DAS IS A MAN WITH ONE THING ON HIS MIND!
I wanted to distance that princess from him.
So that if something ever happens to her, maybe Meliodas will...
Jenna, you of all people must know how I feel!
!!
The reason why Meliodas would sacrifice himself for the princess...
...is for one reason alone.

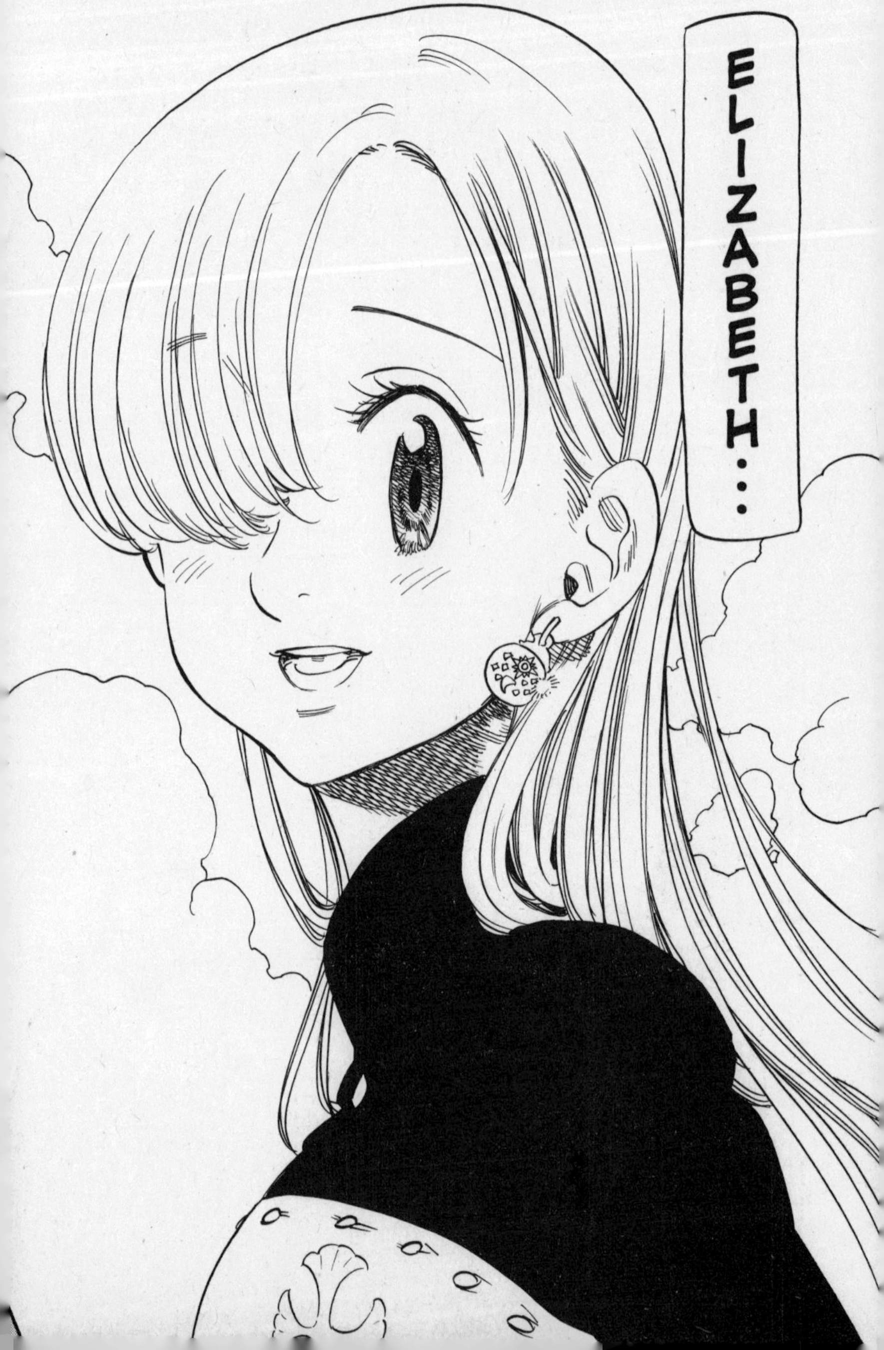
ELIZABETH...

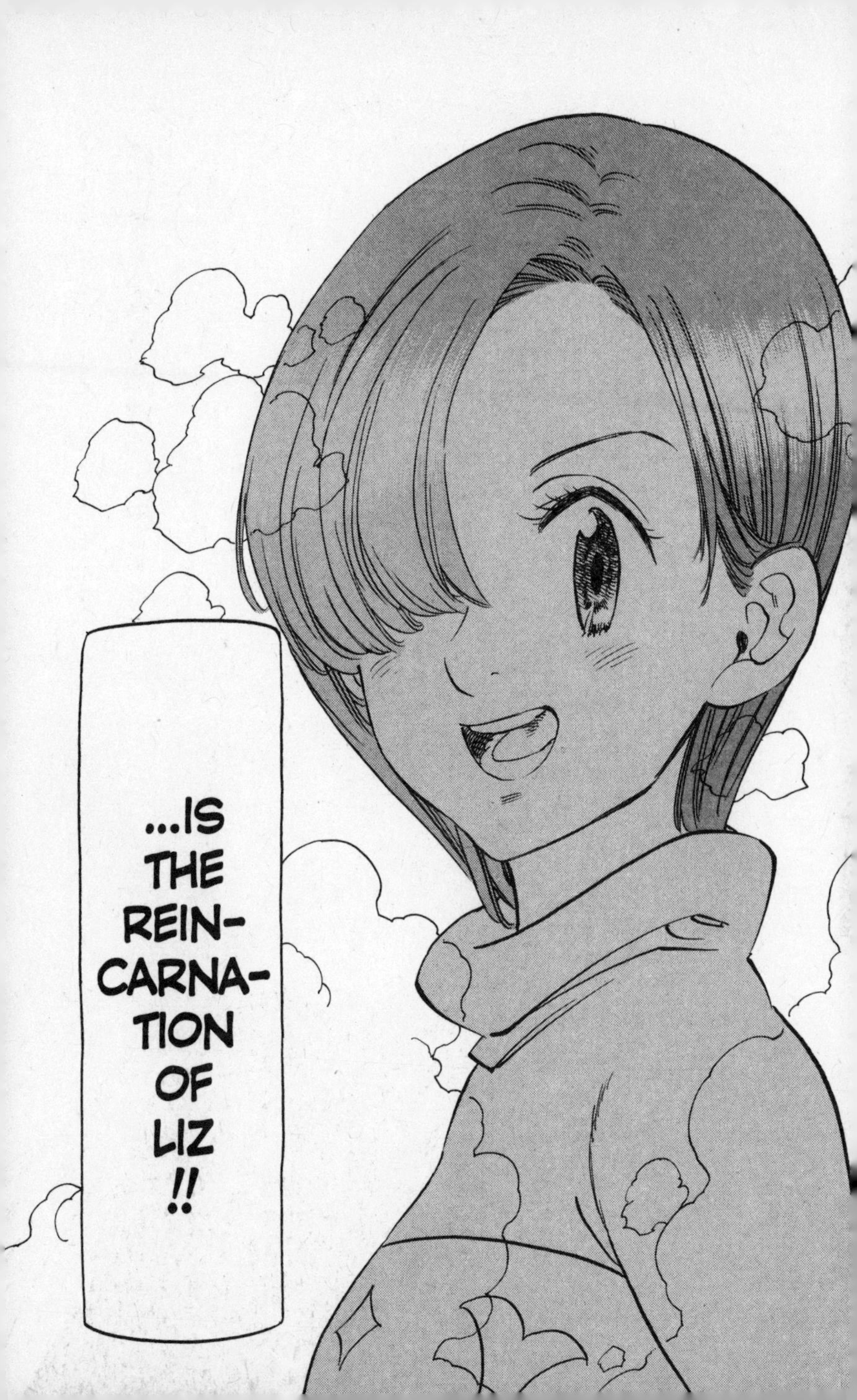
...IS THE REIN-CARNA-TION OF LIZ !!

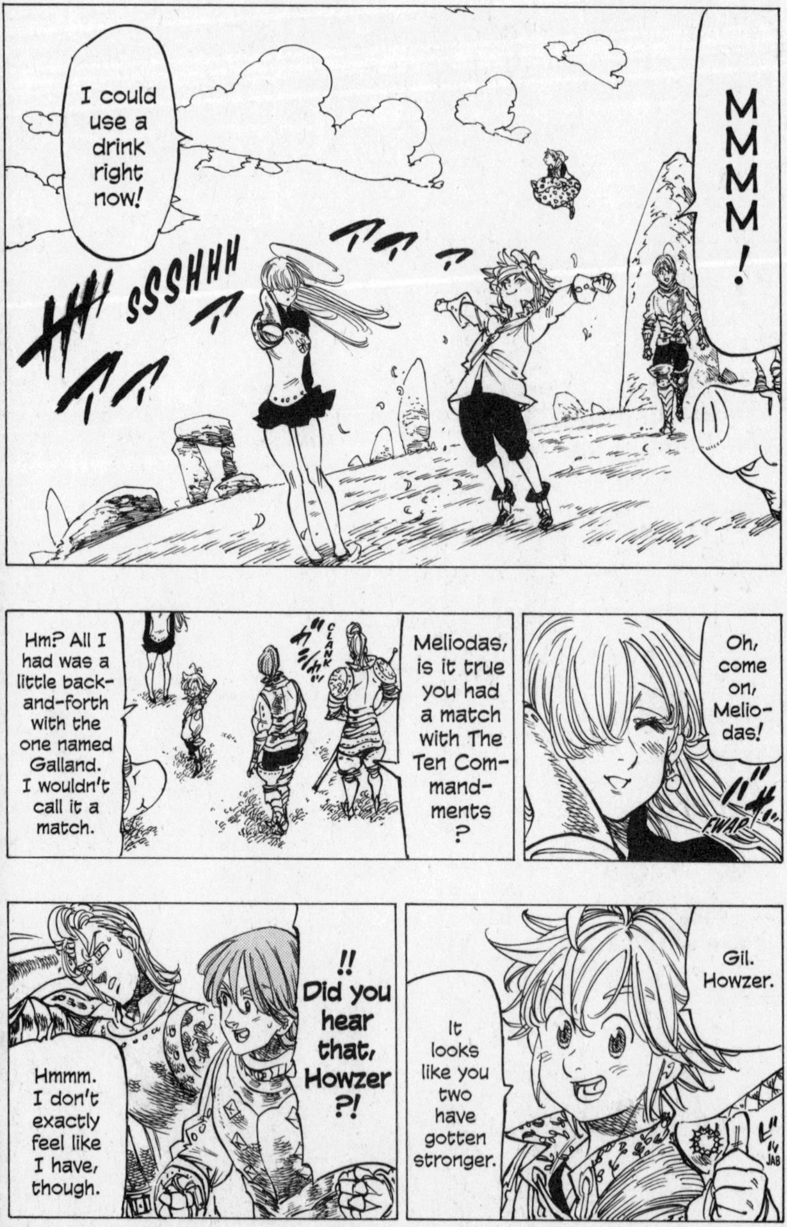
MMMM!
I could use a drink right now!
sSSHHH
Oh, come on, Melio-das!
FWAP
Meliodas, is it true you had a match with The Ten Com-mand-ments?
CLANK
Hm? All I had was a little back-and-forth with the one named Galland. I wouldn't call it a match.
Gil. Howzer.
It looks like you two have gotten stronger.
JAB
!! Did you hear that, Howzer?!
Hmmm. I don't exactly feel like I have, though.

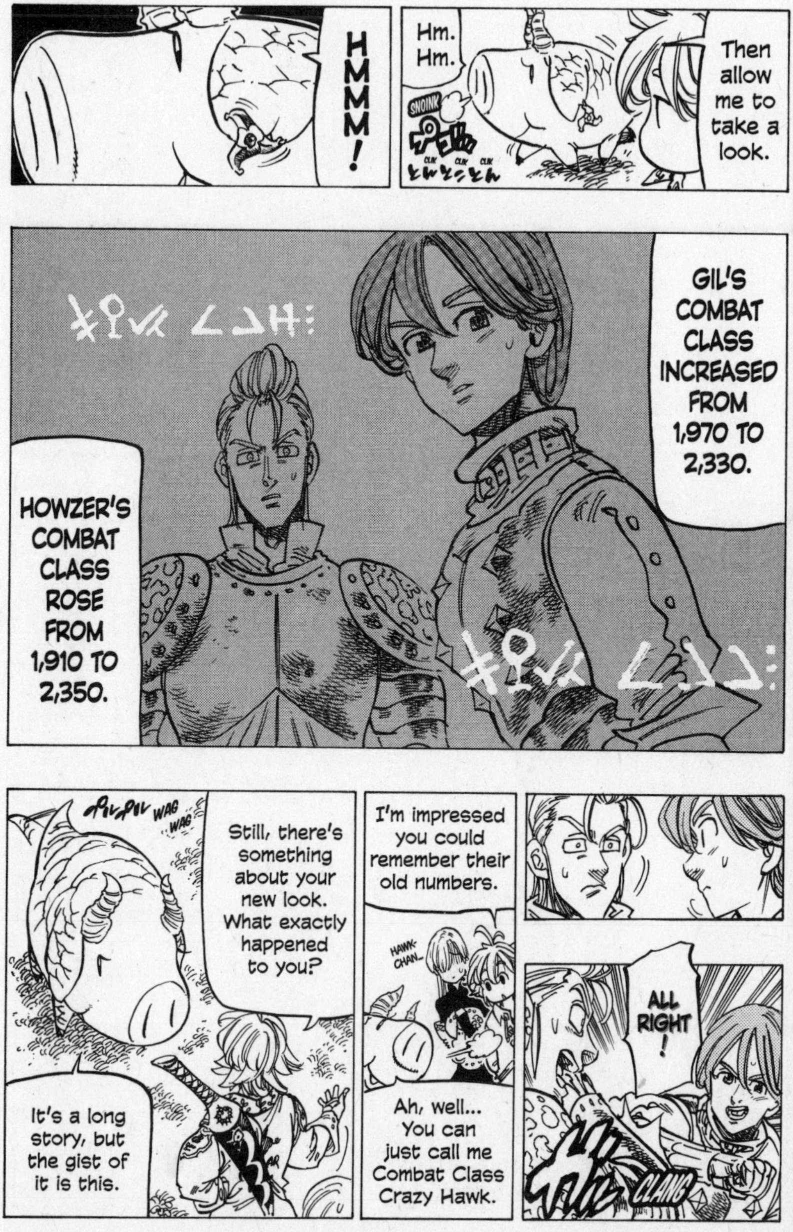
Then allow me to take a look.
Hm. Hm.
SNOINK
CLIK CLIK CLIK
HMMM!
GIL'S COMBAT CLASS INCREASED FROM 1,970 TO 2,330.
HOWZER'S COMBAT CLASS ROSE FROM 1,910 TO 2,350.
ALL RIGHT!
CLANG
I'm impressed you could remember their old numbers.
HAWK-CHAN...
Ah, well... You can just call me Combat Class Crazy Hawk.
WAG WAG
Still, there's something about your new look. What exactly happened to you?
It's a long story, but the gist of it is this.

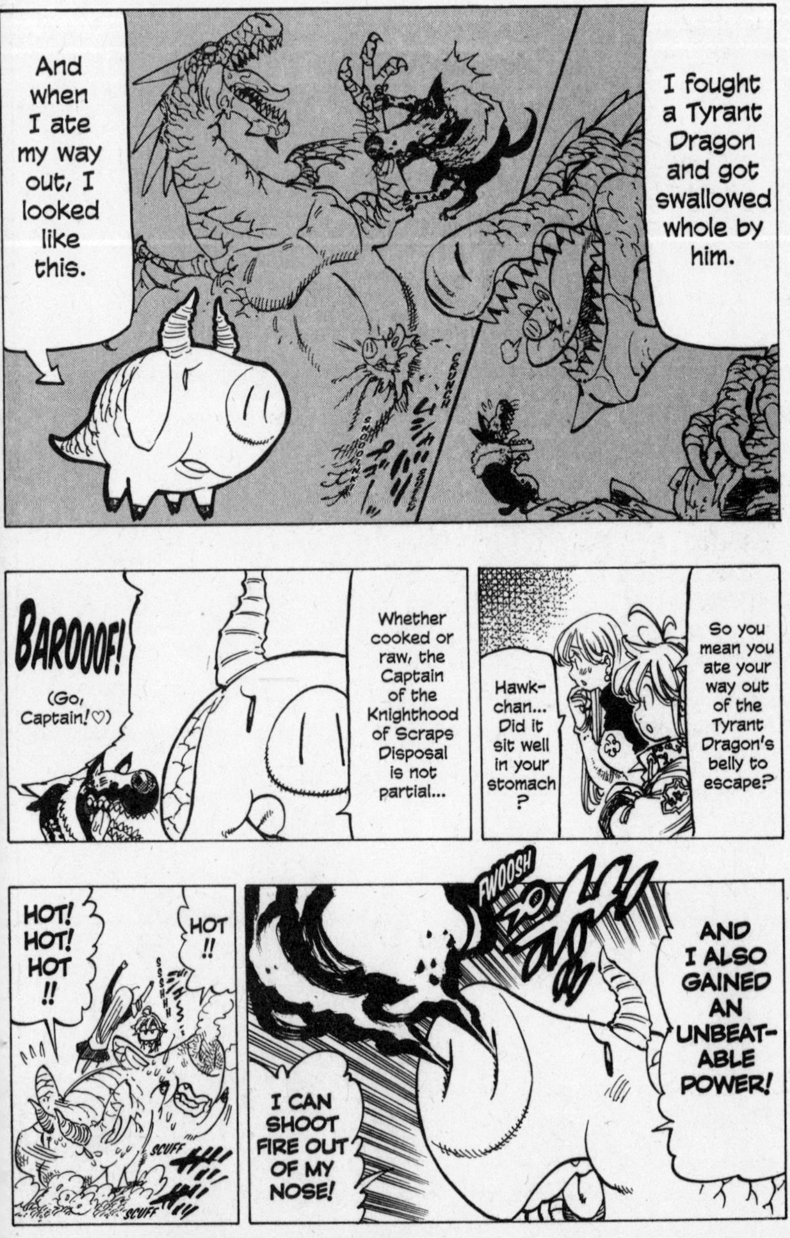
I fought a Tyrant Dragon and got swallowed whole by him.
CRUNCH
And when I ate my way out, I looked like this.
So you mean you ate your way out of the Tyrant Dragon's belly to escape?
Hawk-chan... Did it sit well in your stomach?
Whether cooked or raw, the Captain of the Knighthood of Scraps Disposal is not partial...
BAROOOF!
(Go, Captain!♡)
FWOOSH
AND I ALSO GAINED AN UNBEATABLE POWER!
I CAN SHOOT FIRE OUT OF MY NOSE!
HOT !!
HOT! HOT! HOT !!
SCUFF
SCUFF

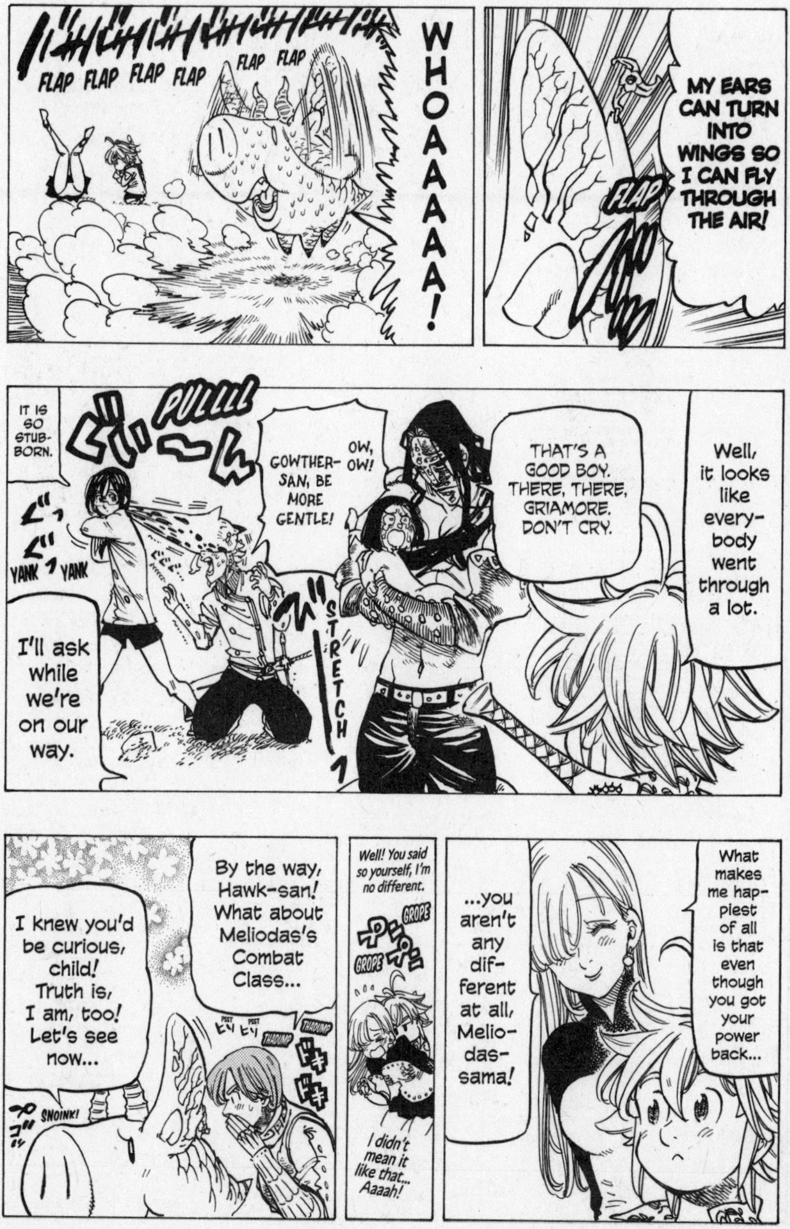
MY EARS CAN TURN INTO WINGS SO I CAN FLY THROUGH THE AIR!
FLAP
FLAP FLAP
FLAP FLAP FLAP FLAP
WHOAAAAAA!
Well, it looks like everybody went through a lot.
THAT'S A GOOD BOY. THERE, THERE, GRIAMORE. DON'T CRY.
OW, OW!
GOWTHER-SAN, BE MORE GENTLE!
PULLL
STRETCH
IT IS SO STUBBORN.
YANK YANK
I'll ask while we're on our way.
What makes me happiest of all is that even though you got your power back...
...you aren't any different at all, Melio-das-sama!
Well! You said so yourself, I'm no different.
GROPE
GROPE
I didn't mean it like that... Aaaah!
By the way, Hawk-san! What about Meliodas's Combat Class...
THADUMP
THADUMP
PSST PSST
I knew you'd be curious, child! Truth is, I am, too! Let's see now...
SNOINK!

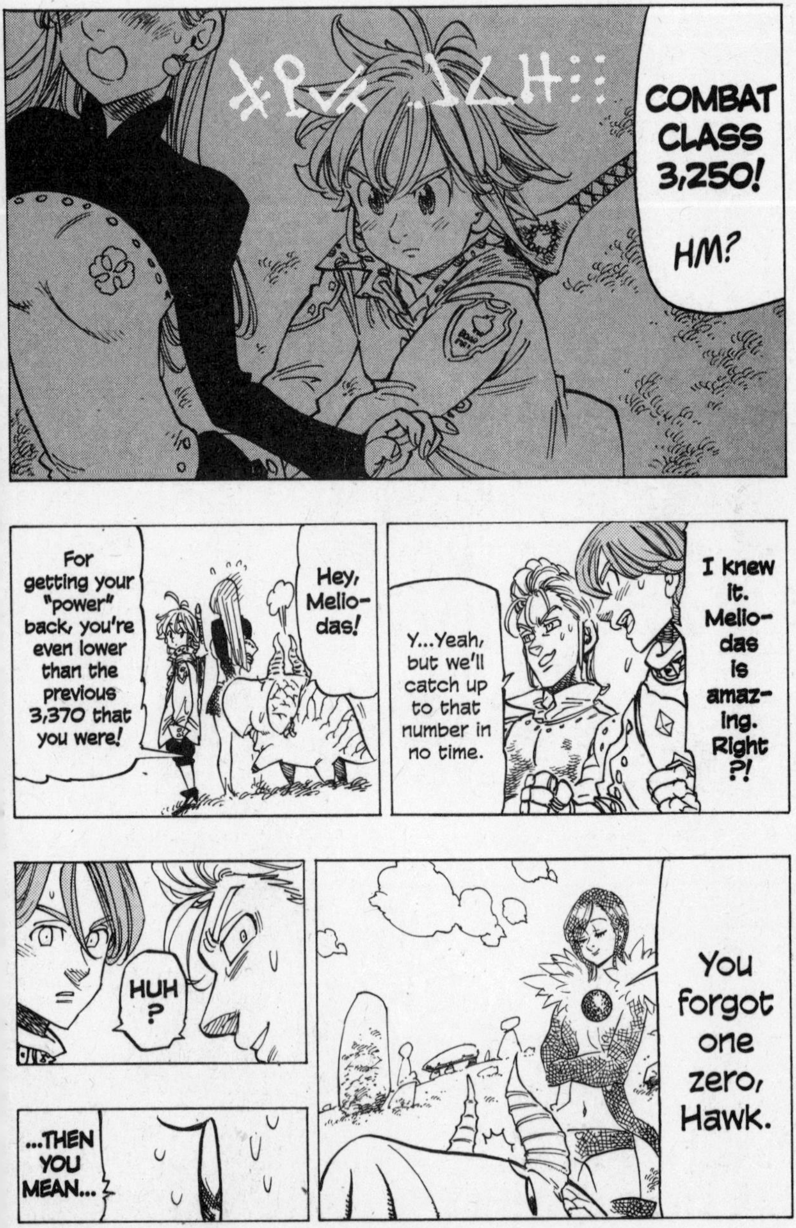
COMBAT CLASS 3,250!
HM?
I knew it. Meliodas is amazing. Right?!
Y...Yeah, but we'll catch up to that number in no time.
Hey, Meliodas!
For getting your "power" back, you're even lower than the previous 3,370 that you were!
You forgot one zero, Hawk.
HUH?
...THEN YOU MEAN...

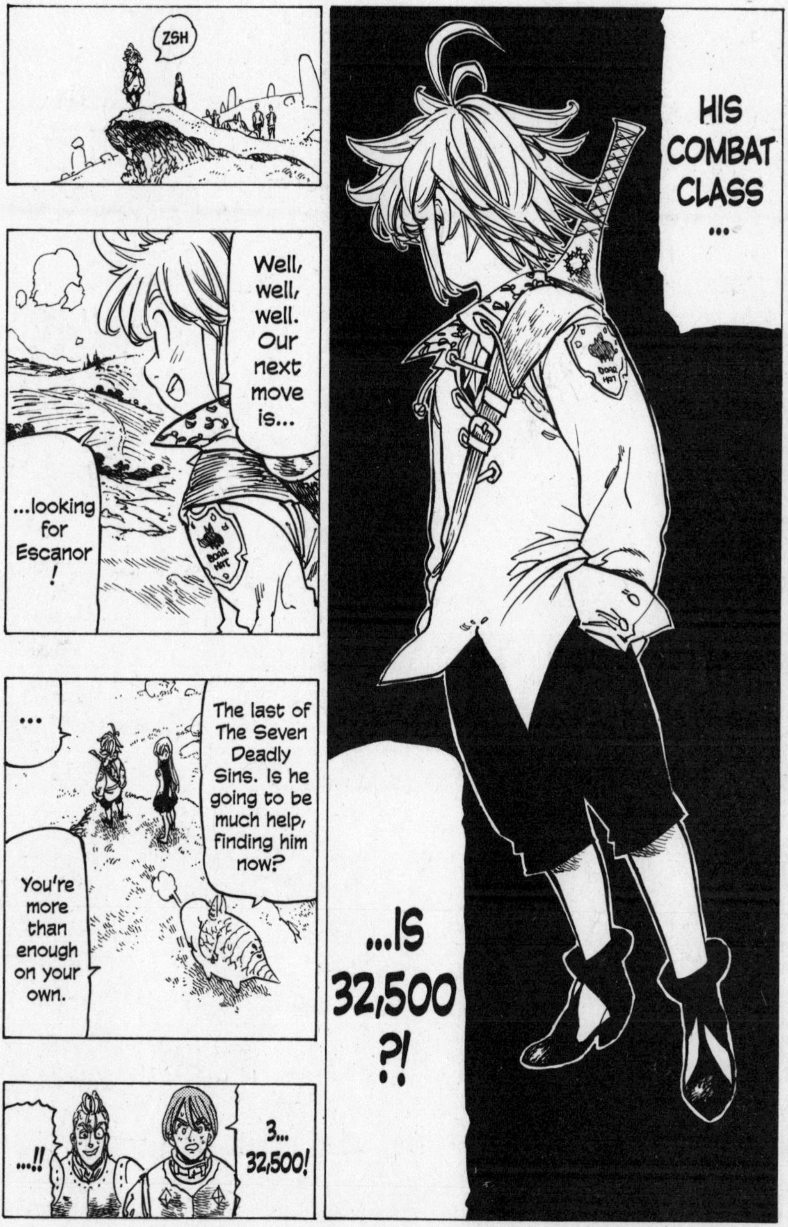
HIS COMBAT CLASS ...
...IS 32,500 ?!
ZSH
Well, well, well. Our next move is...
...looking for Escanor !
The last of The Seven Deadly Sins. Is he going to be much help, finding him now?
...
You're more than enough on your own.
3... 32,500!
...!!

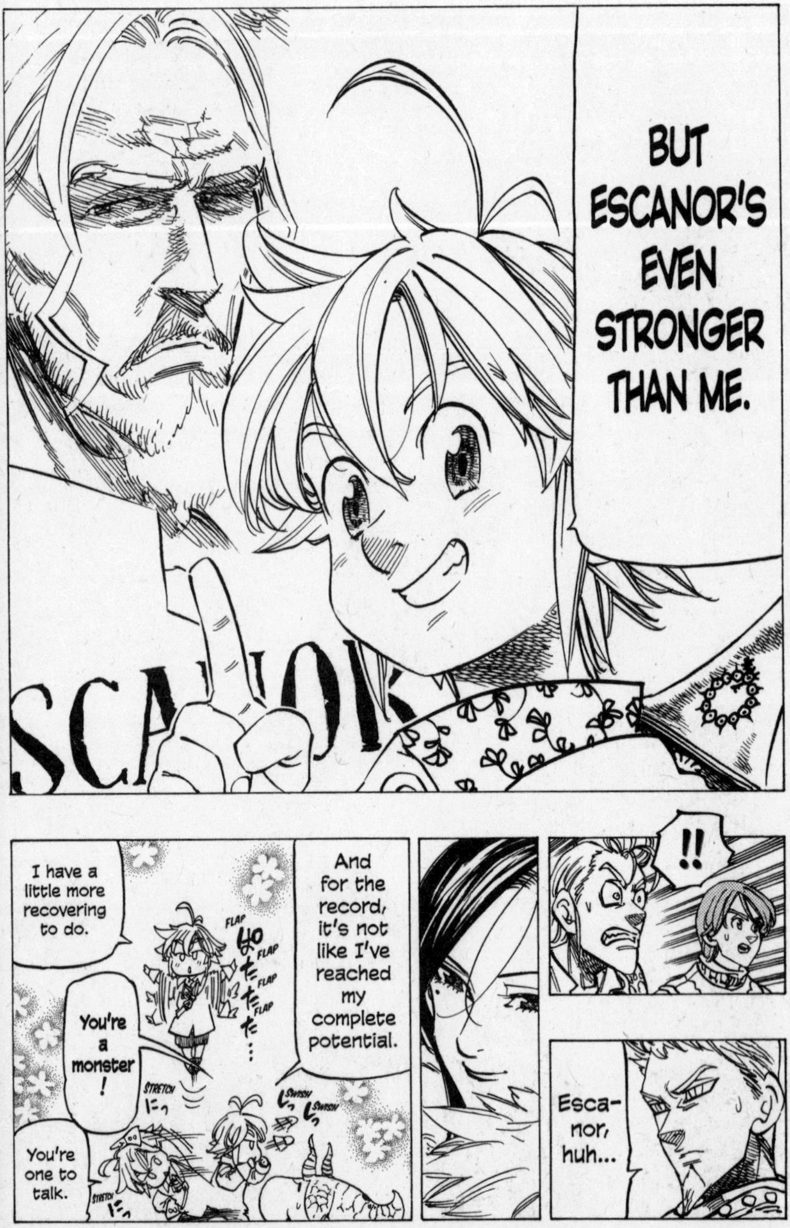

BUT ESCANOR'S EVEN STRONGER THAN ME.
!!
Esca-nor, huh...
And for the record, it's not like I've reached my complete potential.
I have a little more recovering to do.
FLAP
FLAP
FLAP
FLAP
You're a monster!
STRETCH
SWISH
SWISH
You're one to talk.
STRETCH

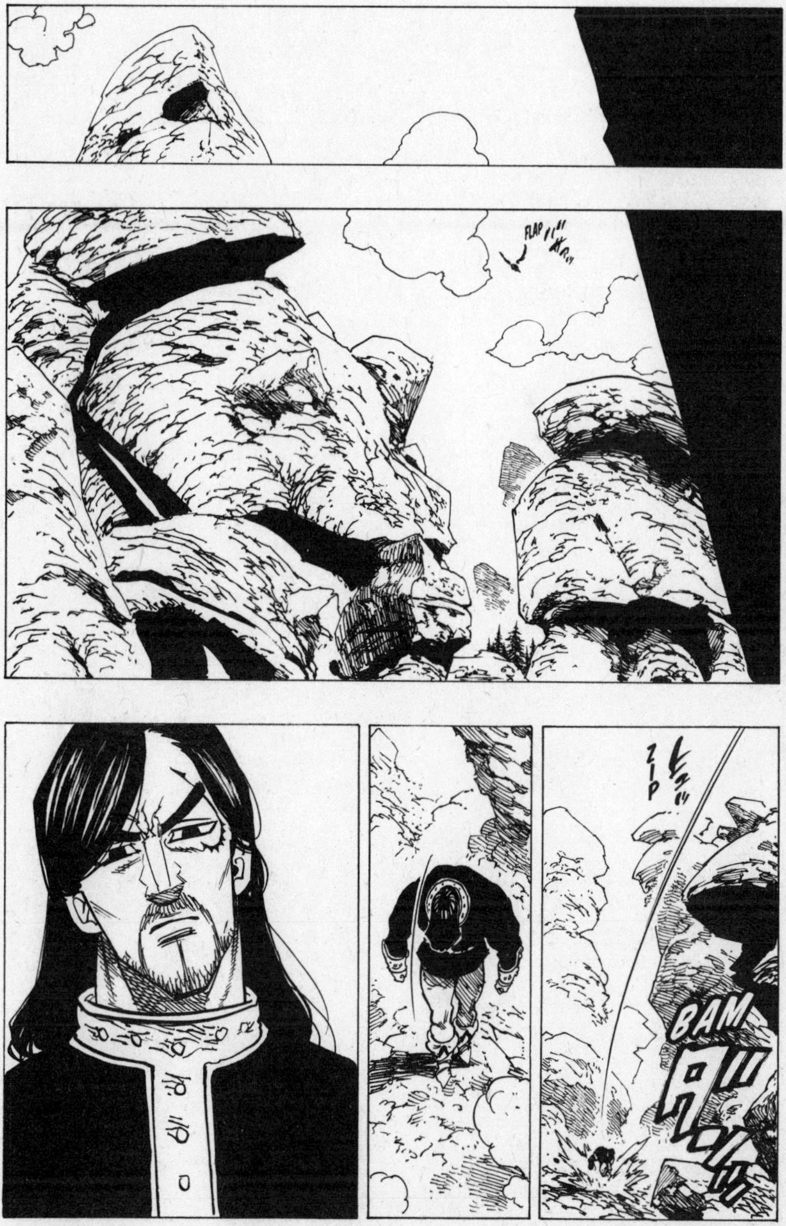
FLAP
ZIP
BAM

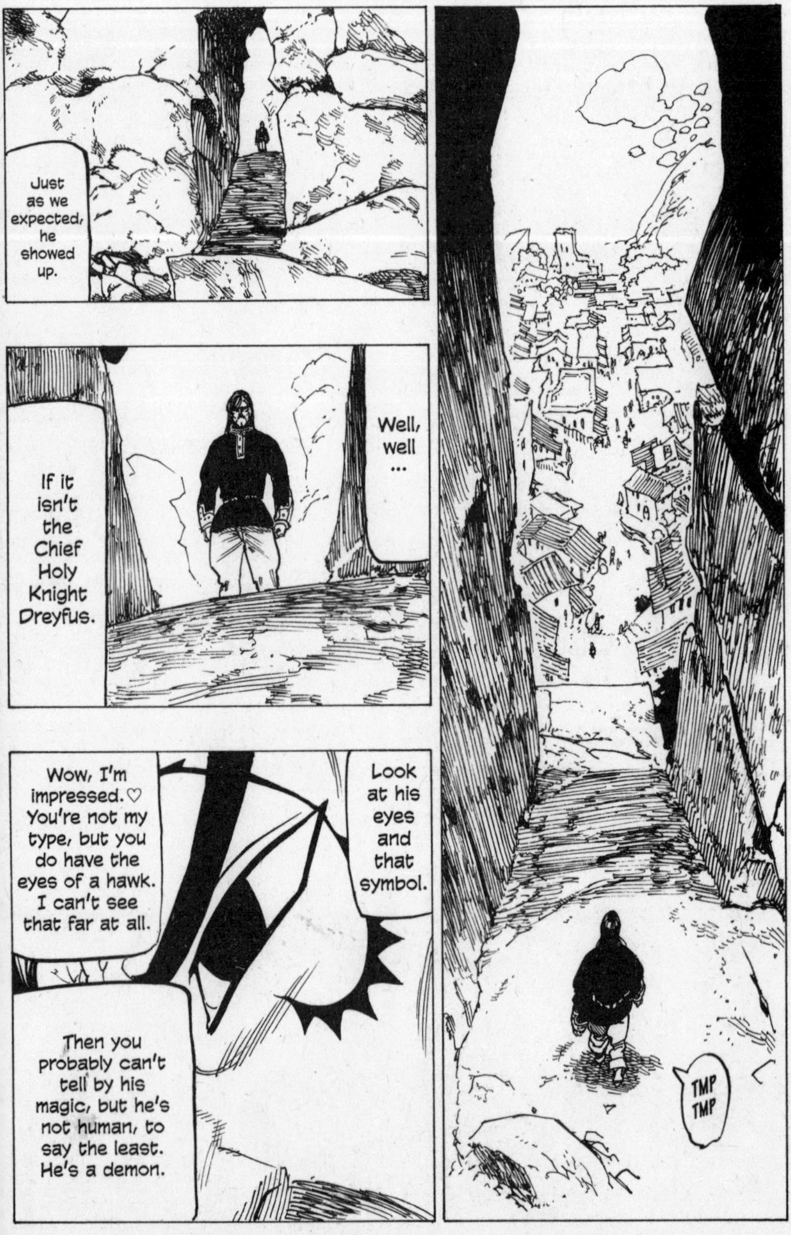
TMP TMP
Just as we expected, he showed up.
Well, well...
If it isn't the Chief Holy Knight Dreyfus.
Look at his eyes and that symbol.
Wow, I'm impressed.♡ You're not my type, but you do have the eyes of a hawk. I can't see that far at all.
Then you probably can't tell by his magic, but he's not human, to say the least. He's a demon.

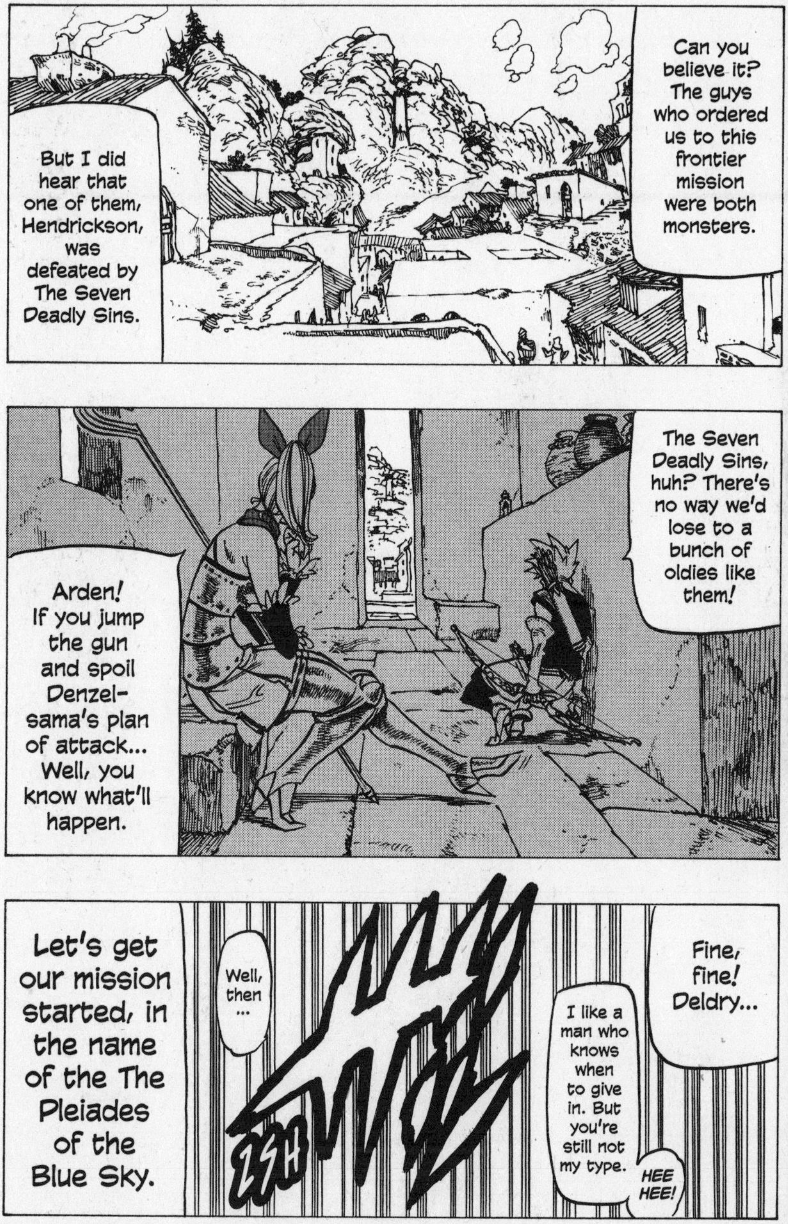
Can you believe it? The guys who ordered us to this frontier mission were both monsters.
But I did hear that one of them, Hendrickson, was defeated by The Seven Deadly Sins.
The Seven Deadly Sins, huh? There's no way we'd lose to a bunch of oldies like them!
Arden! If you jump the gun and spoil Denzel-sama's plan of attack... Well, you know what'll happen.
Fine, fine! Deldry...
I like a man who knows when to give in. But you're still not my type.
HEE HEE!
ZSH
Well, then...
Let's get our mission started, in the name of the The Pleiades of the Blue Sky.

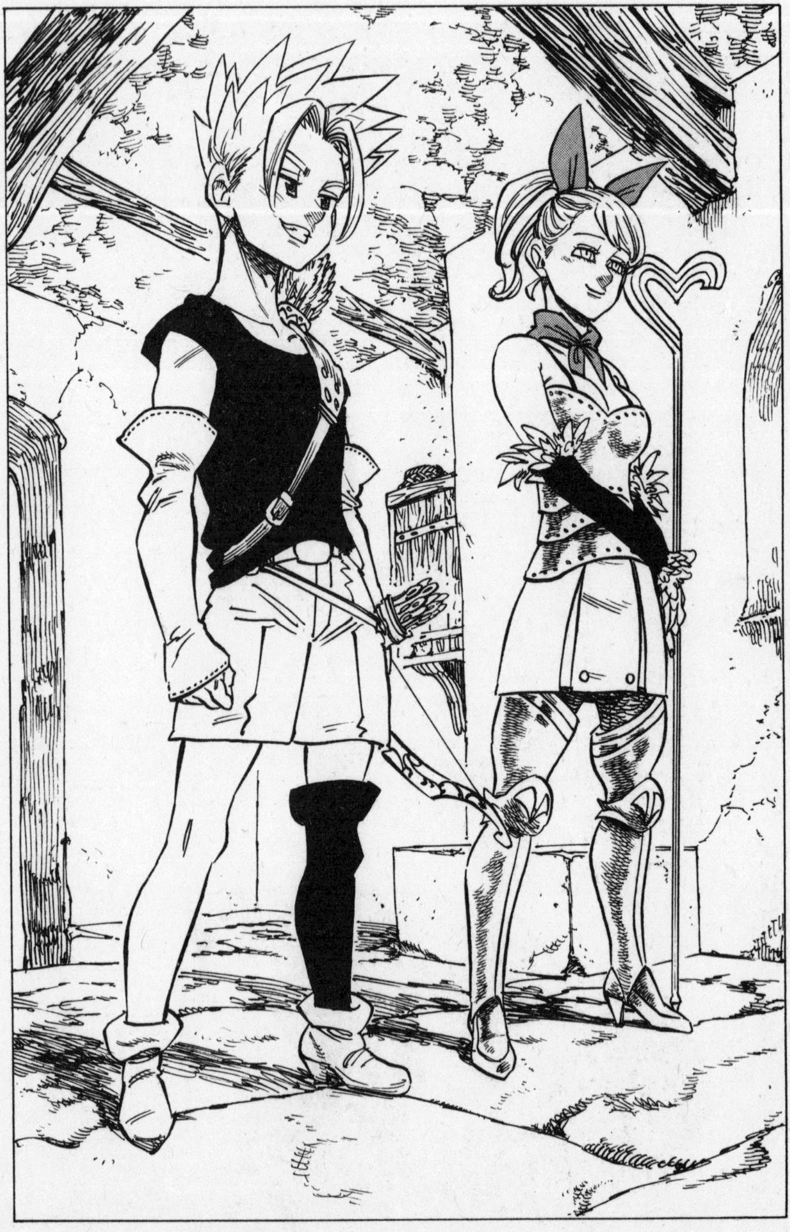

# Chapter 138 - A Fight with Darkness

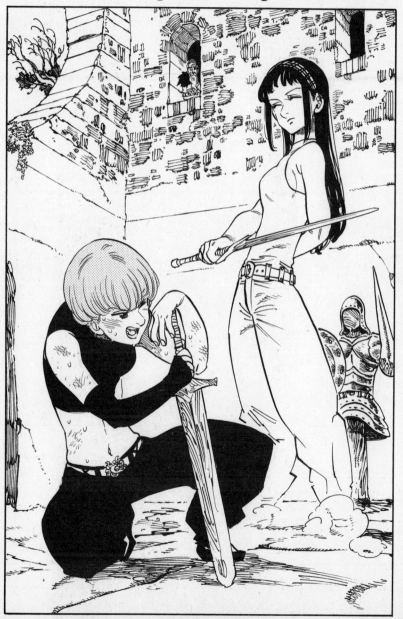

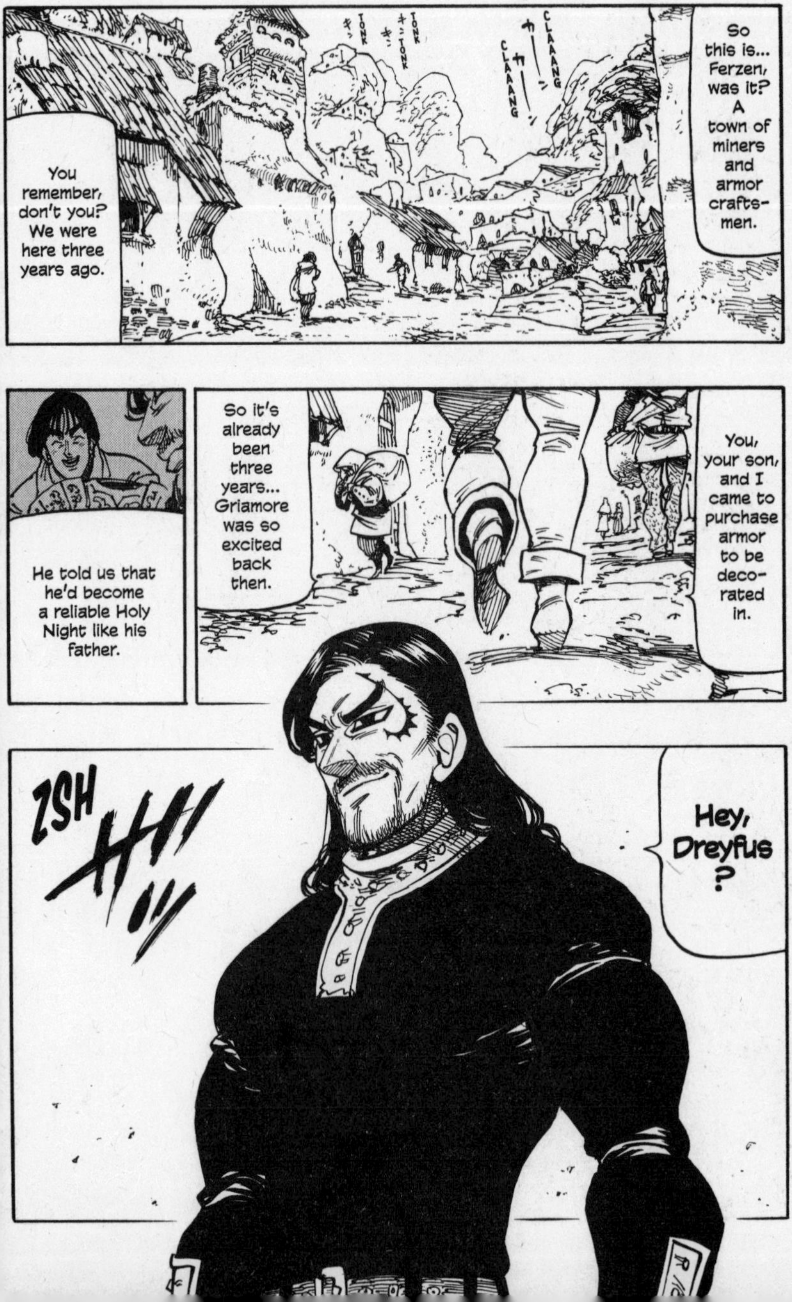
So this is... Ferzen, was it? A town of miners and armor craftsmen.
CLAAANG
CLAAANG
TONK
TONK
TONK
You remember, don't you? We were here three years ago.
You, your son, and I came to purchase armor to be decorated in.
So it's already been three years... Griamore was so excited back then.
He told us that he'd become a reliable Holy Night like his father.
Hey, Dreyfus?
ZSH

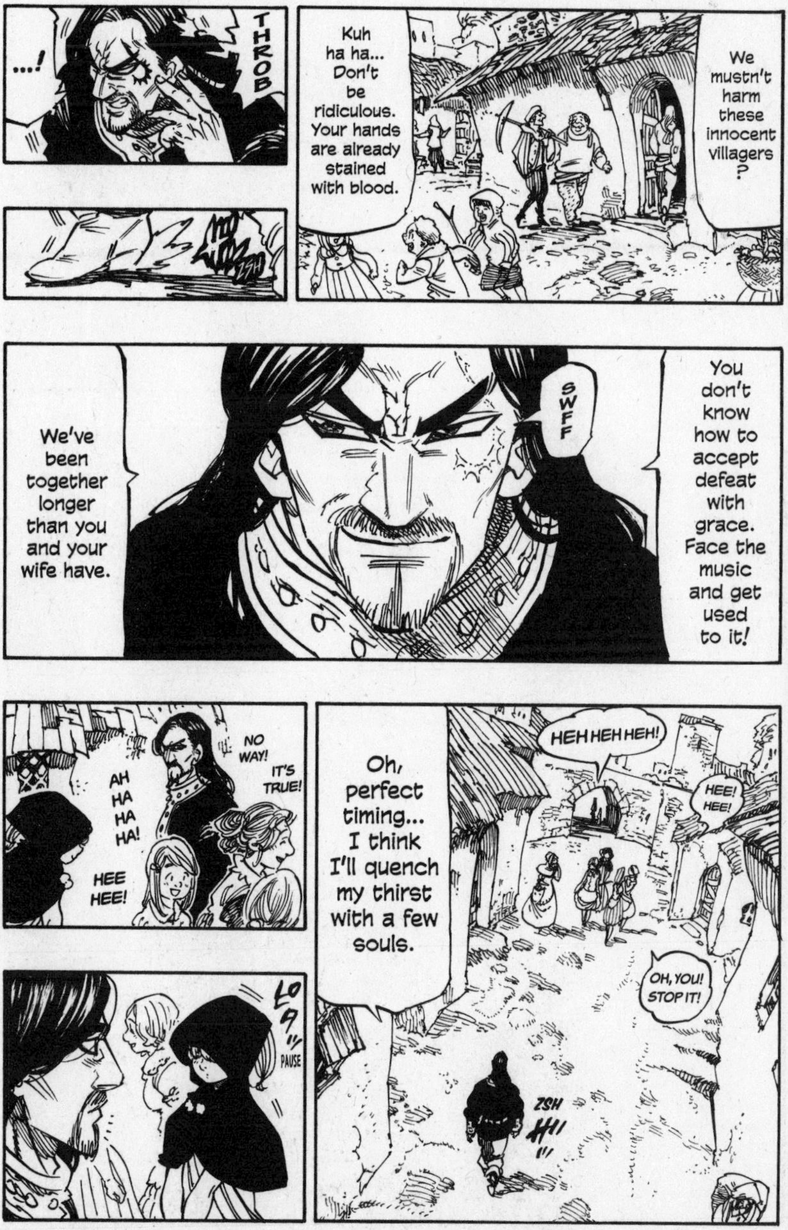
We mustn't harm these innocent villagers?
Kuh ha ha... Don't be ridiculous. Your hands are already stained with blood.
THROB
...!
ZSH
You don't know how to accept defeat with grace. Face the music and get used to it!
SWFF
We've been together longer than you and your wife have.
Oh, perfect timing... I think I'll quench my thirst with a few souls.
HEH HEH HEH!
HEE! HEE!
OH, YOU! STOP IT!
ZSH
NO WAY!
IT'S TRUE!
AH HA HA HA!
HEE HEE!
PAUSE

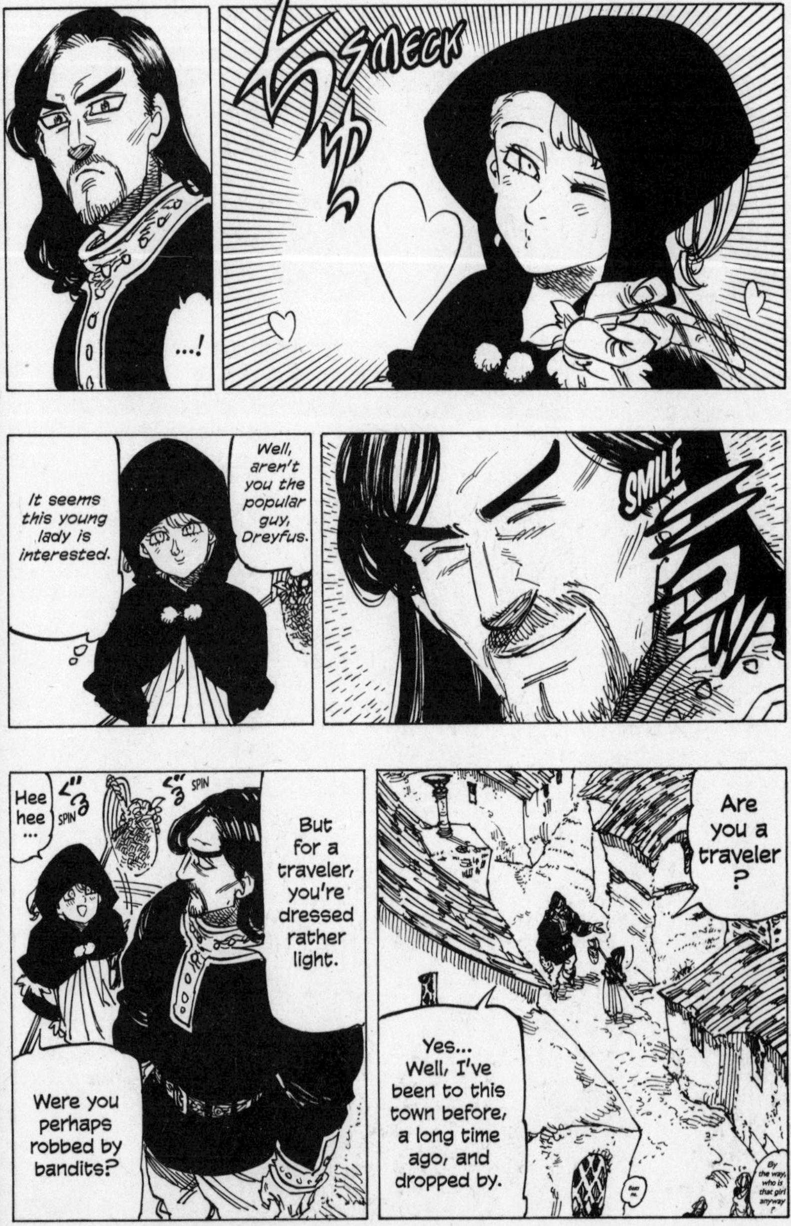
SMECK
...!
SMILE
Well, aren't you the popular guy, Dreyfus.
It seems this young lady is interested.
Are you a traveler?
Yes... Well, I've been to this town before, a long time ago, and dropped by.
By the way, who is that girl anyway?
But for a traveler, you're dressed rather light.
SPIN
SPIN
Hee hee...
Were you perhaps robbed by bandits?

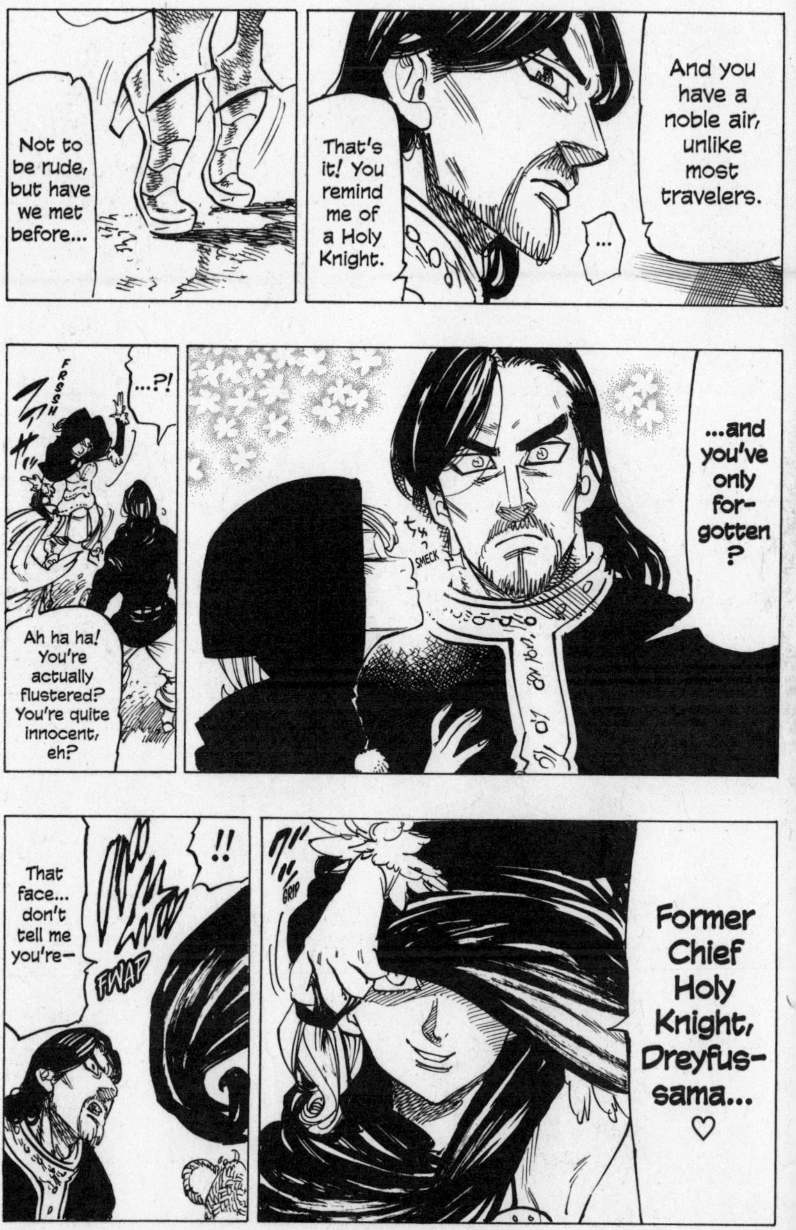
And you have a noble air, unlike most travelers.
...
That's it! You remind me of a Holy Knight.
Not to be rude, but have we met before...
...and you've only forgotten?
SMECK
...?!
FRSSH
Ah ha ha! You're actually flustered? You're quite innocent, eh?
GRIP
Former Chief Holy Knight, Dreyfus-sama... ♡
!!
FWAP
That face... don't tell me you're—

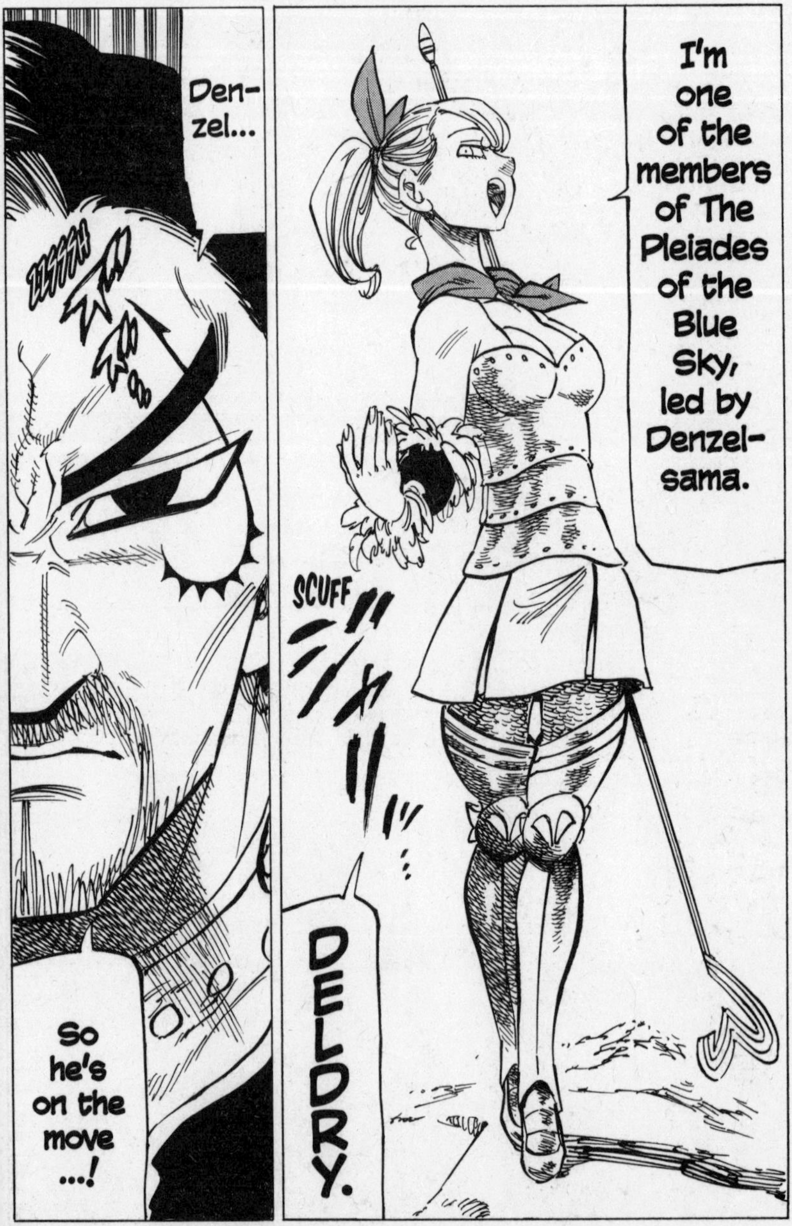
I'm one of the members of The Pleiades of the Blue Sky, led by Denzel-sama.
SCUFF
DELDRY.
Den-zel...
So he's on the move ...!

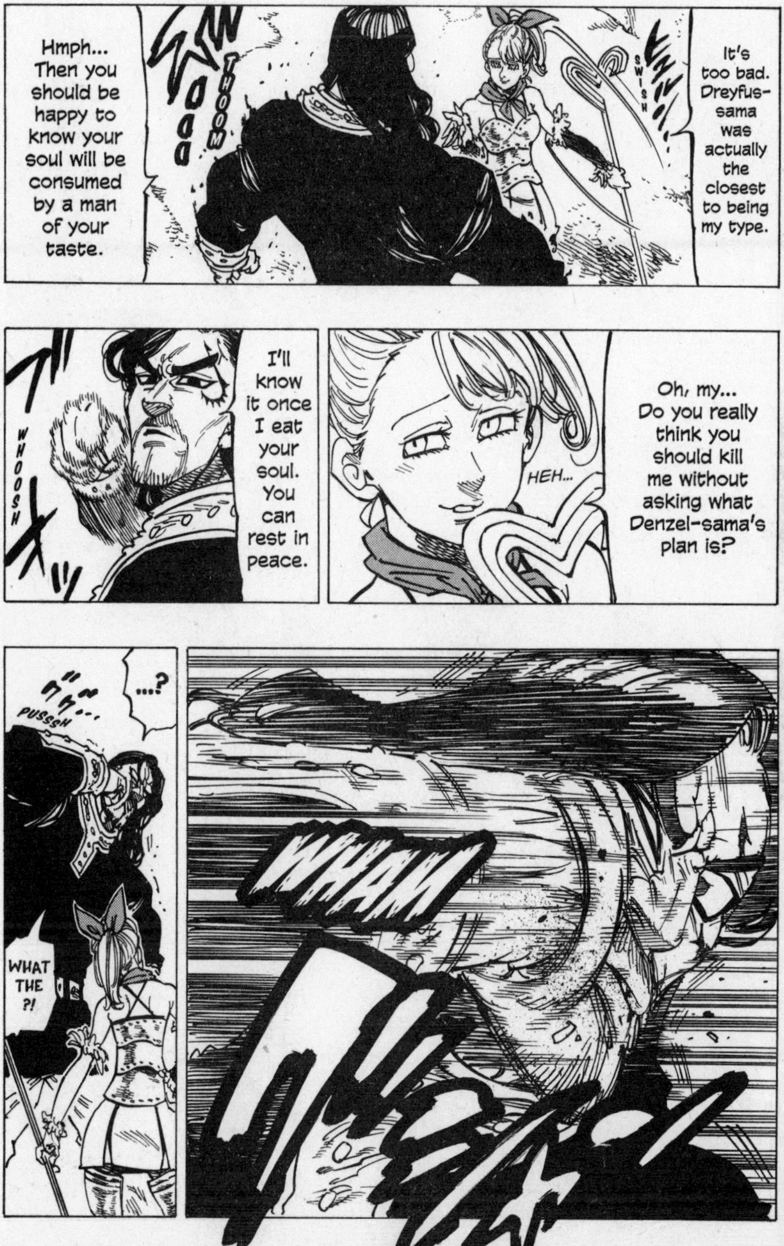
It's too bad. Dreyfus-sama was actually the closest to being my type.
SWISH
THOOM
Hmph... Then you should be happy to know your soul will be consumed by a man of your taste.
Oh, my... Do you really think you should kill me without asking what Denzel-sama's plan is?
HEH...
I'll know it once I eat your soul. You can rest in peace.
WHOOSH
WHAM
...?
PUSSSH
WHAT THE ?!

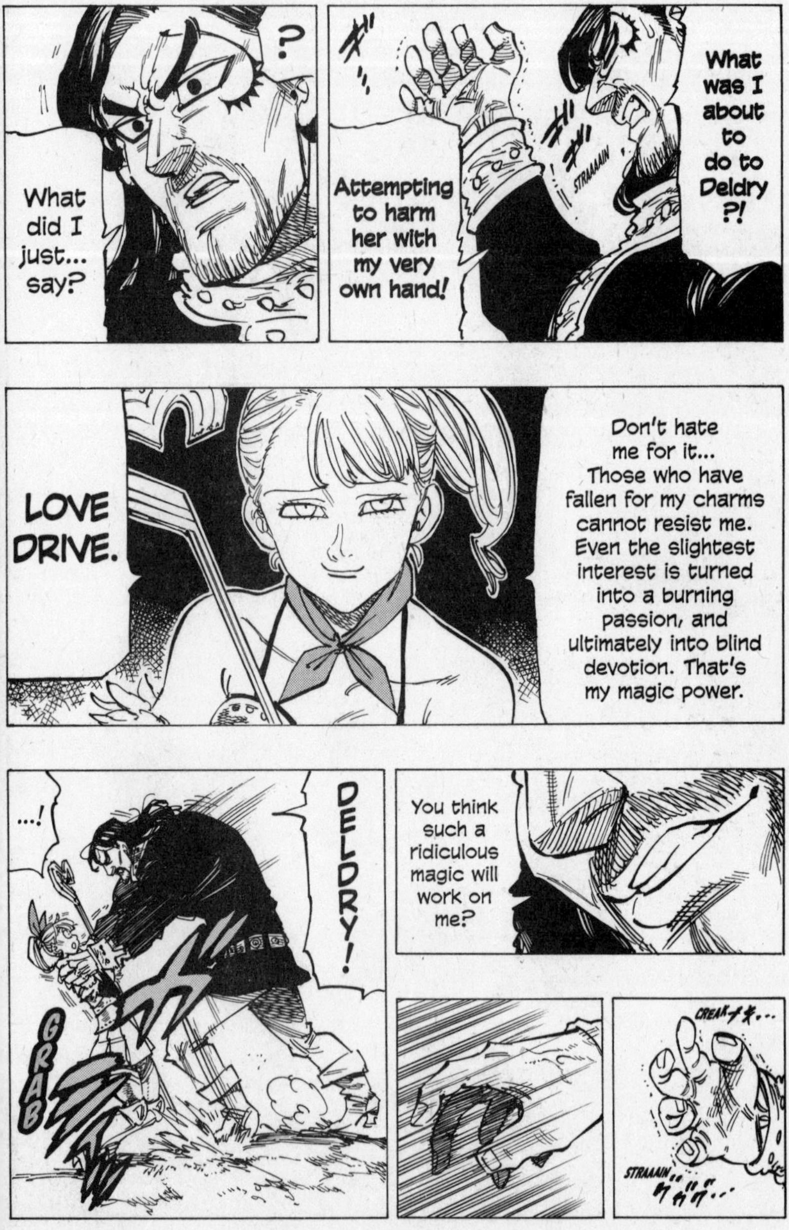
What was I about to do to Deldry?!
STRAAAAIN
Attempting to harm her with my very own hand!
?
What did I just... say?
Don't hate me for it... Those who have fallen for my charms cannot resist me. Even the slightest interest is turned into a burning passion, and ultimately into blind devotion. That's my magic power.
LOVE DRIVE.
You think such a ridiculous magic will work on me?
CREAK...
STRAAAIN...
DELDRY!
...!
GRAB

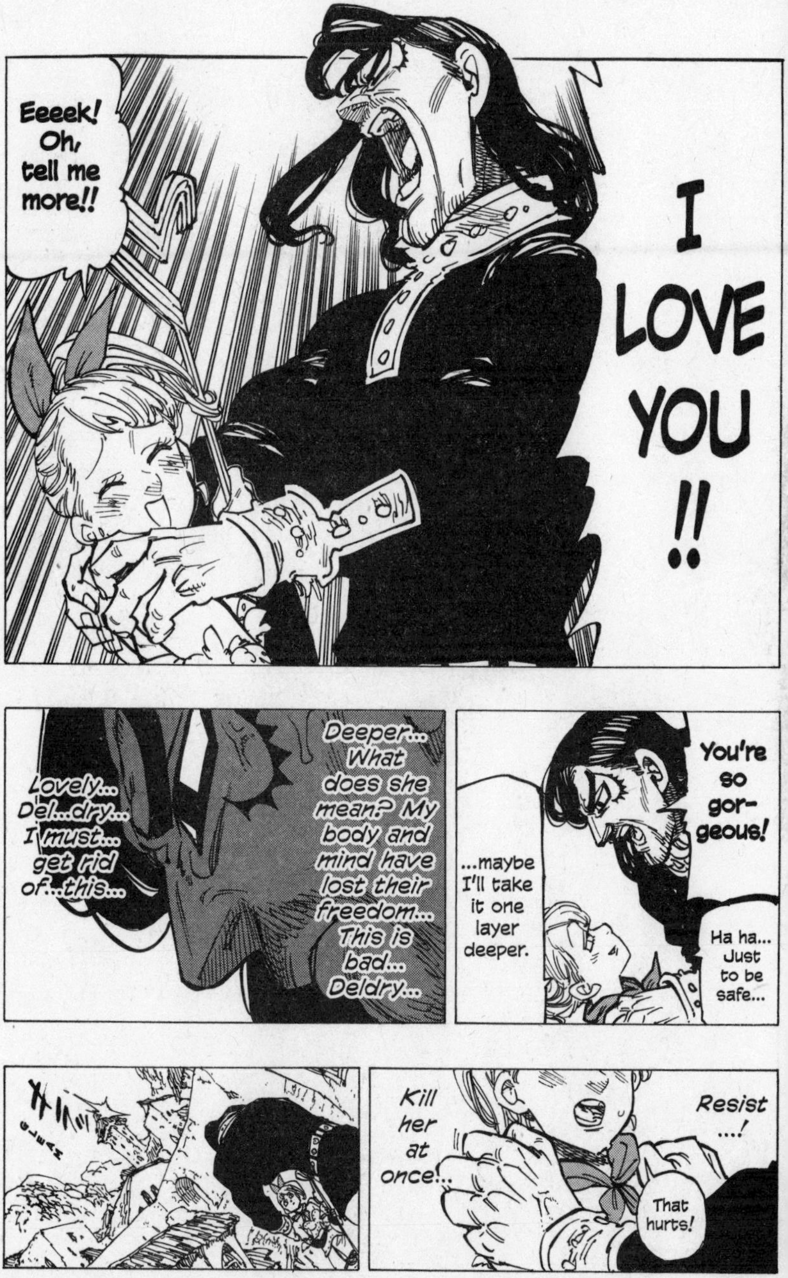
I LOVE YOU!!
Eeeek! Oh, tell me more!!
You're so gor-geous!
Ha ha... Just to be safe...
...maybe I'll take it one layer deeper.
Deeper... What does she mean? My body and mind have lost their freedom... This is bad... Deldry...
Lovely... Del...dry... I must... get rid of...this...
Resist ...!
Kill her at once!...
That hurts!

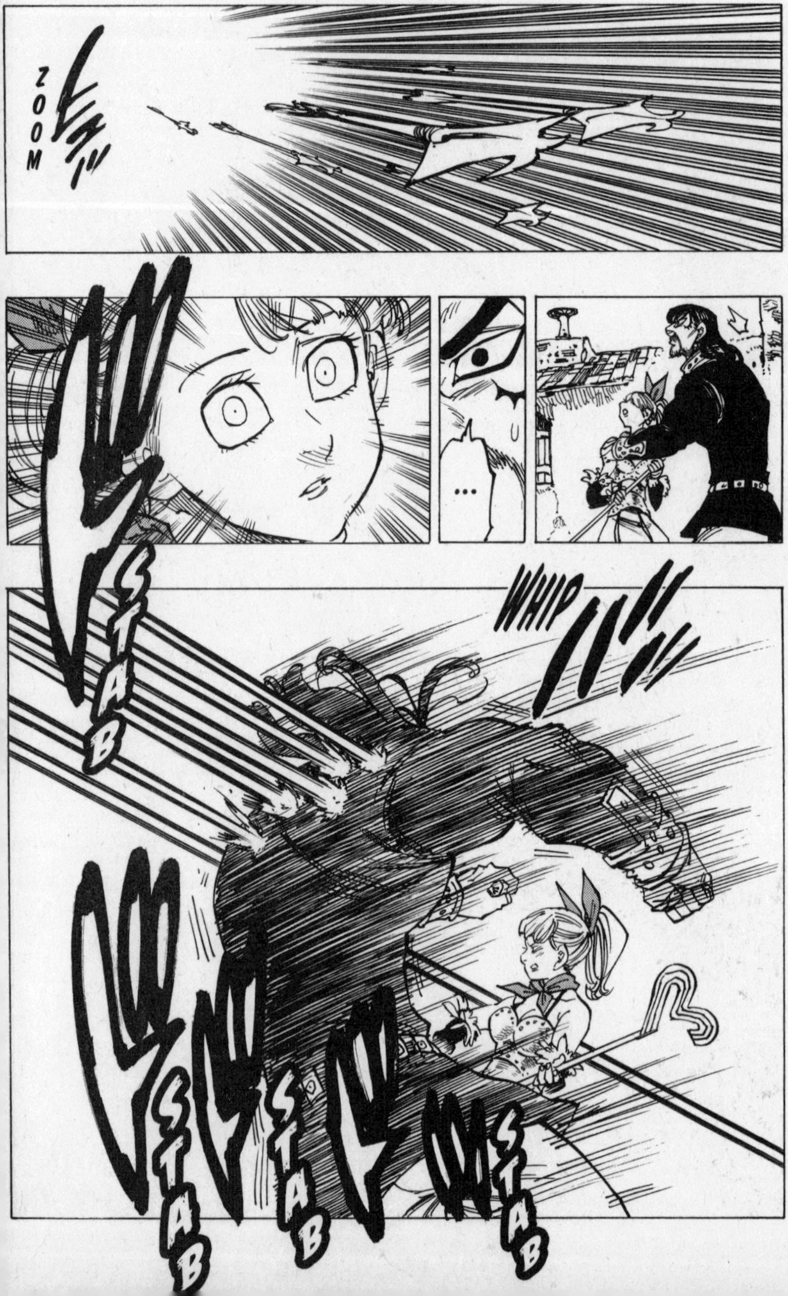
ZOOM
...
WHIP
STAB
STAB
STAB
STAB

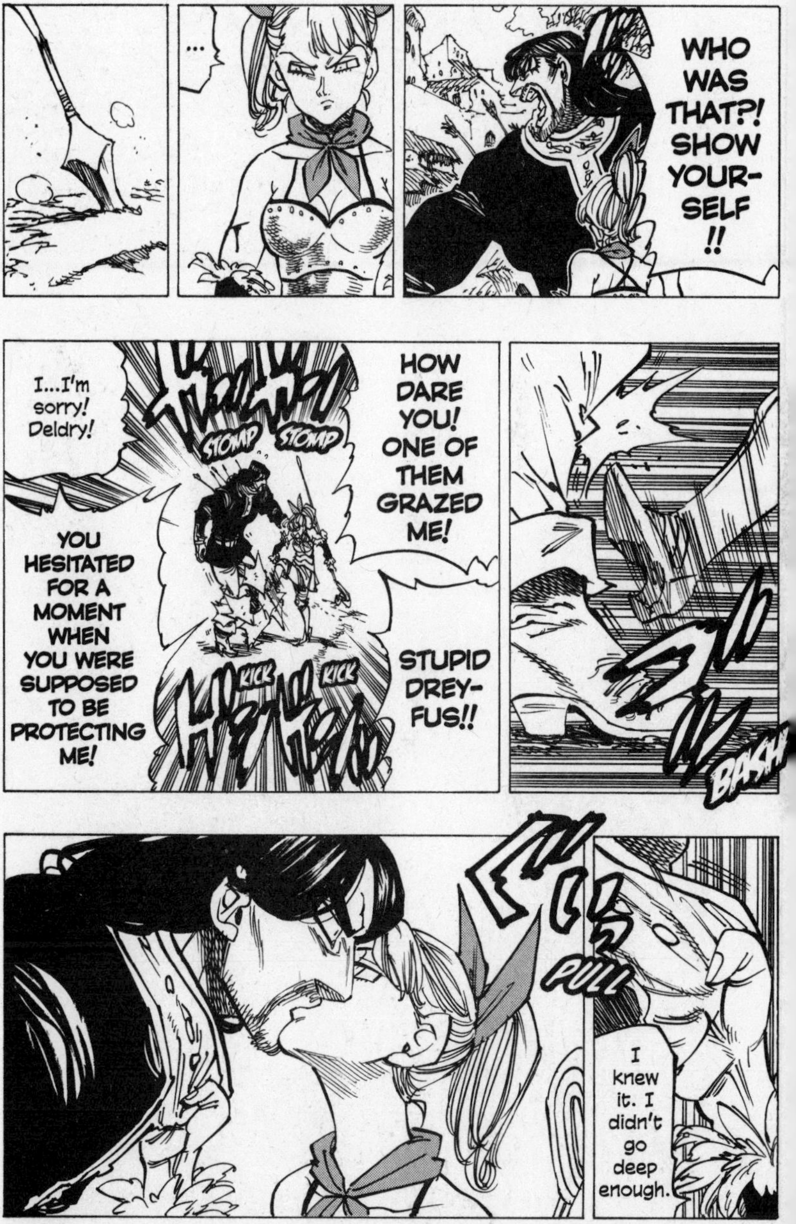
WHO WAS THAT?! SHOW YOURSELF!!
...
BASH
HOW DARE YOU! ONE OF THEM GRAZED ME!
STOMP STOMP
I...I'm sorry! Deldry!
STUPID DREYFUS!!
KICK KICK
YOU HESITATED FOR A MOMENT WHEN YOU WERE SUPPOSED TO BE PROTECTING ME!
I knew it. I didn't go deep enough.
PULL

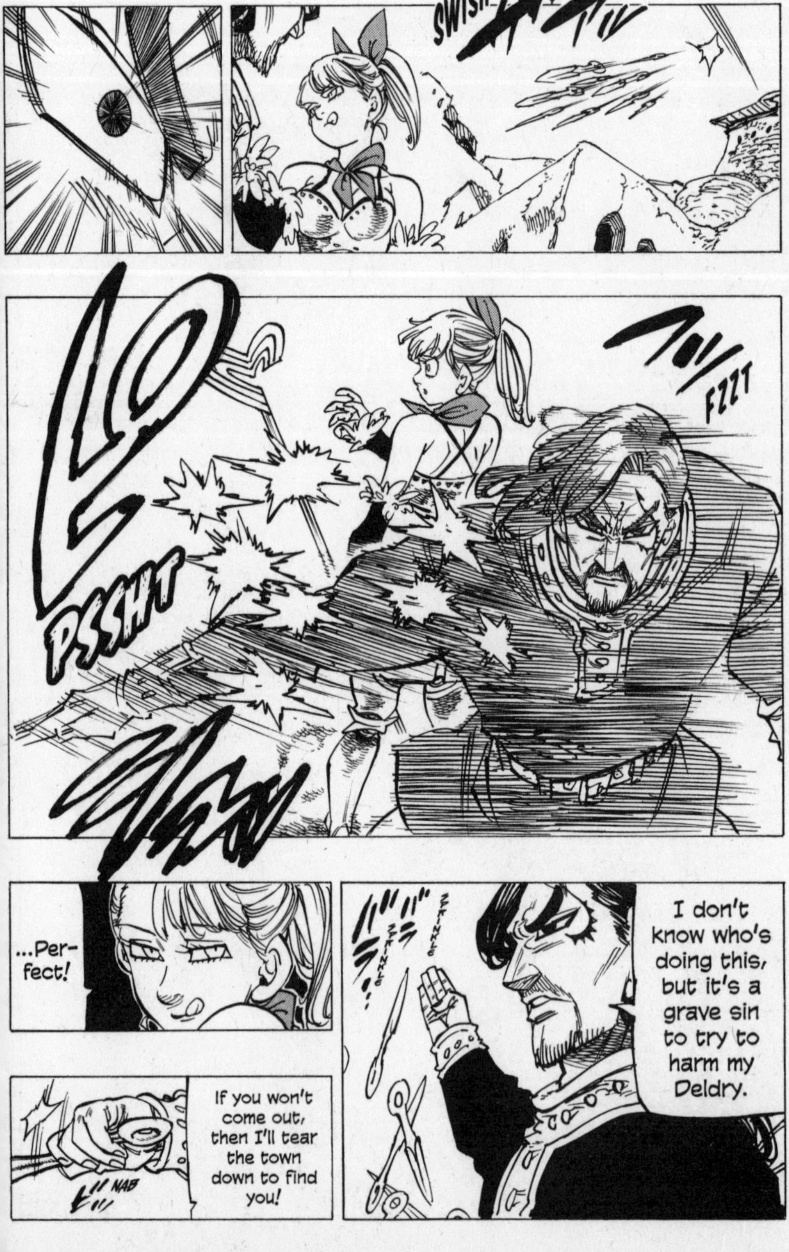
SWISH
FZZT
PSSHT
I don't know who's doing this, but it's a grave sin to try to harm my Deldry.
...Per-fect!
NAB
If you won't come out, then I'll tear the town down to find you!

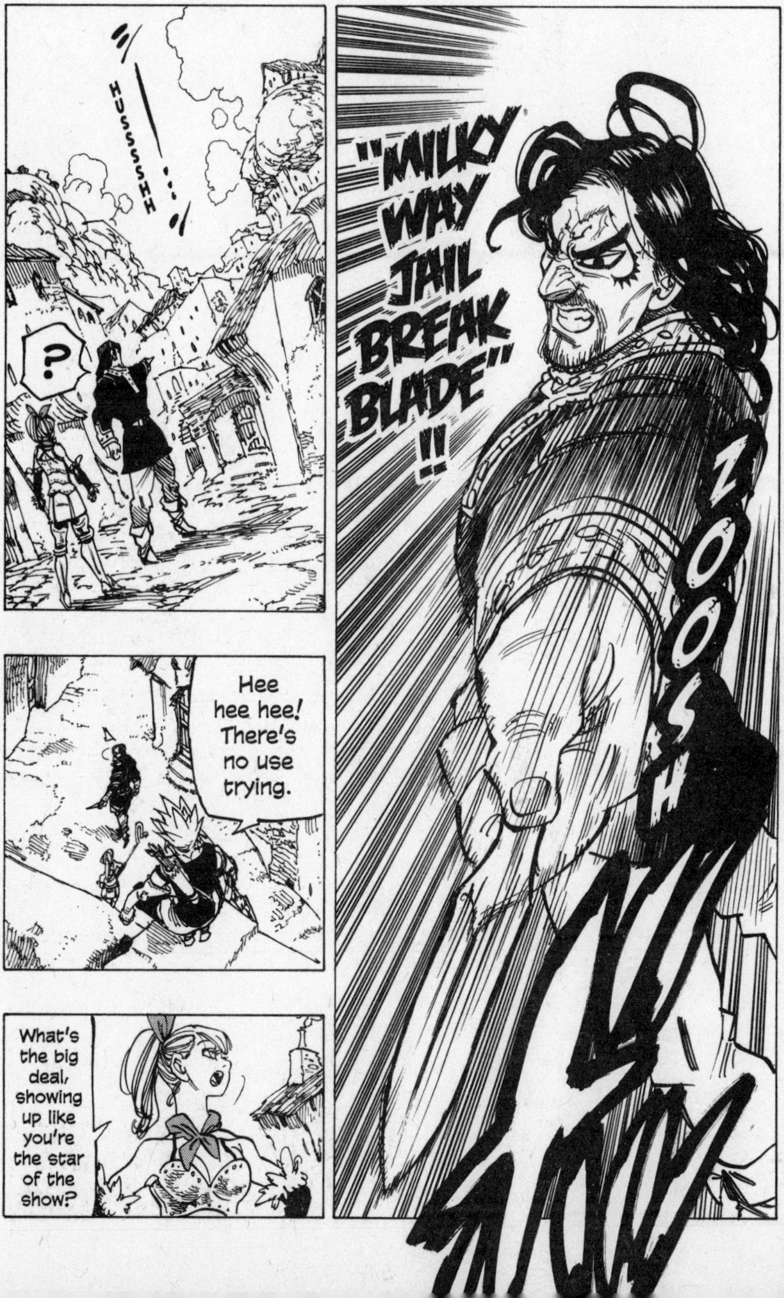
"MILKY WAY JAIL BREAK BLADE"!!
ZOOOSH
HUSSSSHH
?
Hee hee hee! There's no use trying.
What's the big deal, showing up like you're the star of the show?

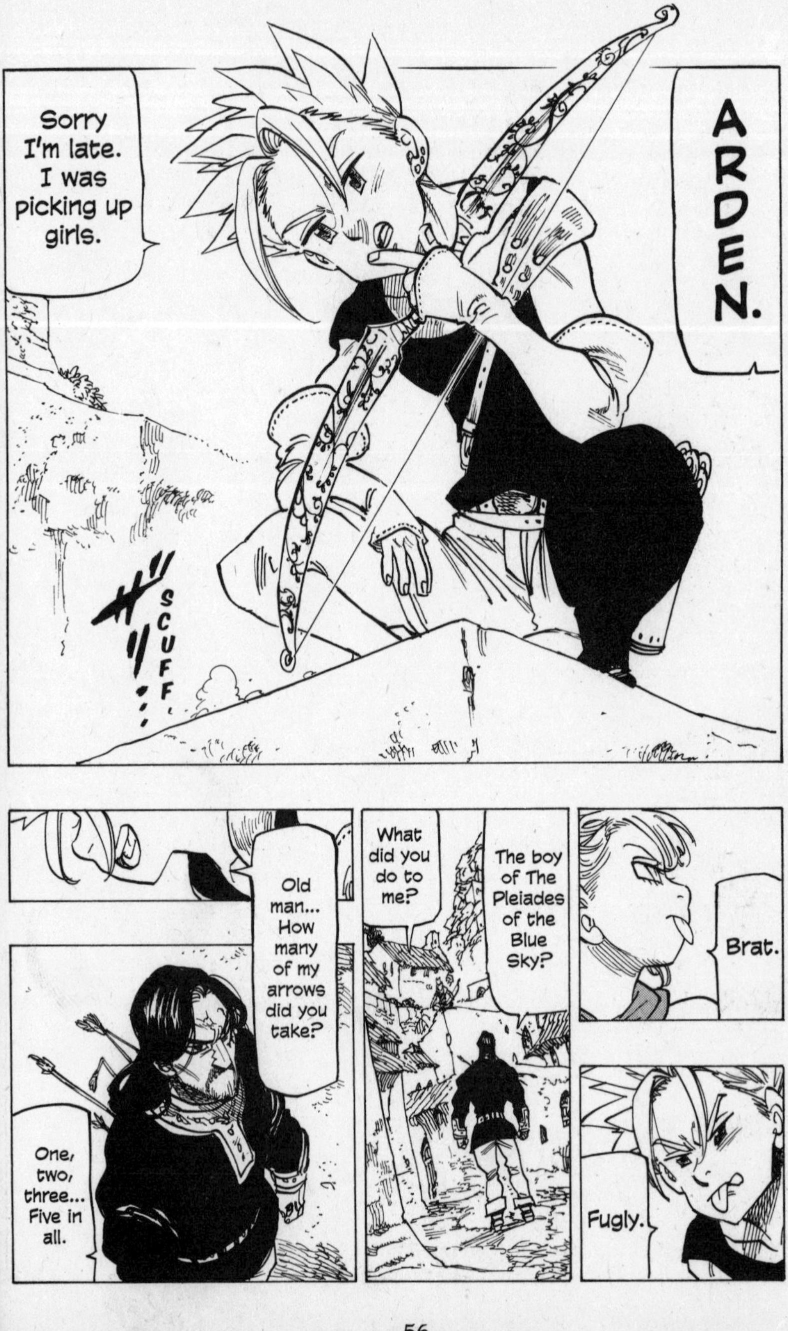
ARDEN.
Sorry I'm late. I was picking up girls.
SCUFF
Brat.
Fugly.
The boy of The Pleiades of the Blue Sky?
What did you do to me?
Old man... How many of my arrows did you take?
One, two, three... Five in all.

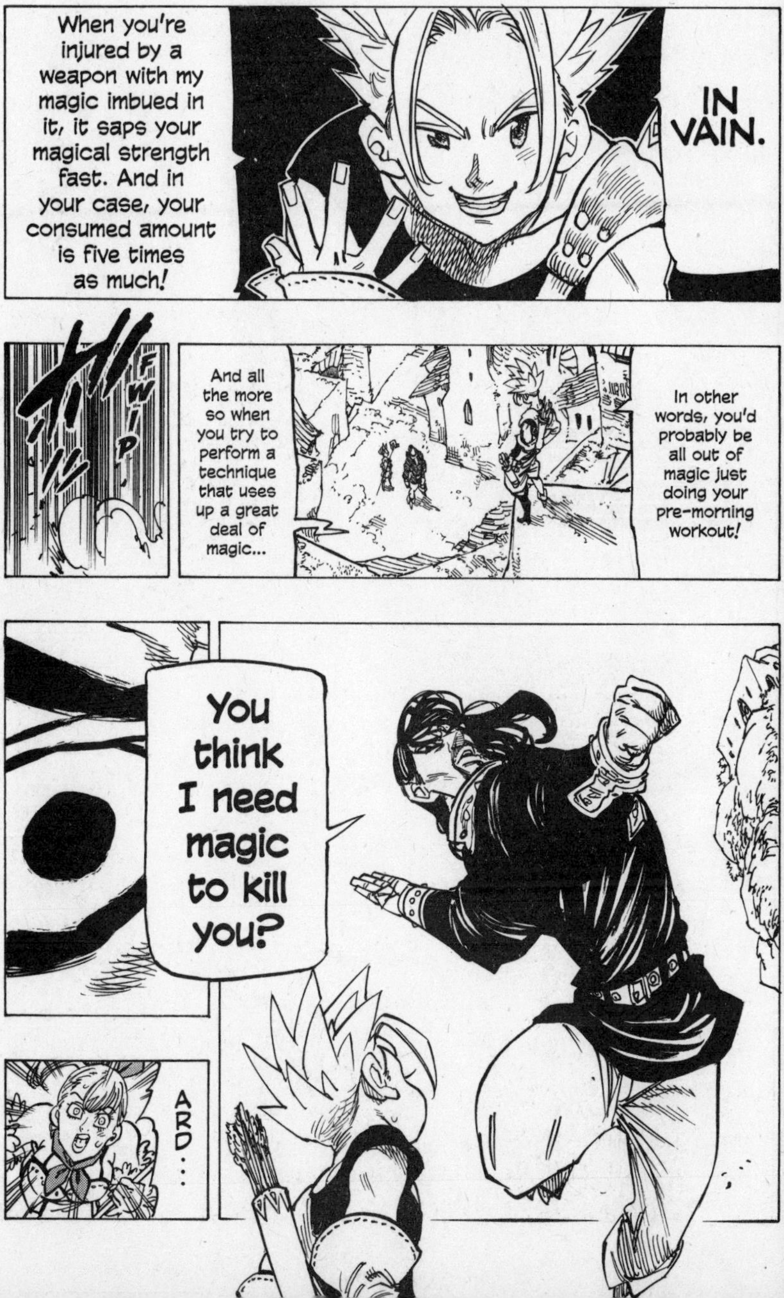
IN VAIN.
When you're injured by a weapon with my magic imbued in it, it saps your magical strength fast. And in your case, your consumed amount is five times as much!
And all the more so when you try to perform a technique that uses up a great deal of magic...
In other words, you'd probably be all out of magic just doing your pre-morning workout!
FWIP
You think I need magic to kill you?
ARD...

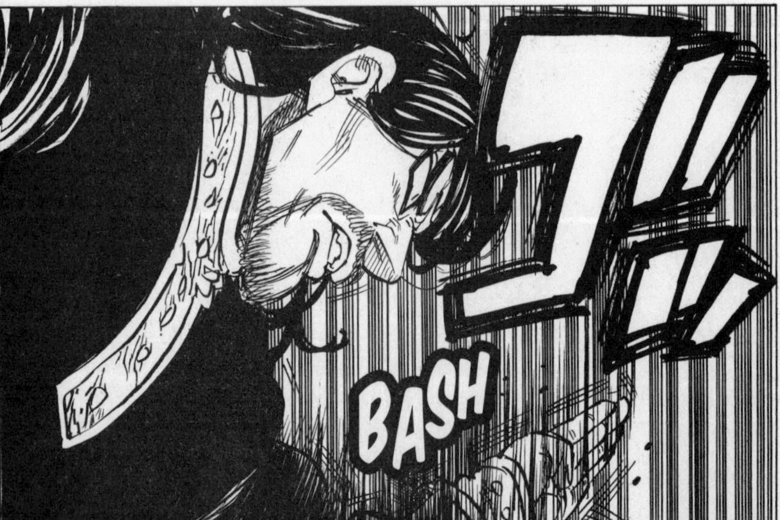
BASH

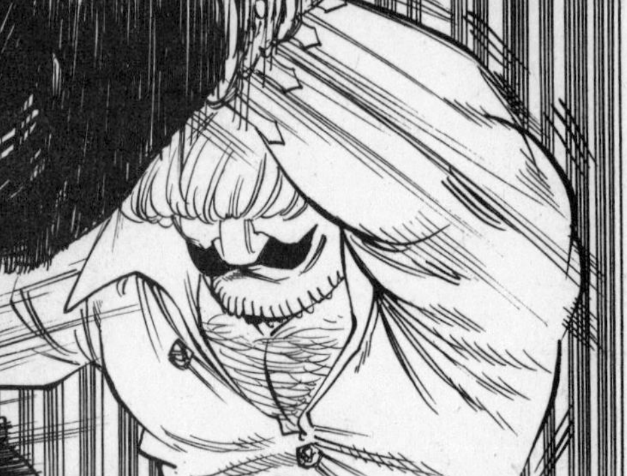
THOOM
WHOOOOM
W... What the ?!

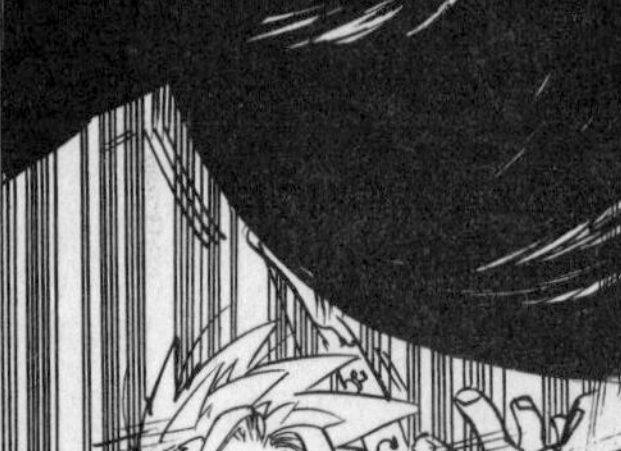
KUH !!

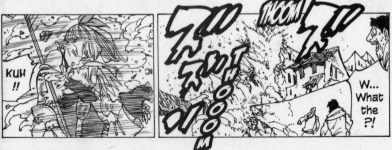

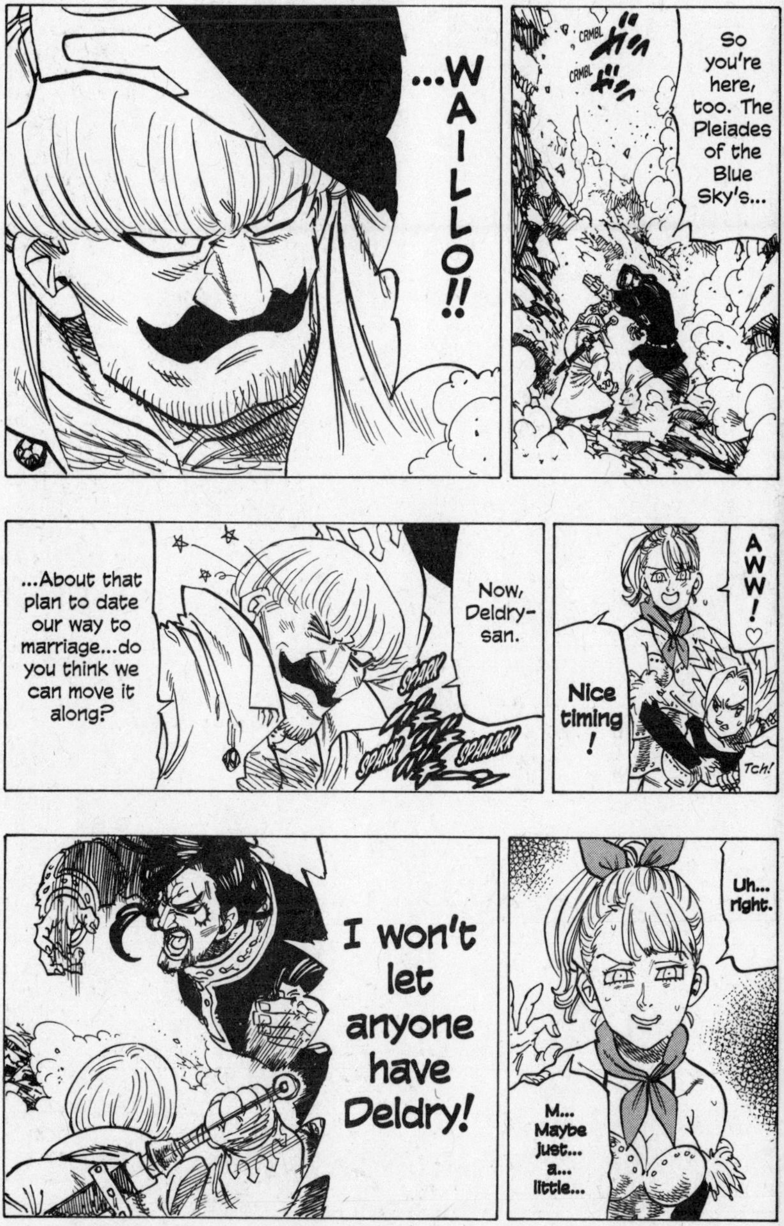
CRMBL
CRMBL
So you're here, too. The Pleiades of the Blue Sky's...
...WAILLO!!
AWW! ♡
Nice timing!
Tch!
Now, Deldry-san.
...About that plan to date our way to marriage...do you think we can move it along?
SPARK
SPARK
SPAAARK
Uh... right.
M... Maybe just... a... little...
I won't let anyone have Deldry!

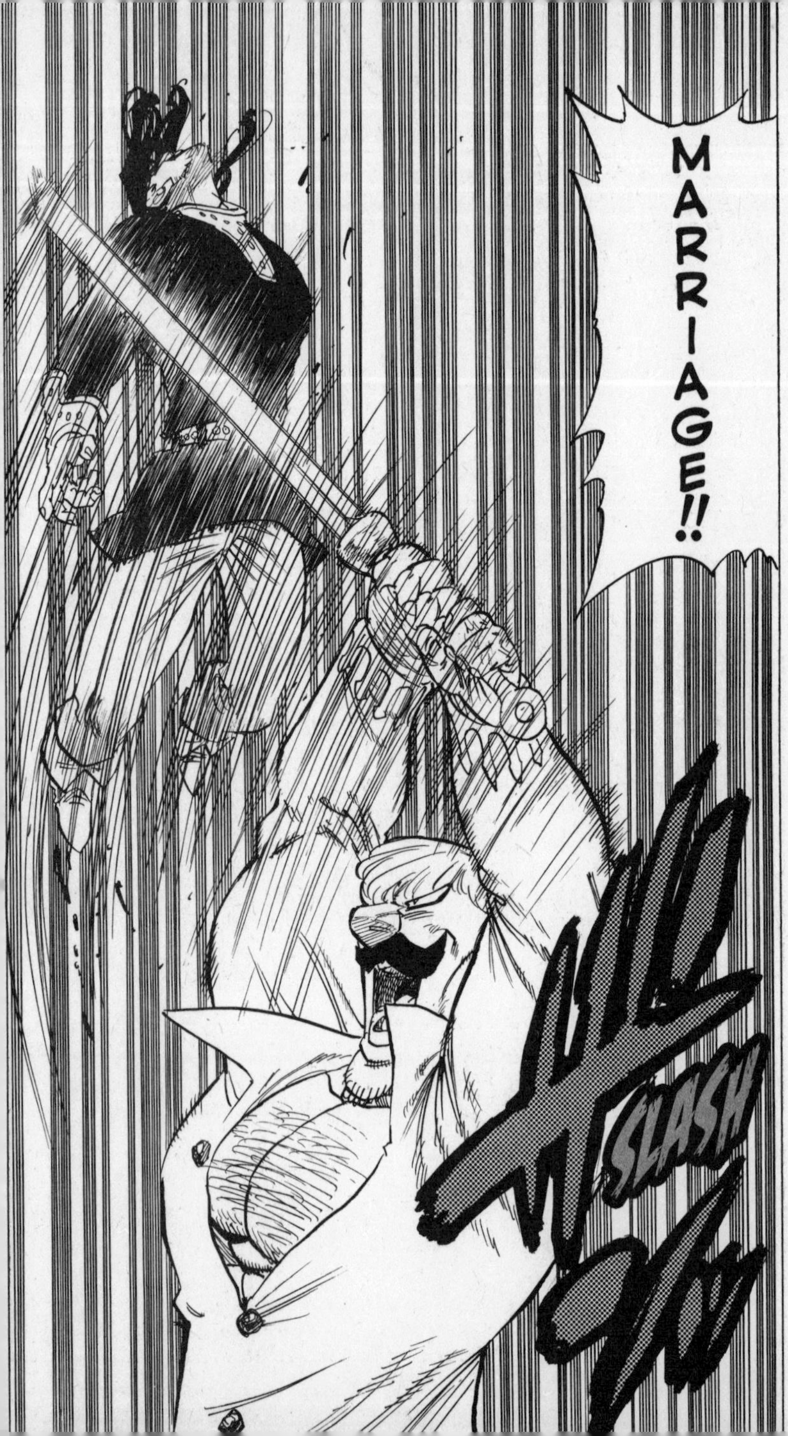
MARRIAGE!!
SLASH

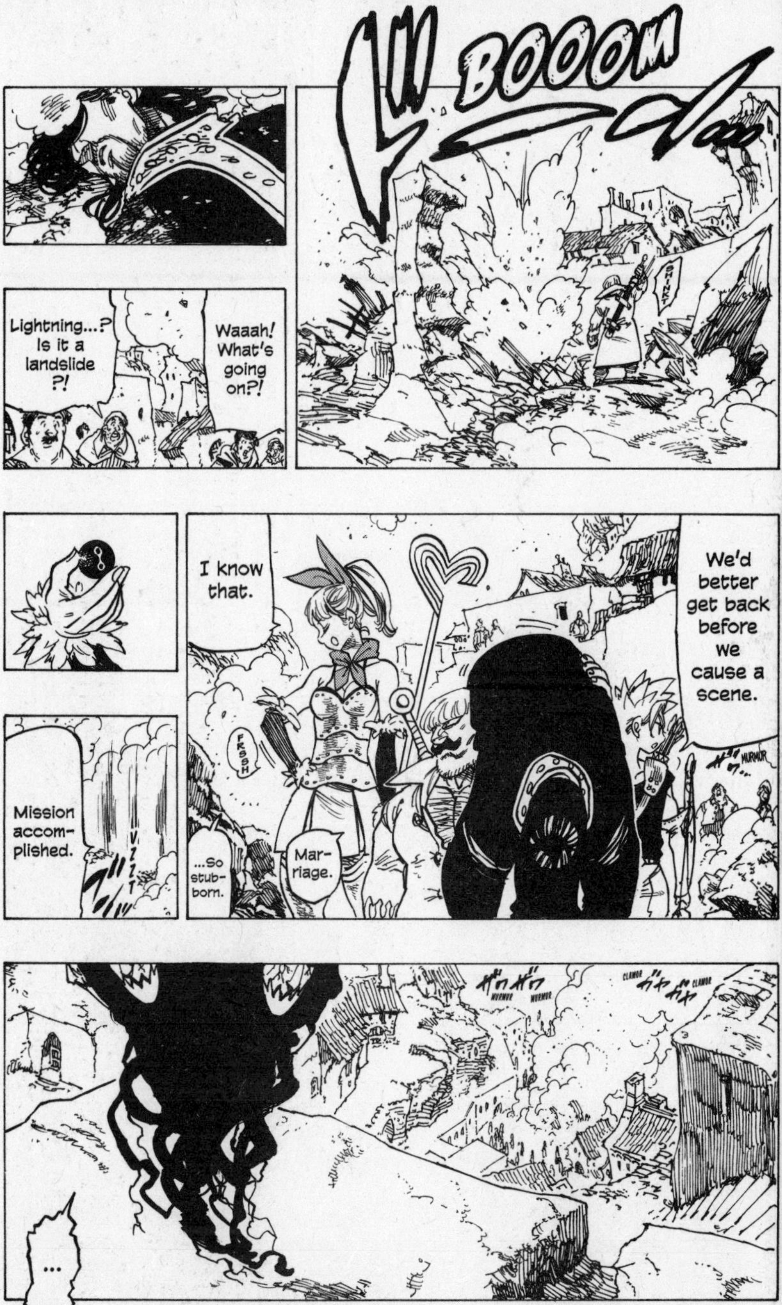
BOOOM
SHINK
Waaah! What's going on?!
Lightning...? Is it a landslide?!
We'd better get back before we cause a scene.
MURMUR
I know that.
FRSSH
Mar-riage.
...So stub-born.
Mission accom-plished.
VZZT
CLAMOR
CLAMOR
MURMUR
MURMUR
...

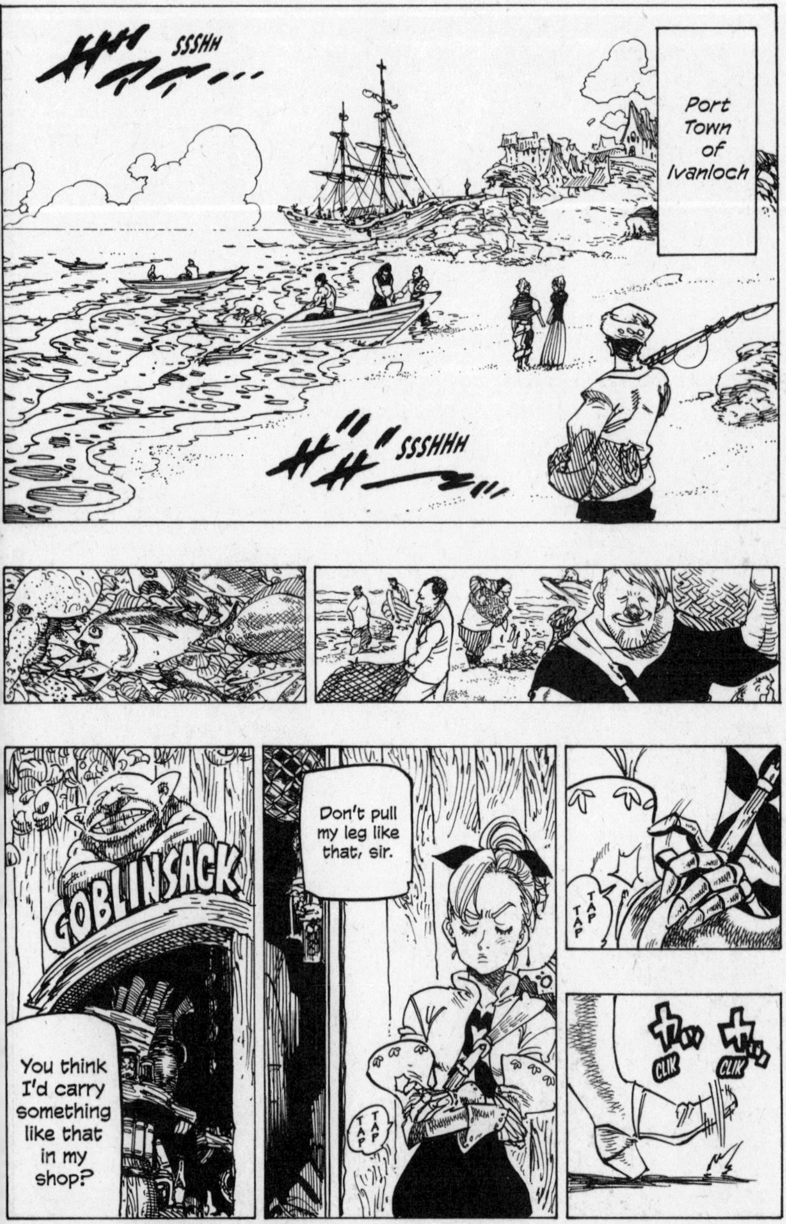
Port Town of Ivanloch
SSSHH
SSSHHH
TAP TAP
CLIK
CLIK
Don't pull my leg like that, sir.
TAP TAP
GOBLIN SACK
You think I'd carry something like that in my shop?

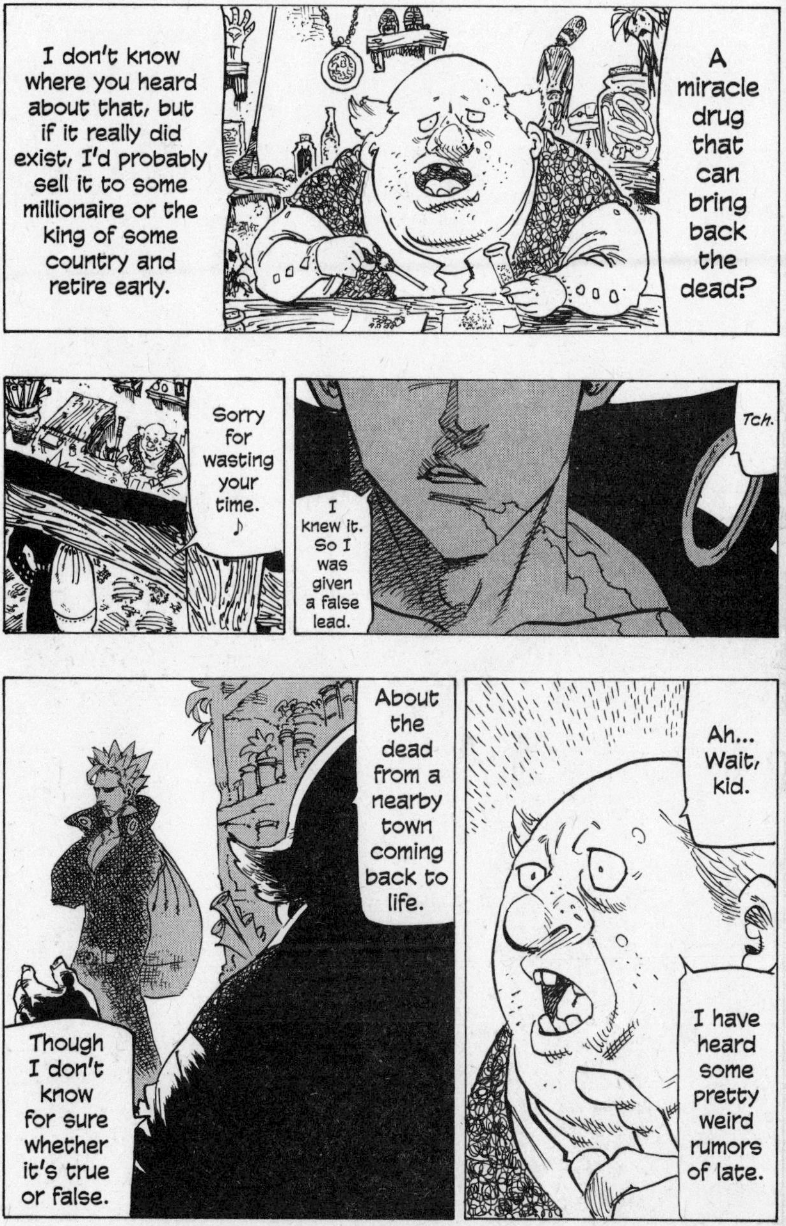
A miracle drug that can bring back the dead?
I don't know where you heard about that, but if it really did exist, I'd probably sell it to some millionaire or the king of some country and retire early.
Tch.
I knew it. So I was given a false lead.
Sorry for wasting your time. ♪
Ah... Wait, kid.
I have heard some pretty weird rumors of late.
About the dead from a nearby town coming back to life.
Though I don't know for sure whether it's true or false.

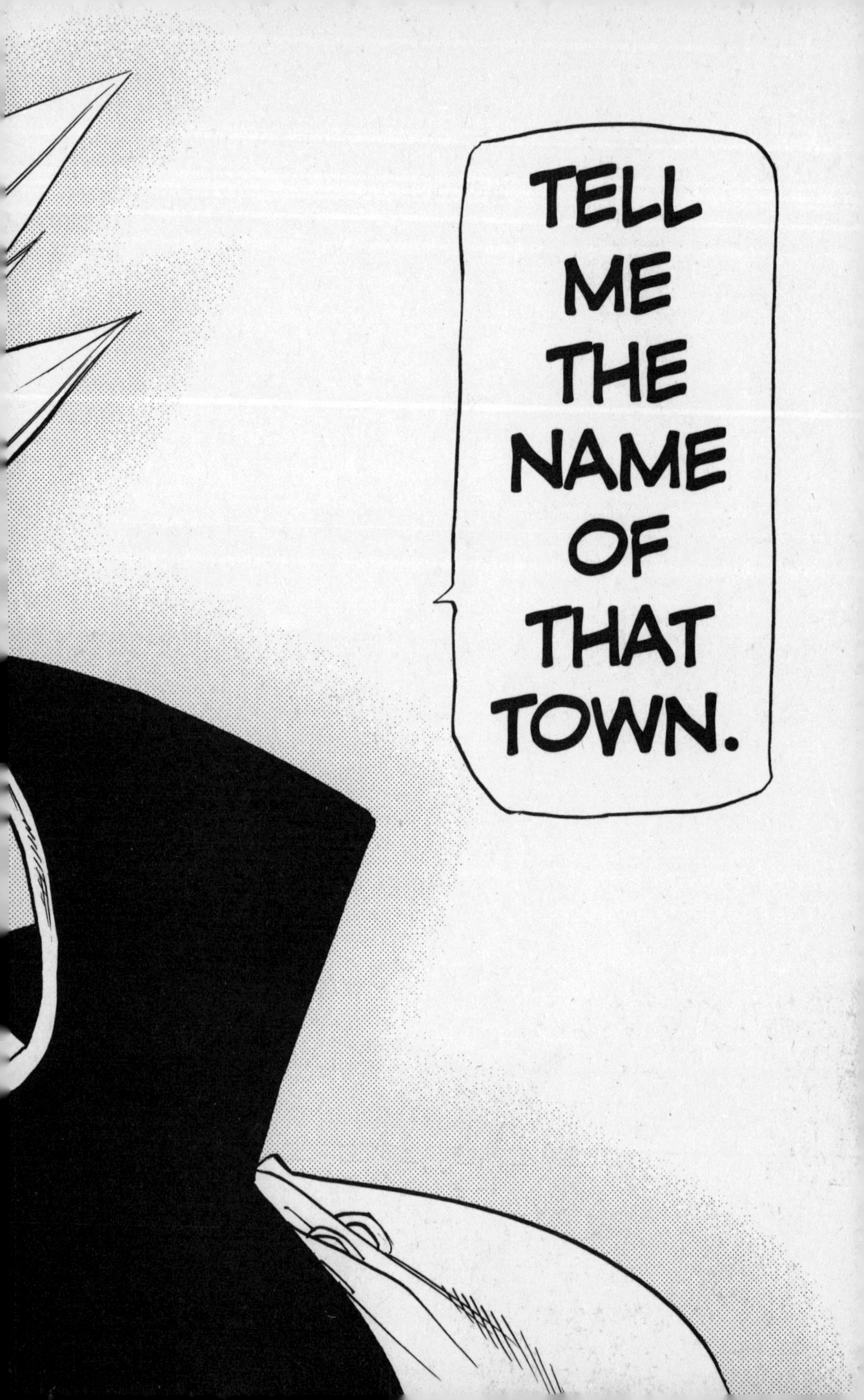
TELL ME THE NAME OF THAT TOWN.

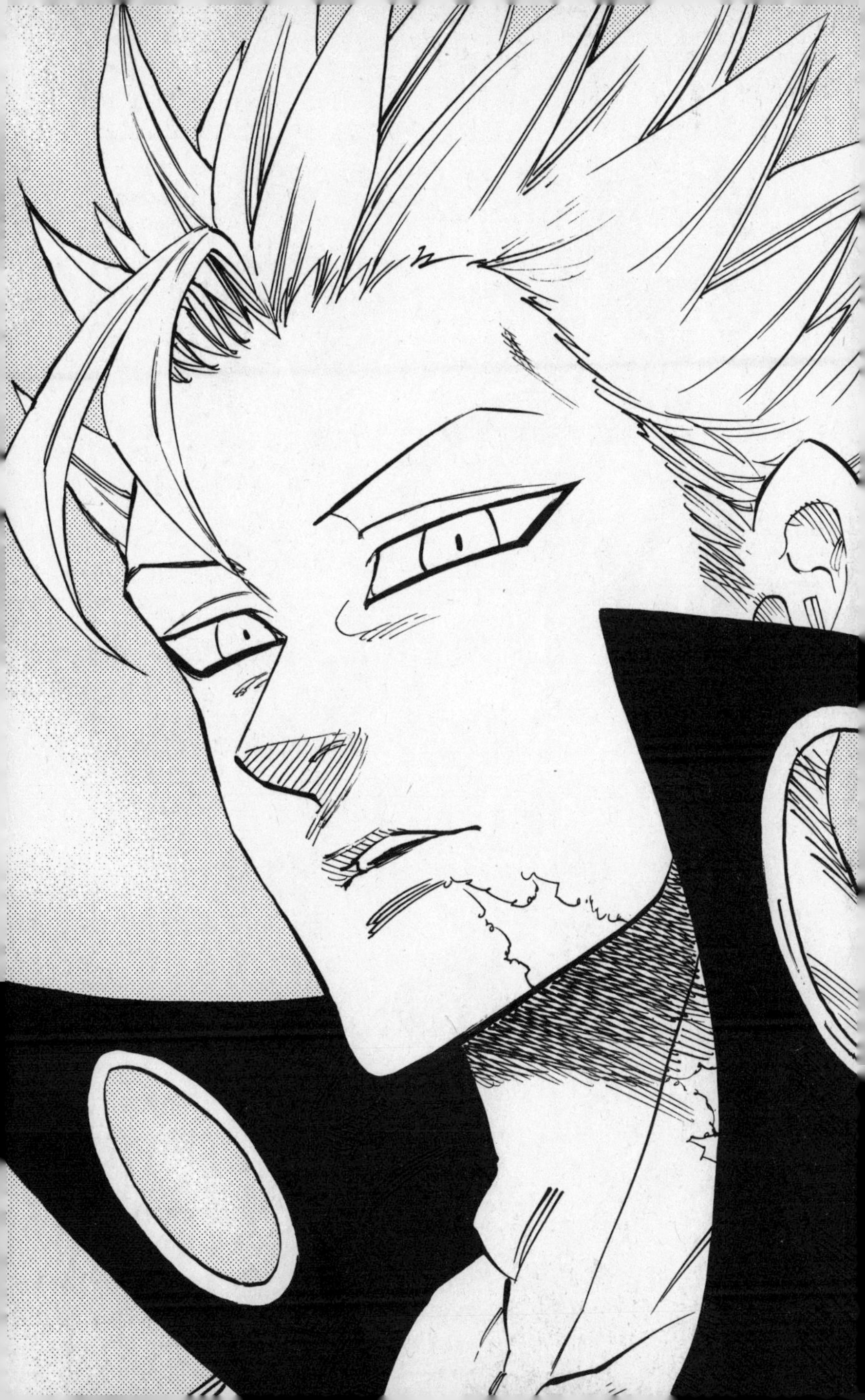

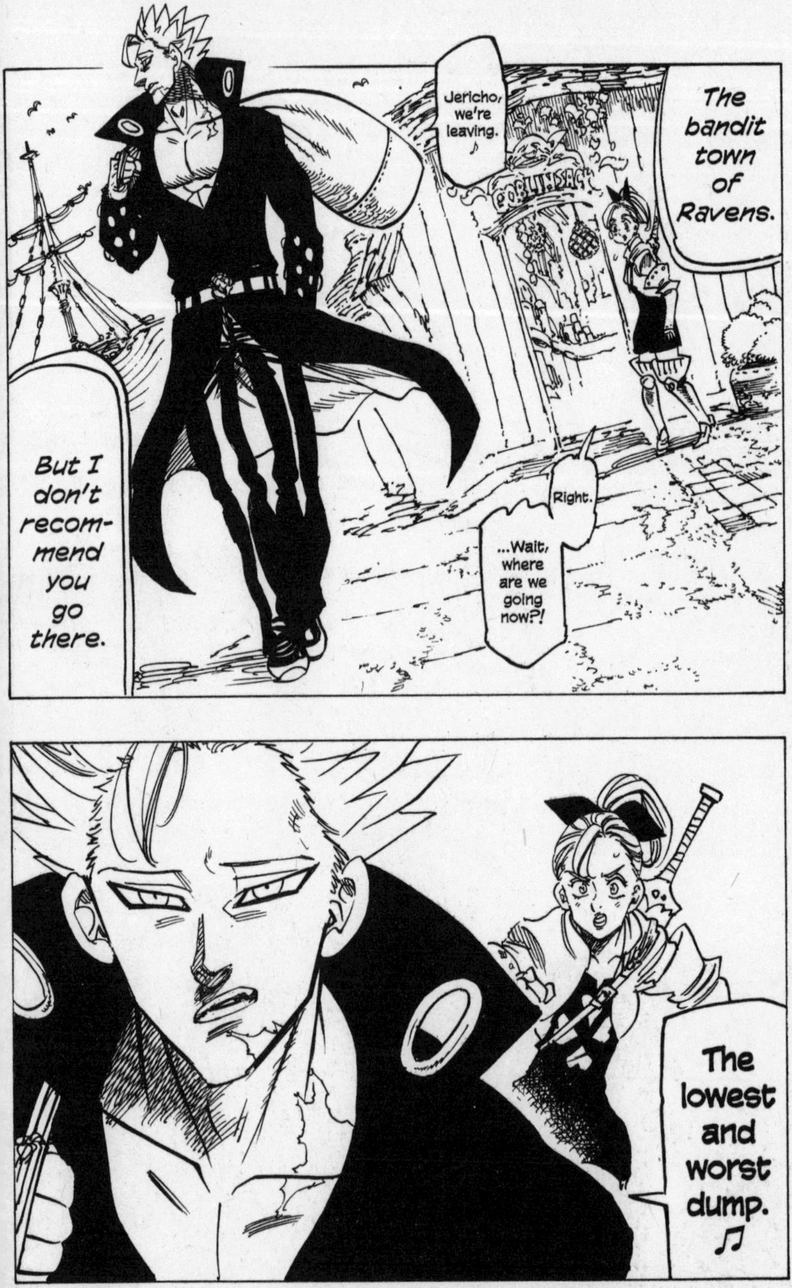
The bandit town of Ravens.
Jericho, we're leaving. ♪
Right.
...Wait, where are we going now?!
But I don't recommend you go there.
The lowest and worst dump. ♫

# Chapter 139 - Tell Me About the Past

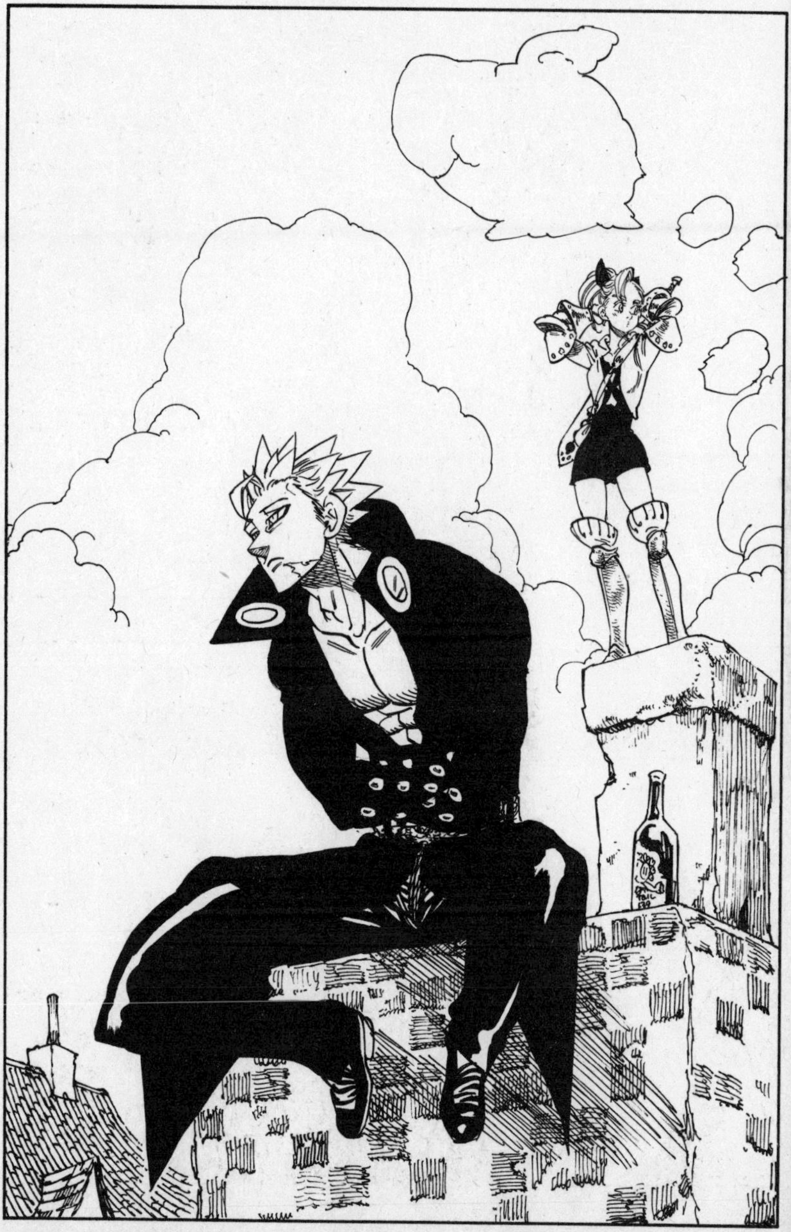

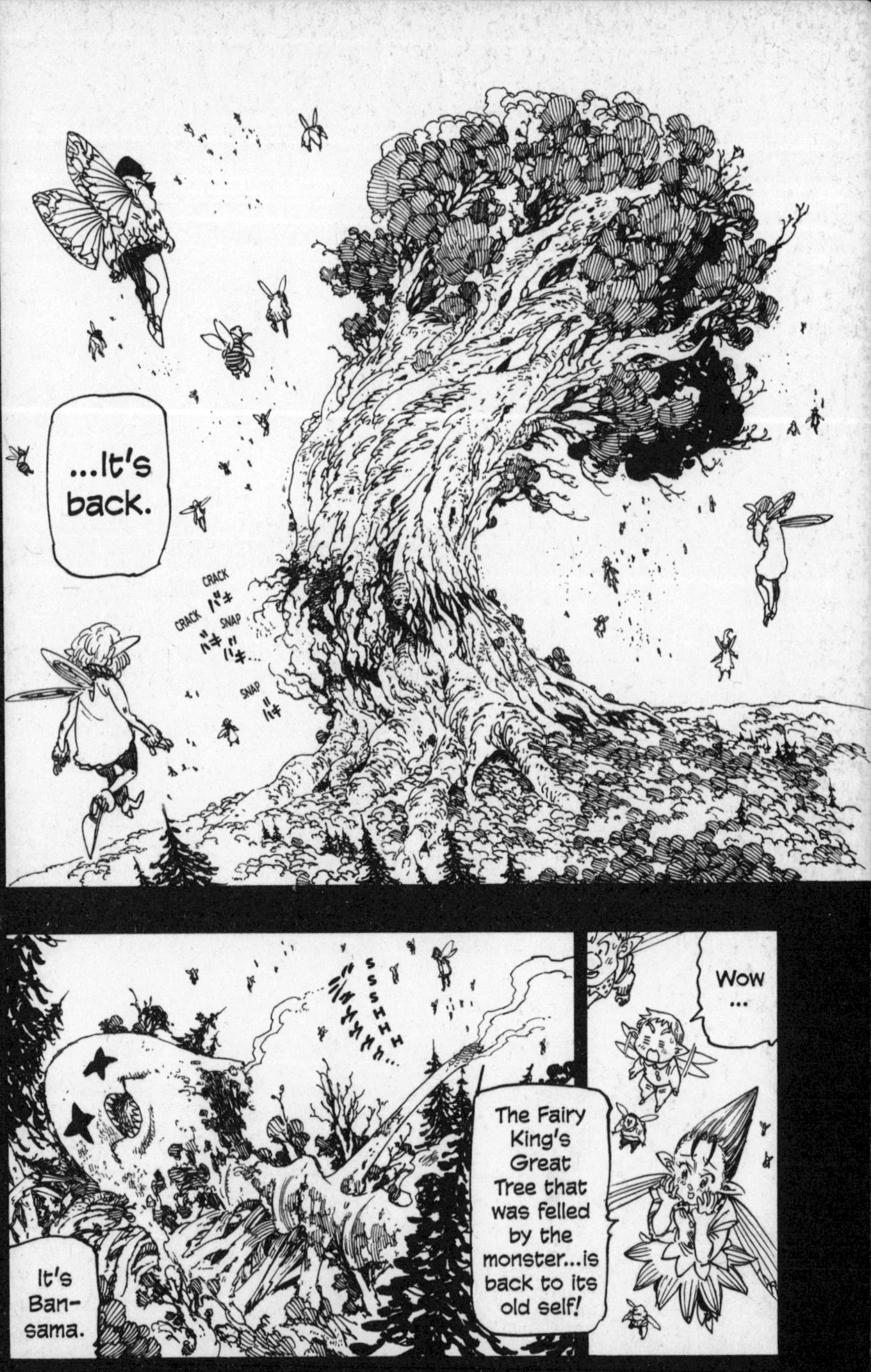
...It's back.
CRACK
バキ
CRACK
SNAP
バキバキ...
SNAP
バキ
Wow ...
The Fairy King's Great Tree that was felled by the monster...is back to its old self!
SSHHHHHH...
It's Ban-sama.

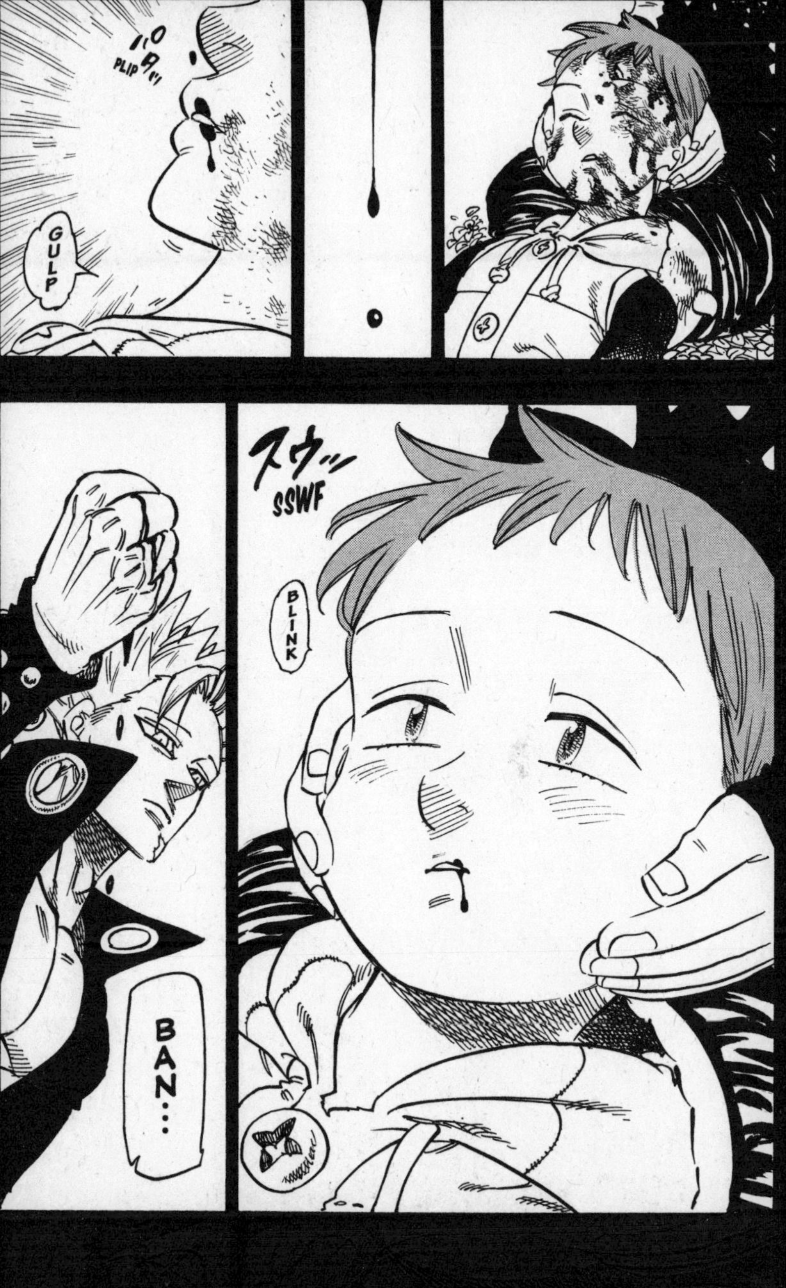
PLIP
GULP
SSWF
BLINK
BAN...

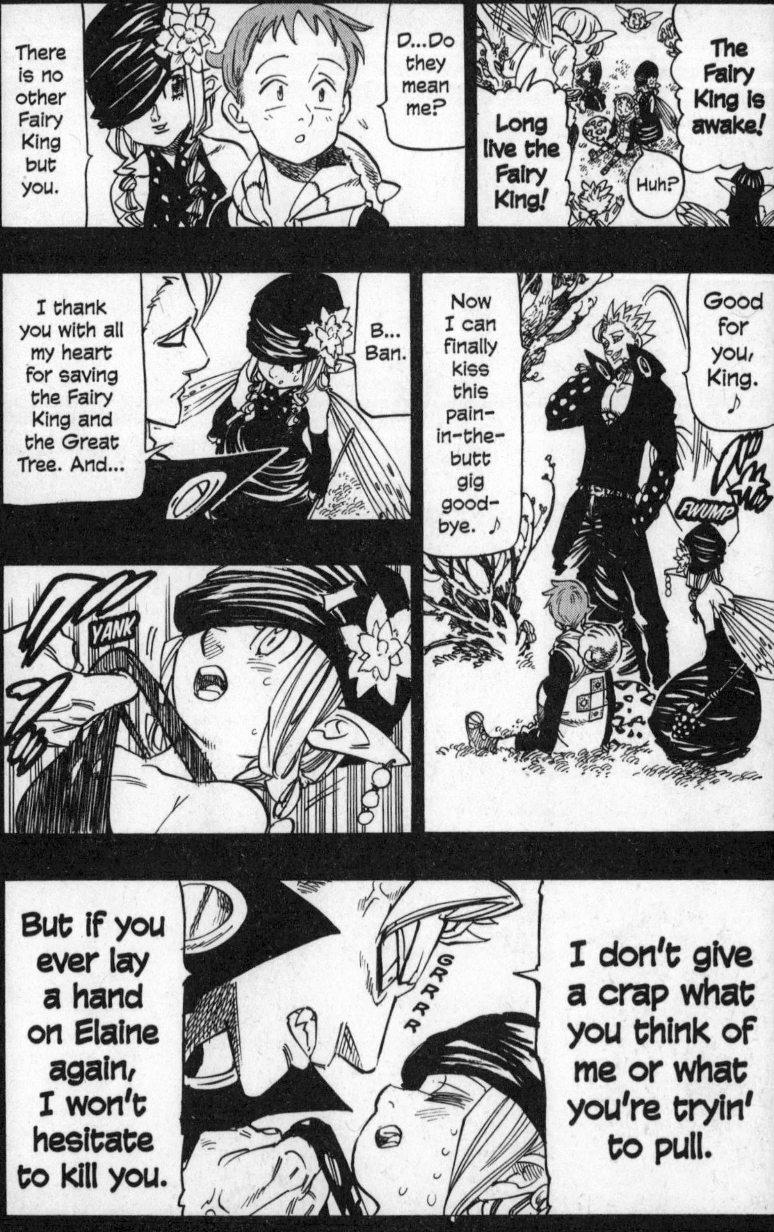

The Fairy King is awake!
Long live the Fairy King!
Huh?
D...Do they mean me?
There is no other Fairy King but you.
Good for you, King. ♪
Now I can finally kiss this pain-in-the-butt gig goodbye. ♪
FWUMP
B... Ban.
I thank you with all my heart for saving the Fairy King and the Great Tree. And...
YANK
I don't give a crap what you think of me or what you're tryin' to pull.
GRRRR
But if you ever lay a hand on Elaine again, I won't hesitate to kill you.

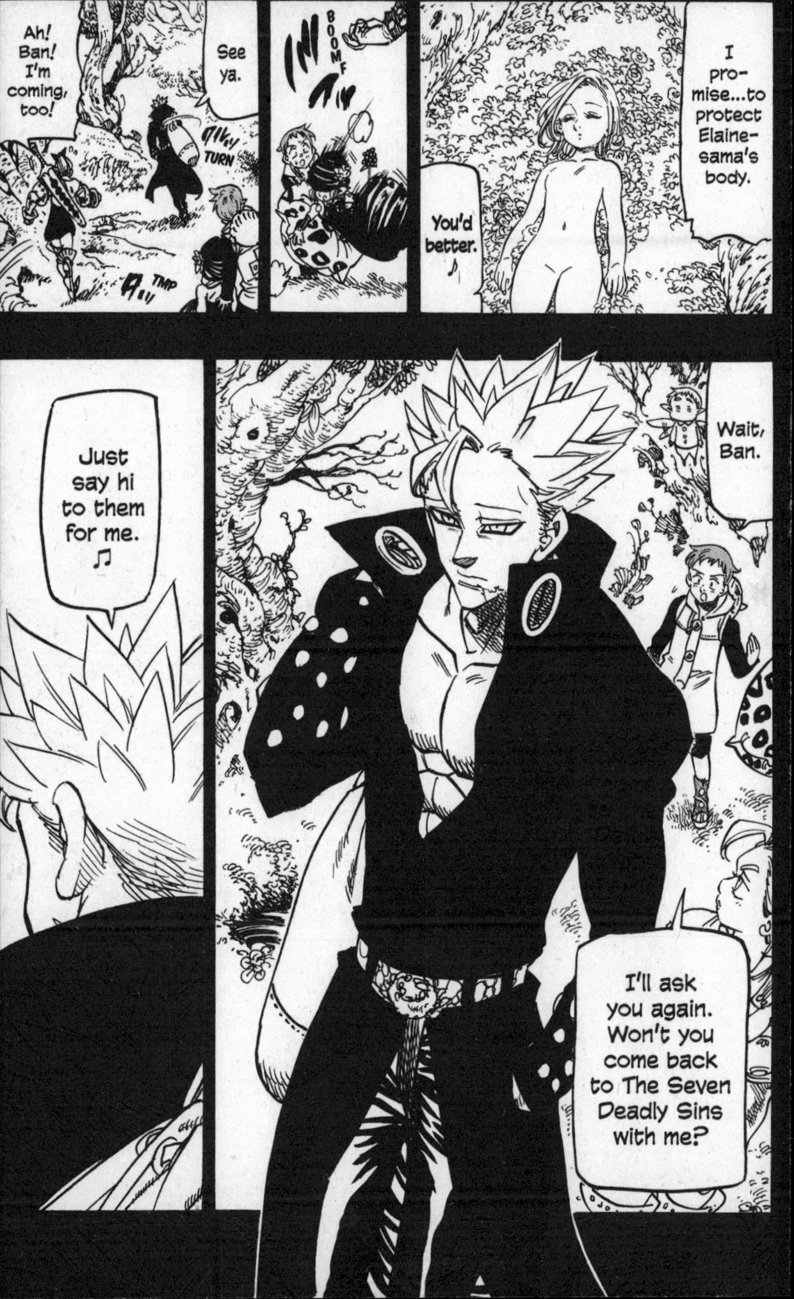
I promise...to protect Elaine-sama's body.
You'd better. ♪
BOOMF
See ya.
TURN
Ah! Ban! I'm coming, too!
TMP
Wait, Ban.
I'll ask you again. Won't you come back to The Seven Deadly Sins with me?
Just say hi to them for me. ♫

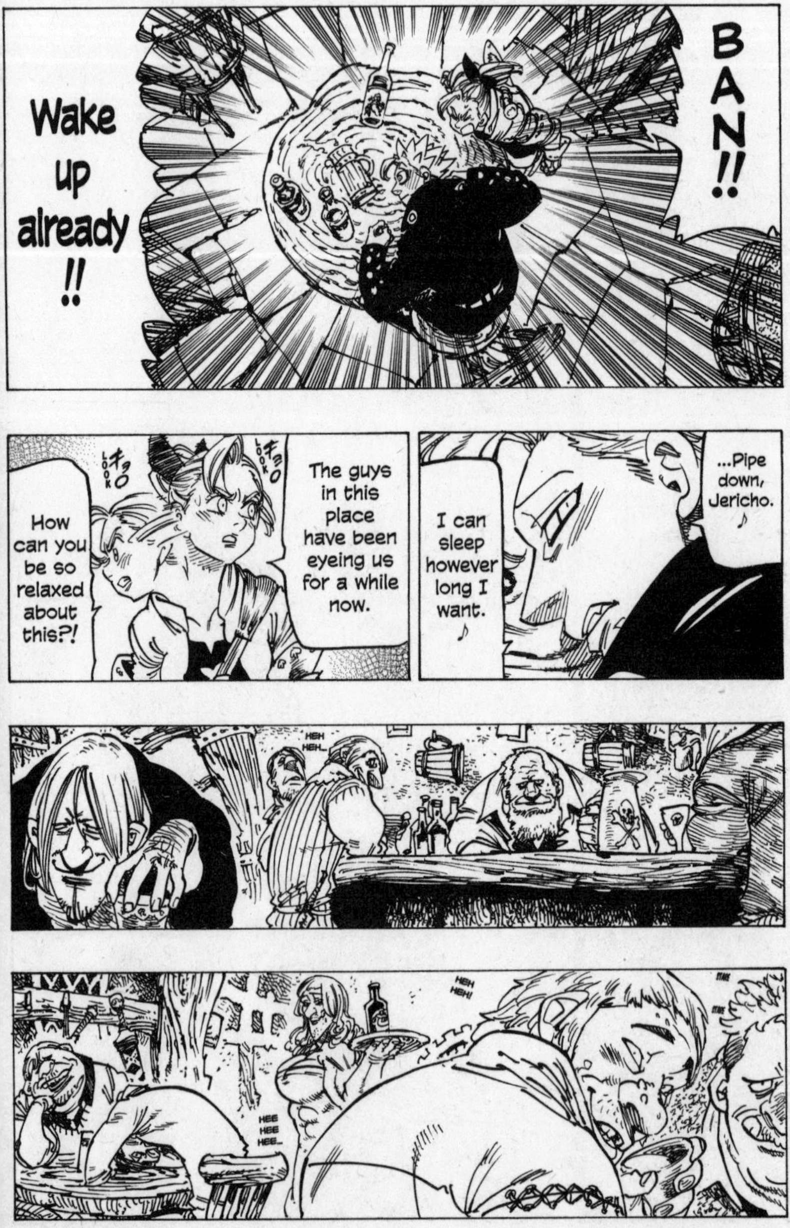
BAN!!
Wake up already!!
...Pipe down, Jericho. ♪
I can sleep however long I want. ♪
LOOK
The guys in this place have been eyeing us for a while now.
LOOK
How can you be so relaxed about this?!
HEH HEH...
STARE
STARE
HEH HEH!
HEE HEE HEE...

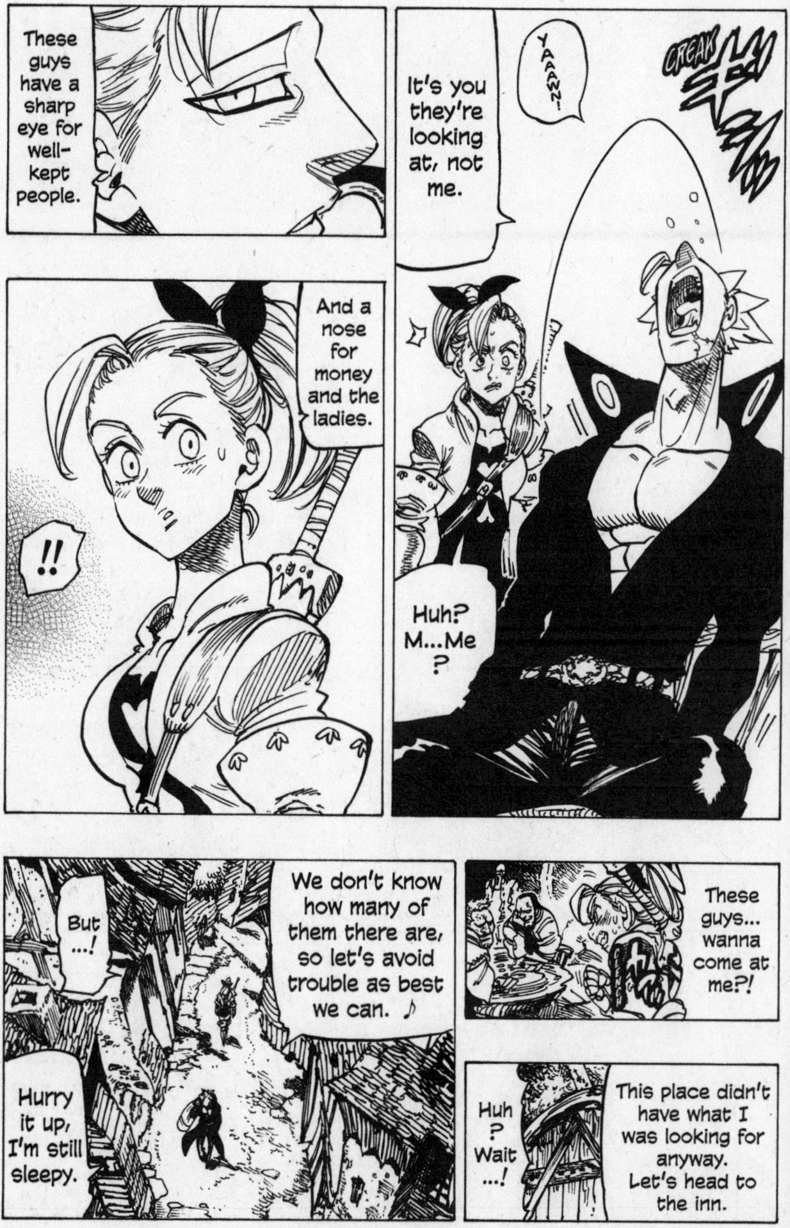
CREAK
YAAAWN!
It's you they're looking at, not me.
Huh? M...Me?
These guys have a sharp eye for well-kept people.
And a nose for money and the ladies.
!!
These guys... wanna come at me?!
This place didn't have what I was looking for anyway. Let's head to the inn.
Huh? Wait...!
We don't know how many of them there are, so let's avoid trouble as best we can. ♪
But...!
Hurry it up, I'm still sleepy.

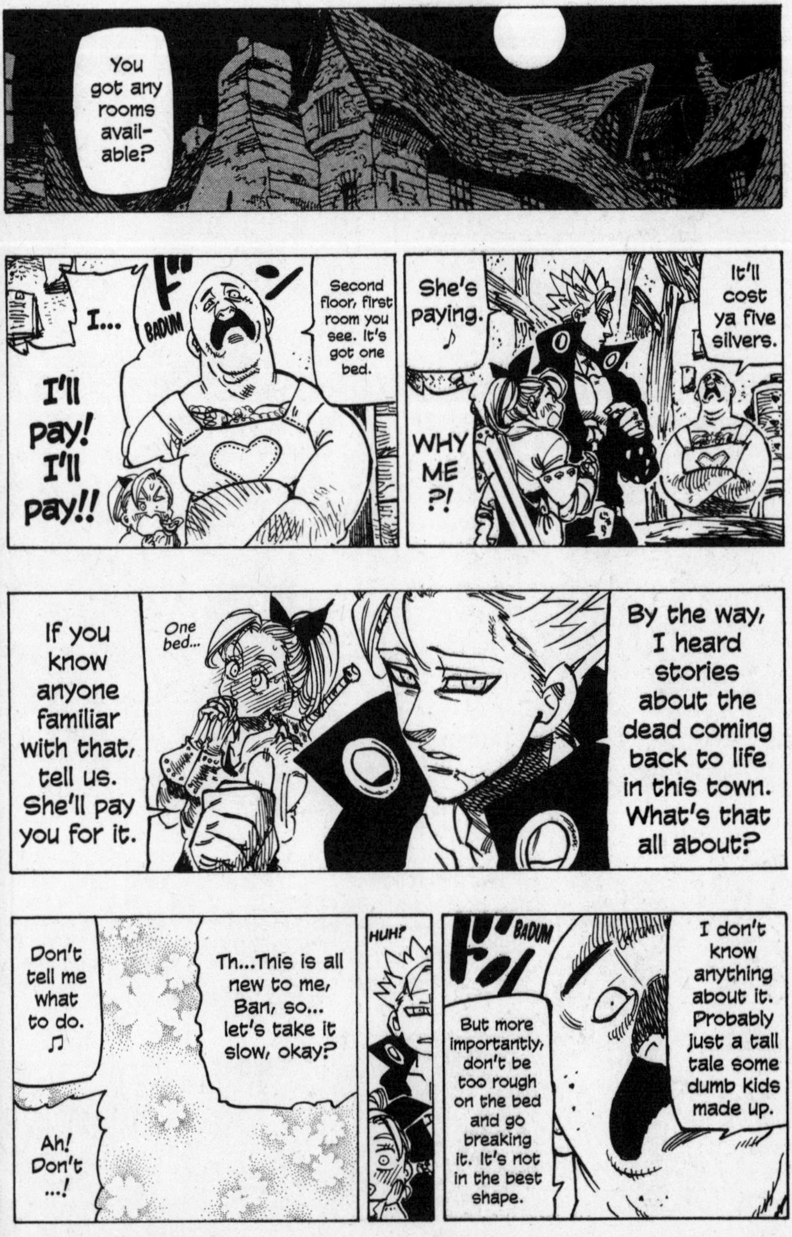
You got any rooms available?
It'll cost ya five silvers.
She's paying. ♪
WHY ME ?!
Second floor, first room you see. It's got one bed.
BADUM
I...
I'll pay! I'll pay!!
By the way, I heard stories about the dead coming back to life in this town. What's that all about?
One bed...
If you know anyone familiar with that, tell us. She'll pay you for it.
I don't know anything about it. Probably just a tall tale some dumb kids made up.
BADUM
But more importantly, don't be too rough on the bed and go breaking it. It's not in the best shape.
HUH?
Th...This is all new to me, Ban, so... let's take it slow, okay?
Don't tell me what to do. ♫
Ah! Don't ...!

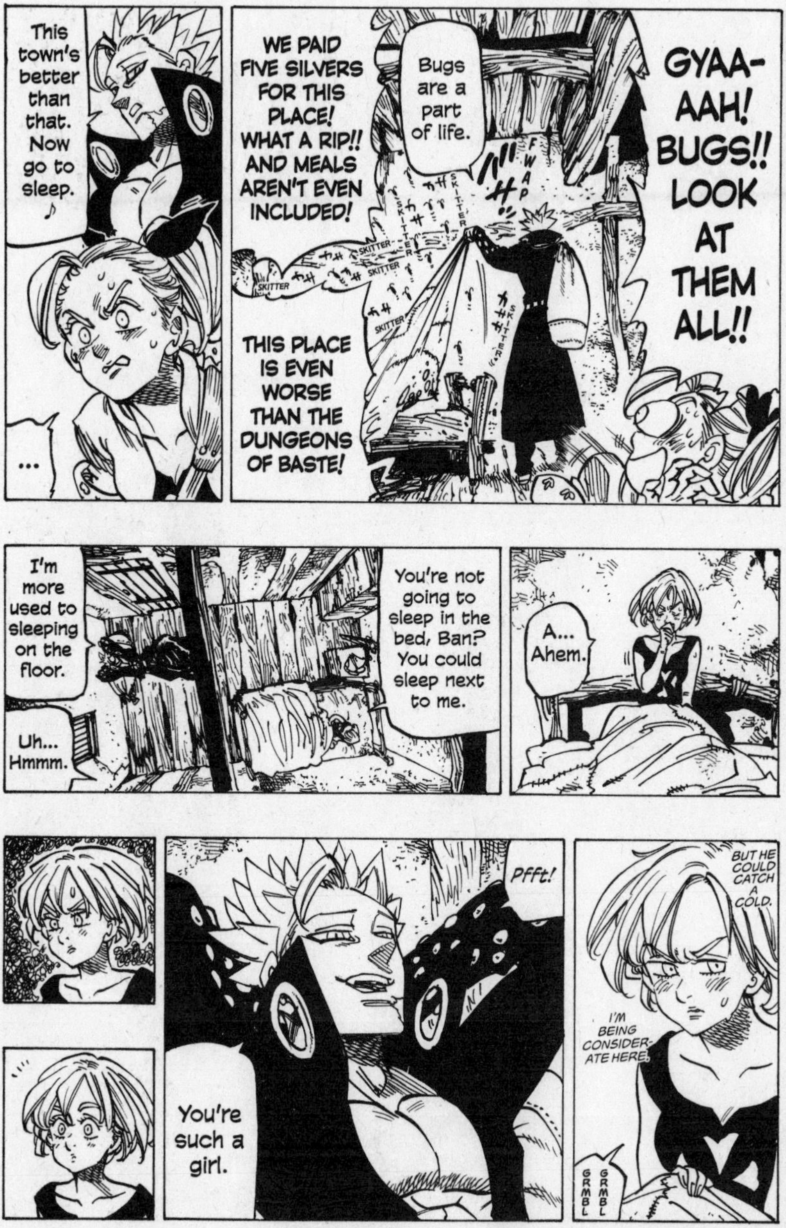
GYAA-AAH! BUGS!! LOOK AT THEM ALL!!
Bugs are a part of life.
FWAP
SKITTER
SKITTER
SKITTER
SKITTER
SKITTER
SKITTER
WE PAID FIVE SILVERS FOR THIS PLACE! WHAT A RIP!! AND MEALS AREN'T EVEN INCLUDED!
THIS PLACE IS EVEN WORSE THAN THE DUNGEONS OF BASTE!
This town's better than that. Now go to sleep. ♪
...
A... Ahem.
You're not going to sleep in the bed, Ban? You could sleep next to me.
I'm more used to sleeping on the floor.
Uh... Hmmm.
BUT HE COULD CATCH A COLD.
I'M BEING CONSIDER-ATE HERE.
GRMBL GRMBL
Pfft!
You're such a girl.

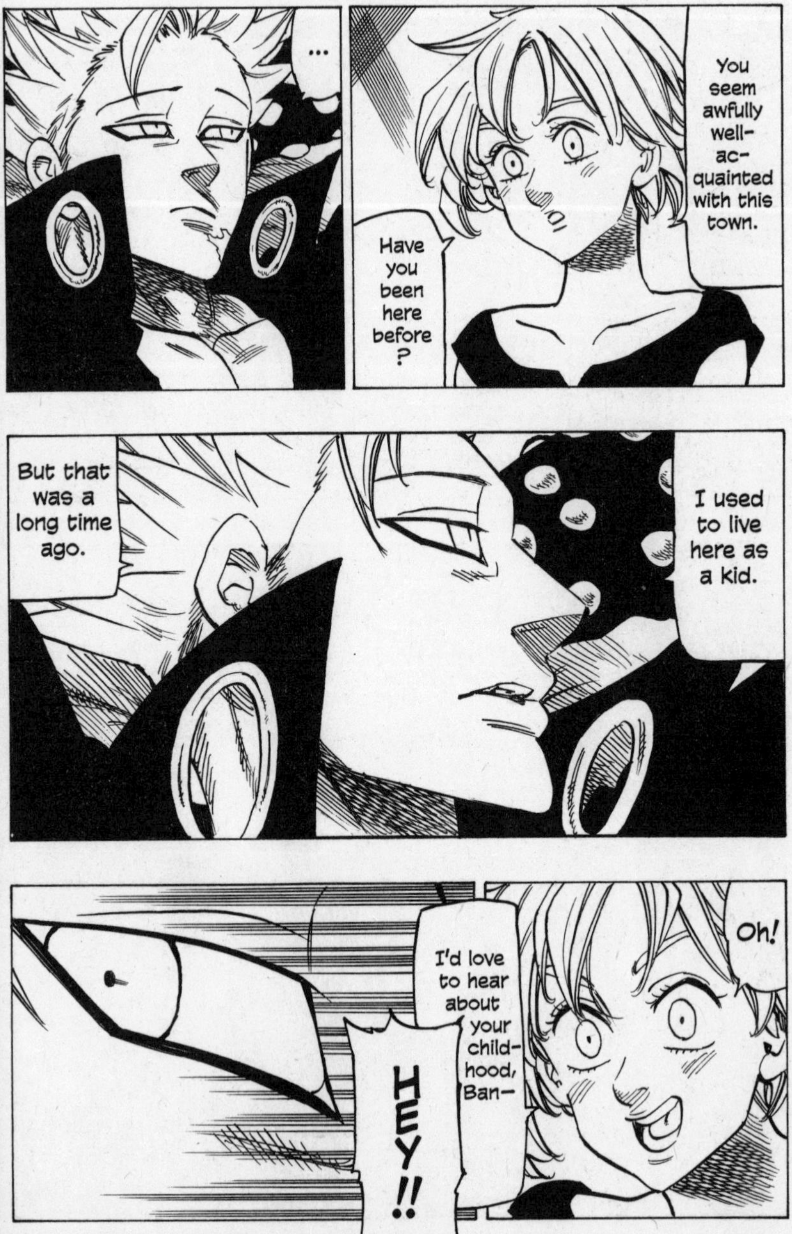
You seem awfully well-acquainted with this town.
Have you been here before?
...
I used to live here as a kid.
But that was a long time ago.
Oh!
I'd love to hear about your childhood, Ban—
HEY!!

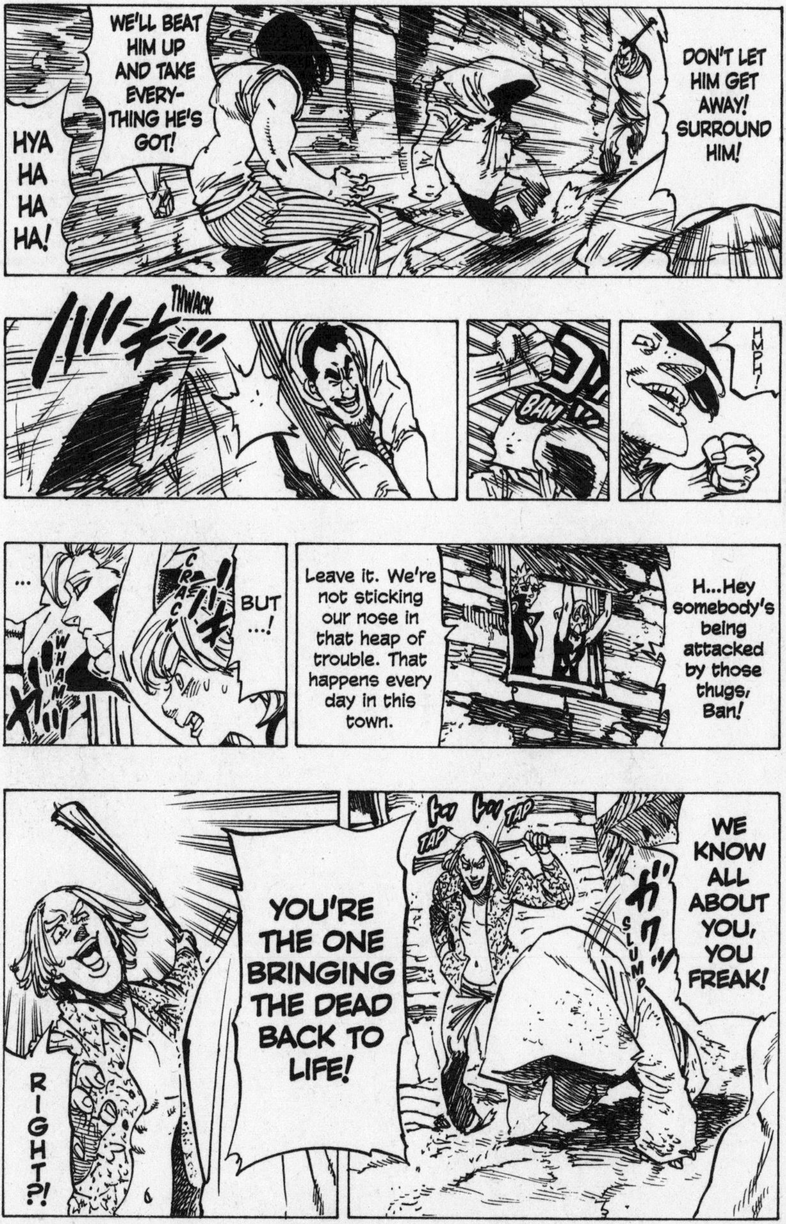
DON'T LET HIM GET AWAY! SURROUND HIM!
WE'LL BEAT HIM UP AND TAKE EVERY-THING HE'S GOT!
HYA HA HA HA!
HMPH!
BAM
THWACK
H...Hey somebody's being attacked by those thugs, Ban!
Leave it. We're not sticking our nose in that heap of trouble. That happens every day in this town.
BUT ...!
CRACK
WHAM
...
WE KNOW ALL ABOUT YOU, YOU FREAK!
SLUMP
TAP
TAP
YOU'RE THE ONE BRINGING THE DEAD BACK TO LIFE!
RIGHT?!

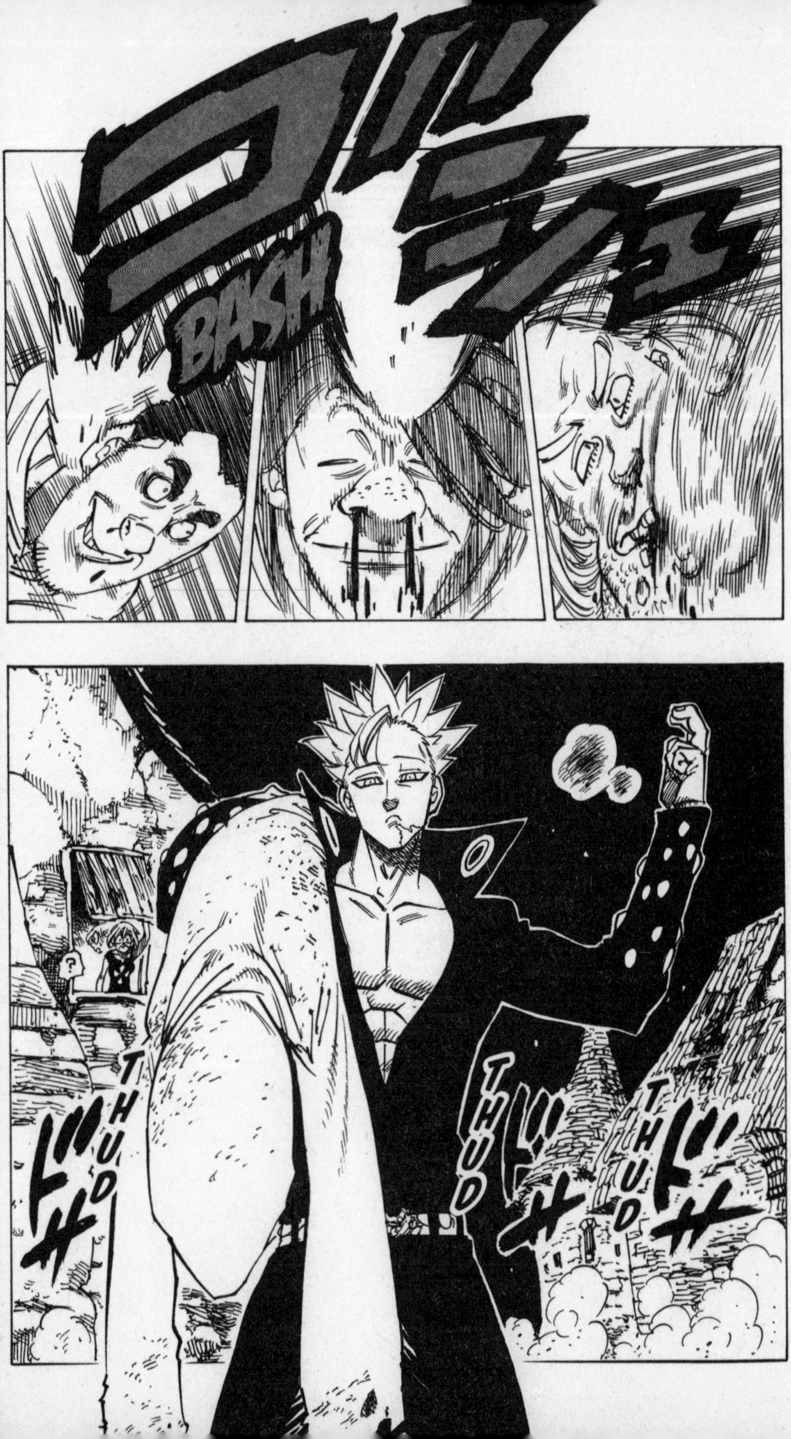
BASH
THUD
THUD
?
THUD

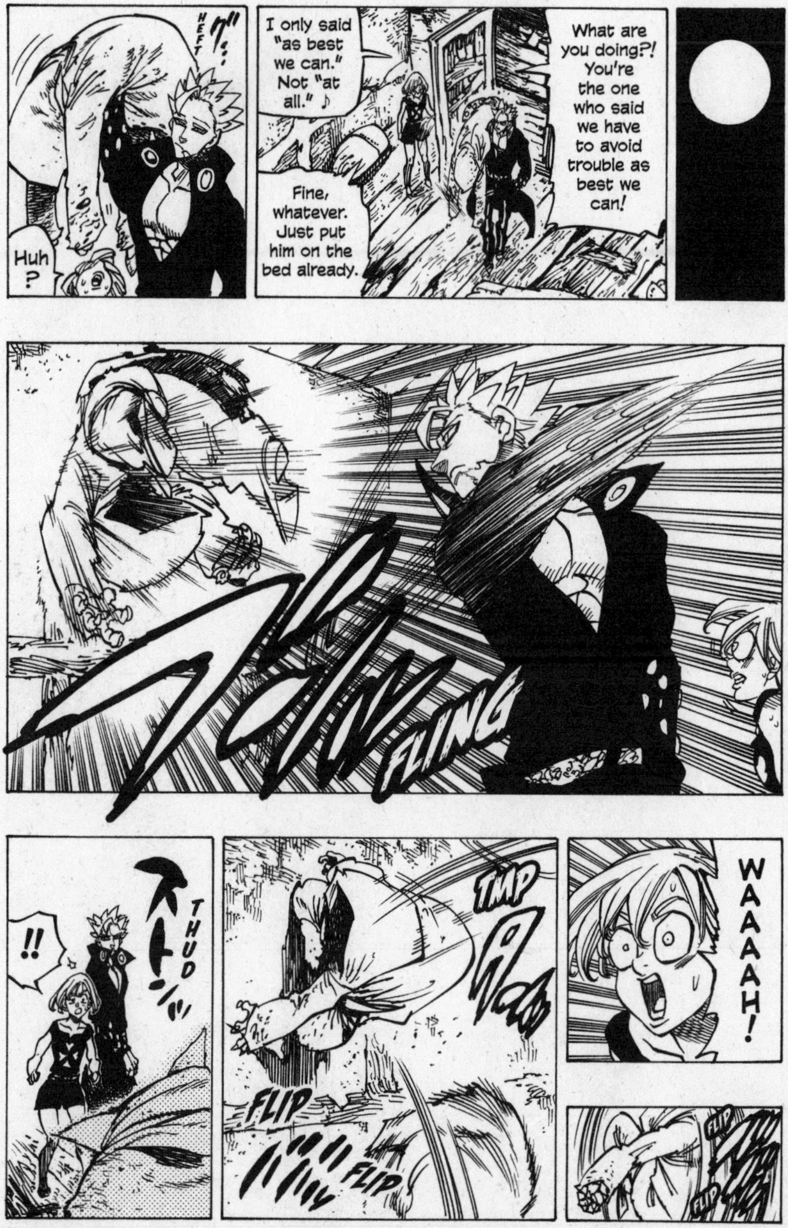
What are you doing?! You're the one who said we have to avoid trouble as best we can!
I only said "as best we can." Not "at all." ♪
Fine, whatever. Just put him on the bed already.
HEFT
Huh?
FLING
WAAAAH!
FLIP
FLIP
TMP
FLIP
FLIP
THUD
!!

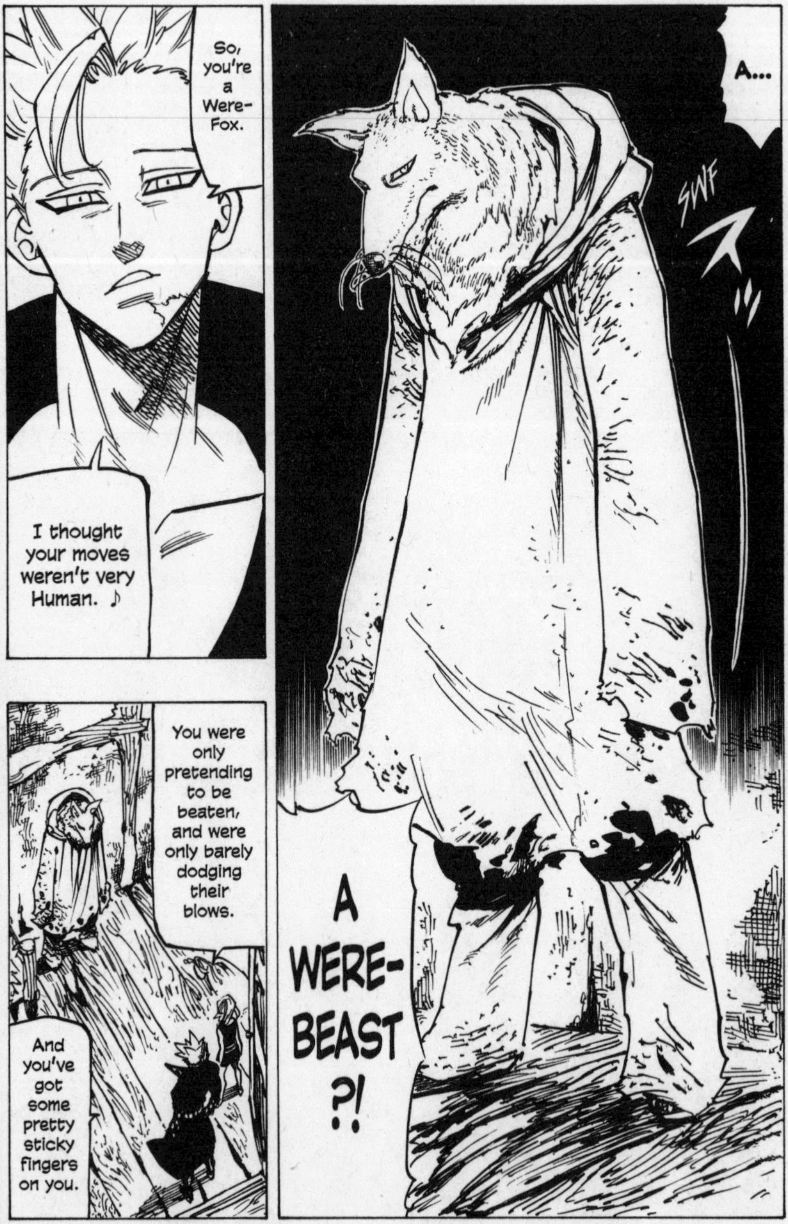
A...
SWF
A WERE-BEAST?!
So, you're a Were-Fox.
I thought your moves weren't very Human. ♪
You were only pretending to be beaten, and were only barely dodging their blows.
And you've got some pretty sticky fingers on you.

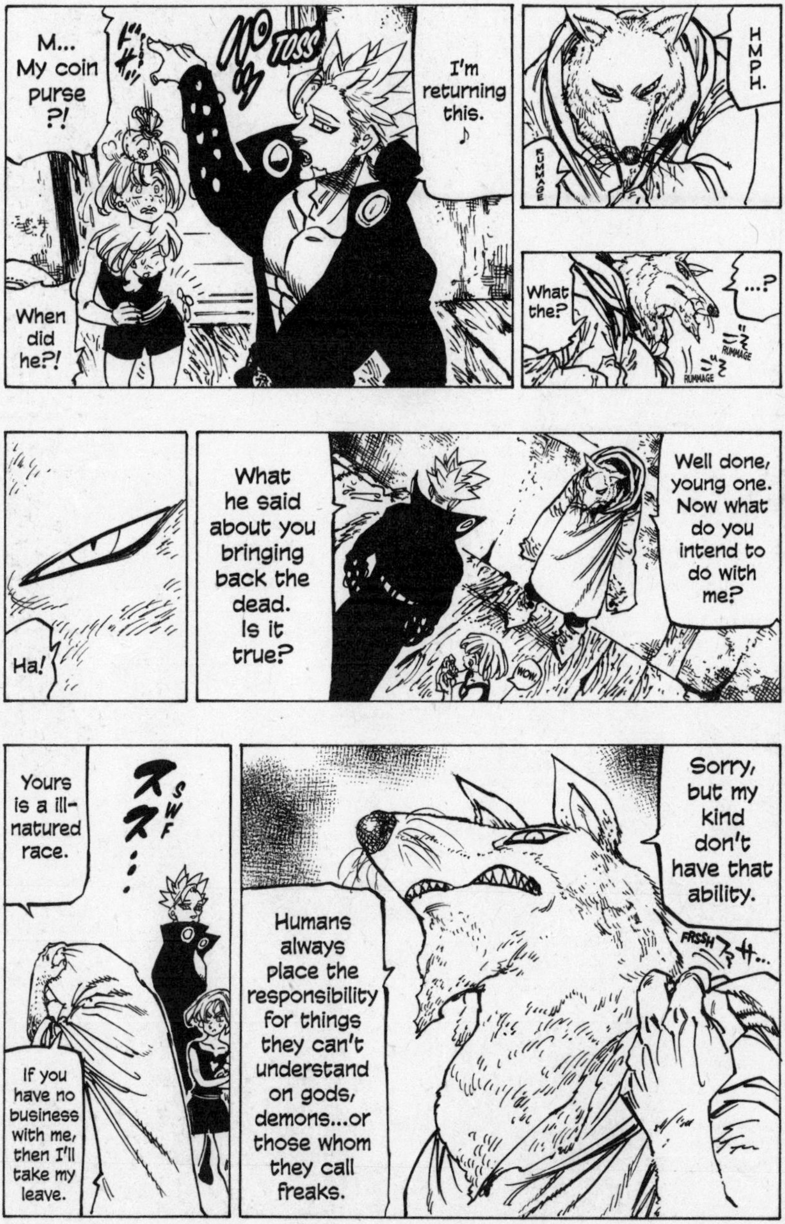
HMPH.
RUMMAGE
...?
What the?
RUMMAGE
RUMMAGE
I'm returning this. ♪
TOSS
M... My coin purse ?!
When did he?!
Well done, young one. Now what do you intend to do with me?
WOW
What he said about you bringing back the dead. Is it true?
Ha!
Sorry, but my kind don't have that ability.
FRSSH
Humans always place the responsibility for things they can't understand on gods, demons...or those whom they call freaks.
Yours is a ill-natured race.
SWF
If you have no business with me, then I'll take my leave.

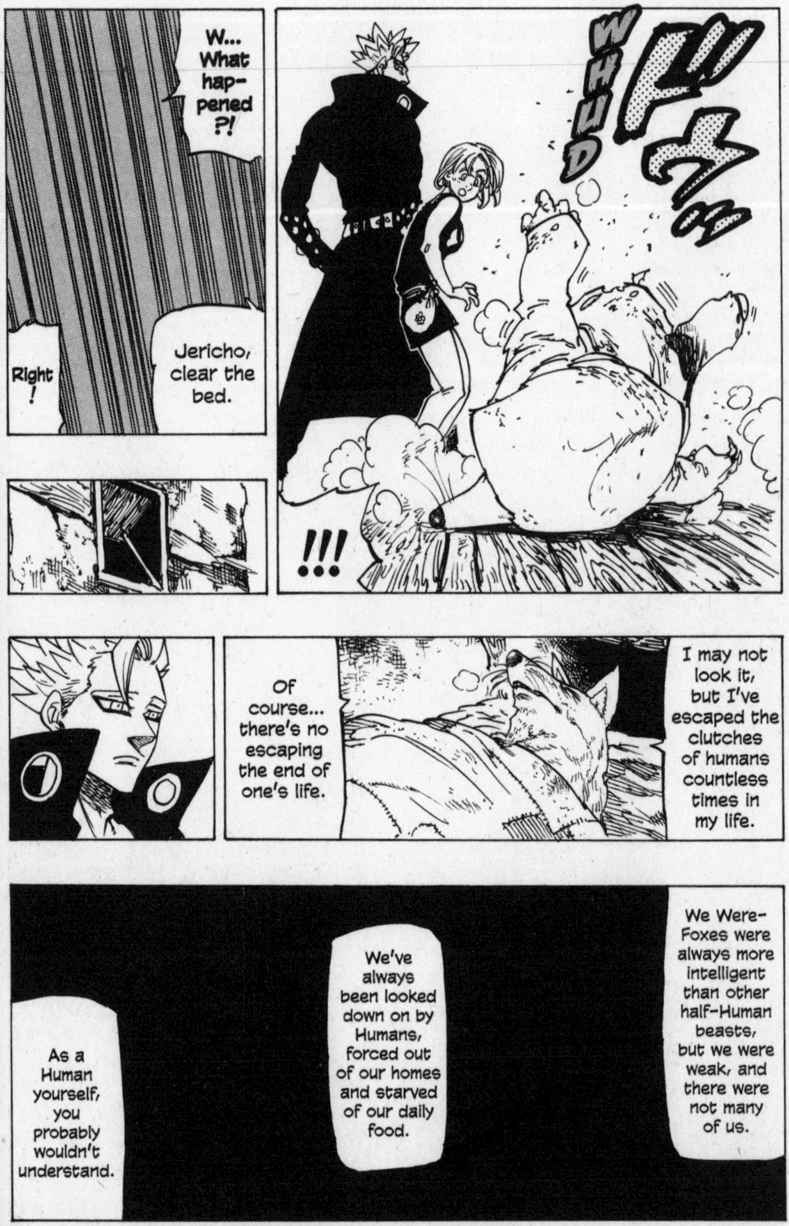
WHUD
!!!
W... What hap-pened?!
Jericho, clear the bed.
Right!
I may not look it, but I've escaped the clutches of humans countless times in my life.
Of course... there's no escaping the end of one's life.
We Were-Foxes were always more intelligent than other half-Human beasts, but we were weak, and there were not many of us.
We've always been looked down on by Humans, forced out of our homes and starved of our daily food.
As a Human yourself, you probably wouldn't understand.

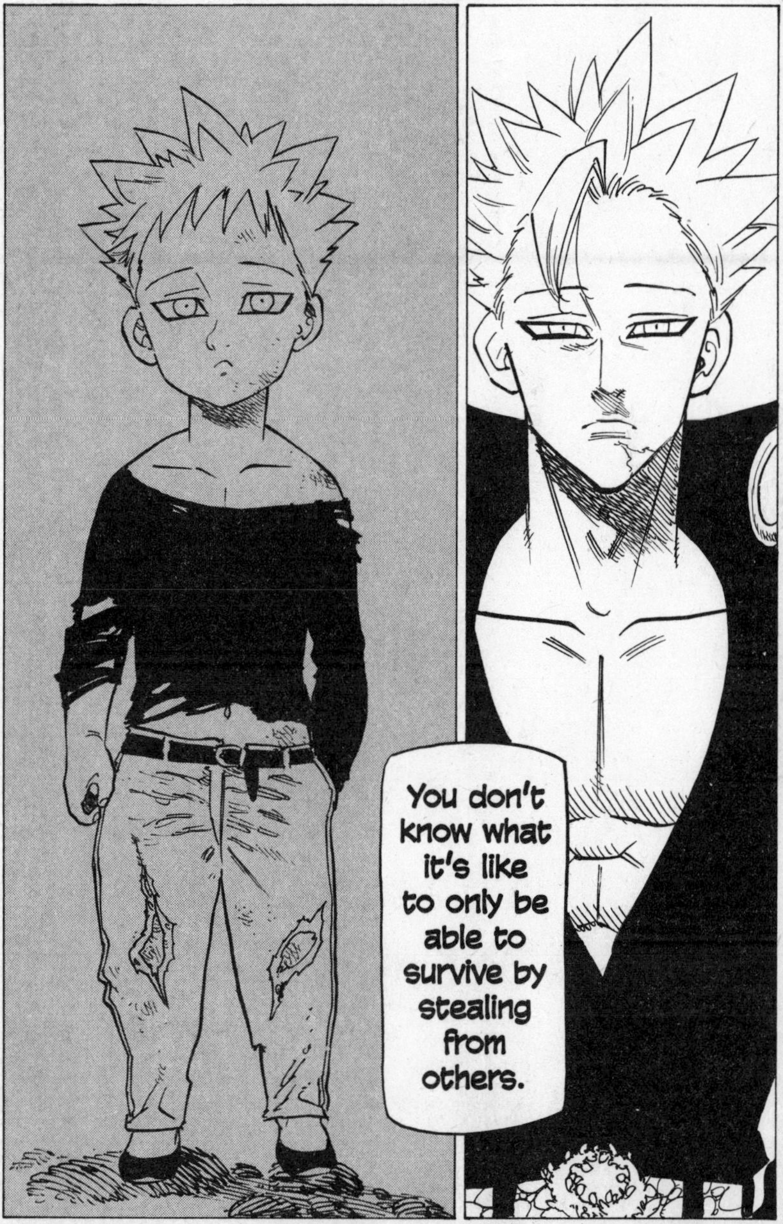
You don't know what it's like to only be able to survive by stealing from others.

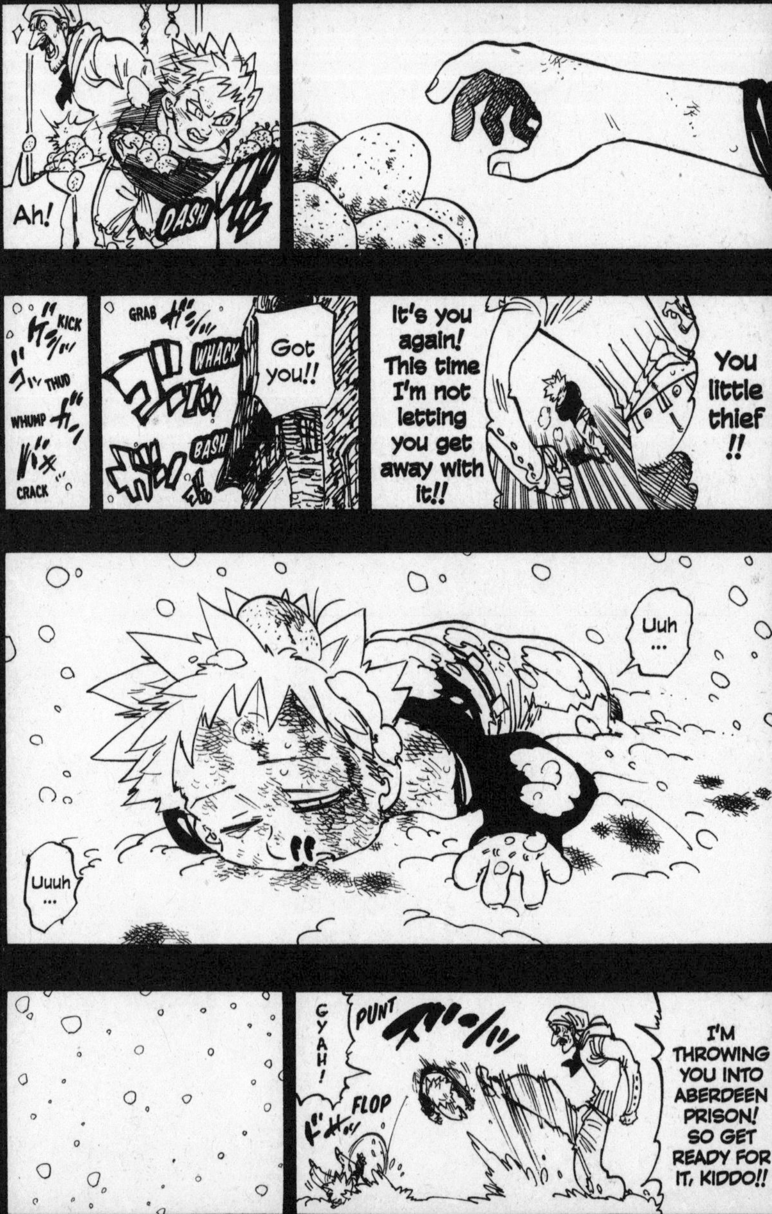
Ah!
DASH
You little thief!!
It's you again! This time I'm not letting you get away with it!!
Got you!!
GRAB
WHACK
BASH
KICK
THUD
WHUMP
CRACK
Uuh...
Uuuh...
I'M THROWING YOU INTO ABERDEEN PRISON! SO GET READY FOR IT, KIDDO!!
PUNT
GYAH!
FLOP

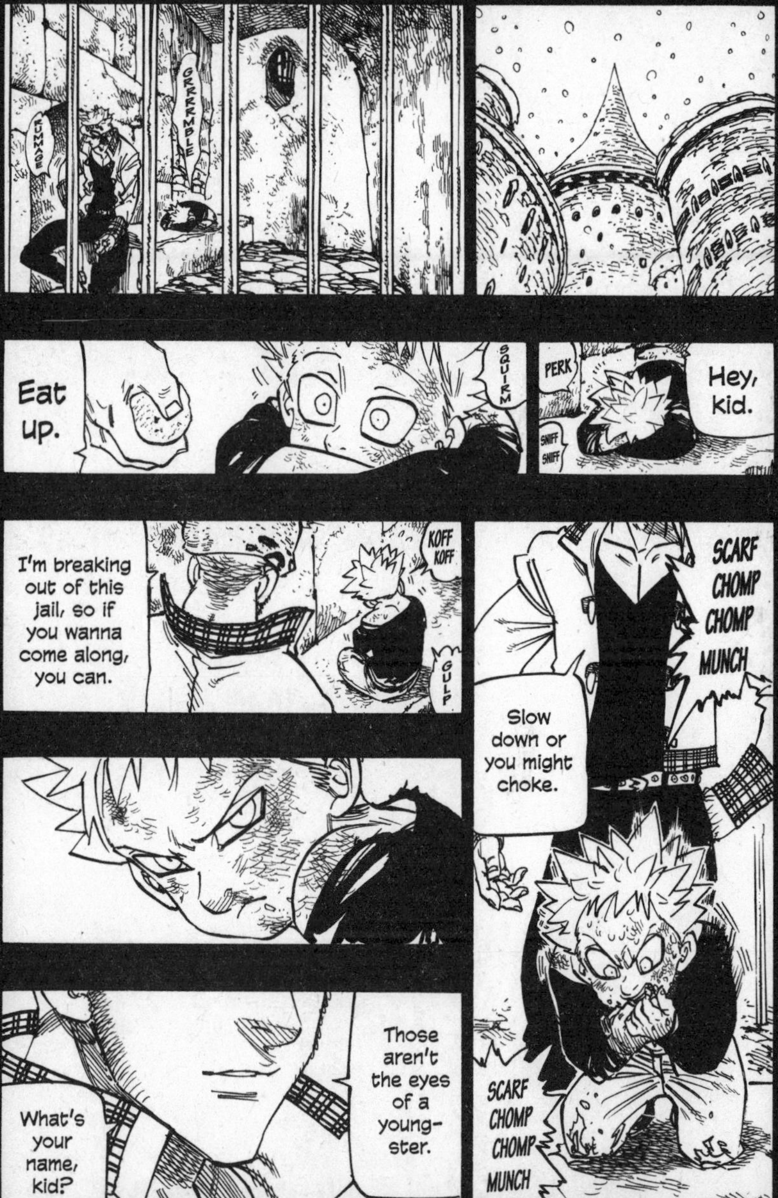
GRRRRMBLE
RUMMAGE
Hey, kid.
PERK
SNIFF SNIFF
SQUIRM
Eat up.
SCARF CHOMP CHOMP MUNCH
Slow down or you might choke.
SCARF CHOMP CHOMP MUNCH
KOFF KOFF
GULP
I'm breaking out of this jail, so if you wanna come along, you can.
Those aren't the eyes of a young-ster.
What's your name, kid?

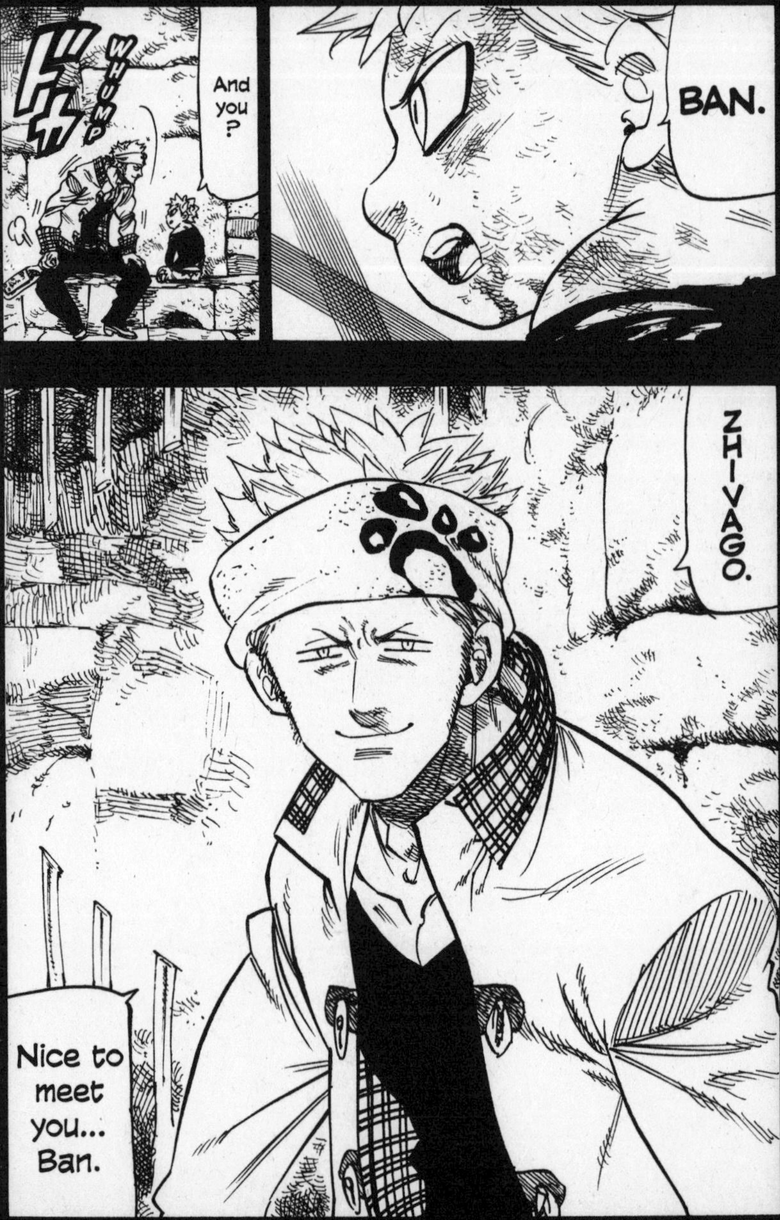

BAN.
And you?
ドサ
WHUMP
ZHIVAGO.
Nice to meet you... Ban.

# Chapter 140 - The Thief & The Boy

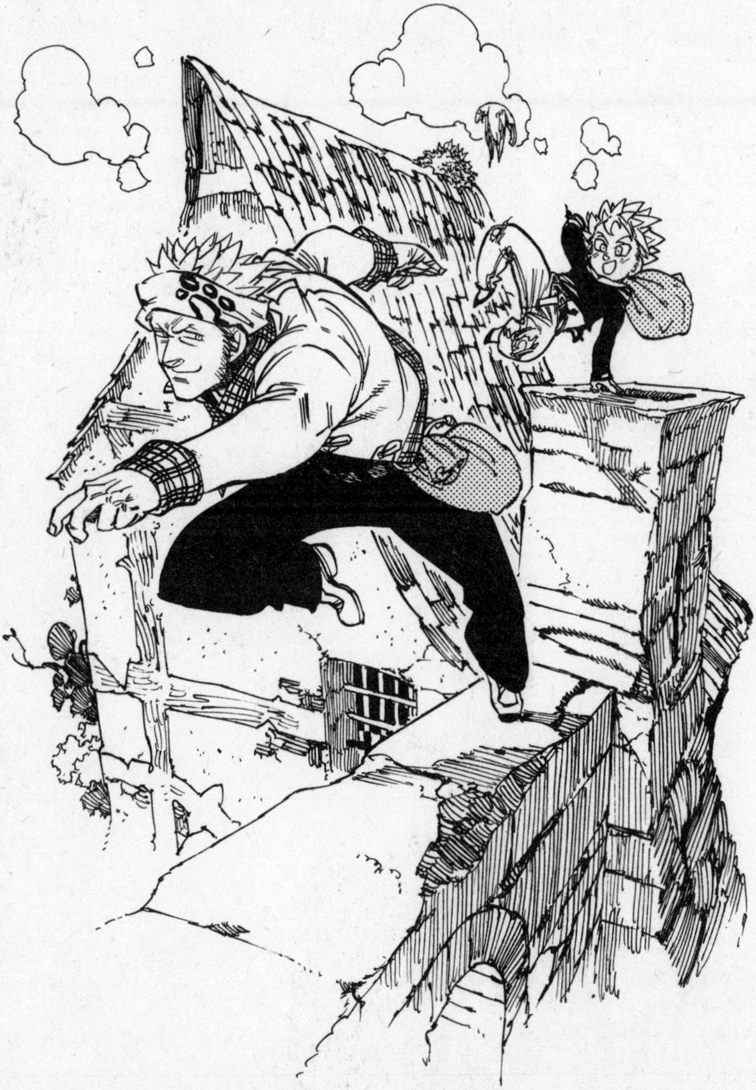

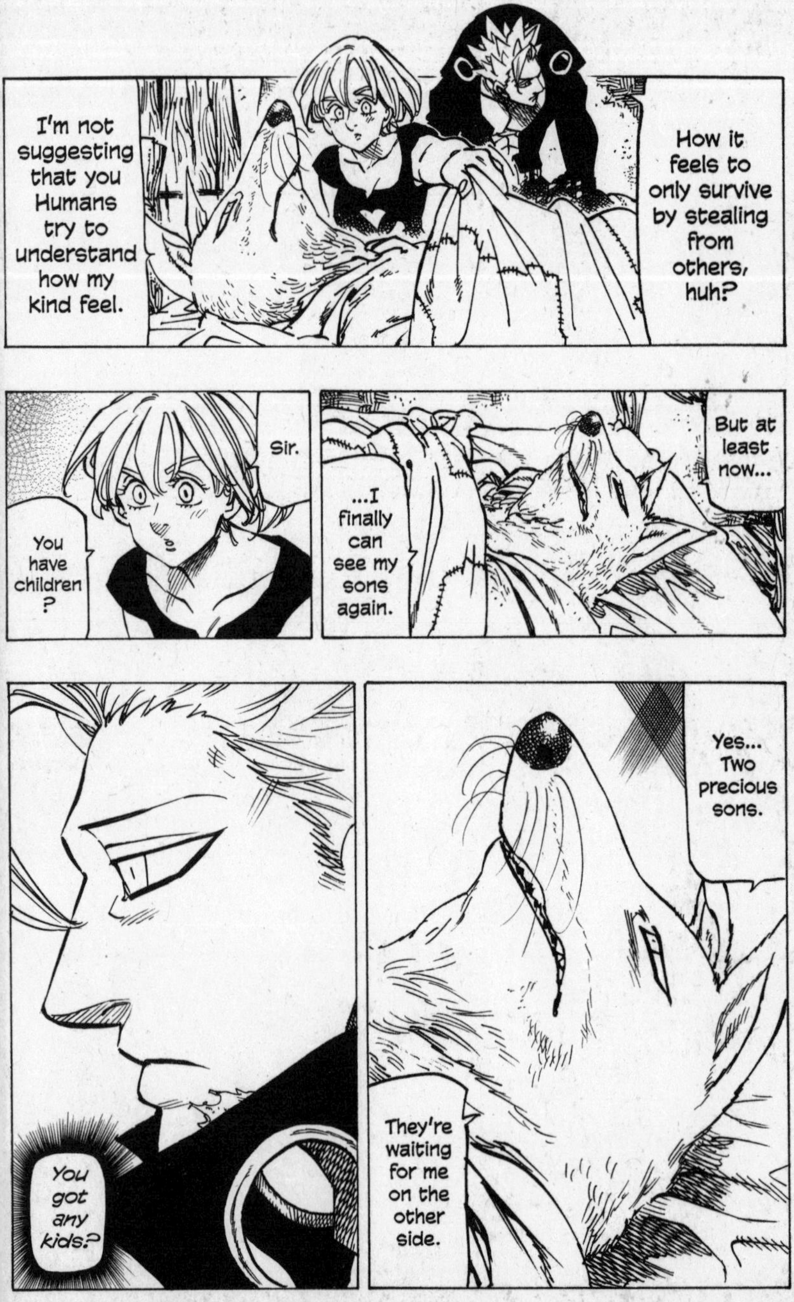
How it feels to only survive by stealing from others, huh?
I'm not suggesting that you Humans try to understand how my kind feel.
But at least now...
...I finally can see my sons again.
Sir.
You have children?
Yes... Two precious sons.
They're waiting for me on the other side.
You got any kids?

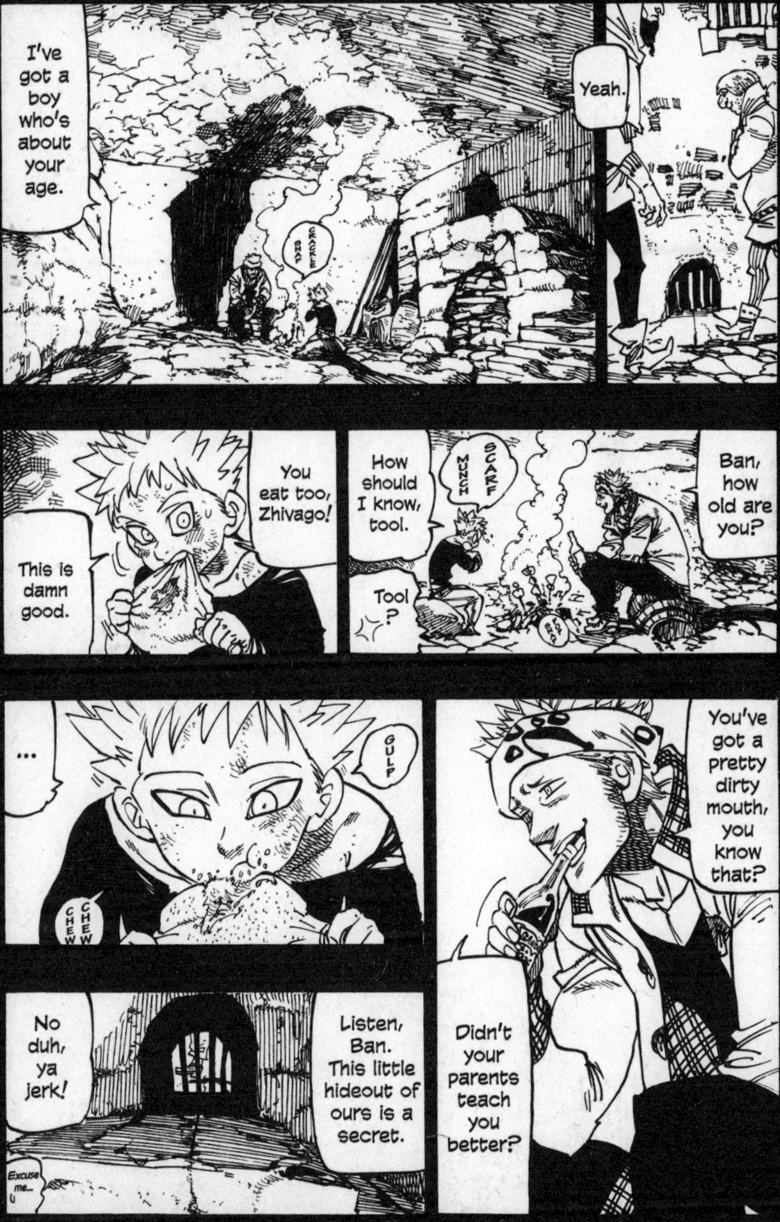
Yeah.
I've got a boy who's about your age.
CRACKLE
SNAP
Ban, how old are you?
SCARF
MUNCH
How should I know, tool.
Tool?
You eat too, Zhivago!
This is damn good.
You've got a pretty dirty mouth, you know that?
Didn't your parents teach you better?
GULP
...
CHEW
CHEW
Listen, Ban. This little hideout of ours is a secret.
No duh, ya jerk!
Excuse me...

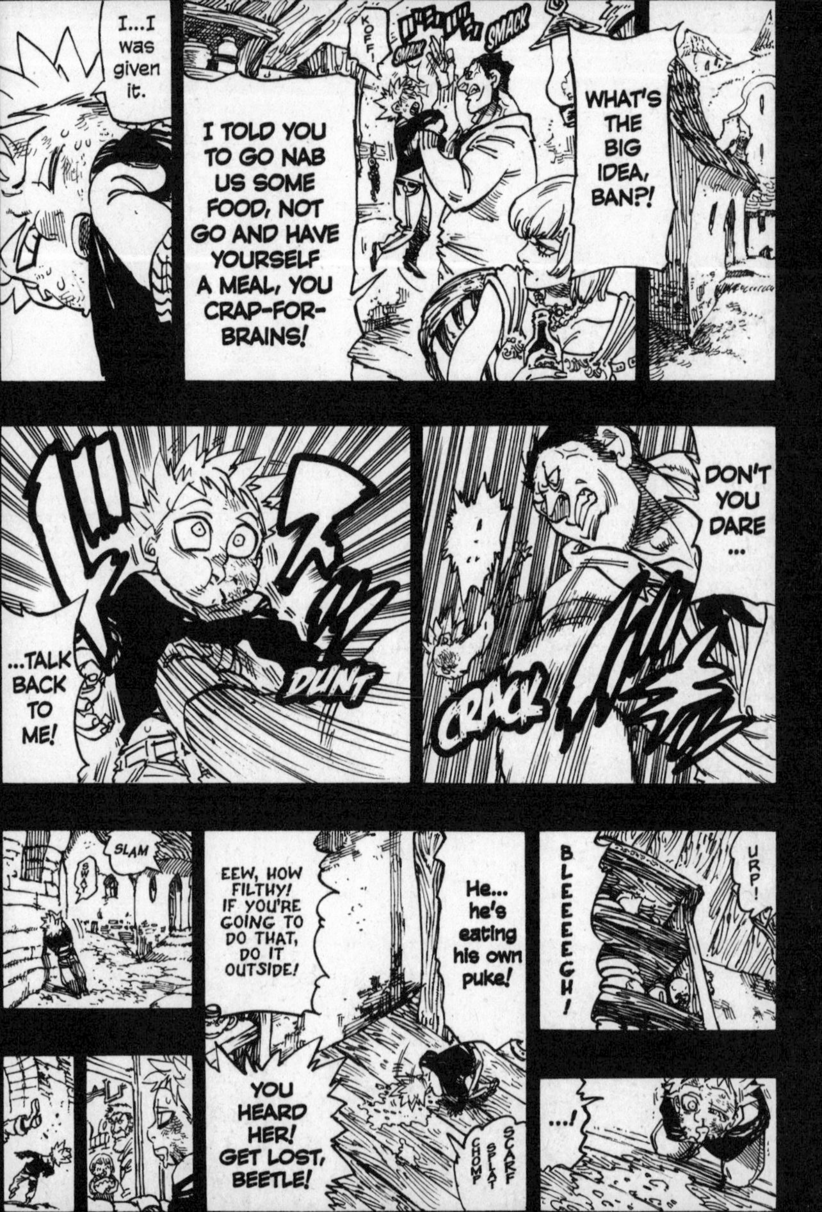
WHAT'S THE BIG IDEA, BAN?!
SMACK
SMACK
KOFF!
I TOLD YOU TO GO NAB US SOME FOOD, NOT GO AND HAVE YOURSELF A MEAL, YOU CRAP-FOR-BRAINS!
I...I was given it.
DON'T YOU DARE ...
CRACK
DUNT
...TALK BACK TO ME!
URP!
BLEEEEEGH!
...!
He... he's eating his own puke!
EEW, HOW FILTHY! IF YOU'RE GOING TO DO THAT, DO IT OUTSIDE!
SCARF
SPLAT
CHOMP
YOU HEARD HER! GET LOST, BEETLE!
SLAM
SWAY

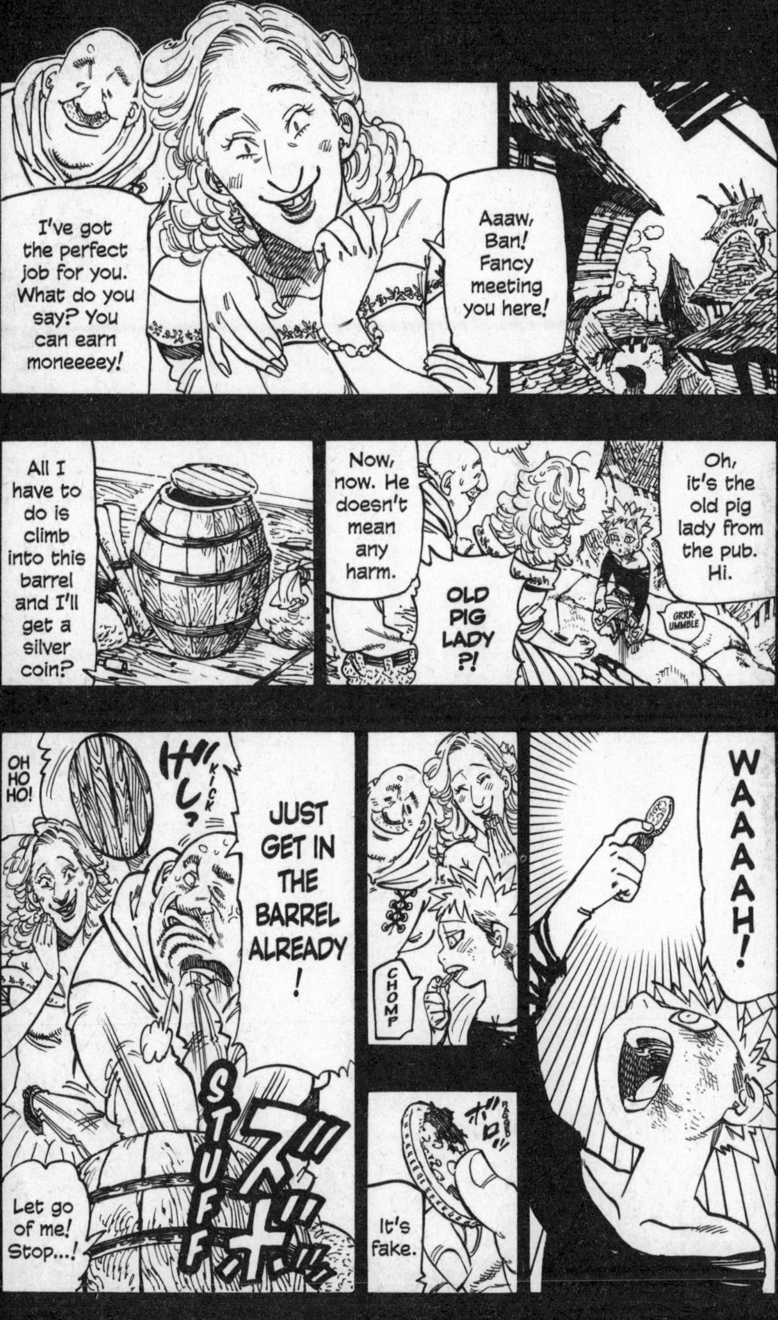

Aaaw, Ban! Fancy meeting you here!
I've got the perfect job for you. What do you say? You can earn moneeeey!
Oh, it's the old pig lady from the pub. Hi.
GRRR-UMMBLE
OLD PIG LADY ?!
Now, now. He doesn't mean any harm.
All I have to do is climb into this barrel and I'll get a silver coin?
WAAAAAH!
CHOMP
RAGGED
It's fake.
OH HO HO!
KICK
JUST GET IN THE BARREL ALREADY!
STUFF
Let go of me! Stop...!

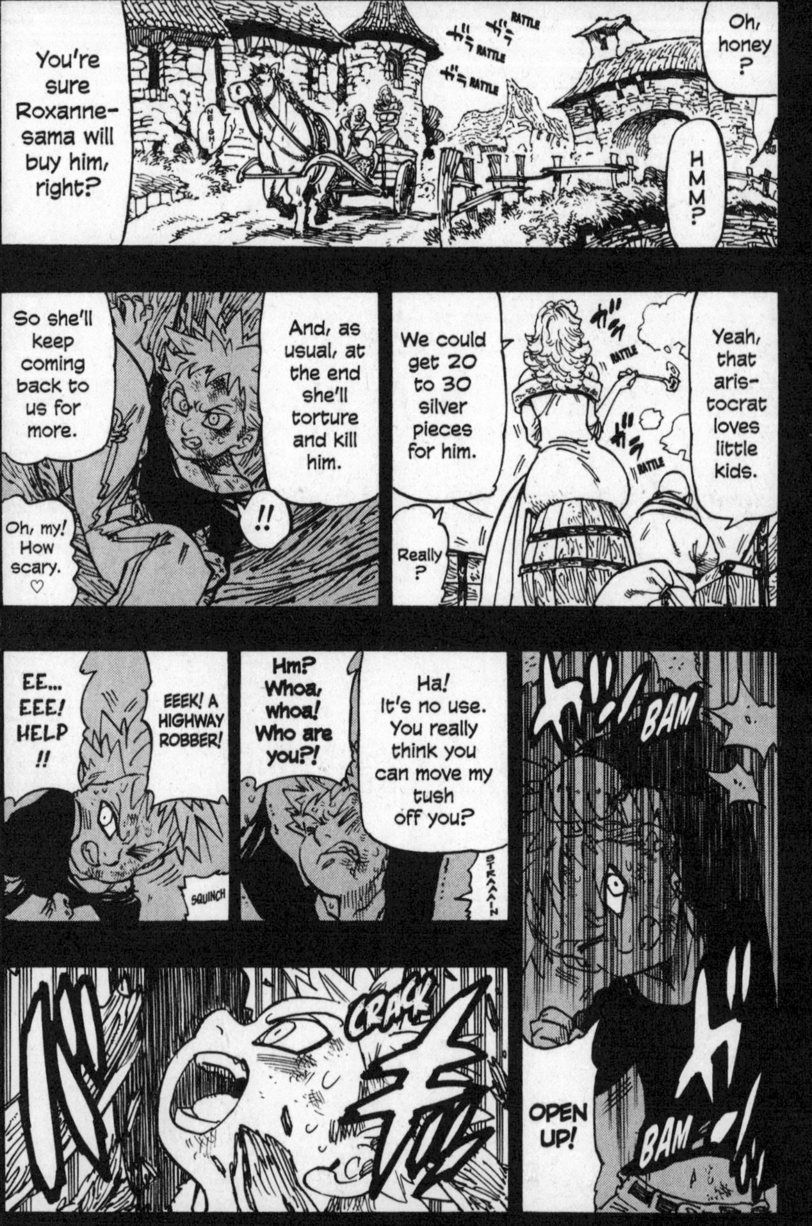
Oh, honey?
RATTLE
RATTLE
RATTLE
HMM?
NEIGH!
You're sure Roxanne-sama will buy him, right?
Yeah, that aris-tocrat loves little kids.
RATTLE
RATTLE
We could get 20 to 30 silver pieces for him.
Really?
And, as usual, at the end she'll torture and kill him.
So she'll keep coming back to us for more.
!!
Oh, my! How scary. ♡
BAM
OPEN UP!
BAM
Ha! It's no use. You really think you can move my tush off you?
Hm? Whoa, whoa! Who are you?!
STRAAAIN
EEEK! A HIGHWAY ROBBER!
EE... EEE! HELP!!
SQUINCH
CRACK

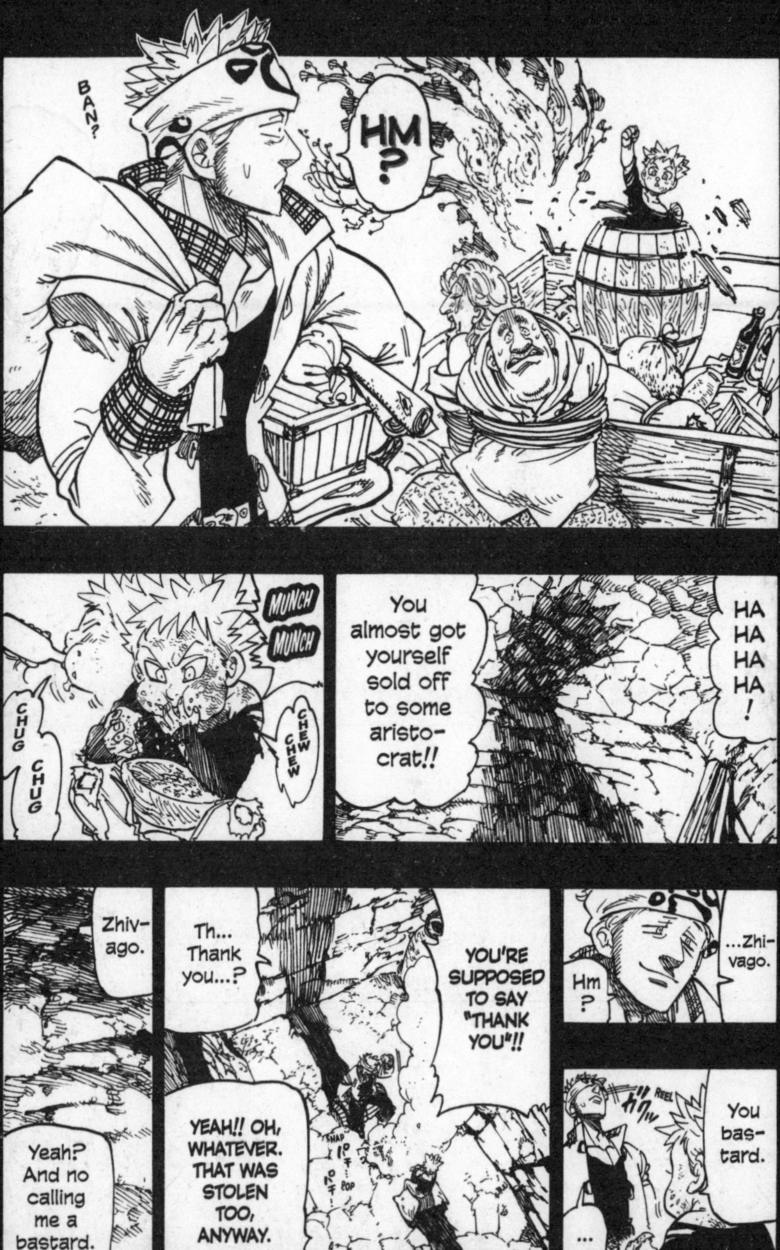
HM?
BAN?
HA HA HA HA!
You almost got yourself sold off to some aristocrat!!
MUNCH
MUNCH
CHEW CHEW
CHUG CHUG
...Zhivago.
Hm?
You bastard.
REEL
...
YOU'RE SUPPOSED TO SAY "THANK YOU"!!
Th... Thank you...?
YEAH!! OH, WHATEVER. THAT WAS STOLEN TOO, ANYWAY.
SNAP
POP
Zhivago.
Yeah? And no calling me a bastard.

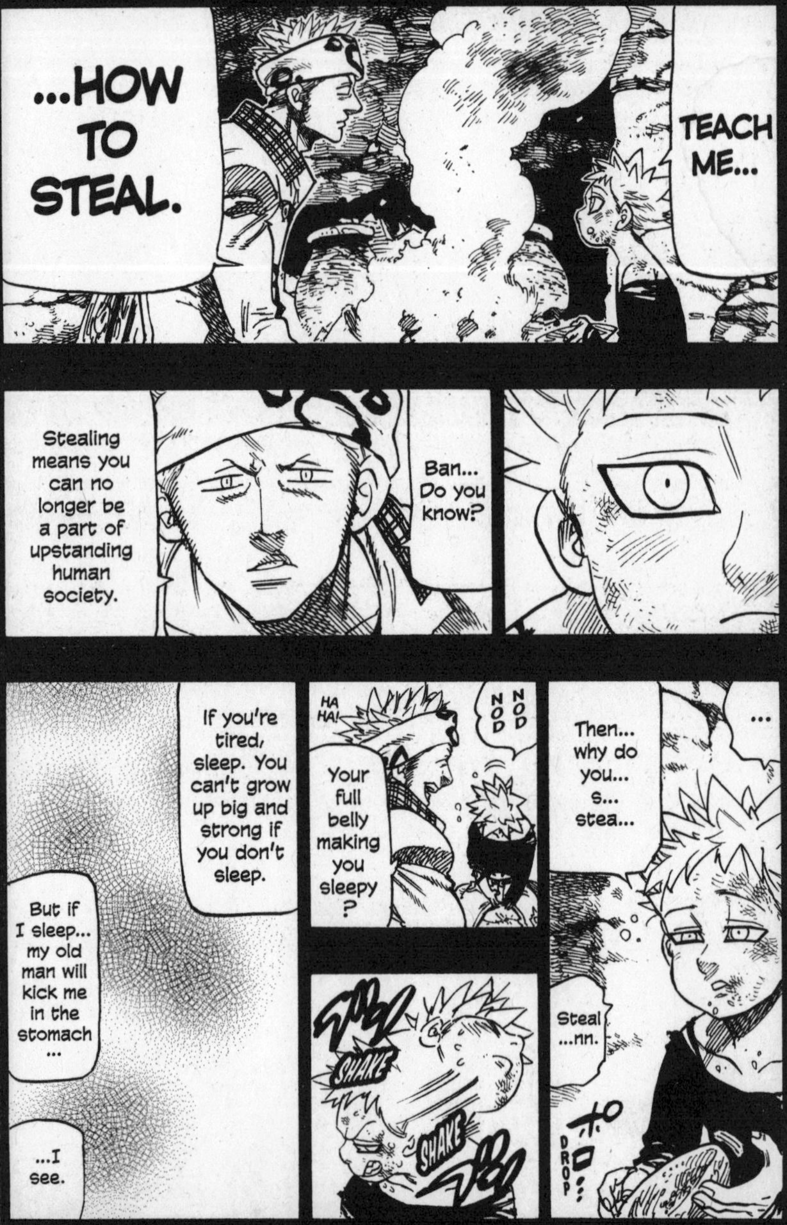
TEACH ME...
...HOW TO STEAL.
Ban... Do you know?
Stealing means you can no longer be a part of upstanding human society.
...
Then... why do you... s... stea...
Steal ...nn.
DROP
NOD NOD
HA HA!
Your full belly making you sleepy?
SHAKE
SHAKE
If you're tired, sleep. You can't grow up big and strong if you don't sleep.
But if I sleep... my old man will kick me in the stomach ...
...I see.

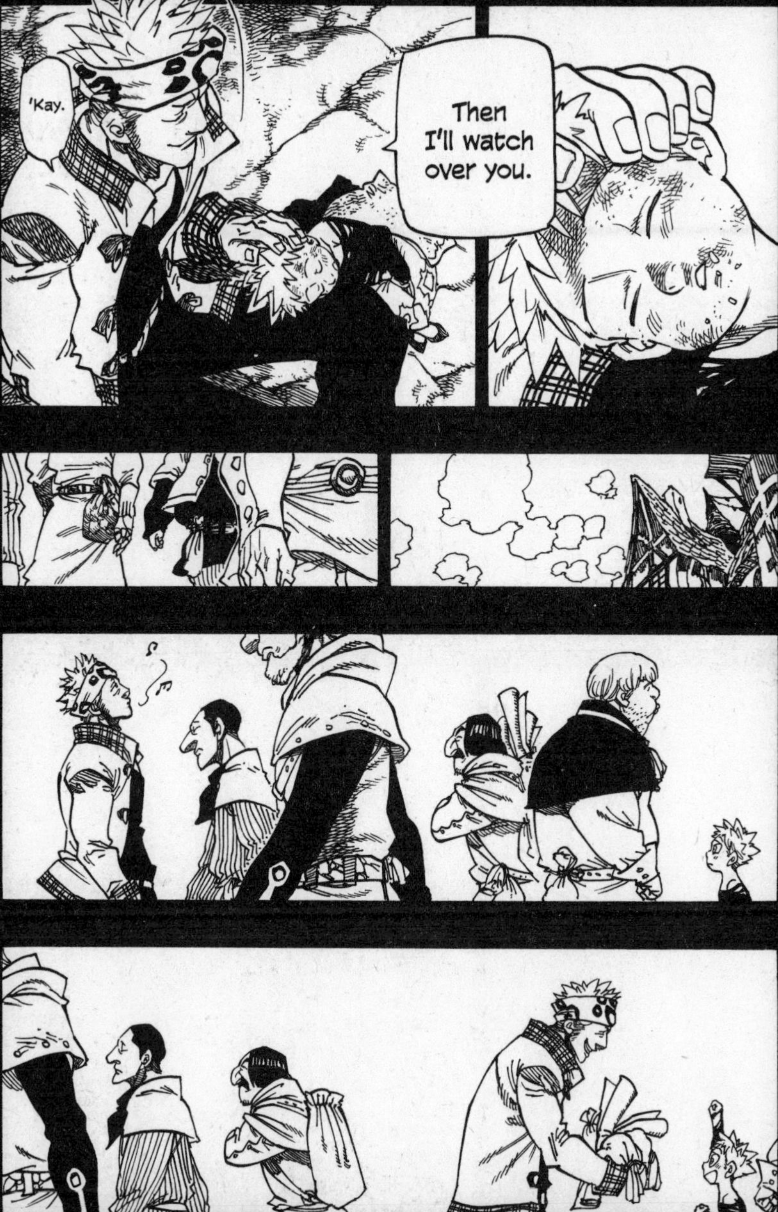
Then I'll watch over you.
'Kay.

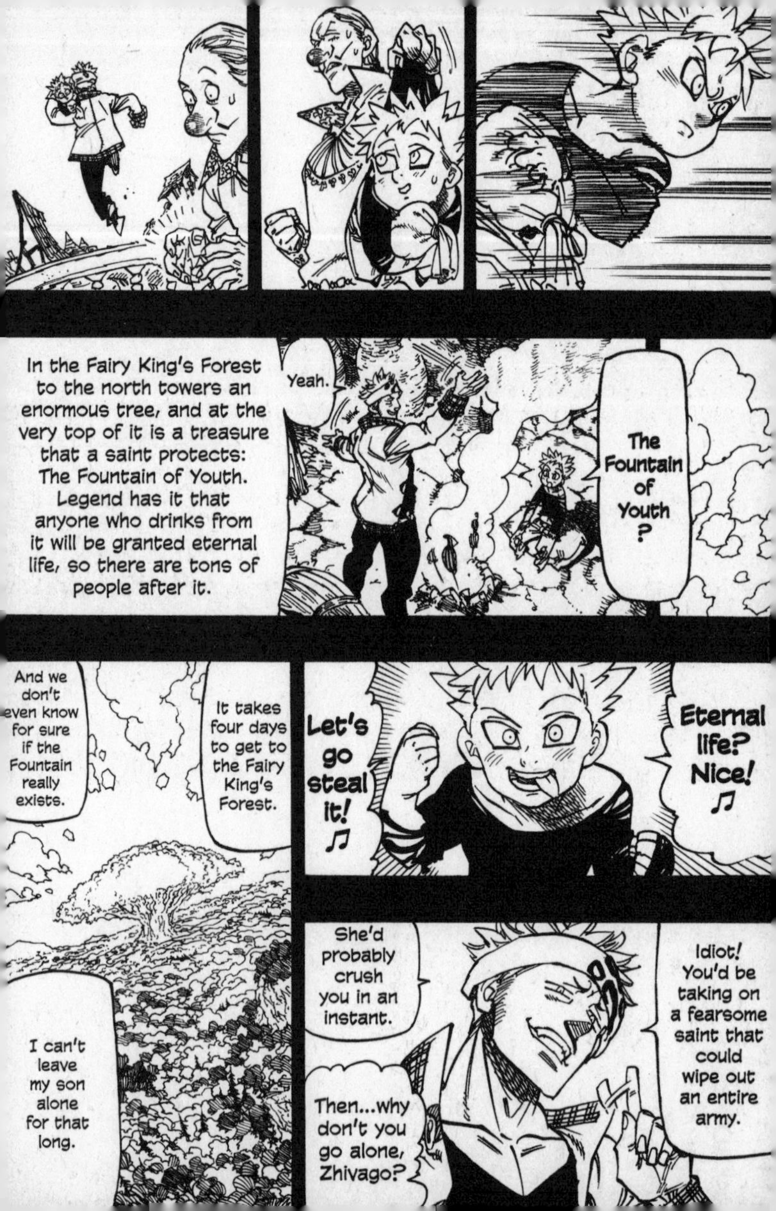
The Fountain of Youth?
Yeah.
In the Fairy King's Forest to the north towers an enormous tree, and at the very top of it is a treasure that a saint protects: The Fountain of Youth. Legend has it that anyone who drinks from it will be granted eternal life, so there are tons of people after it.
Eternal life? Nice! ♫
Let's go steal it! ♫
Idiot! You'd be taking on a fearsome saint that could wipe out an entire army.
She'd probably crush you in an instant.
Then...why don't you go alone, Zhivago?
It takes four days to get to the Fairy King's Forest.
And we don't even know for sure if the Fountain really exists.
I can't leave my son alone for that long.

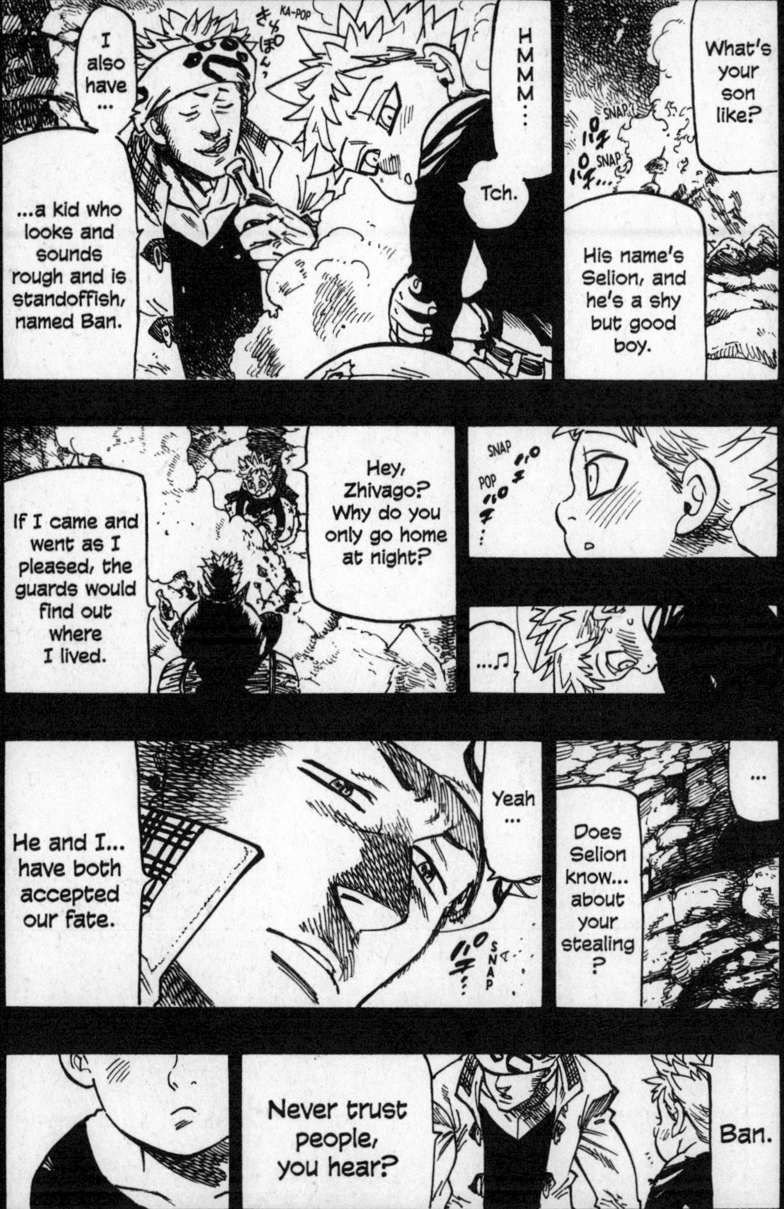

What's your son like?
SNAP
SNAP
His name's Selion, and he's a shy but good boy.
HMMM...
KA-POP
I also have...
Tch.
...a kid who looks and sounds rough and is standoffish, named Ban.
SNAP
POP
...♪
Hey, Zhivago? Why do you only go home at night?
If I came and went as I pleased, the guards would find out where I lived.
...
Does Selion know... about your stealing?
Yeah...
SNAP
He and I... have both accepted our fate.
Ban.
Never trust people, you hear?

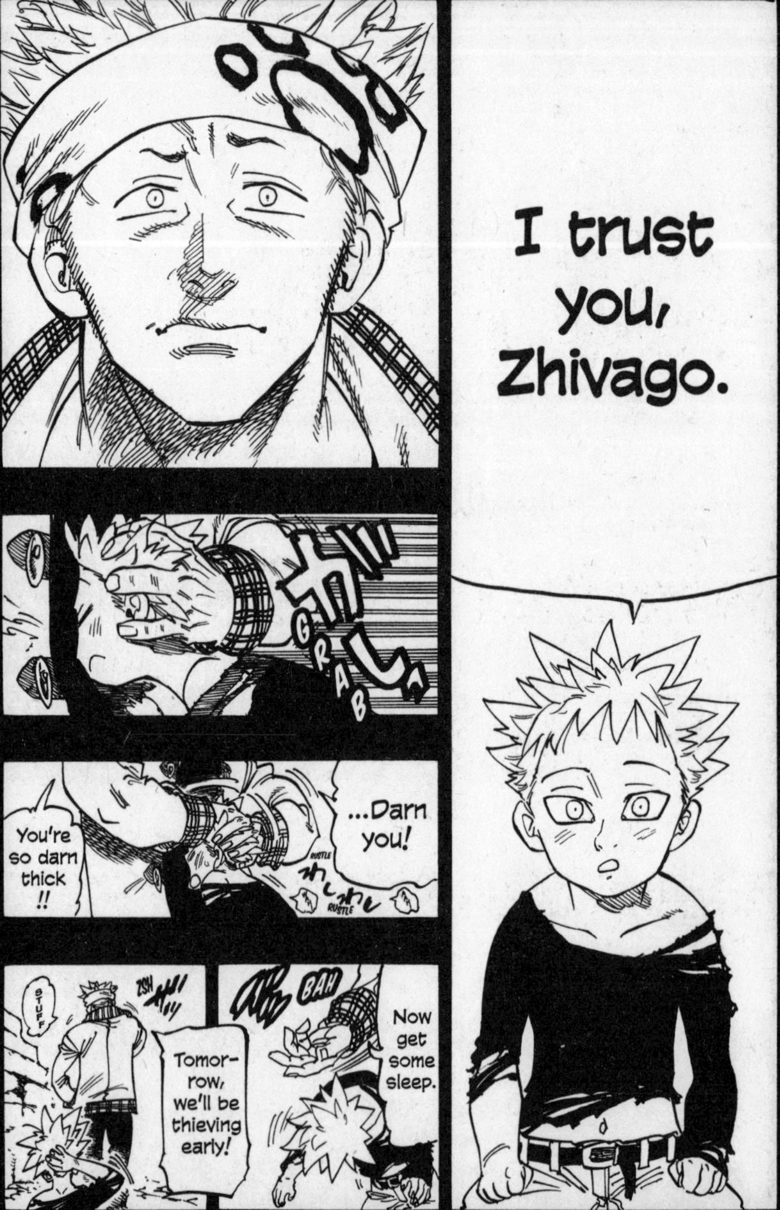
I trust you, Zhivago.
GRAB
...Darn you!
RUSTLE
RUSTLE
You're so darn thick!!
BAH
Now get some sleep.
ZSH
STUFF
Tomor-row, we'll be thieving early!

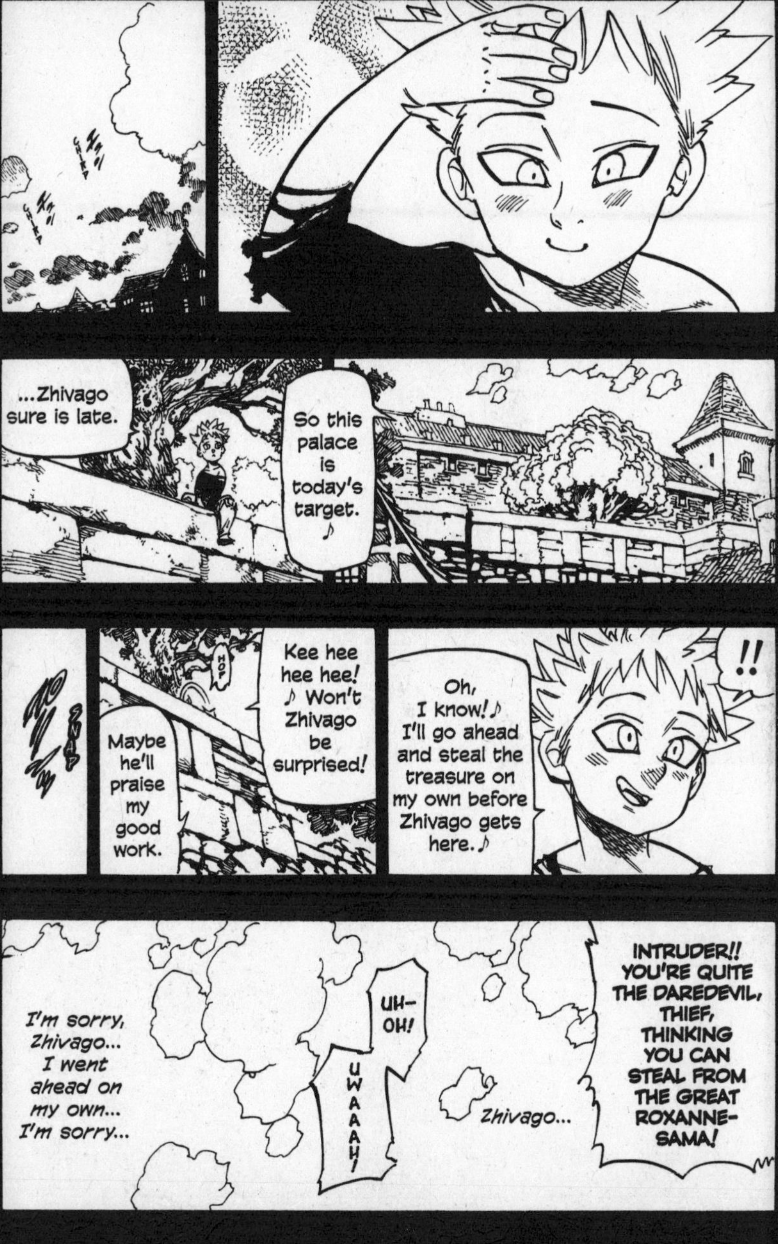
CHIRP
CHIRP
So this palace is today's target. ♪
...Zhivago sure is late.
!!
Oh, I know!♪ I'll go ahead and steal the treasure on my own before Zhivago gets here.♪
HOP
Kee hee hee hee! ♪ Won't Zhivago be surprised!
Maybe he'll praise my good work.
SNAP
INTRUDER!! YOU'RE QUITE THE DAREDEVIL, THIEF, THINKING YOU CAN STEAL FROM THE GREAT ROXANNE-SAMA!
Zhivago...
UH-OH!
UWAAAAH!
I'm sorry, Zhivago... I went ahead on my own... I'm sorry...

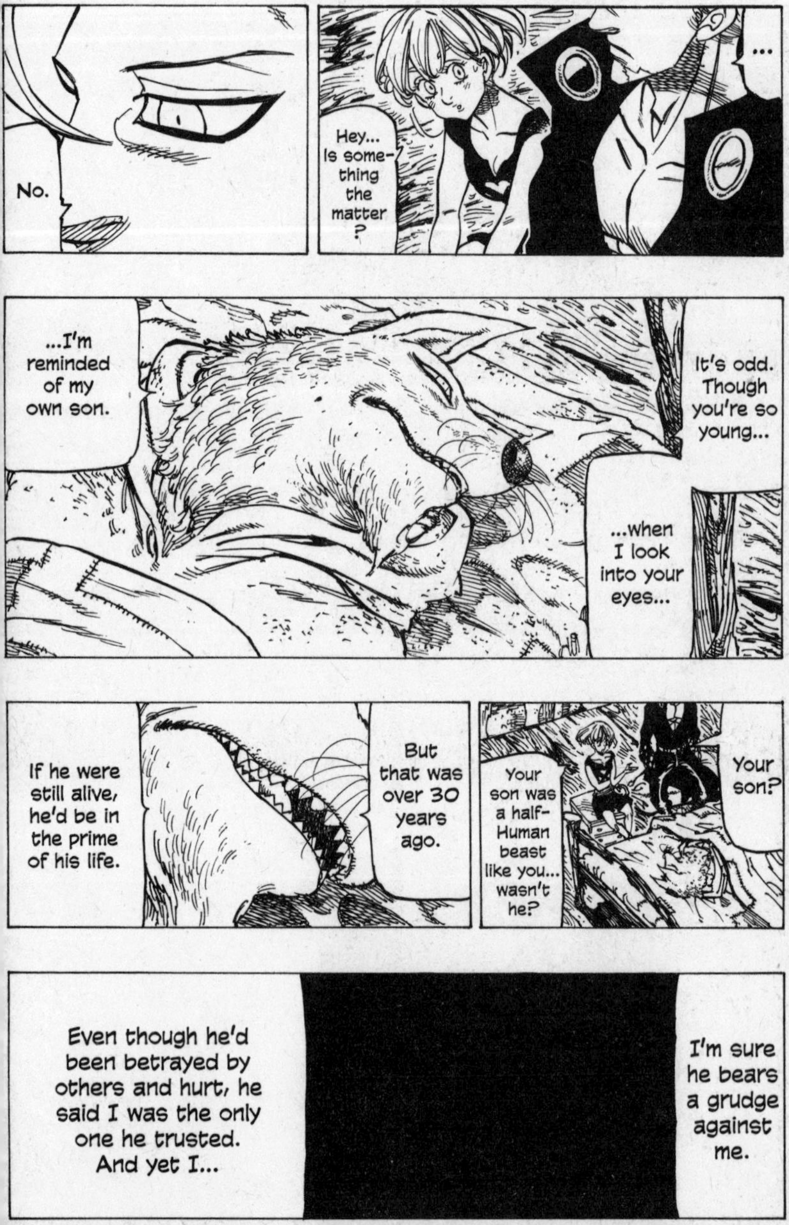
...
Hey... Is something the matter?
No.
It's odd. Though you're so young...
...when I look into your eyes...
...I'm reminded of my own son.
Your son?
Your son was a half-Human beast like you... wasn't he?
But that was over 30 years ago.
If he were still alive, he'd be in the prime of his life.
I'm sure he bears a grudge against me.
Even though he'd been betrayed by others and hurt, he said I was the only one he trusted. And yet I...

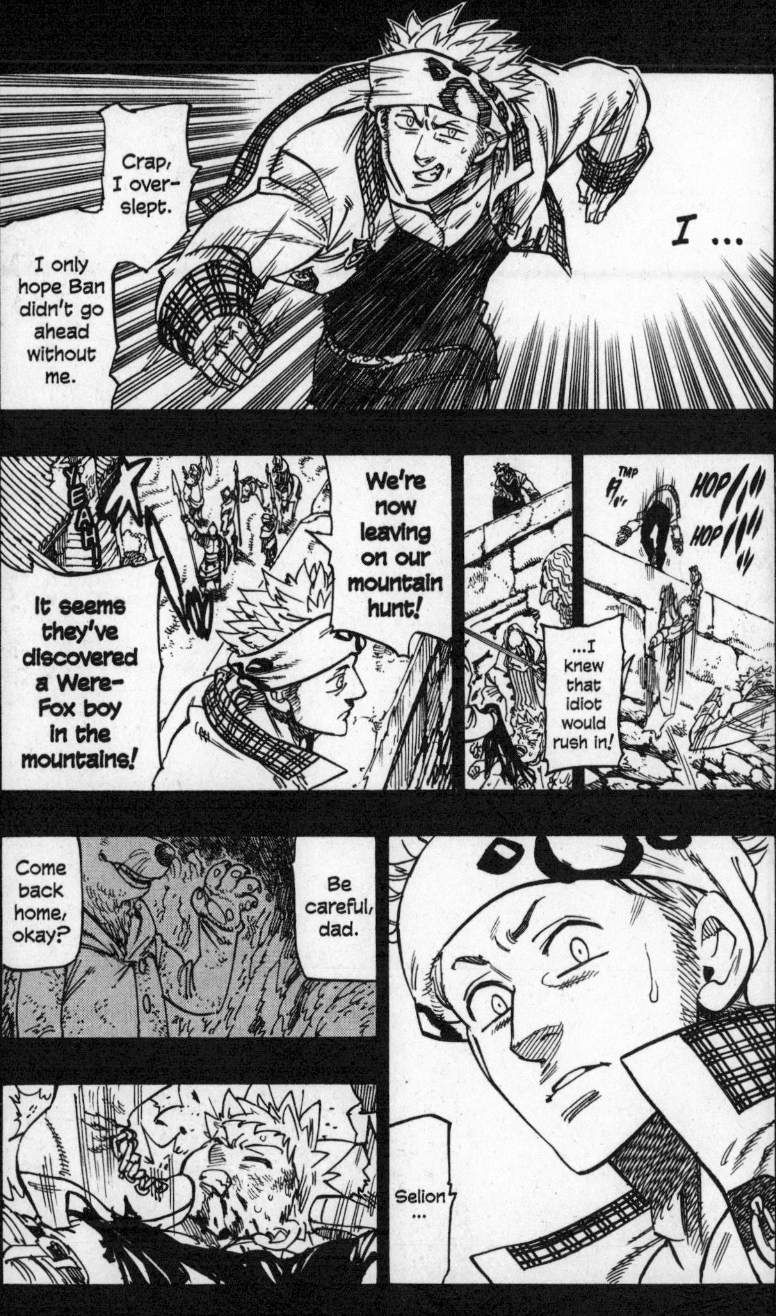
Crap, I over-slept.
I only hope Ban didn't go ahead without me.
I ...
TMP
HOP HOP
...I knew that idiot would rush in!
We're now leaving on our mountain hunt!
YEAH
It seems they've discovered a Were-Fox boy in the mountains!
Selion ...
Be careful, dad.
Come back home, okay?

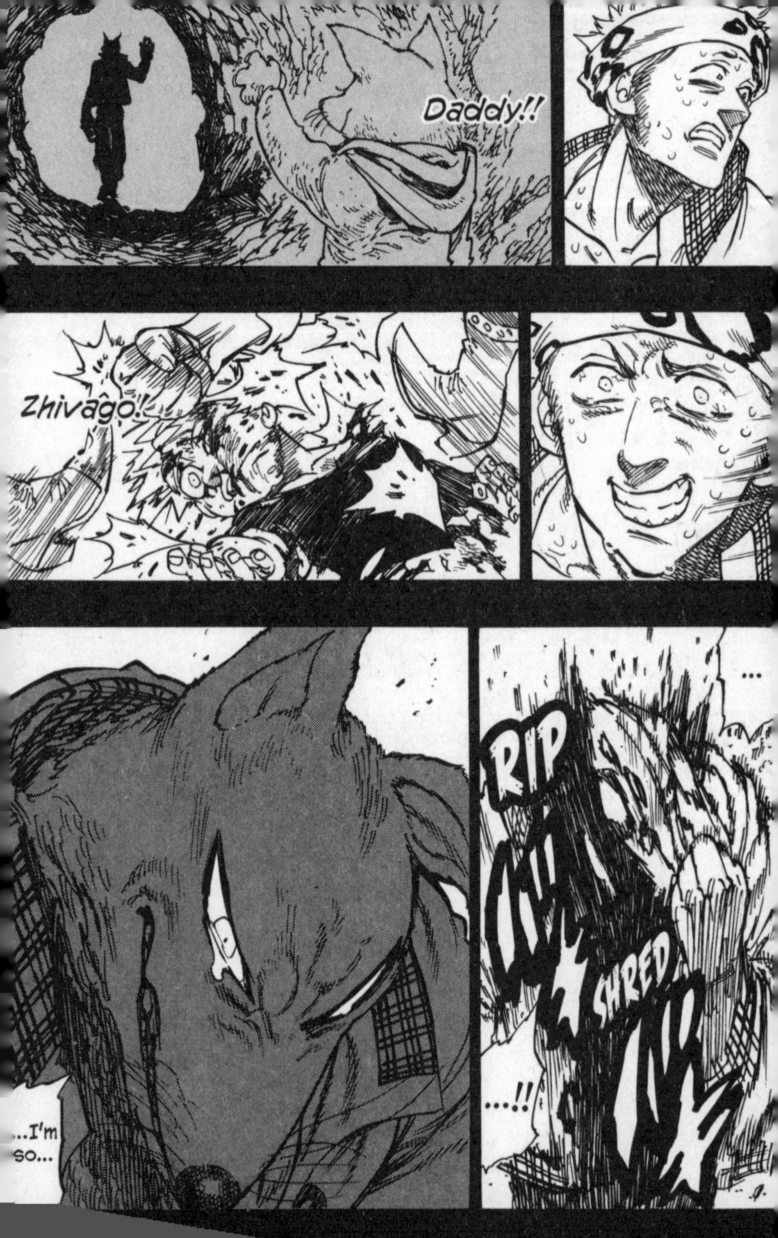
Daddy!!
Zhivago!!
...
RIP
SHRED
...!!
...I'm so...

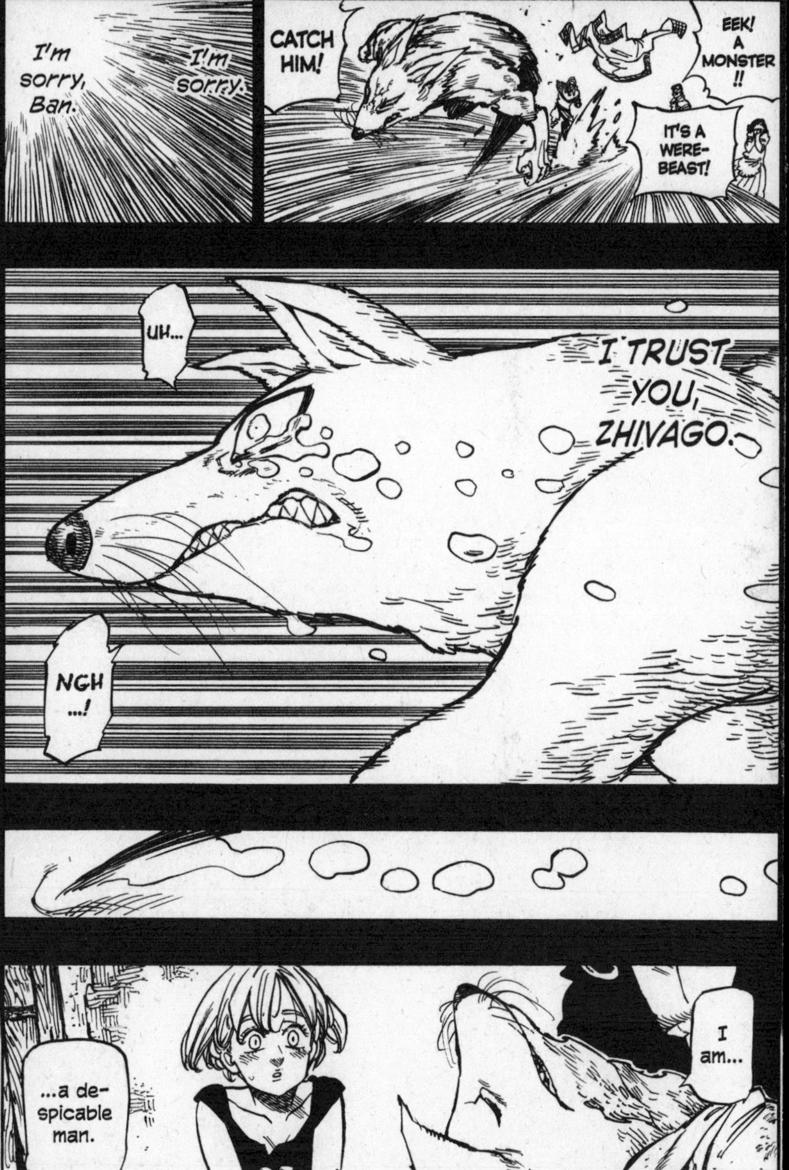
EEK! A MONSTER!!
CATCH HIM!
IT'S A WERE-BEAST!
I'm sorry.
I'm sorry, Ban.
I TRUST YOU, ZHIVAGO.
UH...
NGH ...!
I am...
...a despicable man.

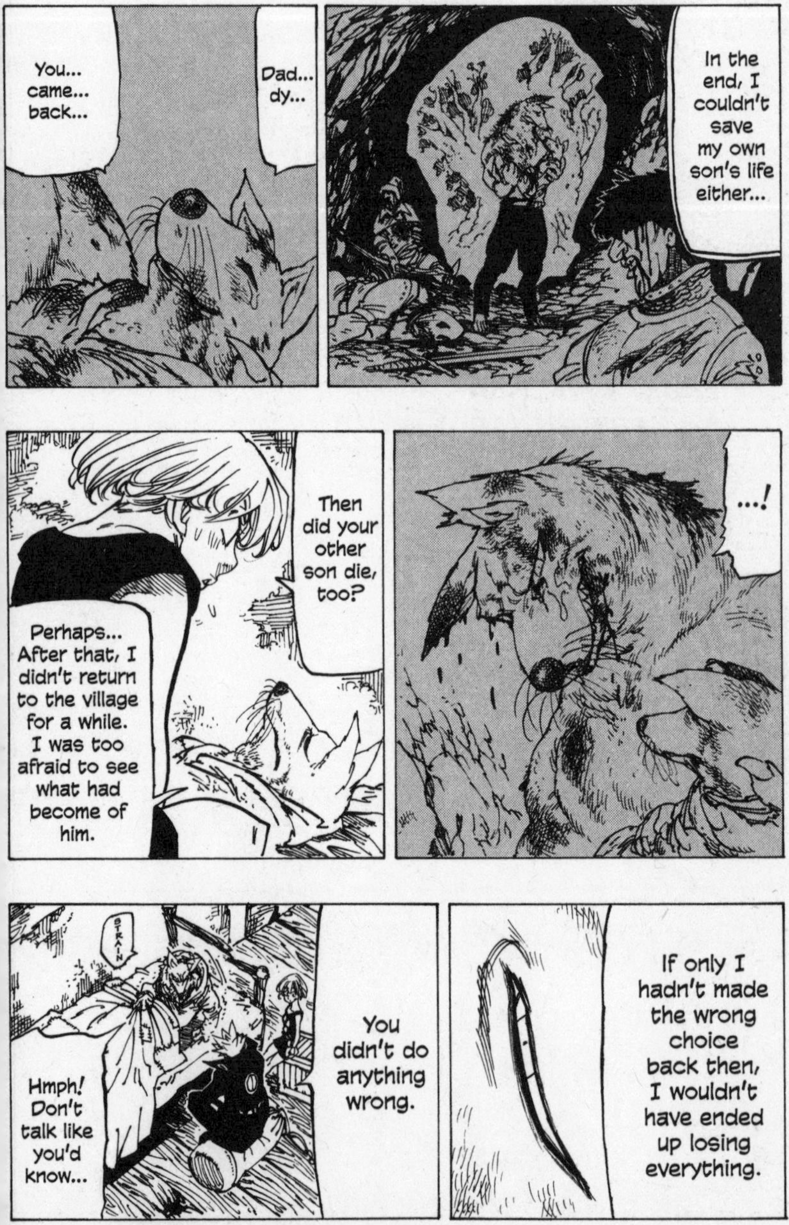
In the end, I couldn't save my own son's life either...
Dad... dy...
You... came... back...
...!
Then did your other son die, too?
Perhaps... After that, I didn't return to the village for a while. I was too afraid to see what had become of him.
If only I hadn't made the wrong choice back then, I wouldn't have ended up losing everything.
You didn't do anything wrong.
STRAIN
Hmph! Don't talk like you'd know...

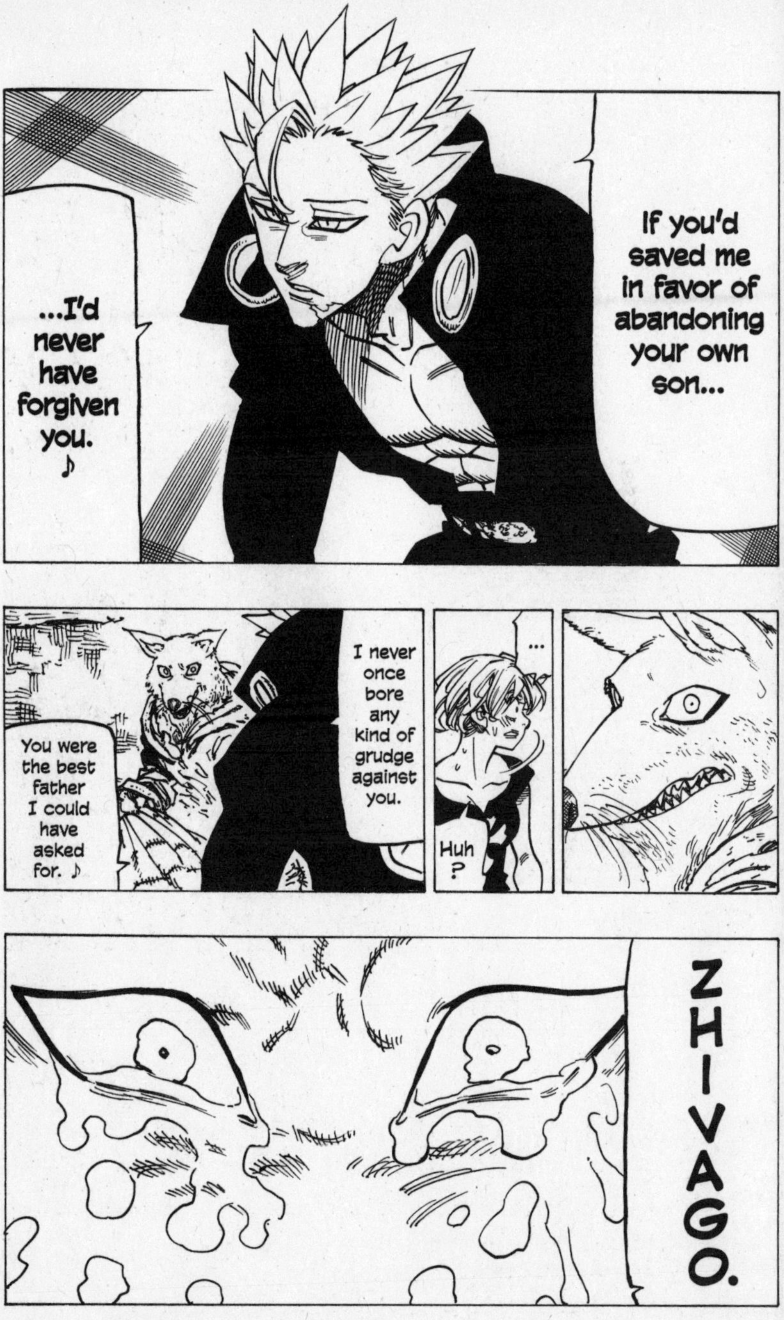
If you'd saved me in favor of abandoning your own son...
...I'd never have forgiven you. ♪
...
Huh?
I never once bore any kind of grudge against you.
You were the best father I could have asked for. ♪
ZHIVAGO.

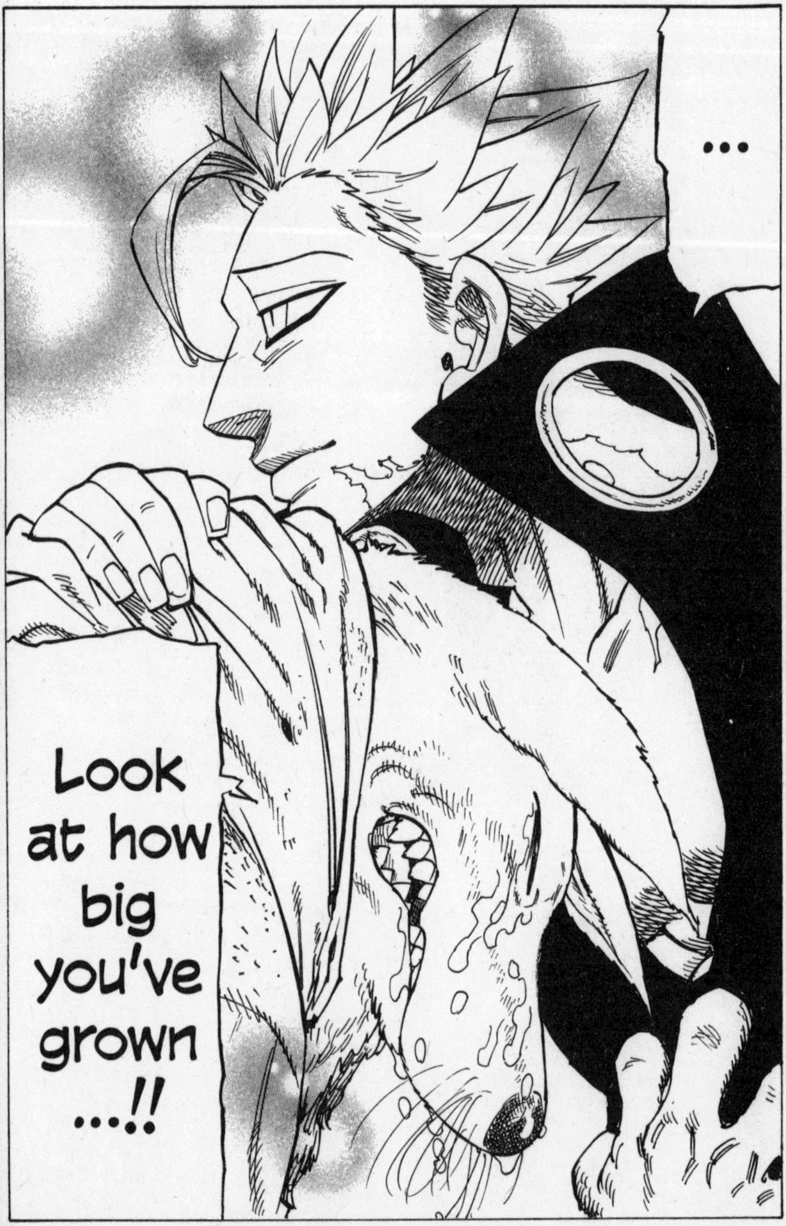
...
Look at how big you've grown ...!!

# Chapter 141 - Father & Son

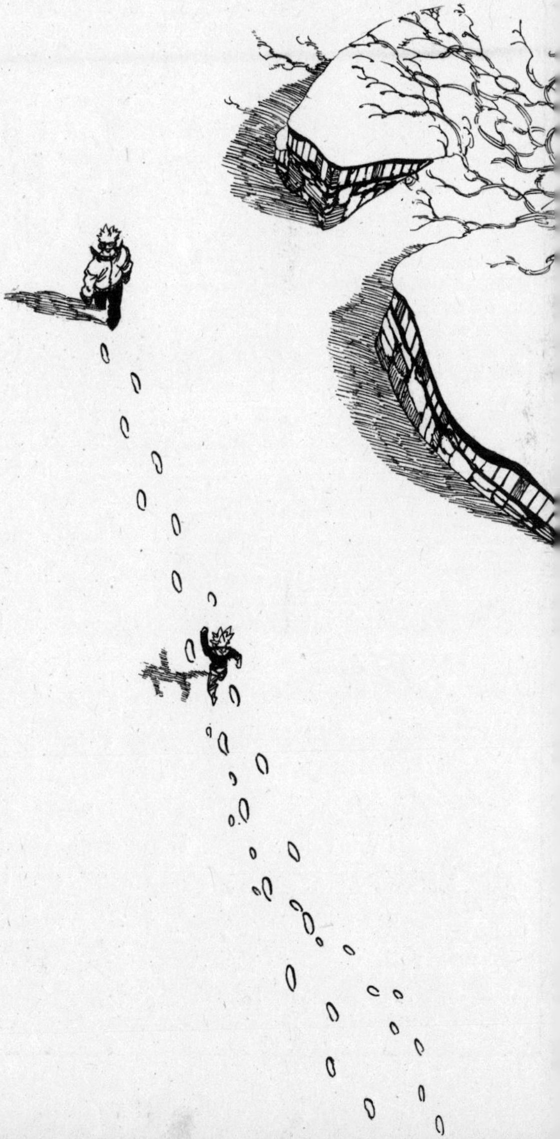

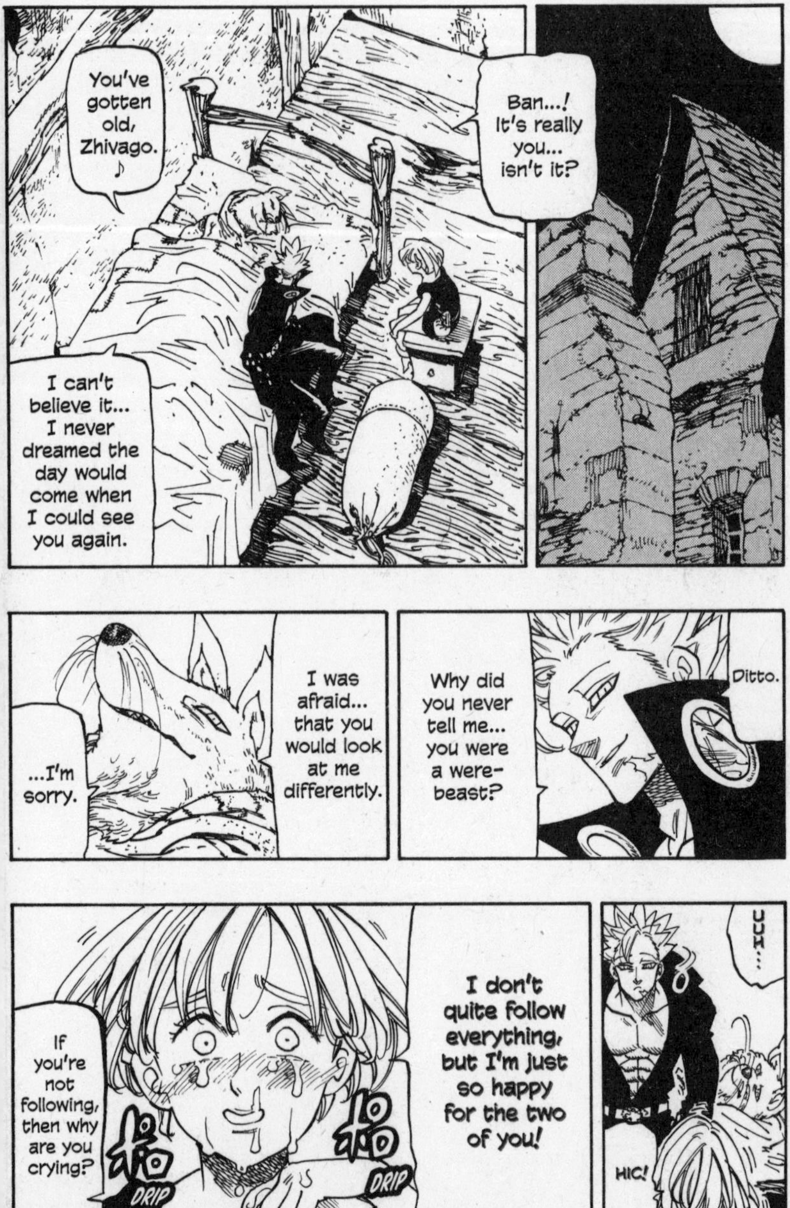
Ban...! It's really you... isn't it?
You've gotten old, Zhivago. ♪
I can't believe it... I never dreamed the day would come when I could see you again.
Ditto.
Why did you never tell me... you were a were-beast?
I was afraid... that you would look at me differently.
...I'm sorry.
UUH...
HIC!
I don't quite follow everything, but I'm just so happy for the two of you!
DRIP
DRIP
If you're not following, then why are you crying?

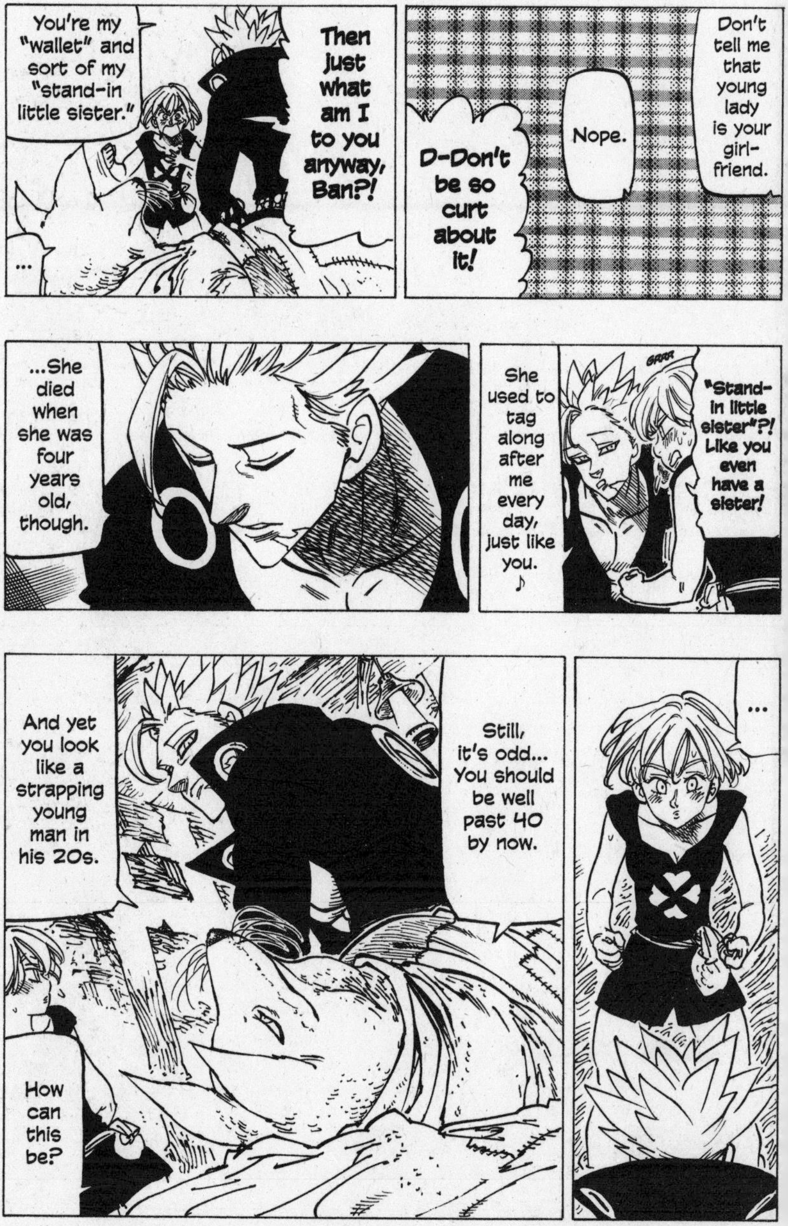
Don't tell me that young lady is your girl-friend.
Nope.
D-Don't be so curt about it!
Then just what am I to you anyway, Ban?!
You're my "wallet" and sort of my "stand-in little sister."
...
GRRR
"Stand-in little sister"?! Like you even have a sister!
She used to tag along after me every day, just like you. ♪
...She died when she was four years old, though.
...
Still, it's odd... You should be well past 40 by now.
And yet you look like a strapping young man in his 20s.
How can this be?

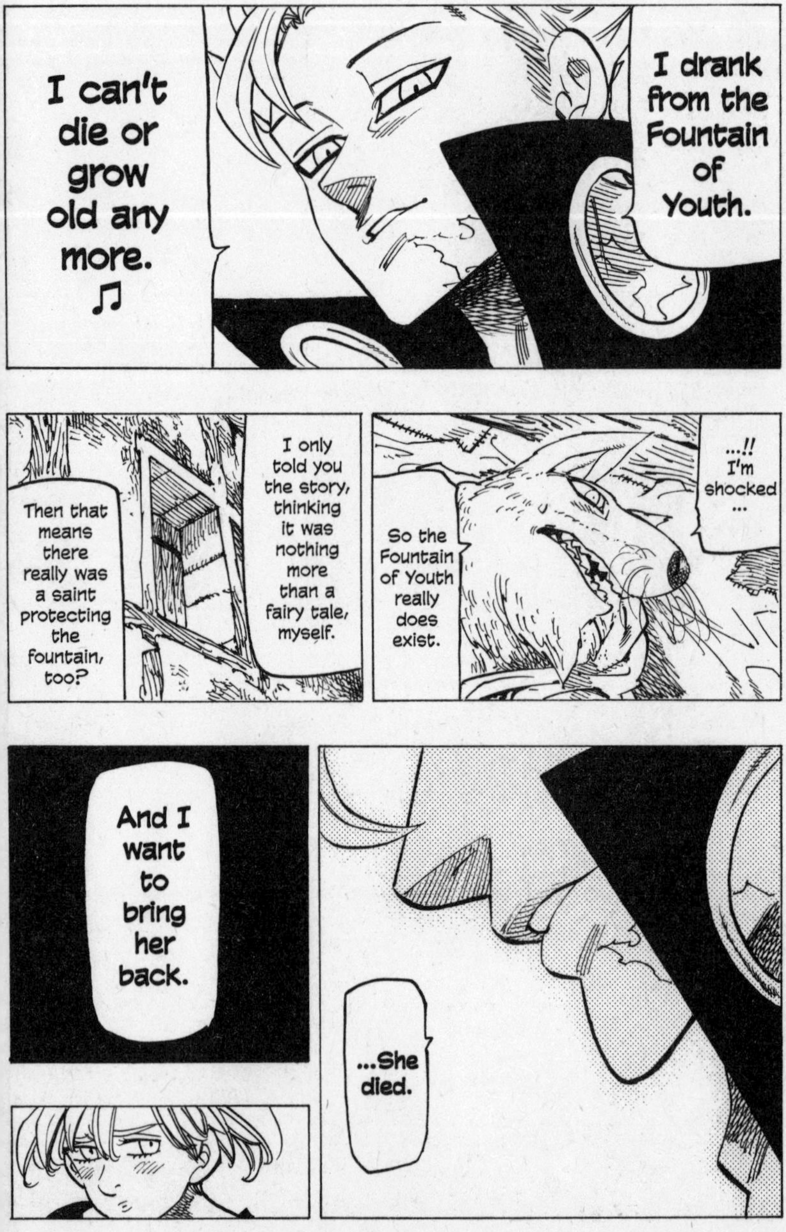
I drank from the Fountain of Youth.
I can't die or grow old any more. ♫
...!! I'm shocked ...
So the Fountain of Youth really does exist.
I only told you the story, thinking it was nothing more than a fairy tale, myself.
Then that means there really was a saint protecting the fountain, too?
...She died.
And I want to bring her back.

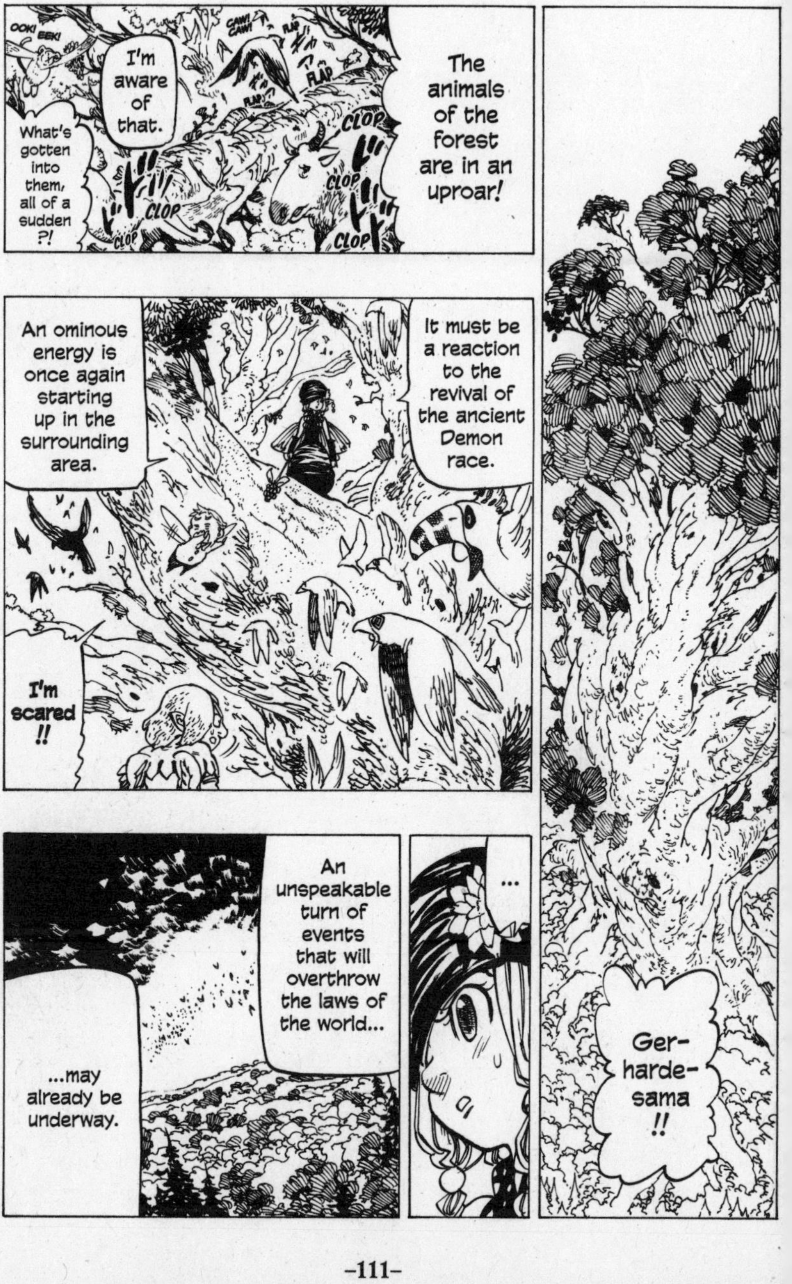
Ger-harde-sama!!
The animals of the forest are in an uproar!
CAW! CAW!
FLAP
FLAP
FLAP
I'm aware of that.
OOK! EEK!
CLOP
CLOP
CLOP
CLOP
CLOP
What's gotten into them, all of a sudden?!
It must be a reaction to the revival of the ancient Demon race.
An ominous energy is once again starting up in the surrounding area.
I'm scared!!
...
An unspeakable turn of events that will overthrow the laws of the world...
...may already be underway.

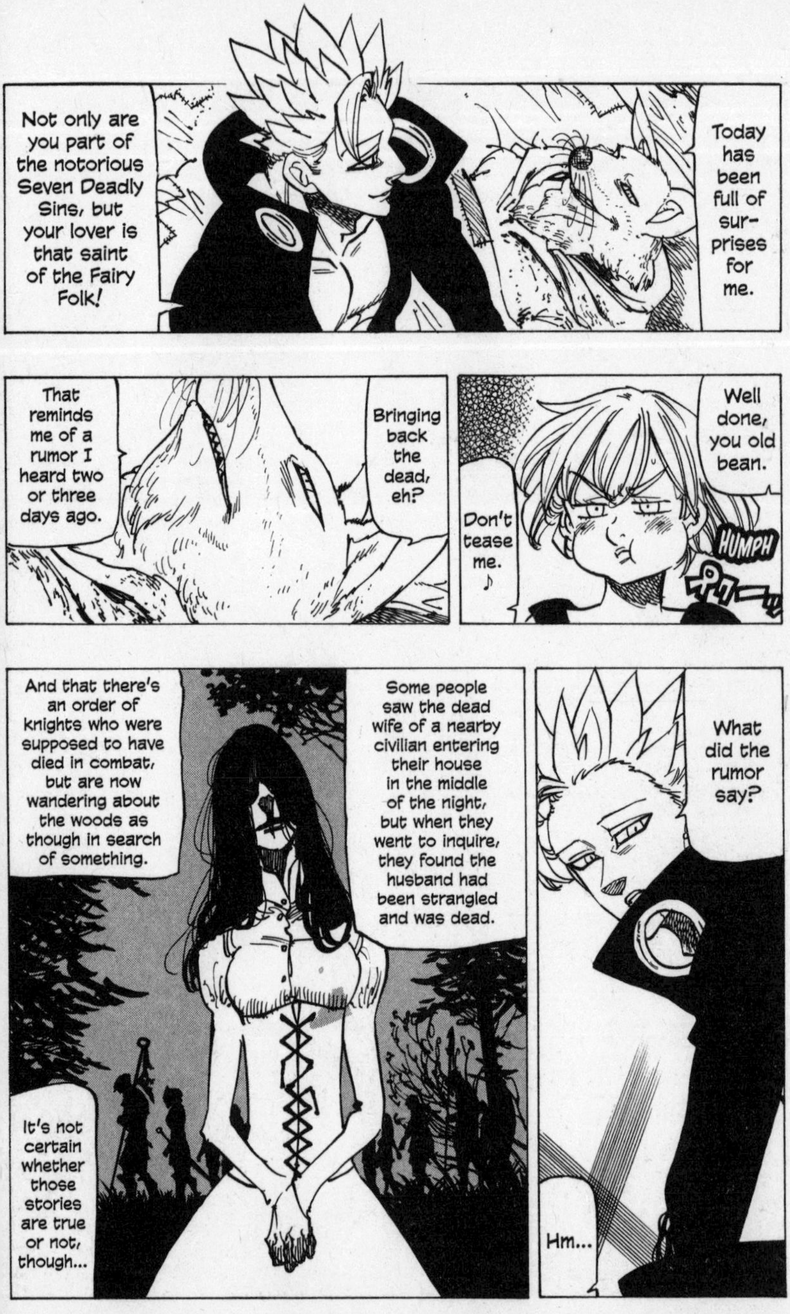
Today has been full of sur-prises for me.
Not only are you part of the notorious Seven Deadly Sins, but your lover is that saint of the Fairy Folk!
Well done, you old bean.
Don't tease me. ♪
HUMPH
Bringing back the dead, eh?
That reminds me of a rumor I heard two or three days ago.
What did the rumor say?
Hm...
Some people saw the dead wife of a nearby civilian entering their house in the middle of the night, but when they went to inquire, they found the husband had been strangled and was dead.
And that there's an order of knights who were supposed to have died in combat, but are now wandering about the woods as though in search of something.
It's not certain whether those stories are true or not, though...

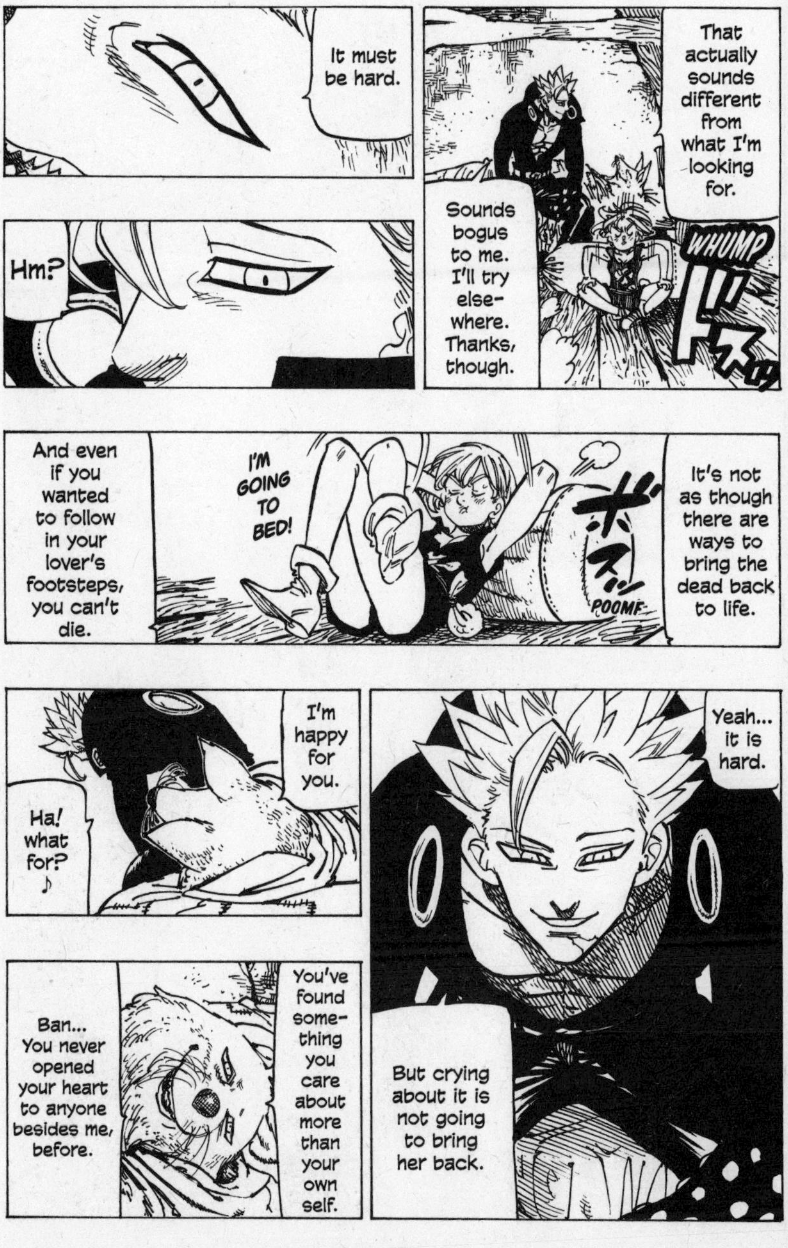
That actually sounds different from what I'm looking for.
Sounds bogus to me. I'll try elsewhere. Thanks, though.
WHUMP
It must be hard.
Hm?
It's not as though there are ways to bring the dead back to life.
POOMF
I'M GOING TO BED!
And even if you wanted to follow in your lover's footsteps, you can't die.
Yeah... it is hard.
But crying about it is not going to bring her back.
I'm happy for you.
Ha! what for? ♪
You've found something you care about more than your own self.
Ban... You never opened your heart to anyone besides me, before.

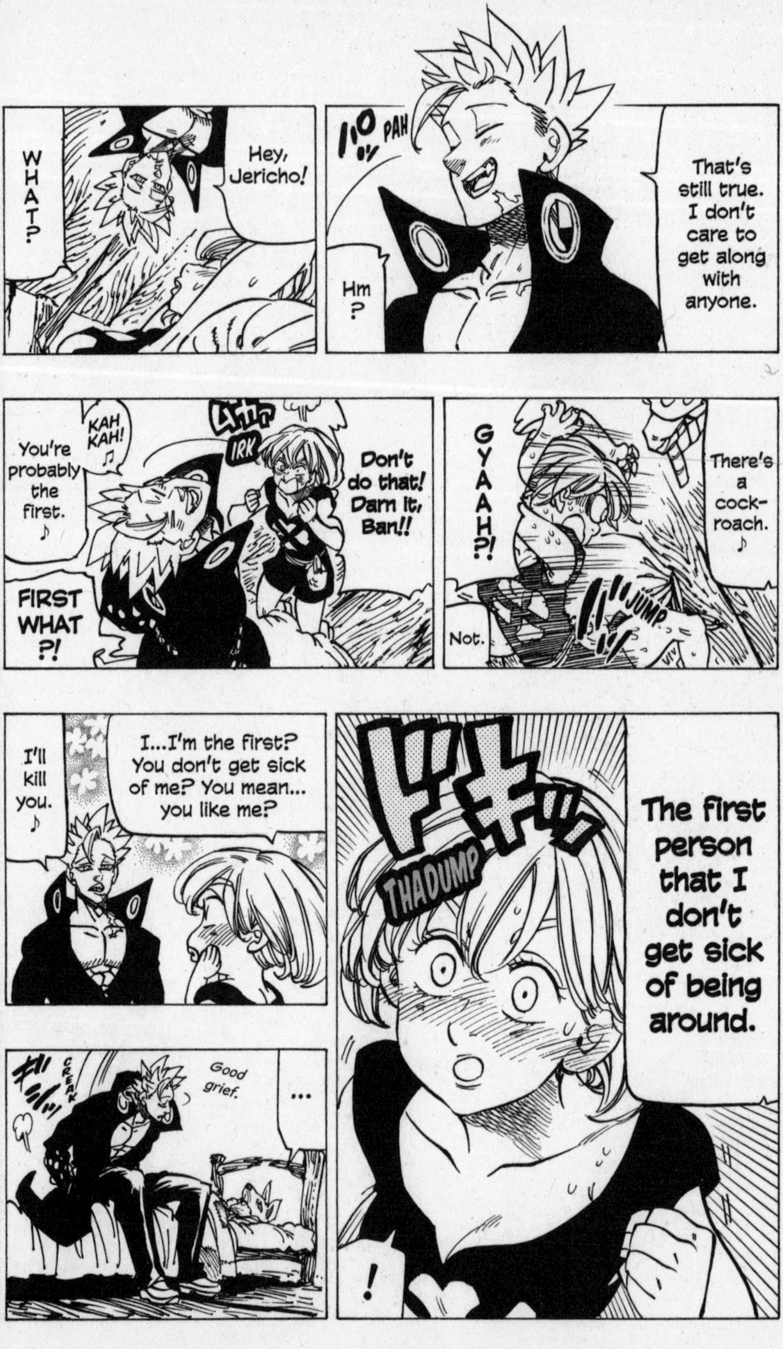
PAH
That's still true. I don't care to get along with anyone.
Hm?
Hey, Jericho!
WHAT?
There's a cockroach. ♪
GYAAAH?!
JUMP
Not.
Don't do that! Darn it, Ban!!
IRK
KAH KAH! ♫
You're probably the first. ♪
FIRST WHAT?!
ドキッ
THADUMP
The first person that I don't get sick of being around.
!
I...I'm the first? You don't get sick of me? You mean... you like me?
I'll kill you. ♪
...
Good grief.
CREAK

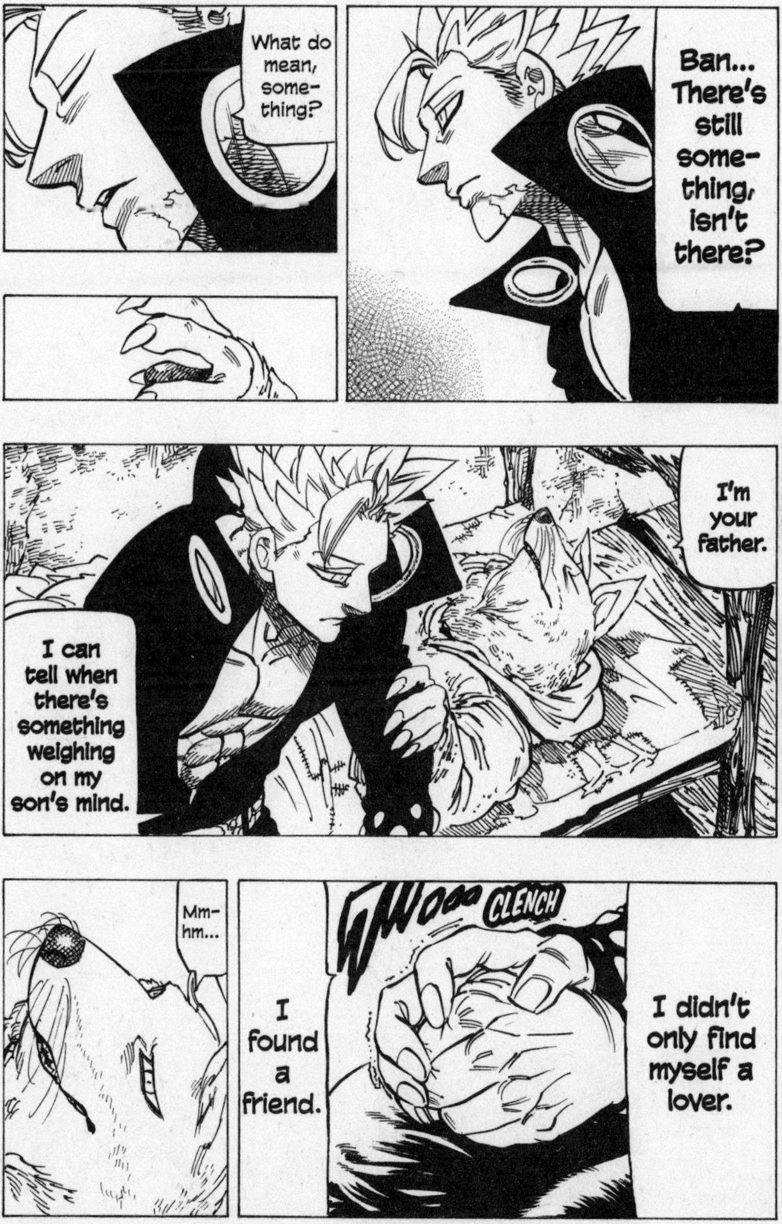
Ban... There's still some-thing, isn't there?
What do mean, some-thing?
I'm your father.
I can tell when there's something weighing on my son's mind.
CLENCH
I didn't only find myself a lover.
I found a friend.
Mm-hm...

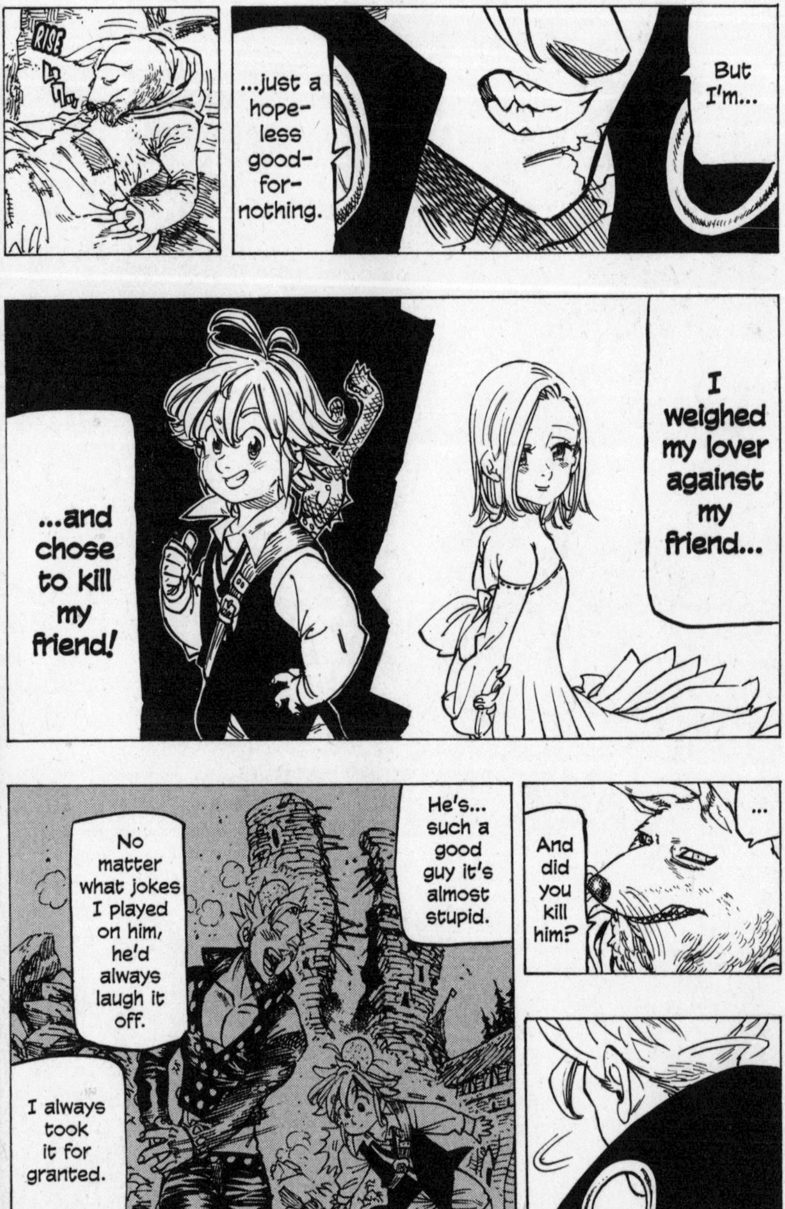
But I'm...
...just a hopeless good-for-nothing.
RISE
I weighed my lover against my friend...
...and chose to kill my friend!
...
And did you kill him?
He's... such a good guy it's almost stupid.
No matter what jokes I played on him, he'd always laugh it off.
I always took it for granted.

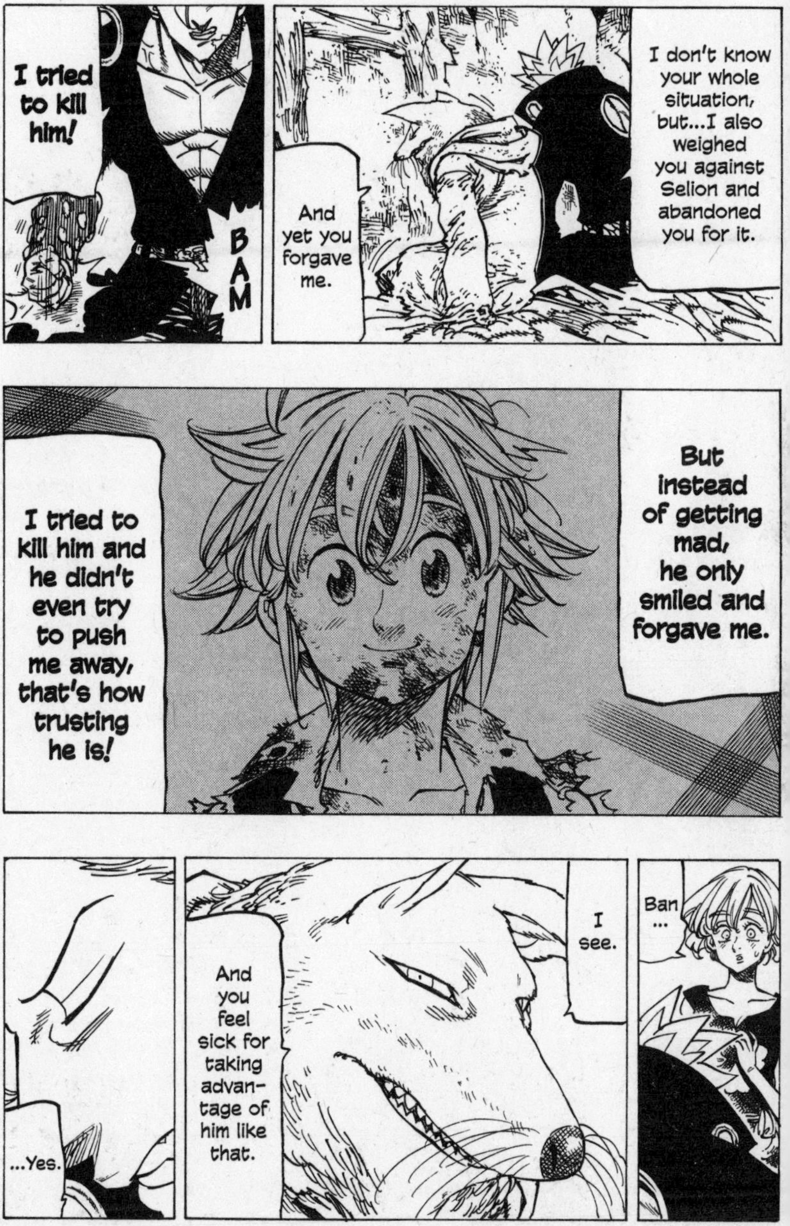
I don't know your whole situation, but...I also weighed you against Selion and abandoned you for it.
And yet you forgave me.
I tried to kill him!
BAM
But instead of getting mad, he only smiled and forgave me.
I tried to kill him and he didn't even try to push me away, that's how trusting he is!
Ban...
I see.
And you feel sick for taking advantage of him like that.
...Yes.

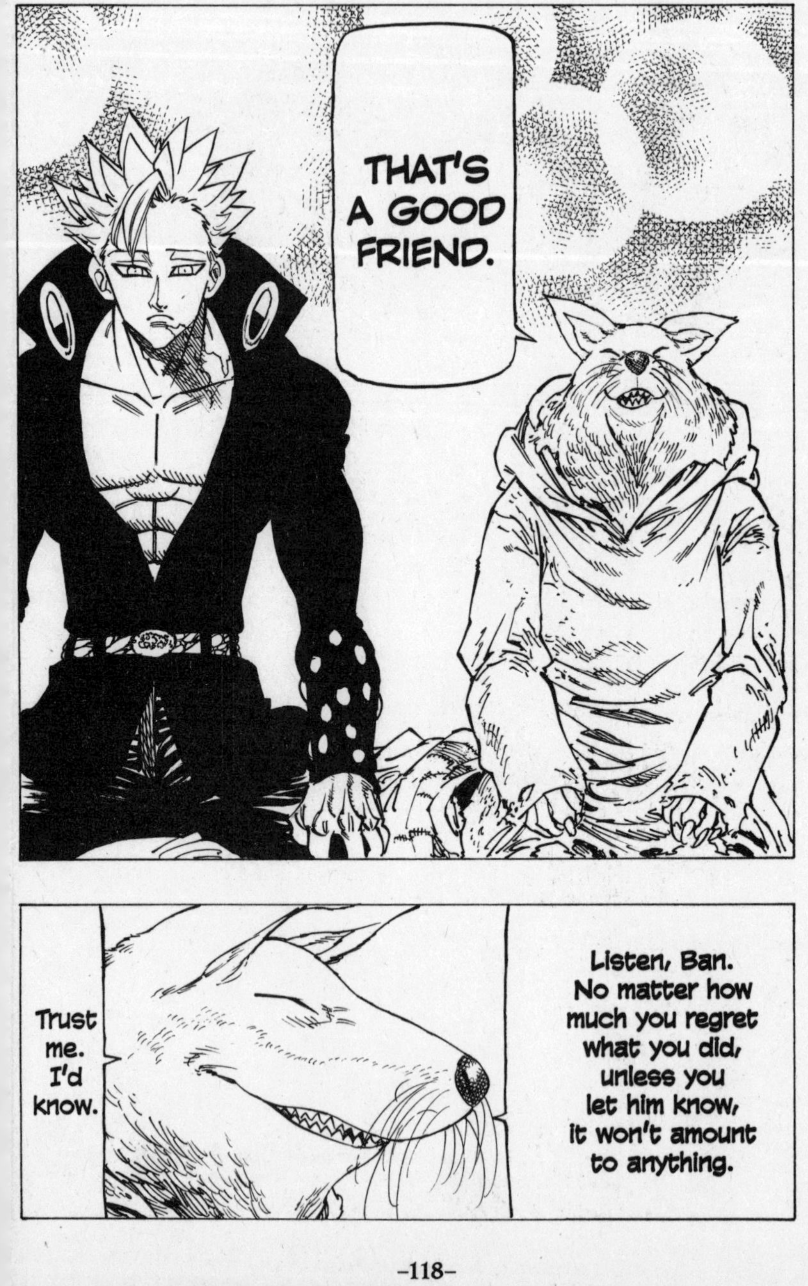
THAT'S A GOOD FRIEND.
Listen, Ban. No matter how much you regret what you did, unless you let him know, it won't amount to anything.
Trust me. I'd know.

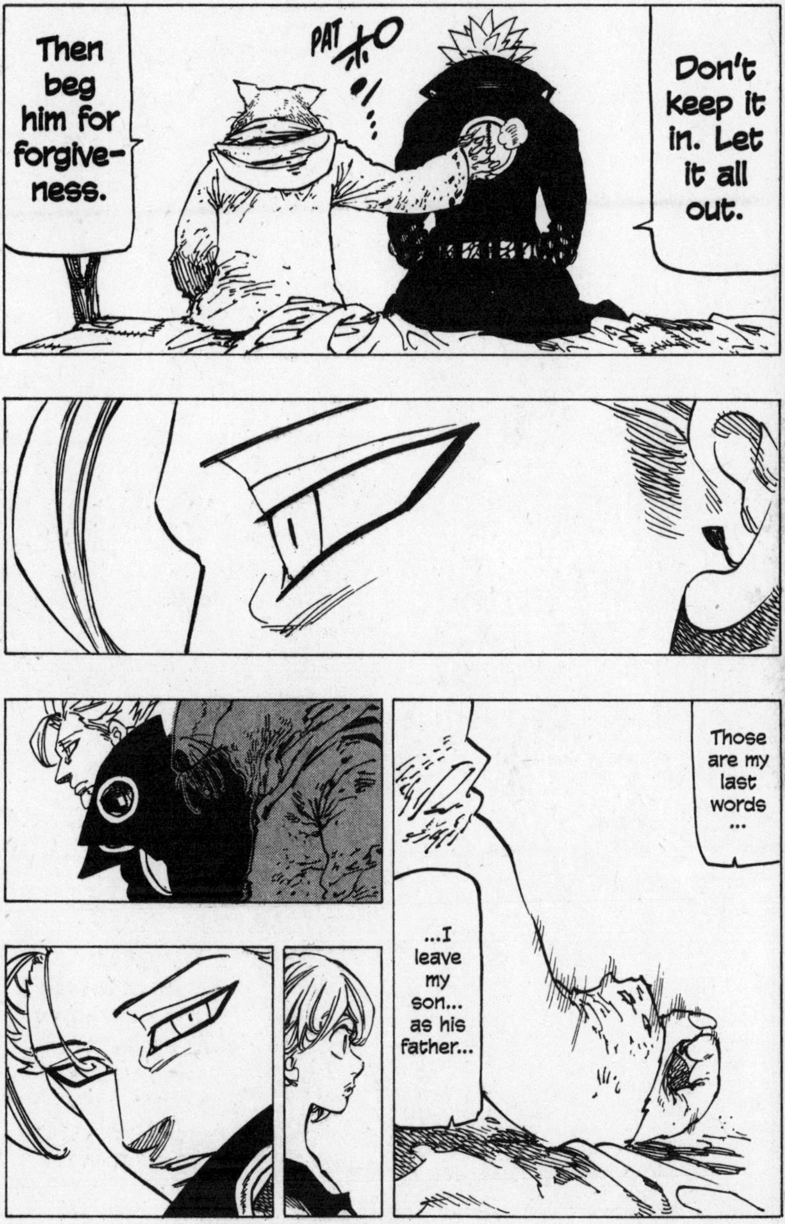
Don't keep it in. Let it all out.
PAT
Then beg him for forgive-ness.
Those are my last words ...
...I leave my son... as his father...

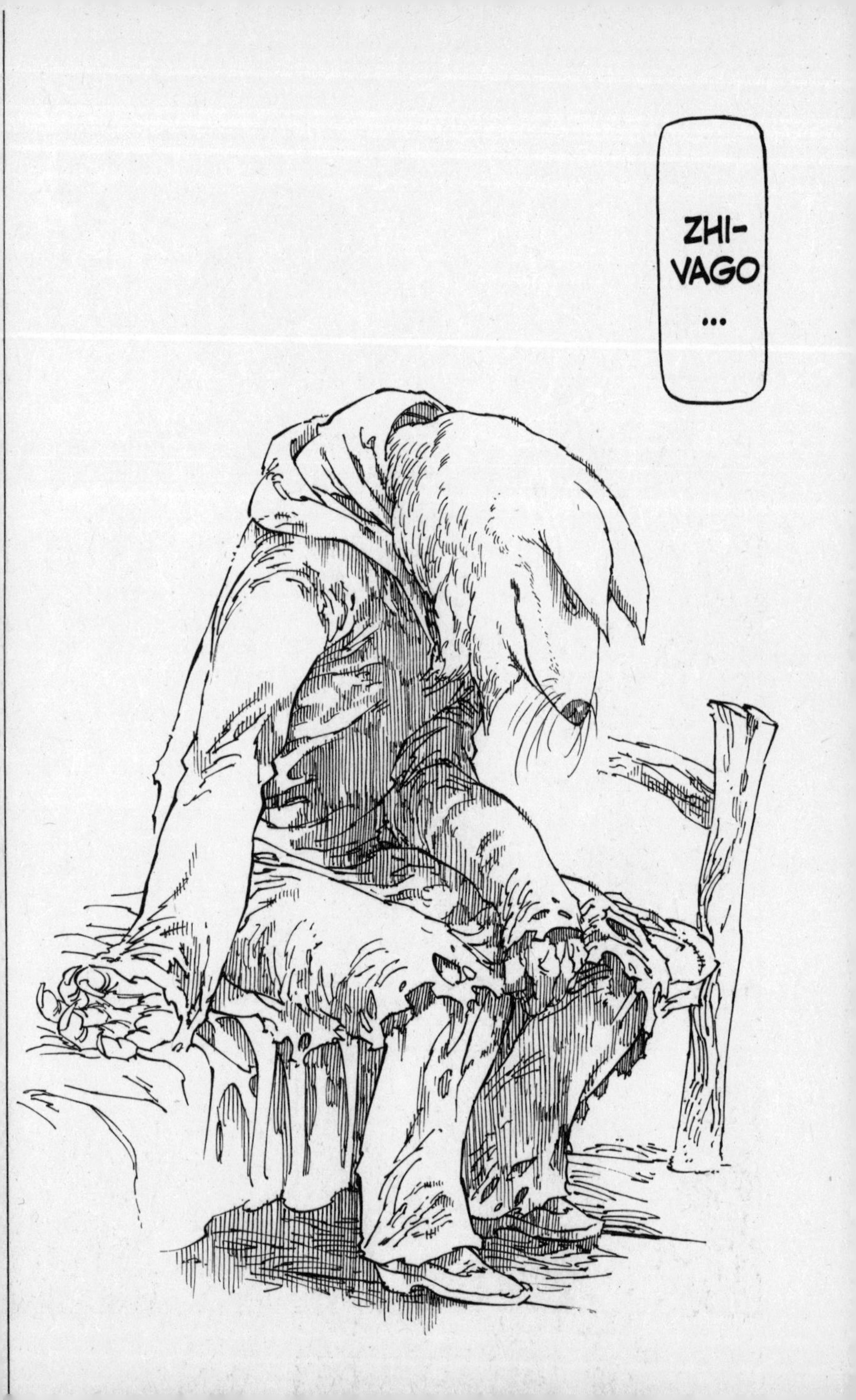
ZHI-
VAGO
...

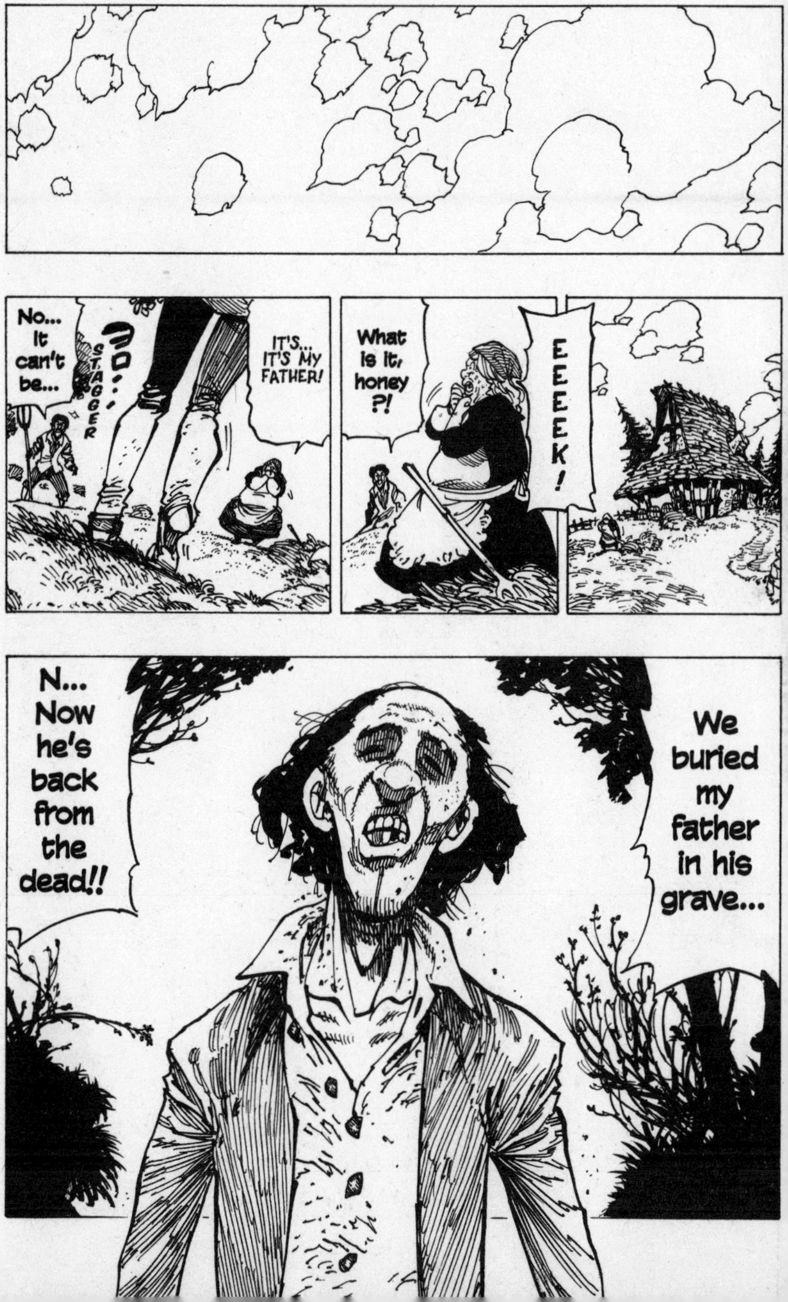
EEEEEK!
What is it, honey?!
IT'S... IT'S MY FATHER!
STAGGER
No... It can't be...
We buried my father in his grave...
N... Now he's back from the dead!!

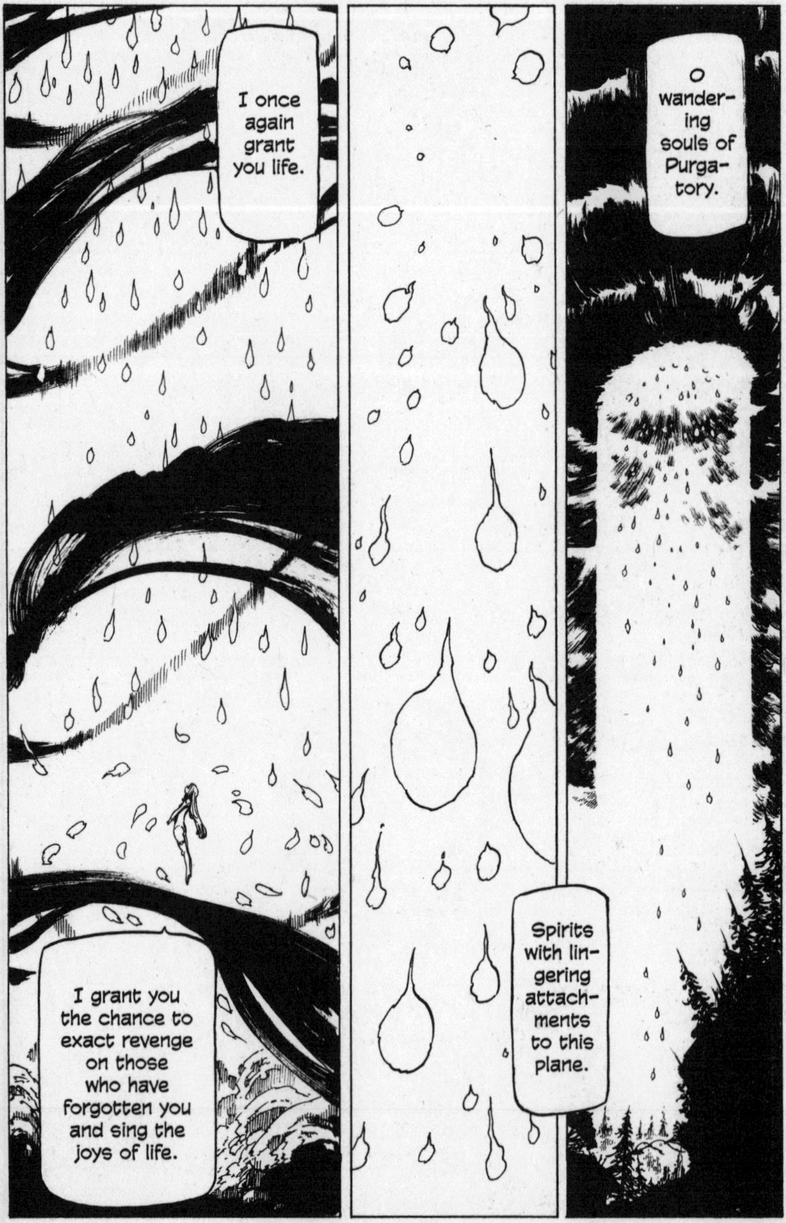
O wander-ing souls of Purga-tory.
Spirits with lin-gering attach-ments to this plane.
I once again grant you life.
I grant you the chance to exact revenge on those who have forgotten you and sing the joys of life.

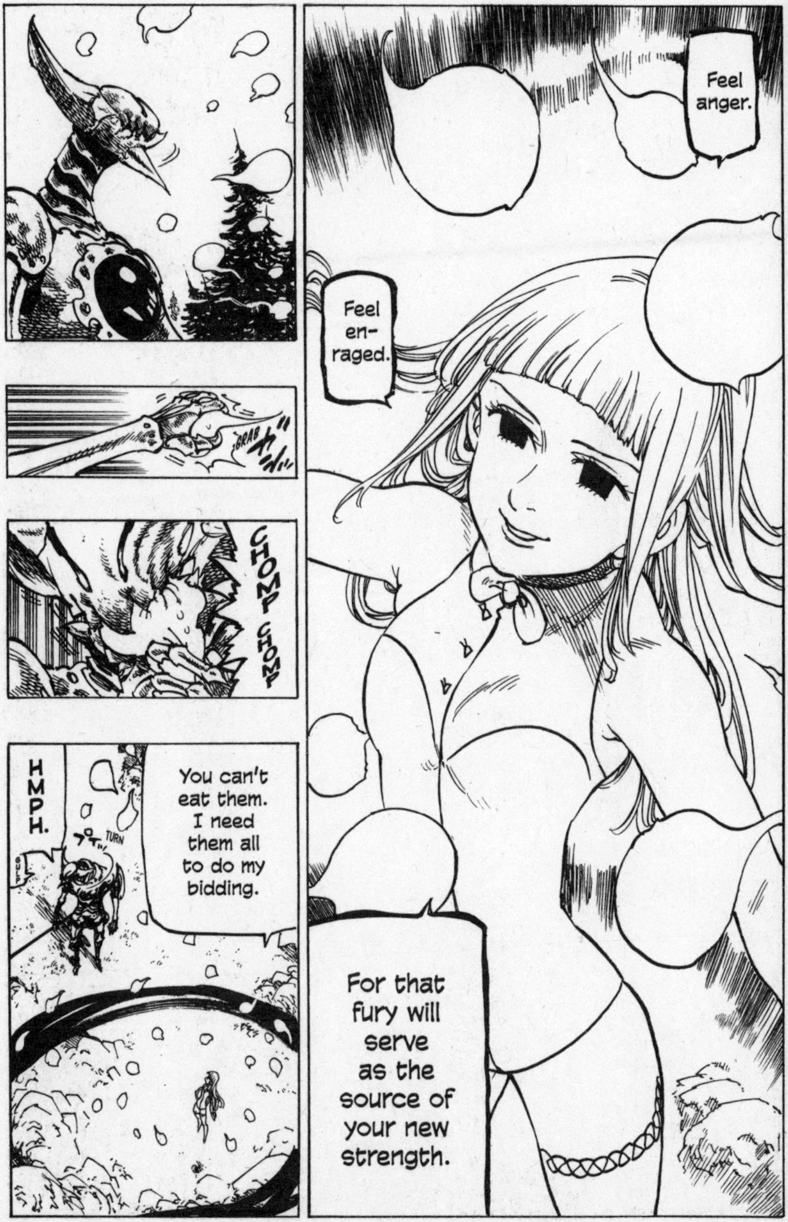
Feel anger.
Feel en-raged.
For that fury will serve as the source of your new strength.
GRAB
CHOMP CHOMP
HMPH.
TURN
You can't eat them. I need them all to do my bidding.

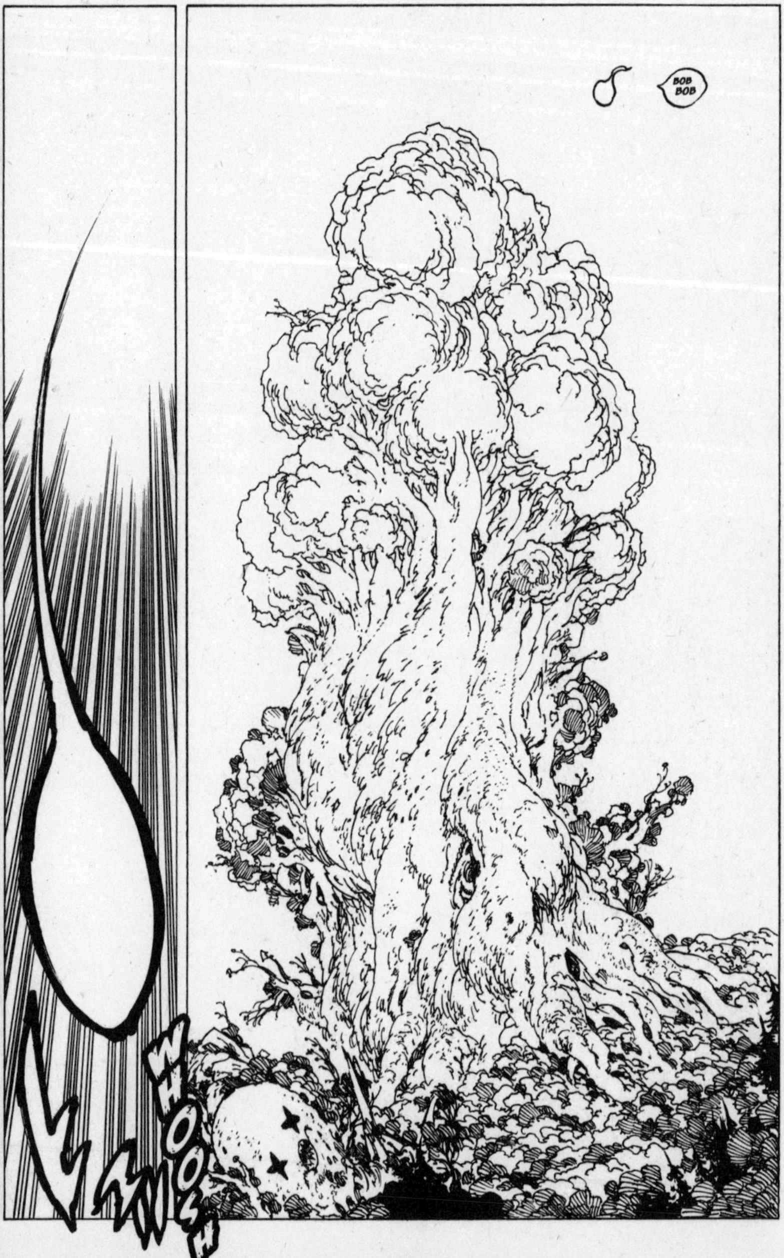
BOB
BOB
WHOOSH

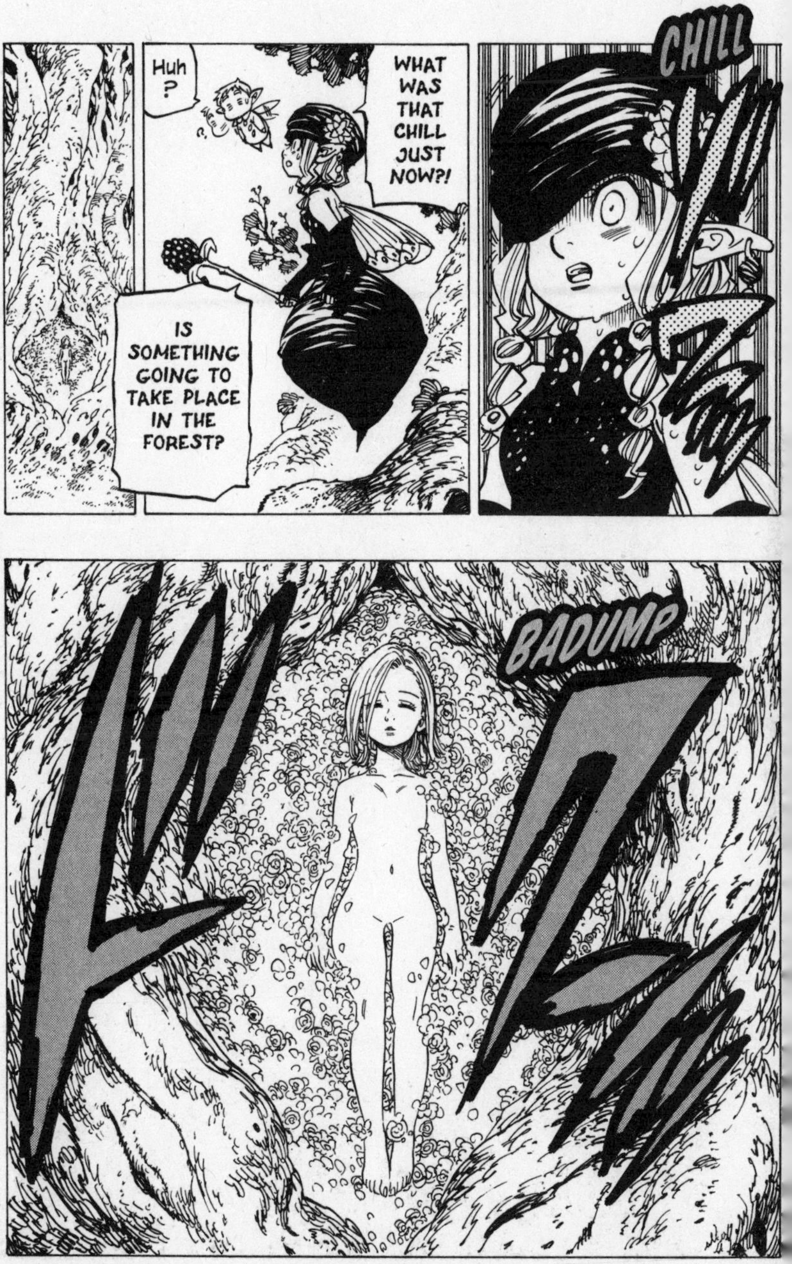
CHILL
WHAT WAS THAT CHILL JUST NOW?!
Huh ?
IS SOMETHING GOING TO TAKE PLACE IN THE FOREST?
BADUMP

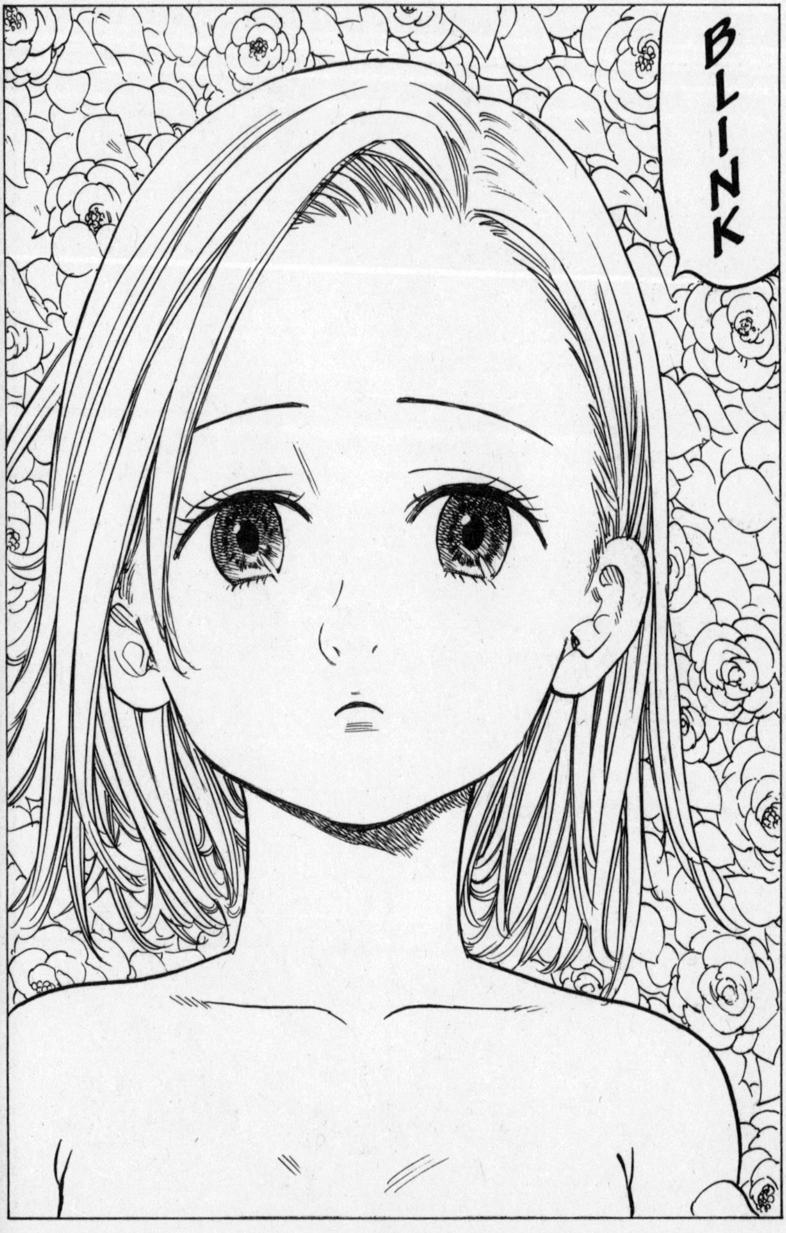
BLINK

## Chapter 142 - Where Love is Found

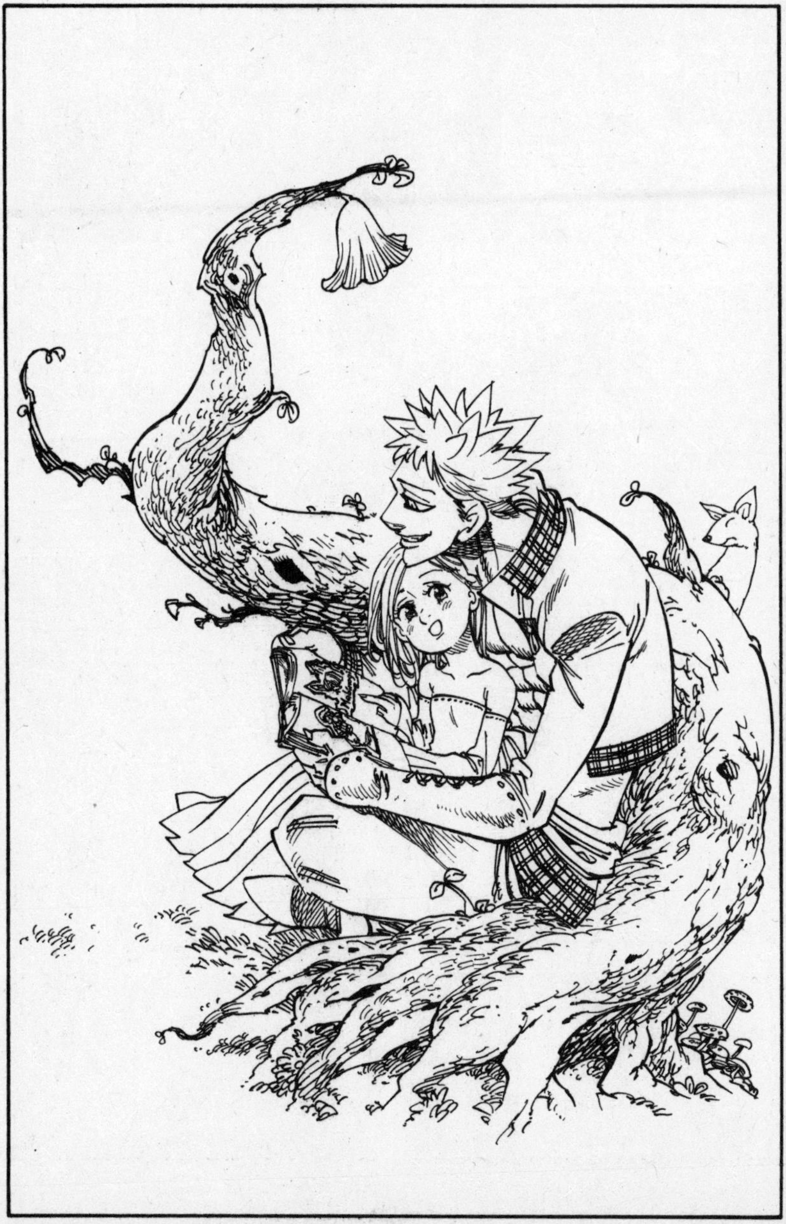

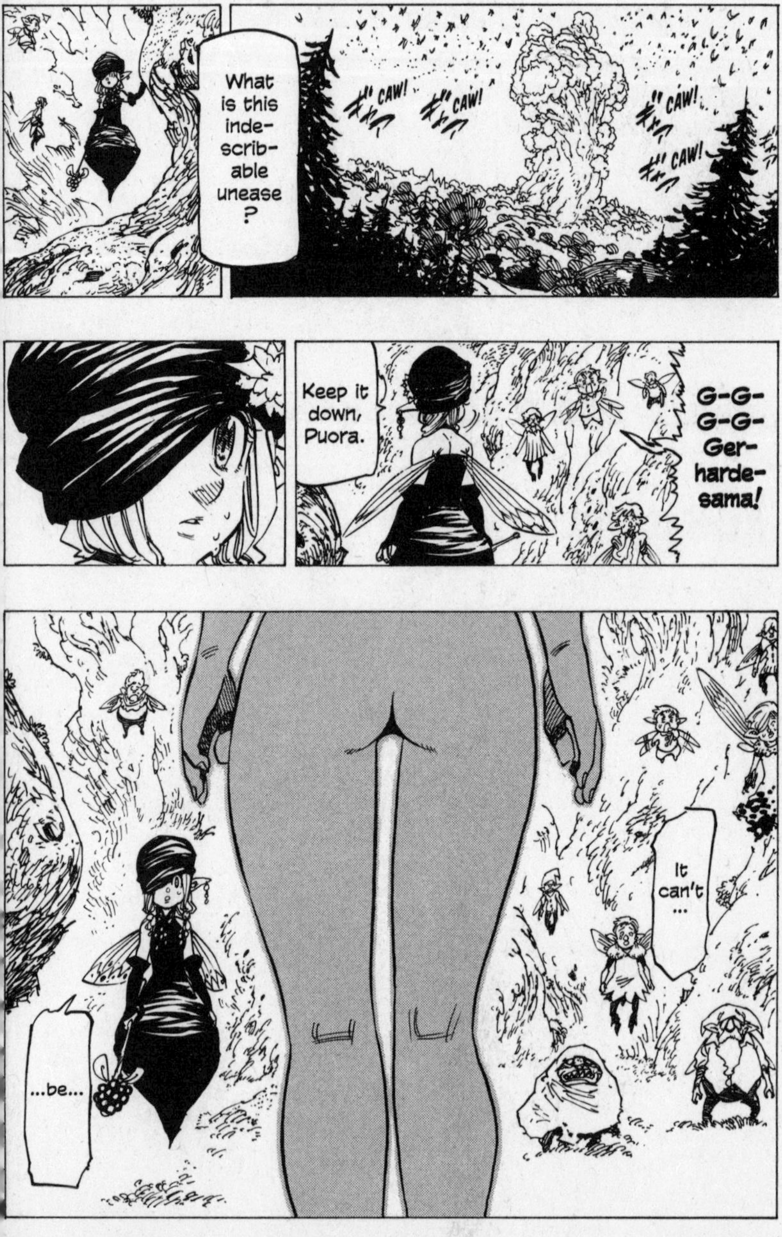
CAW!
CAW!
CAW!
CAW!
What is this indescribable unease?
G-G-G-G-Gerhardesama!
Keep it down, Puora.
It can't...
...be...

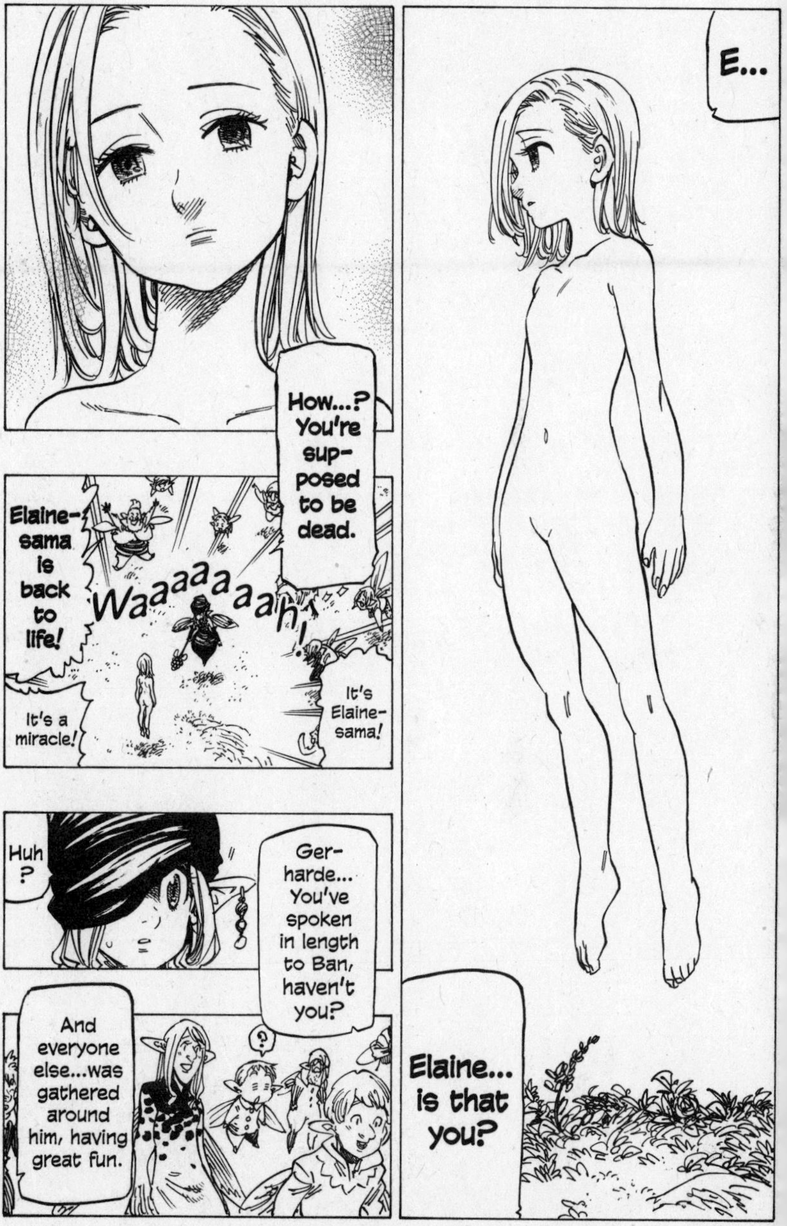
E...
Elaine... is that you?
How...? You're sup-posed to be dead.
Waaaaaaaah!
It's Elaine-sama!
Elaine-sama is back to life!
It's a miracle!
Ger-harde... You've spoken in length to Ban, haven't you?
Huh?
And everyone else...was gathered around him, having great fun.
?

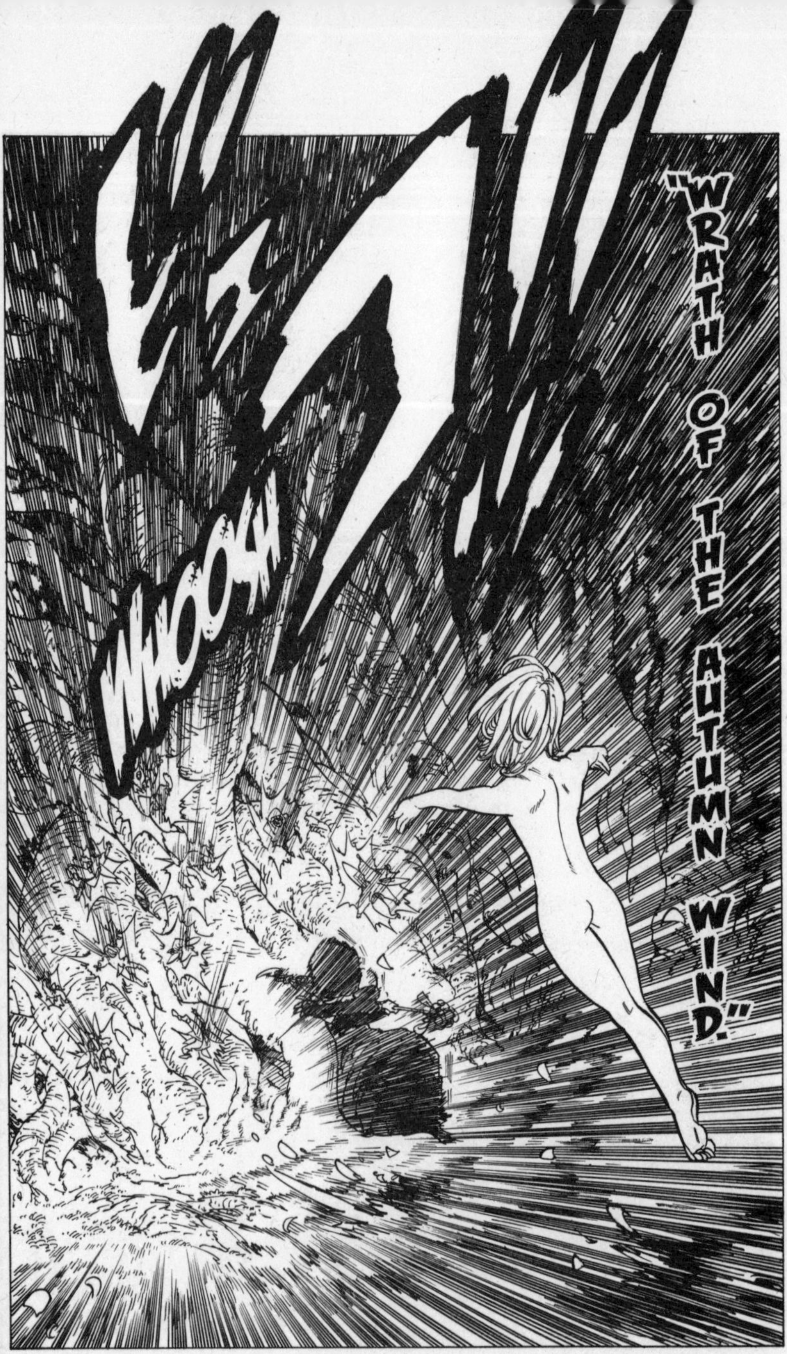
"WRATH OF THE AUTUMN WIND."
WHOOSH

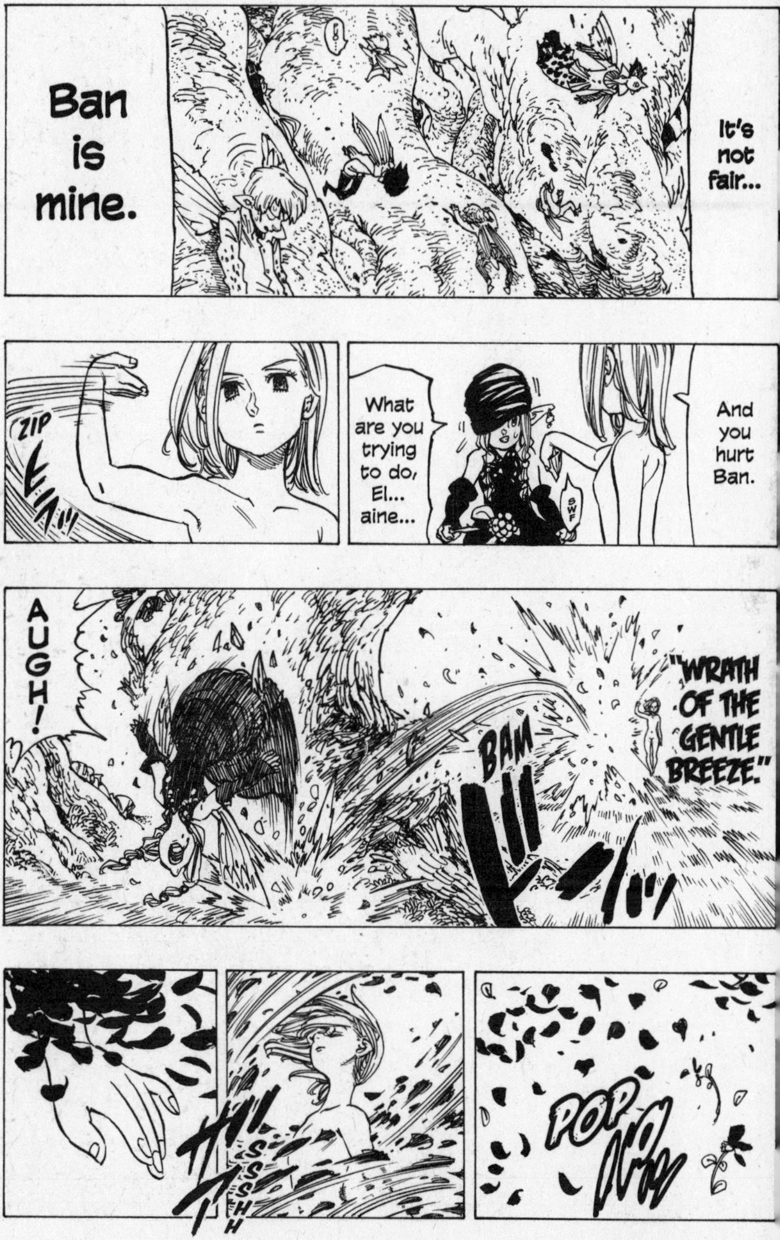
It's not fair...
Ban is mine.
And you hurt Ban.
What are you trying to do, El... aine...
SWF
ZIP
"WRATH OF THE GENTLE BREEZE."
BAM
AUGH!
POP
SSSSHH

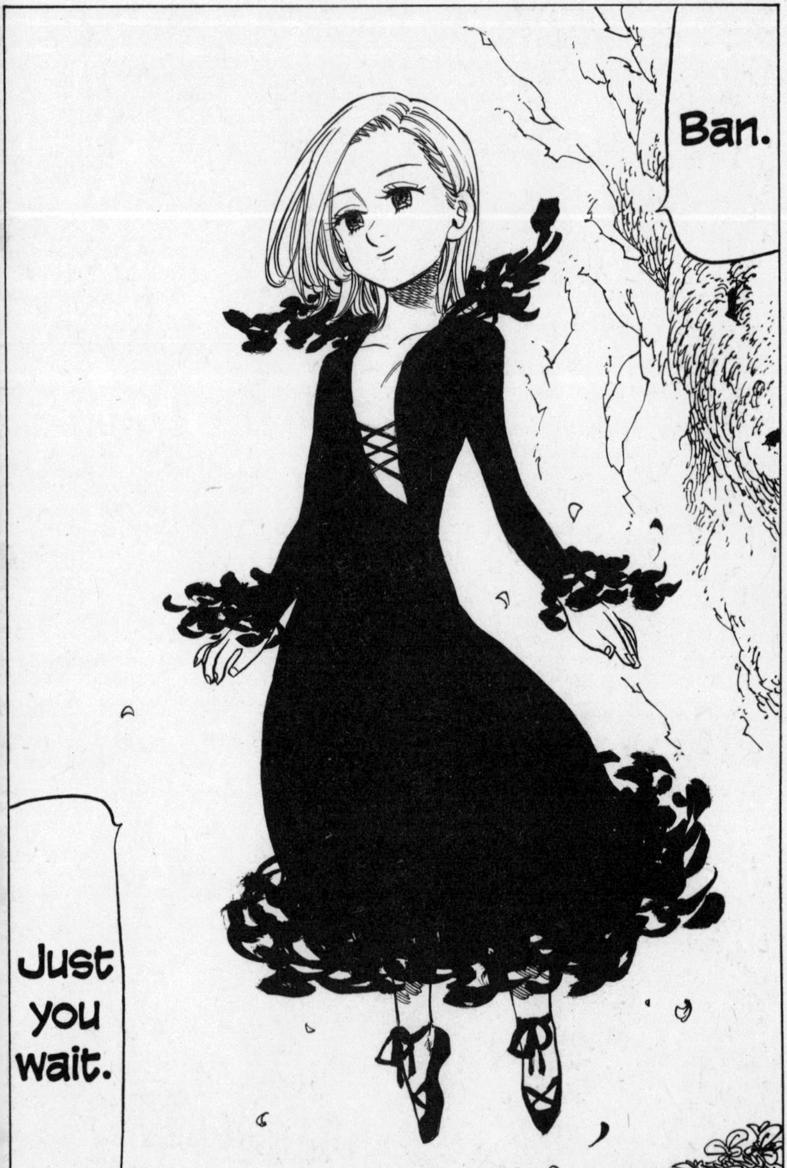
Ban.
Just you wait.

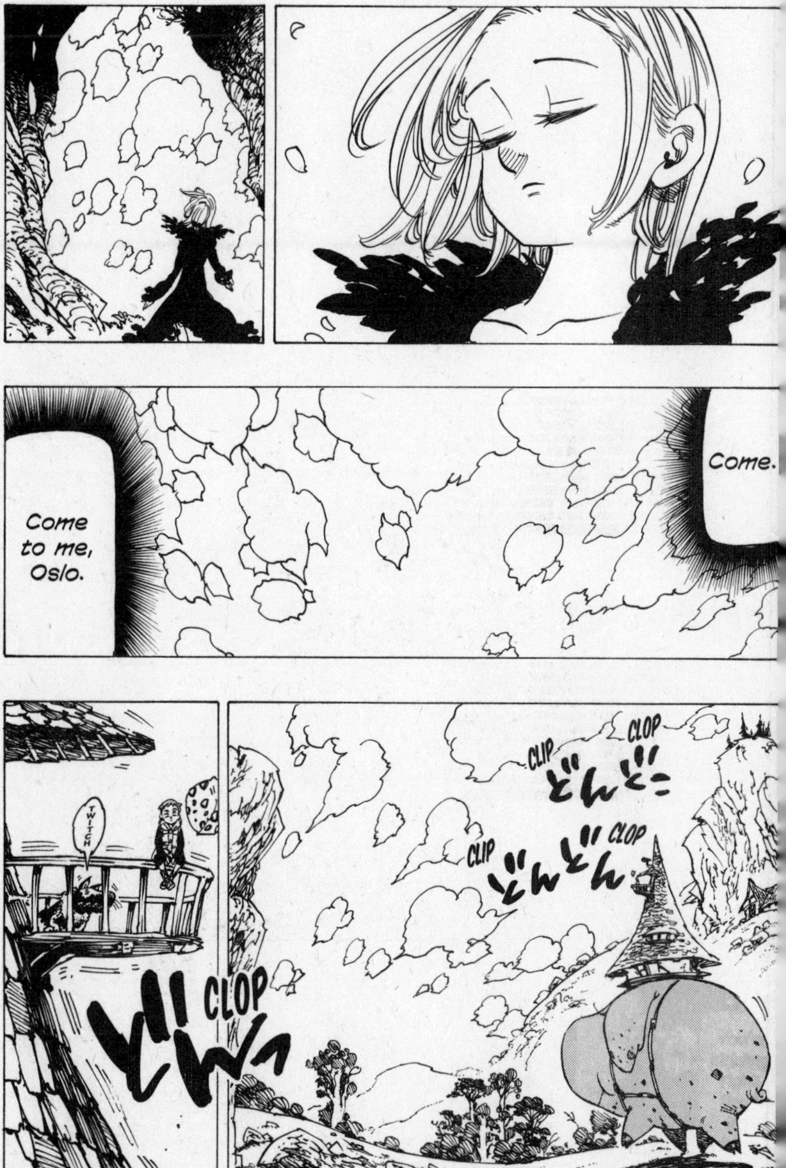
Come.
Come to me, Oslo.
CLOP
CLIP
CLOP
CLIP
TWITCH
CLOP

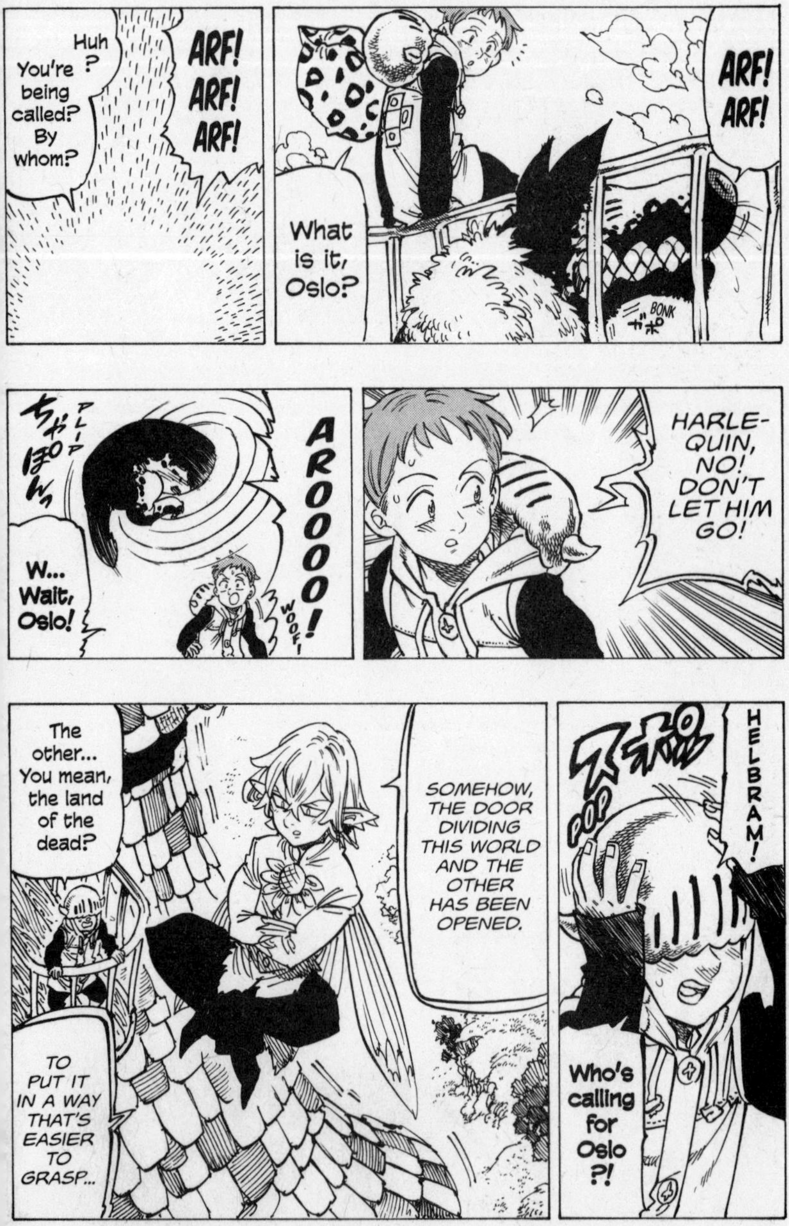
ARF! ARF!
What is it, Oslo?
BONK
ARF! ARF! ARF!
Huh? You're being called? By whom?
HARLE-QUIN, NO! DON'T LET HIM GO!
AROOOOO!
WOOF!
PLIP
W... Wait, Oslo!
HELBRAM!
POP
Who's calling for Oslo?!
SOMEHOW, THE DOOR DIVIDING THIS WORLD AND THE OTHER HAS BEEN OPENED.
The other... You mean, the land of the dead?
TO PUT IT IN A WAY THAT'S EASIER TO GRASP...

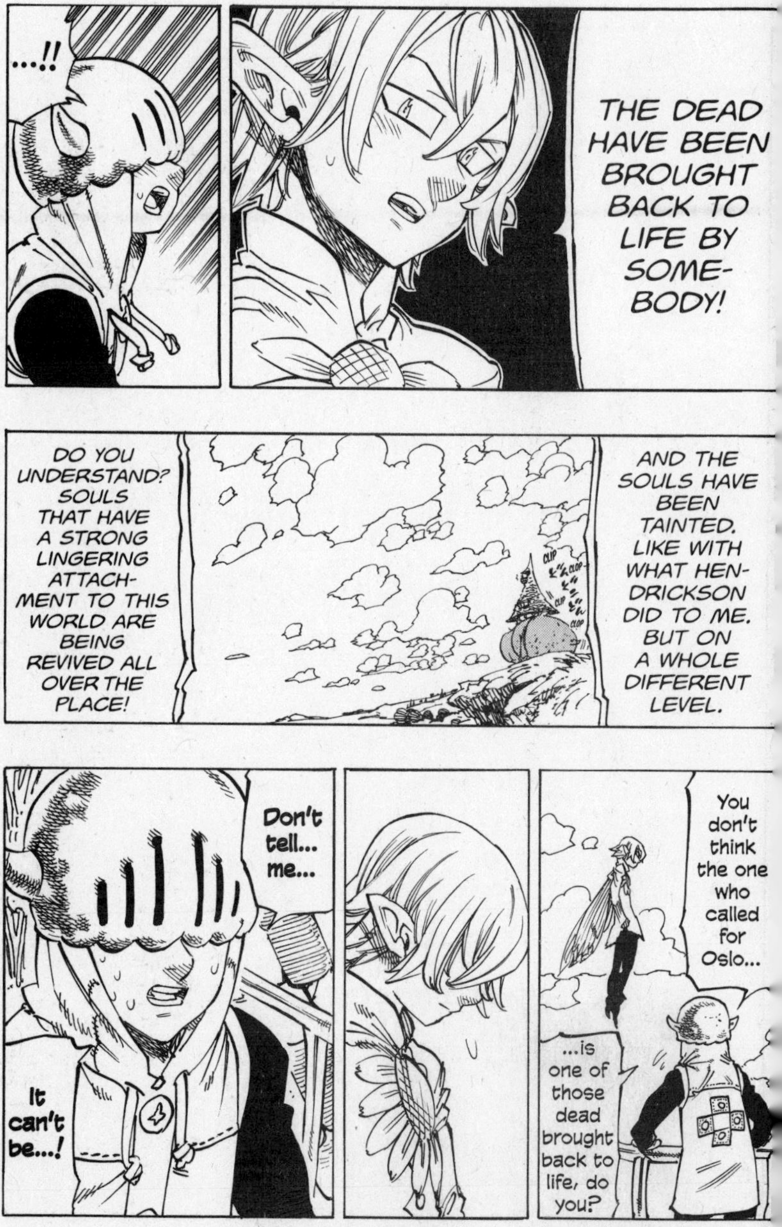
THE DEAD HAVE BEEN BROUGHT BACK TO LIFE BY SOME-BODY!
...!!
AND THE SOULS HAVE BEEN TAINTED. LIKE WITH WHAT HEN-DRICKSON DID TO ME. BUT ON A WHOLE DIFFERENT LEVEL.
CLIP CLOP CLIP CLOP
DO YOU UNDERSTAND? SOULS THAT HAVE A STRONG LINGERING ATTACH-MENT TO THIS WORLD ARE BEING REVIVED ALL OVER THE PLACE!
You don't think the one who called for Oslo...
...is one of those dead brought back to life, do you?
Don't tell... me...
It can't be...!

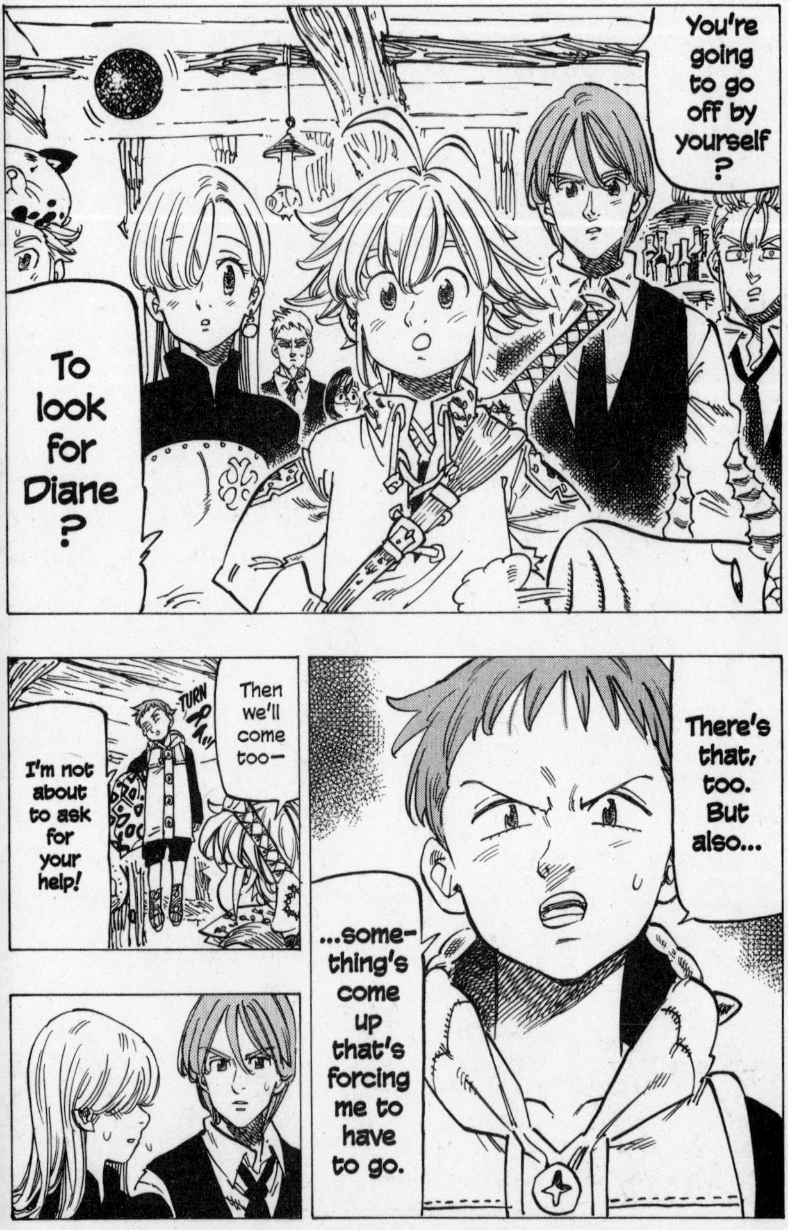
You're going to go off by yourself?
To look for Diane?
There's that, too. But also...
...something's come up that's forcing me to have to go.
Then we'll come too—
TURN
I'm not about to ask for your help!

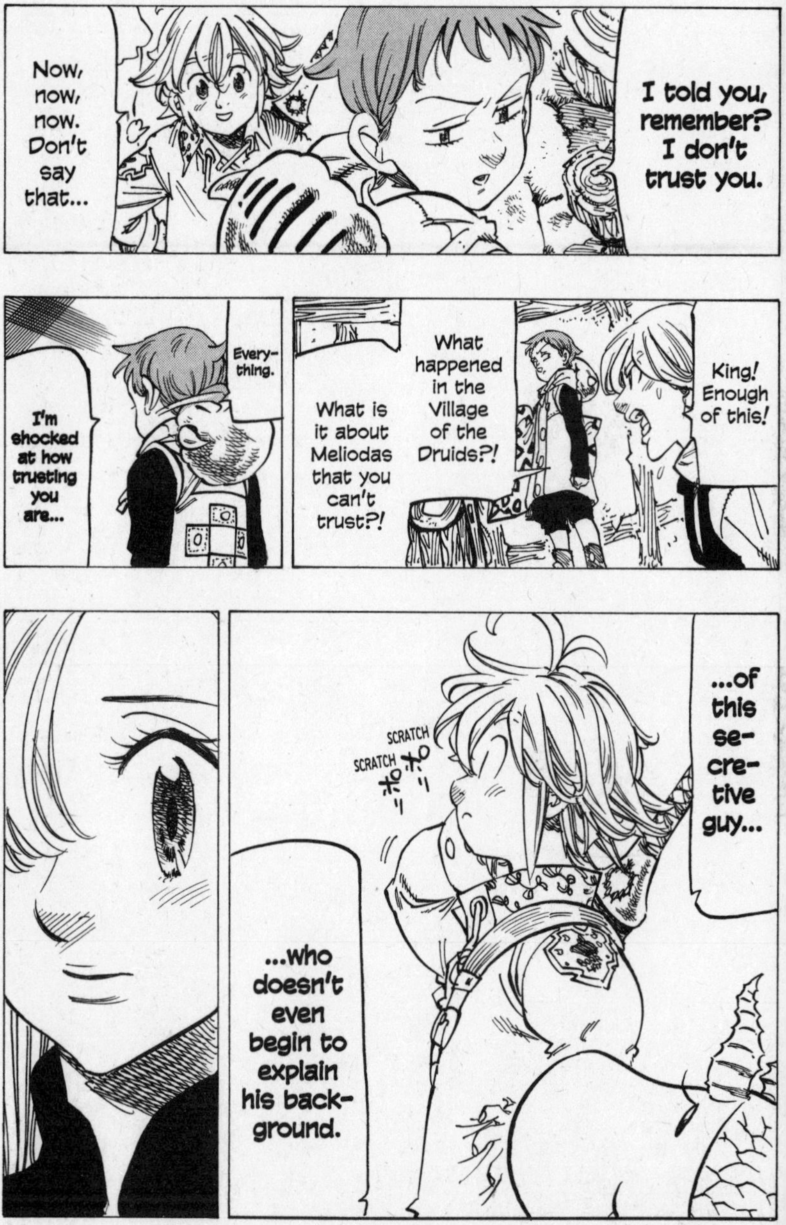
I told you, remember? I don't trust you.
Now, now, now. Don't say that...
King! Enough of this!
What happened in the Village of the Druids?!
What is it about Meliodas that you can't trust?!
Every-thing.
I'm shocked at how trusting you are...
...of this se-cre-tive guy...
SCRATCH
SCRATCH
...who doesn't even begin to explain his back-ground.

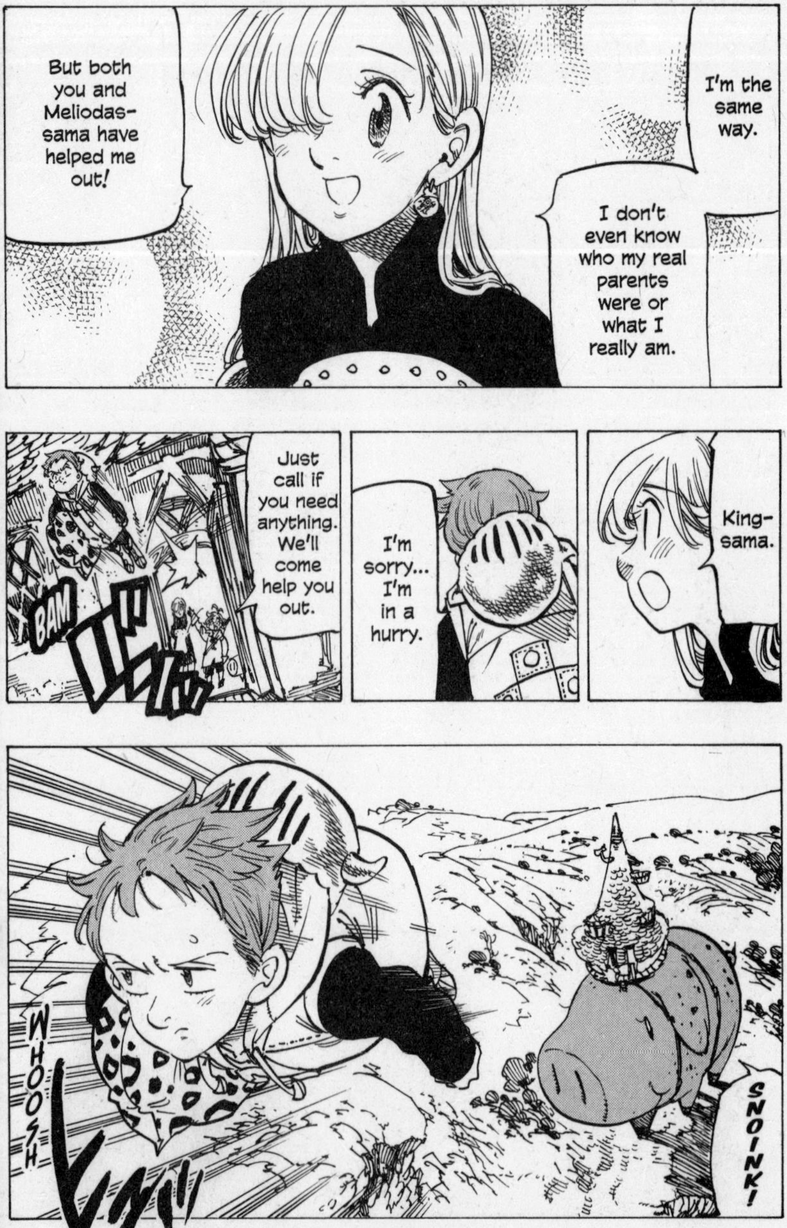
I'm the same way.
I don't even know who my real parents were or what I really am.
But both you and Meliodas-sama have helped me out!
King-sama.
I'm sorry... I'm in a hurry.
Just call if you need anything. We'll come help you out.
BAM
SNOINK!
WHOOSH

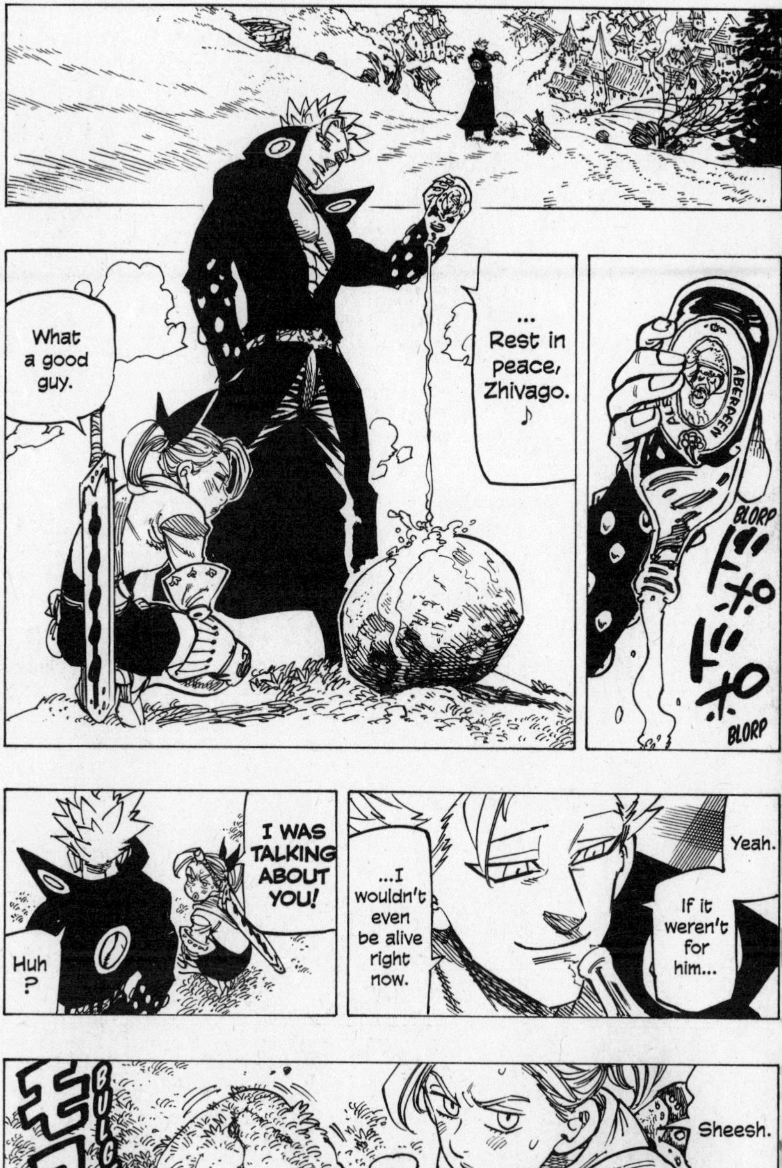
ABERDEEN
BLORP
BLORP
... Rest in peace, Zhivago. ♪
What a good guy.
Yeah.
If it weren't for him...
...I wouldn't even be alive right now.
I WAS TALKING ABOUT YOU!
Huh?
Sheesh.
He's so thick.
BULGE

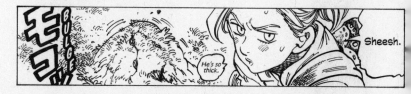

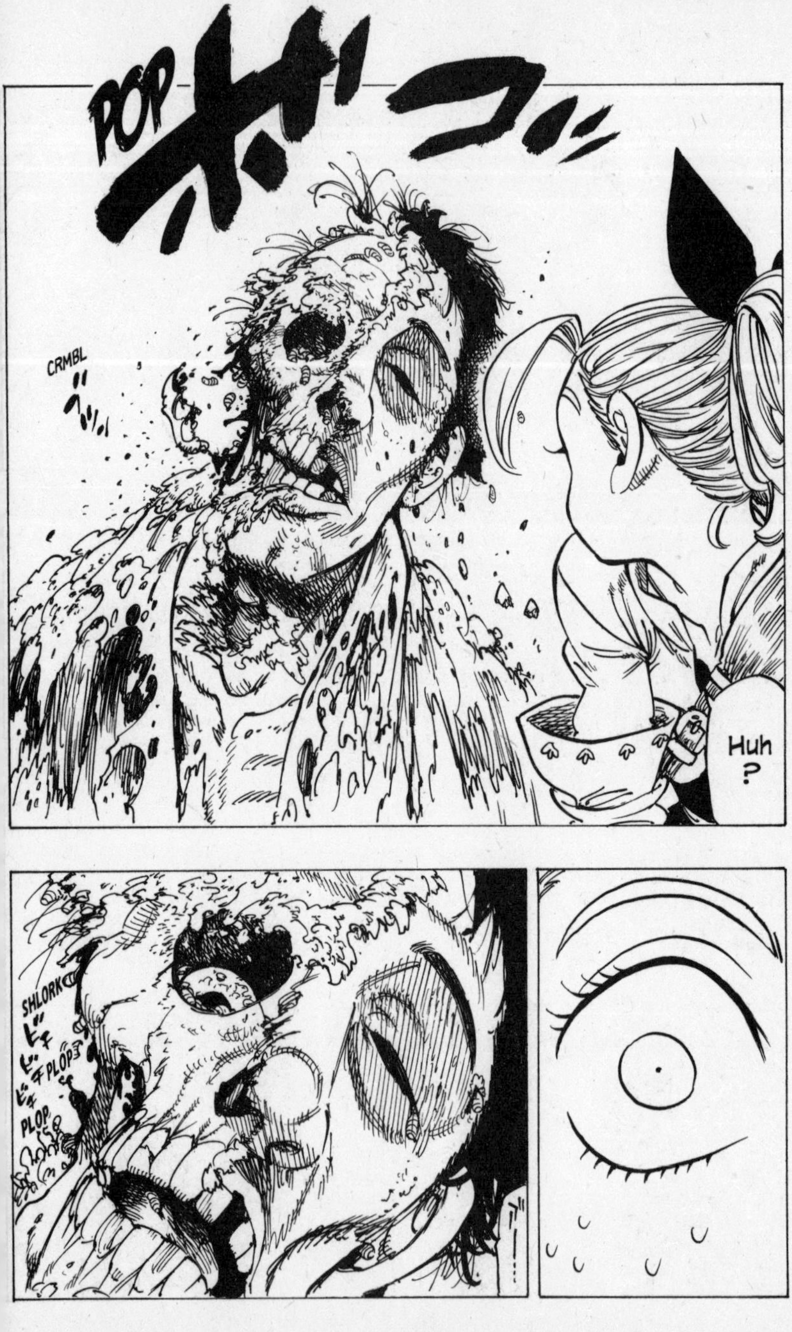
POP
CRMBL
Huh?
SHLORK
PLOP
PLOP

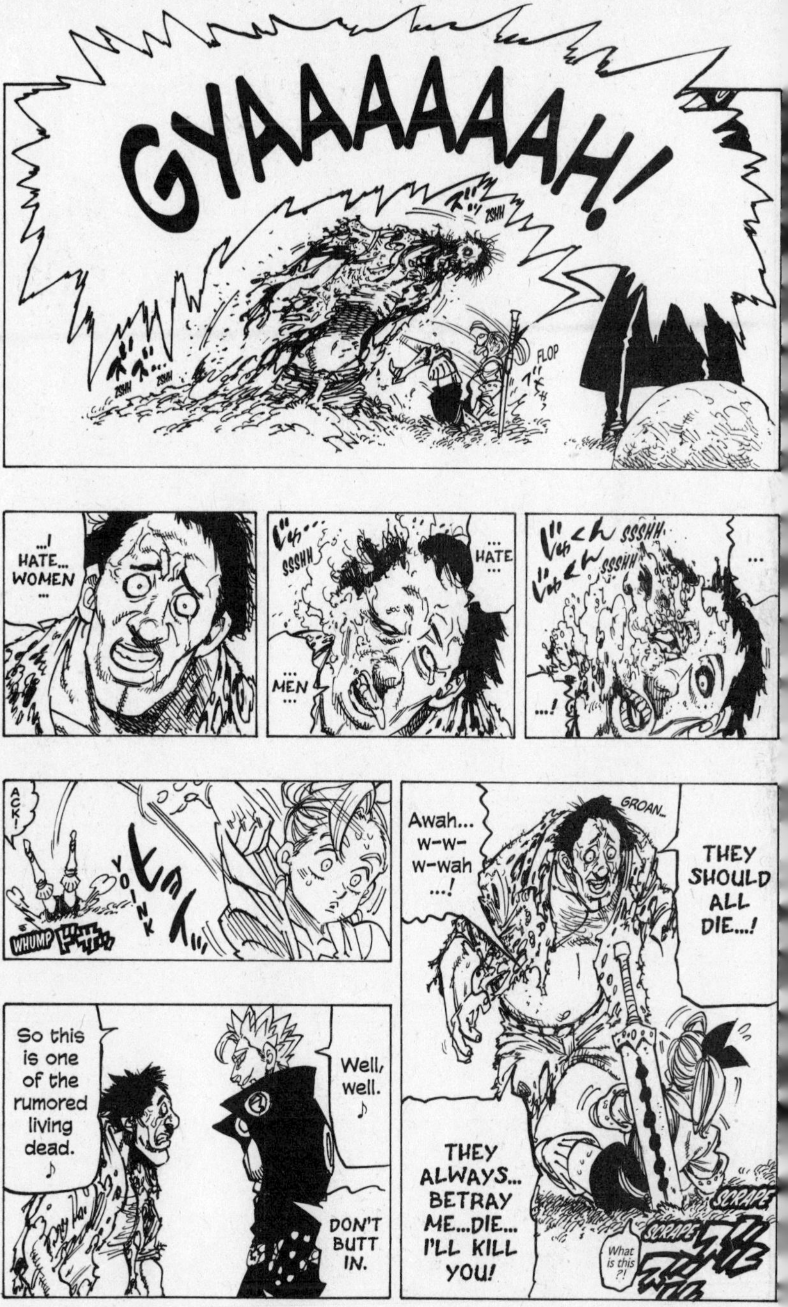
GYAAAAAAH!
ZSHH
ZSHH
ZSHH
FLOP
...
SSSHH
SSSHH
...!
...HATE...
SSSHH
...MEN...
...I HATE... WOMEN...
GROAN...
THEY SHOULD ALL DIE...!
Awah... w-w-w-wah...!
THEY ALWAYS... BETRAY ME...DIE... I'LL KILL YOU!
SCRAPE
SCRAPE
What is this?!
ACK!
YOINK
WHUMP
Well, well. ♪
So this is one of the rumored living dead. ♪
DON'T BUTT IN.

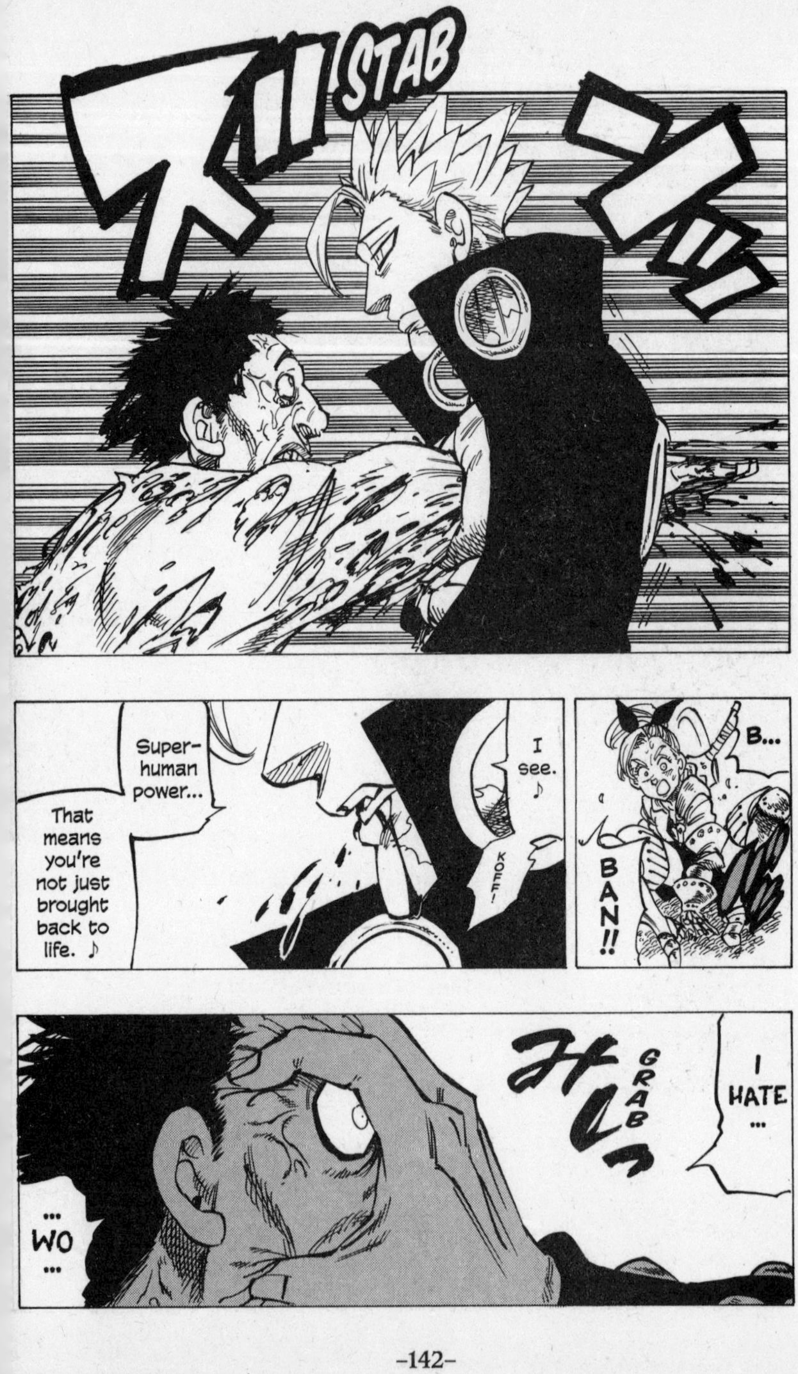
STAB
B...
BAN!!
I see. ♪
KOFF!
Super-human power...
That means you're not just brought back to life. ♪
I HATE...
GRAB
...WO...

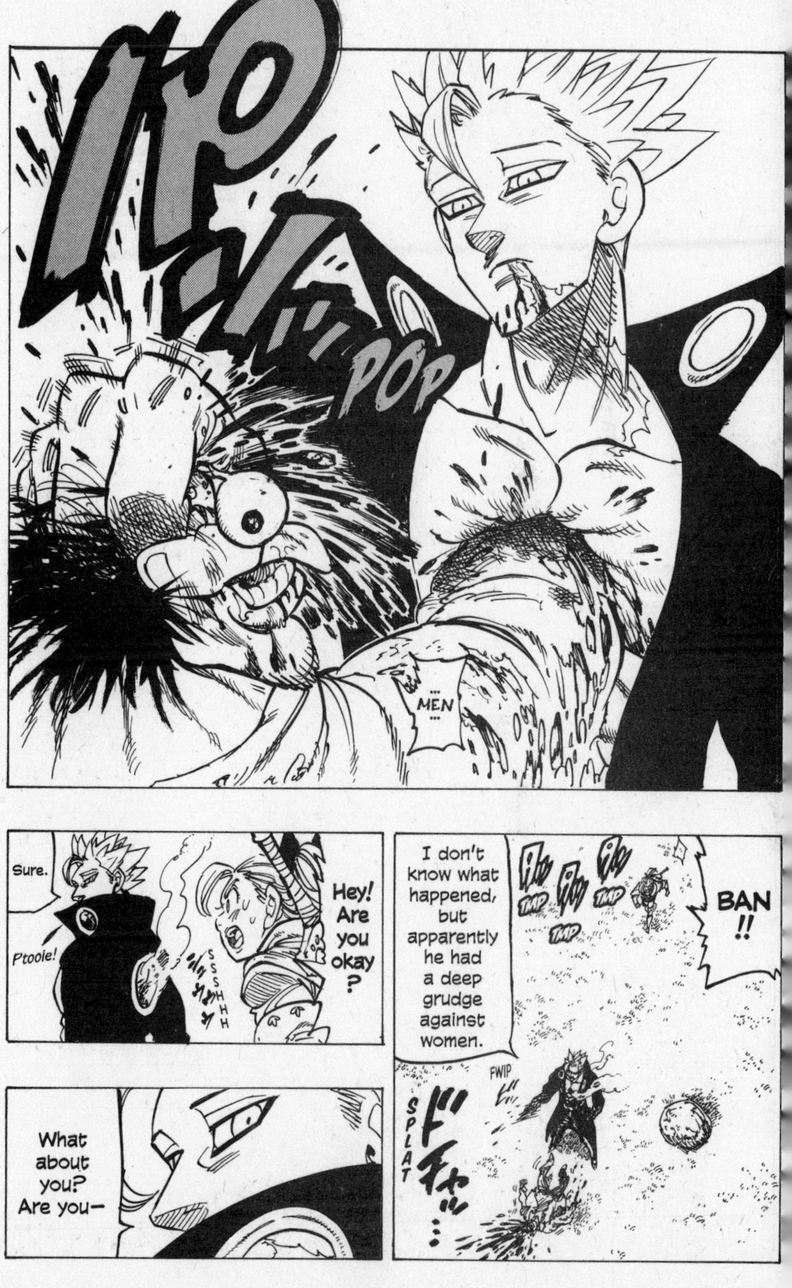
POP
...MEN...
BAN!!
TMP TMP TMP TMP
I don't know what happened, but apparently he had a deep grudge against women.
Hey! Are you okay?
SSSHHH
Sure.
Ptooie!
FWIP
SPLAT
What about you? Are you—

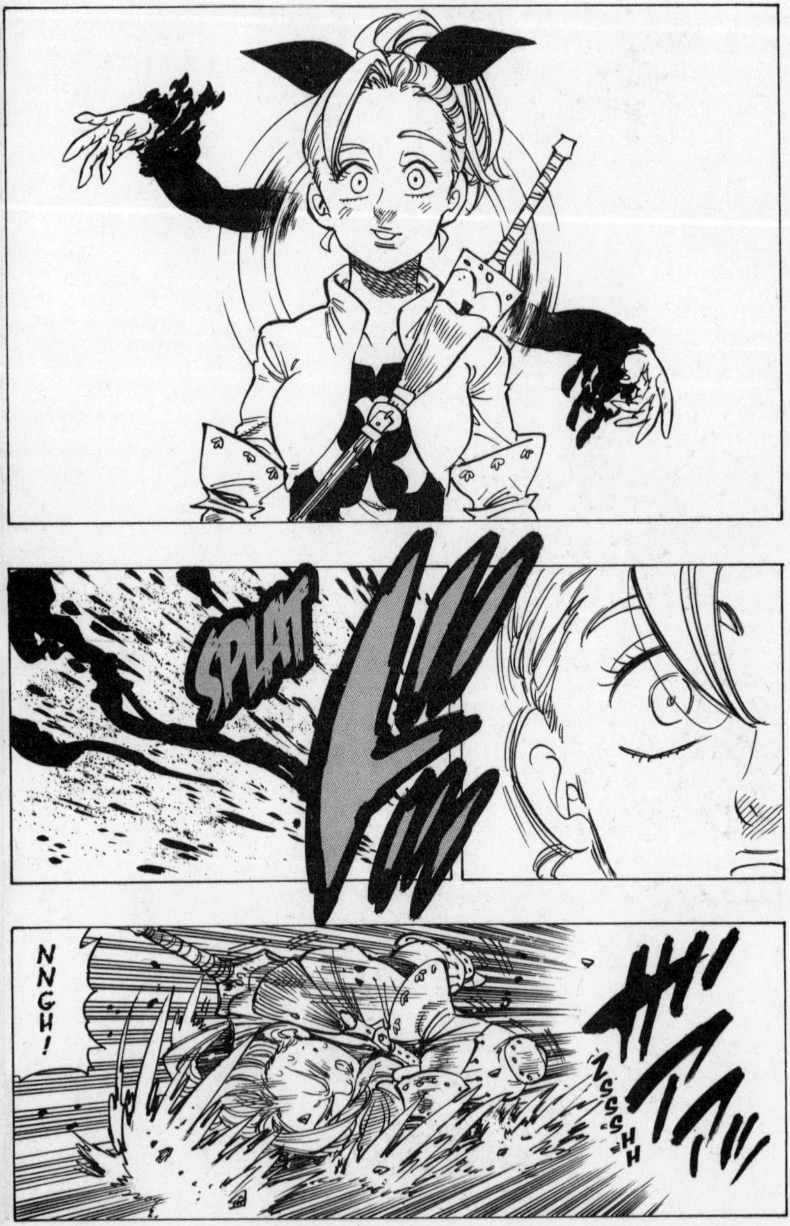
SPLAT
ZSSSHH
NNGH!

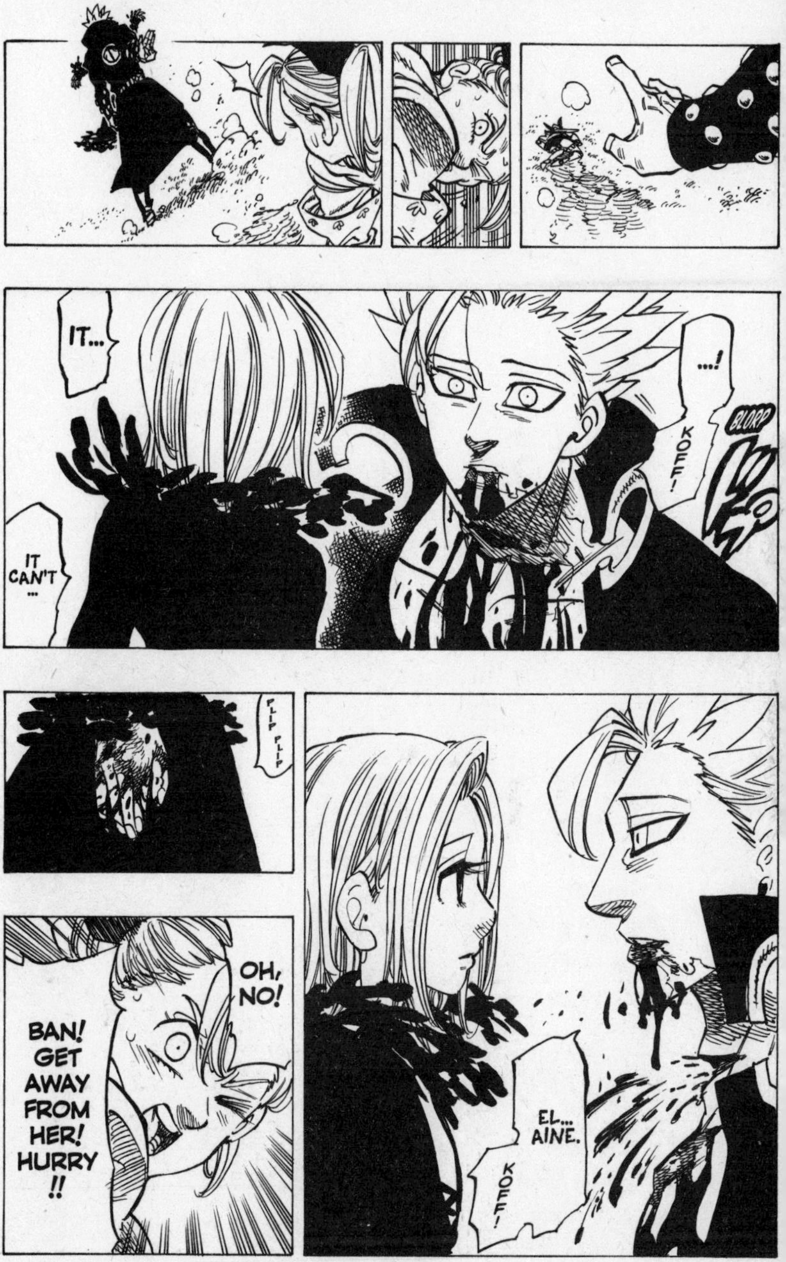
BLORP
...!
KOFF!
IT...
IT CAN'T ...
EL... AINE.
KOFF!
PLIP PLIP
OH, NO!
BAN! GET AWAY FROM HER! HURRY !!

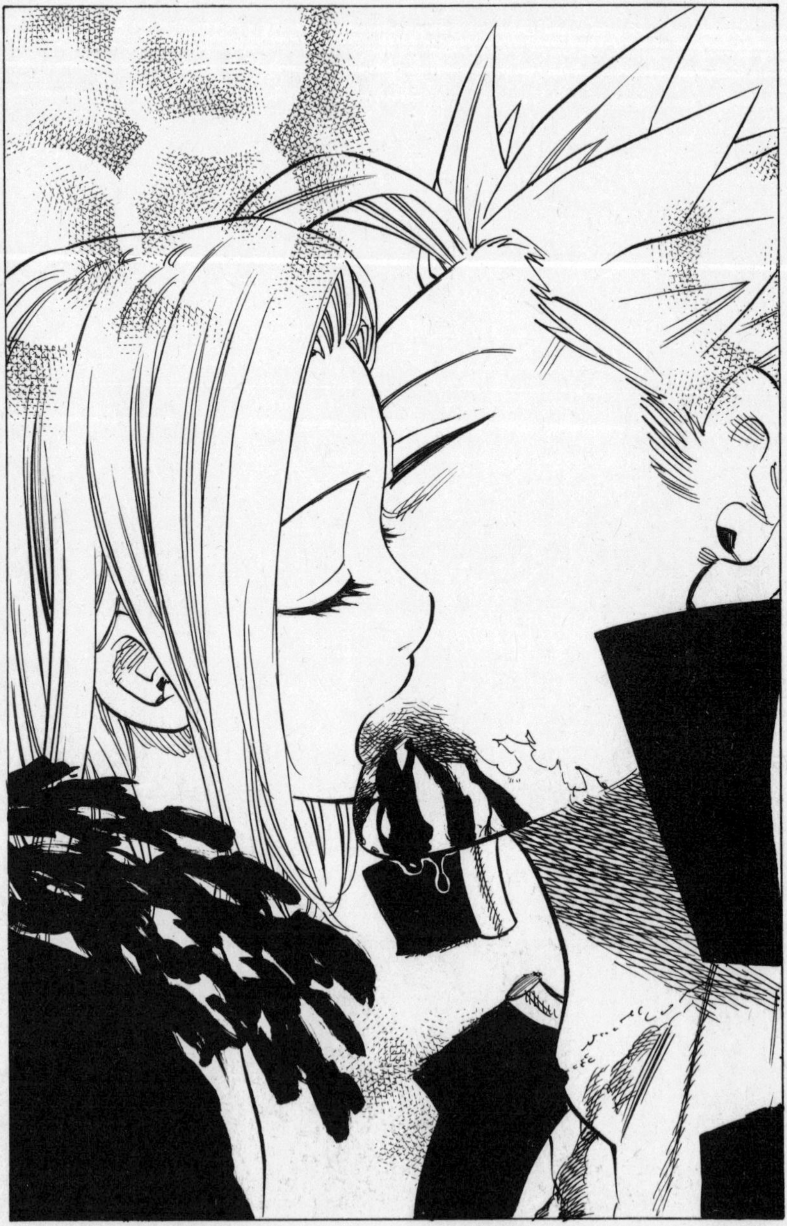

# Chapter 143 - The Saint's Shriek

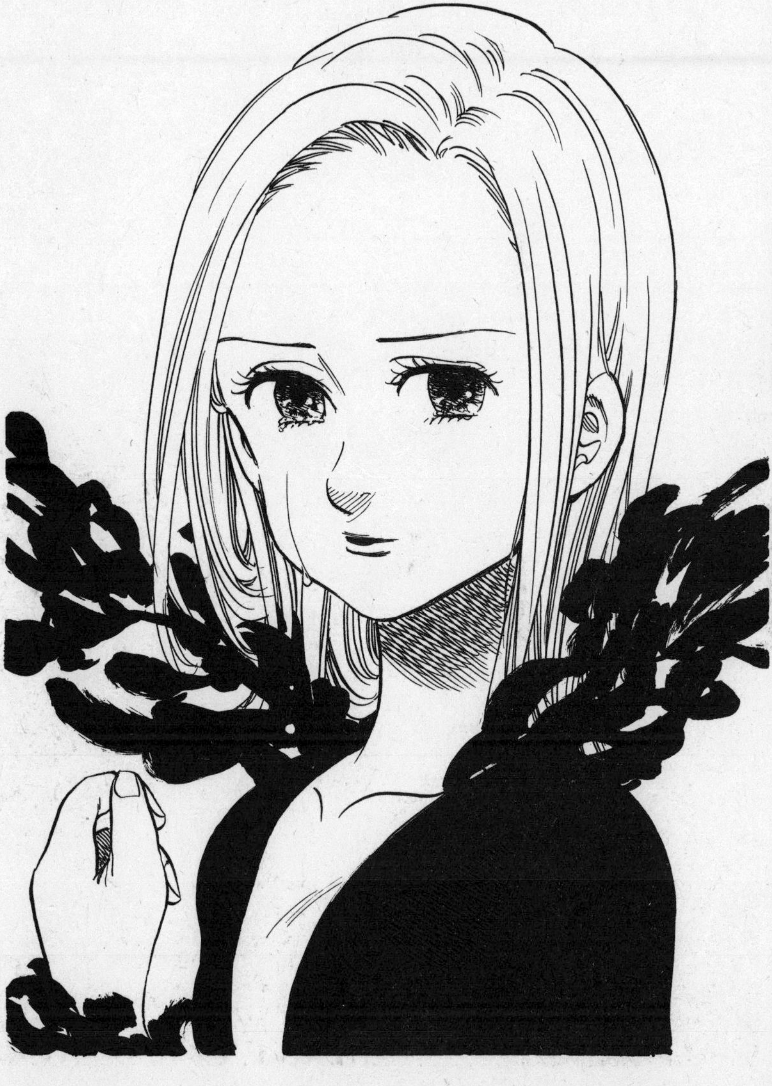

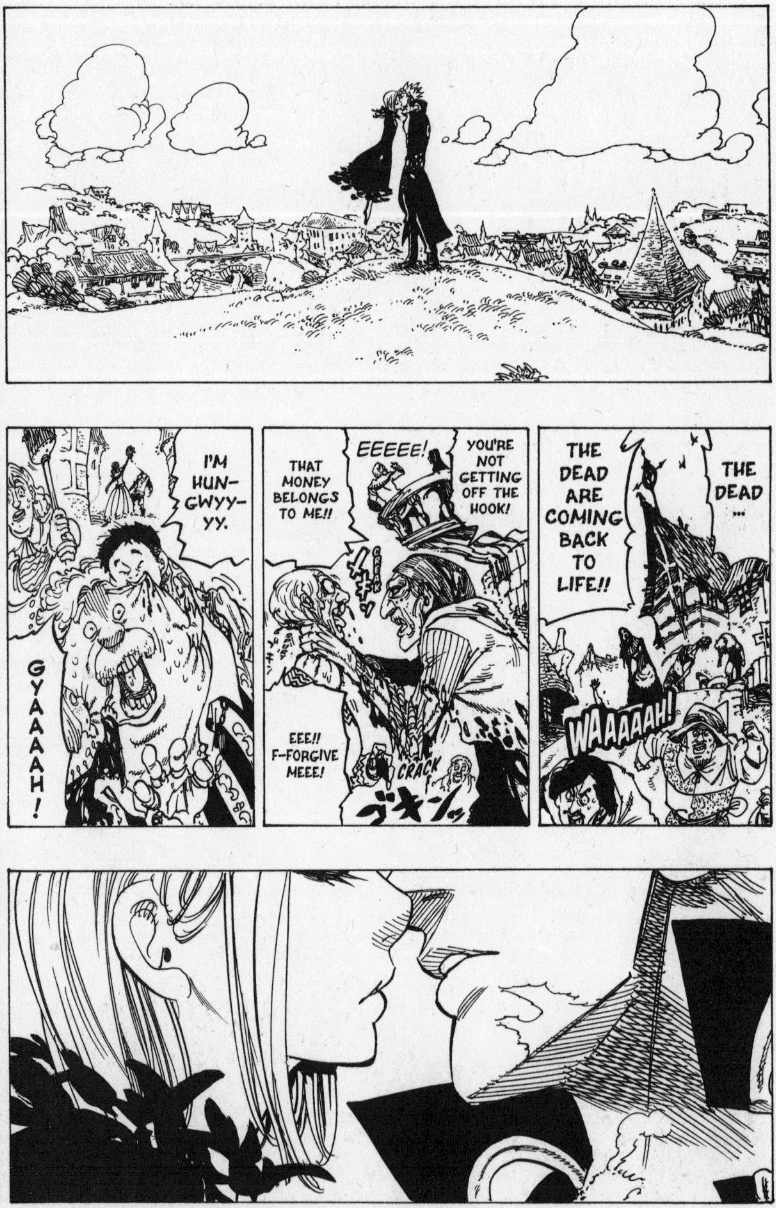
THE DEAD ...
THE DEAD ARE COMING BACK TO LIFE!!
WAAAAAH!
YOU'RE NOT GETTING OFF THE HOOK!
EEEEE!
THAT MONEY BELONGS TO ME!!
CREAK
EEE!! F-FORGIVE MEEE!
CRACK
I'M HUN-GWYY-YY.
GYAAAAH!

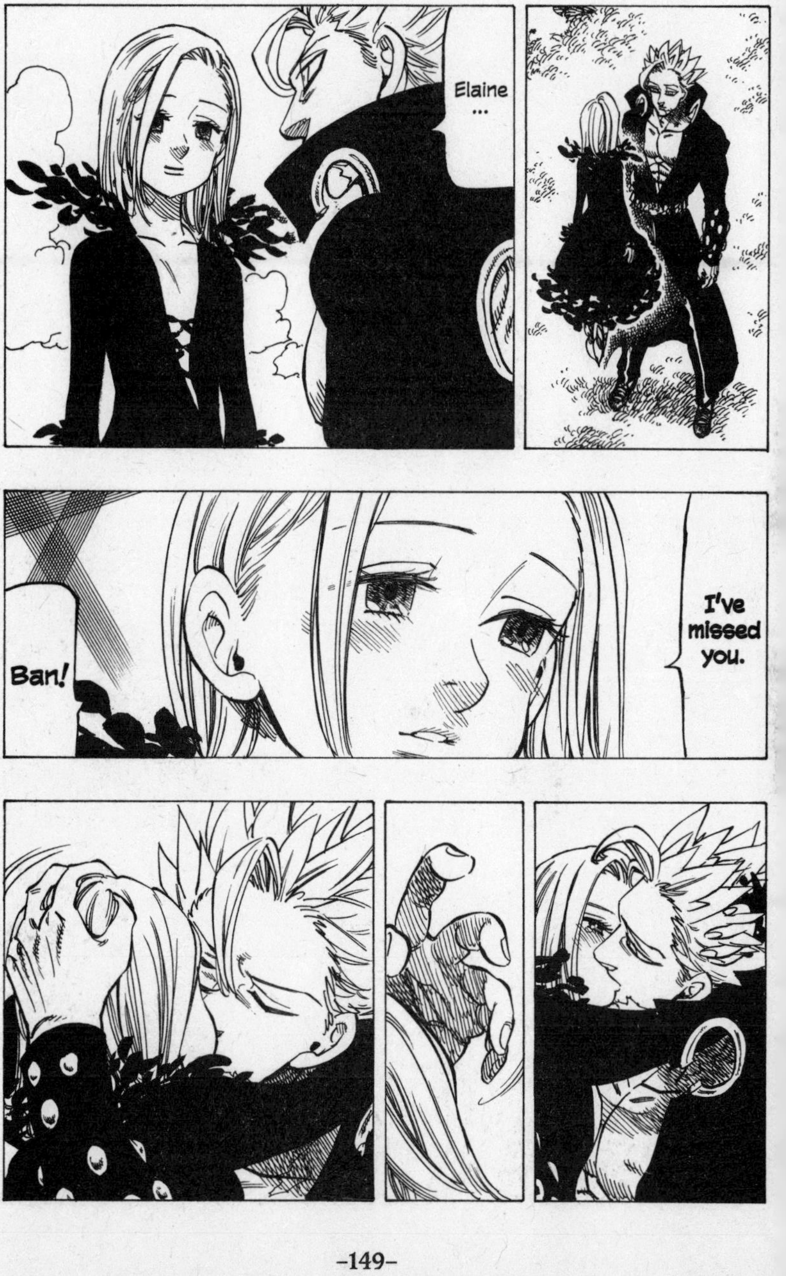
Elaine ...
I've missed you.
Ban!

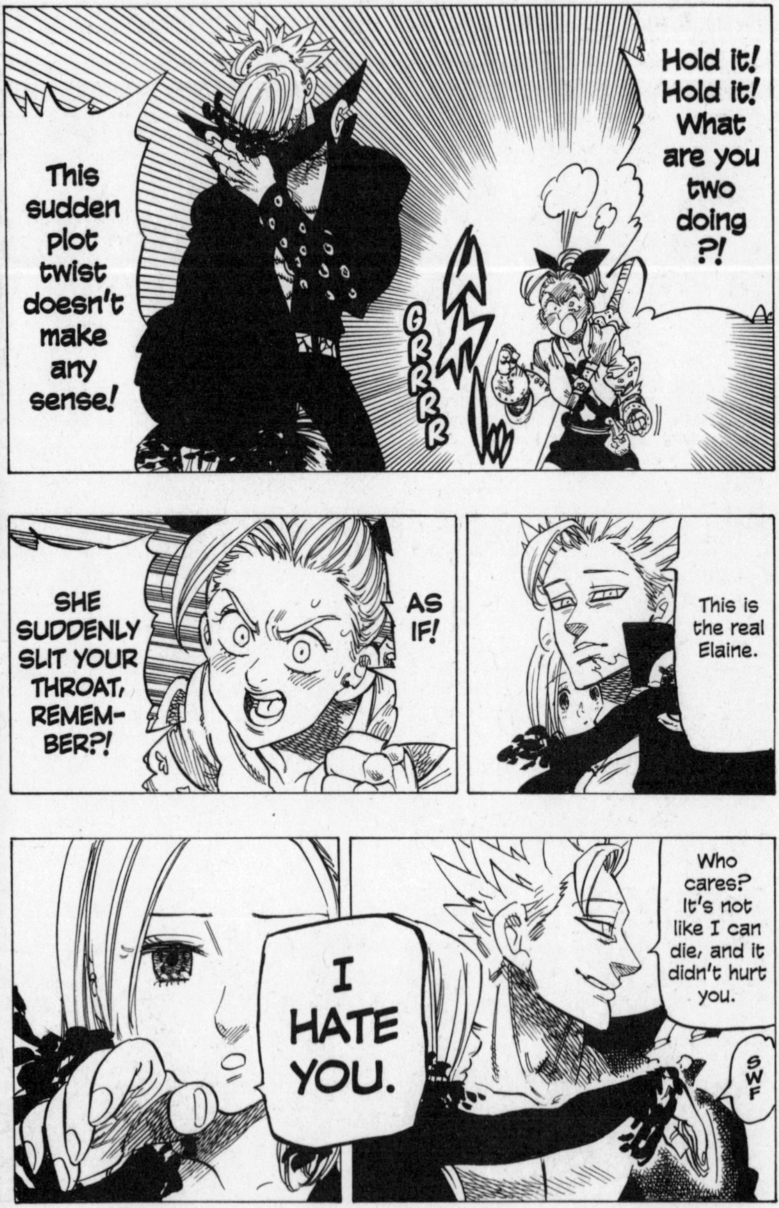
Hold it! Hold it! What are you two doing?!
GRRRR
This sudden plot twist doesn't make any sense!
This is the real Elaine.
AS IF!
SHE SUDDENLY SLIT YOUR THROAT, REMEMBER?!
Who cares? It's not like I can die, and it didn't hurt you.
SWF
I HATE YOU.

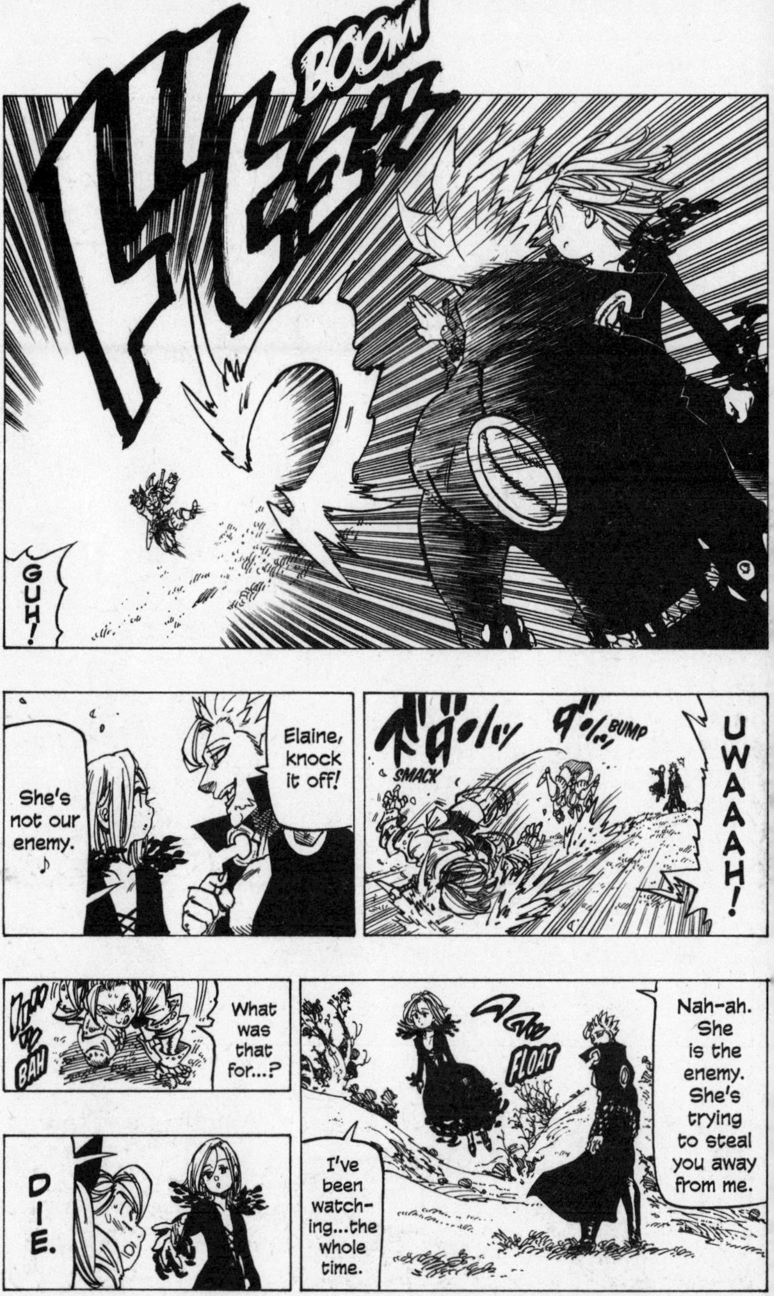
BOOM
GUH!
BUMP
SMACK
UWAAAH!
Elaine, knock it off!
She's not our enemy. ♪
Nah-ah. She is the enemy. She's trying to steal you away from me.
FLOAT
I've been watching...the whole time.
What was that for...?
BAH
DIE.

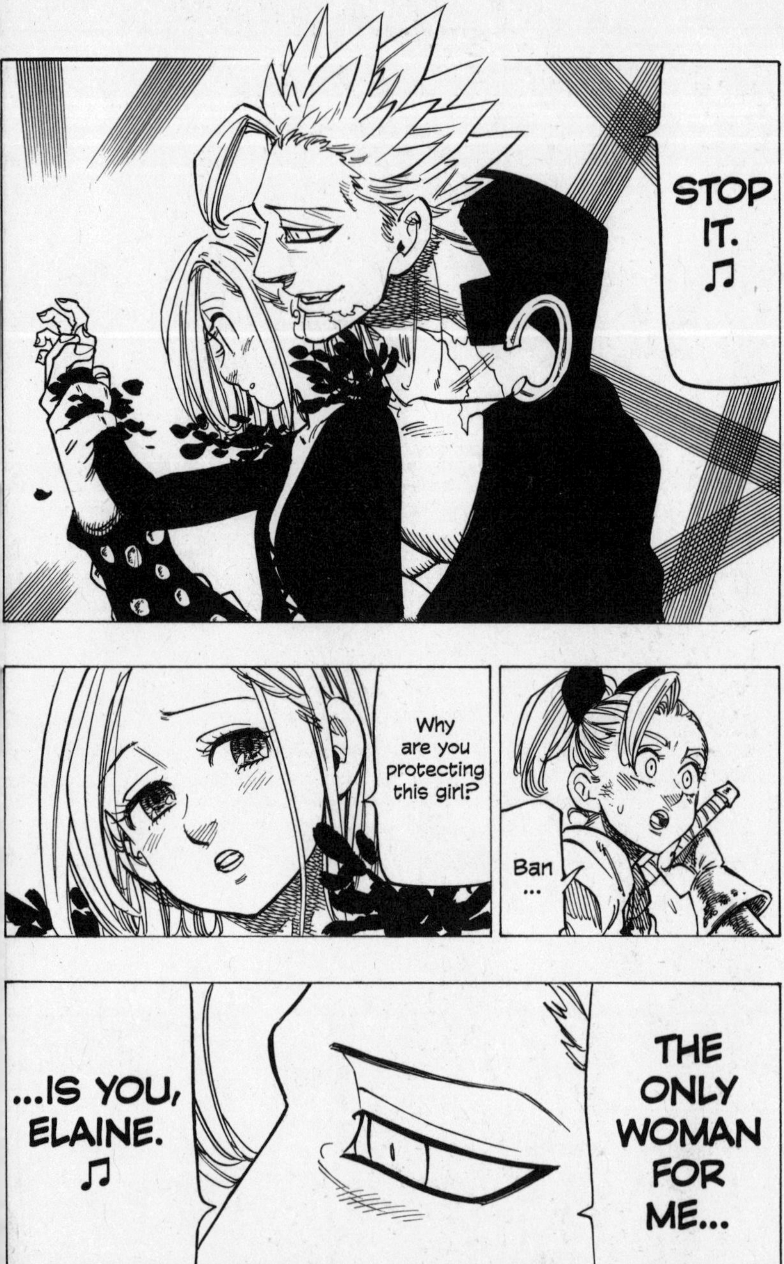
STOP IT. ♫
Ban ...
Why are you protecting this girl?
THE ONLY WOMAN FOR ME...
...IS YOU, ELAINE. ♫

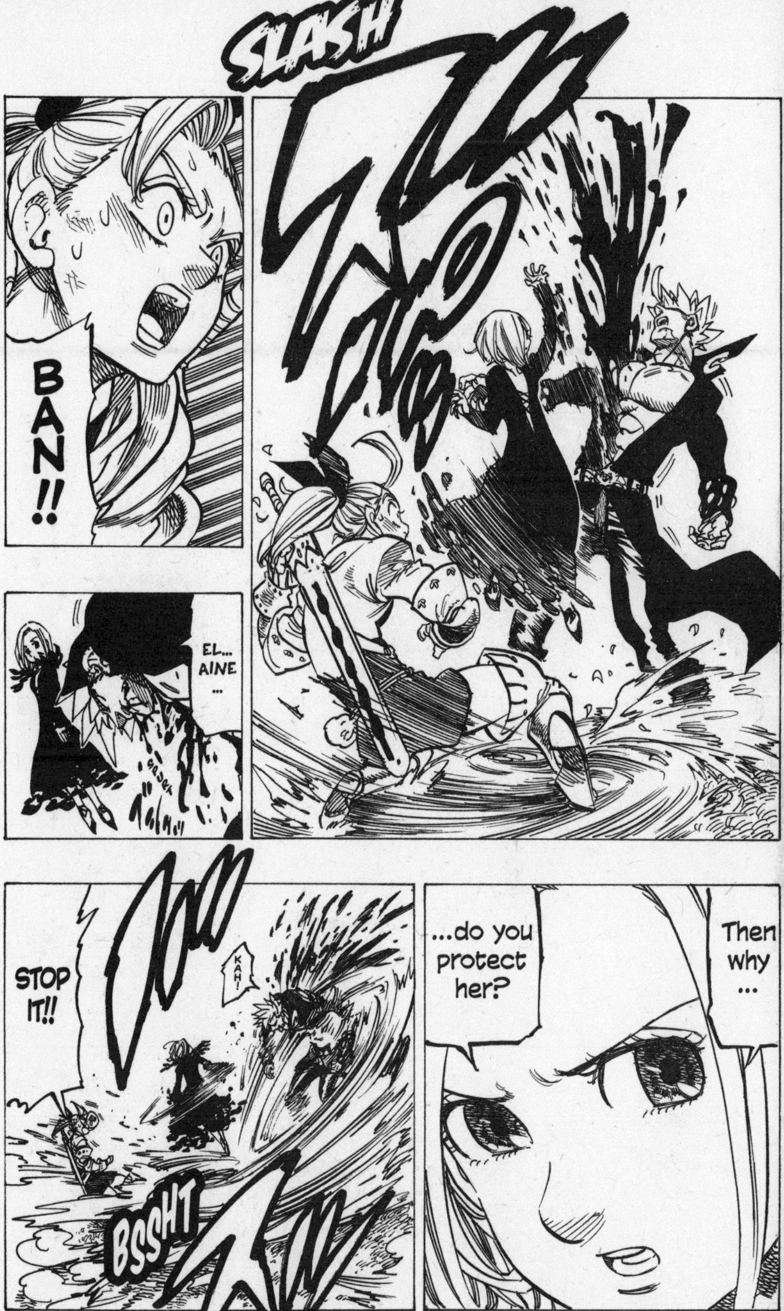
SLASH
BAN!!
EL... AINE ...
Then why ...
...do you protect her?
STOP IT!!
KAH!
BSSHT

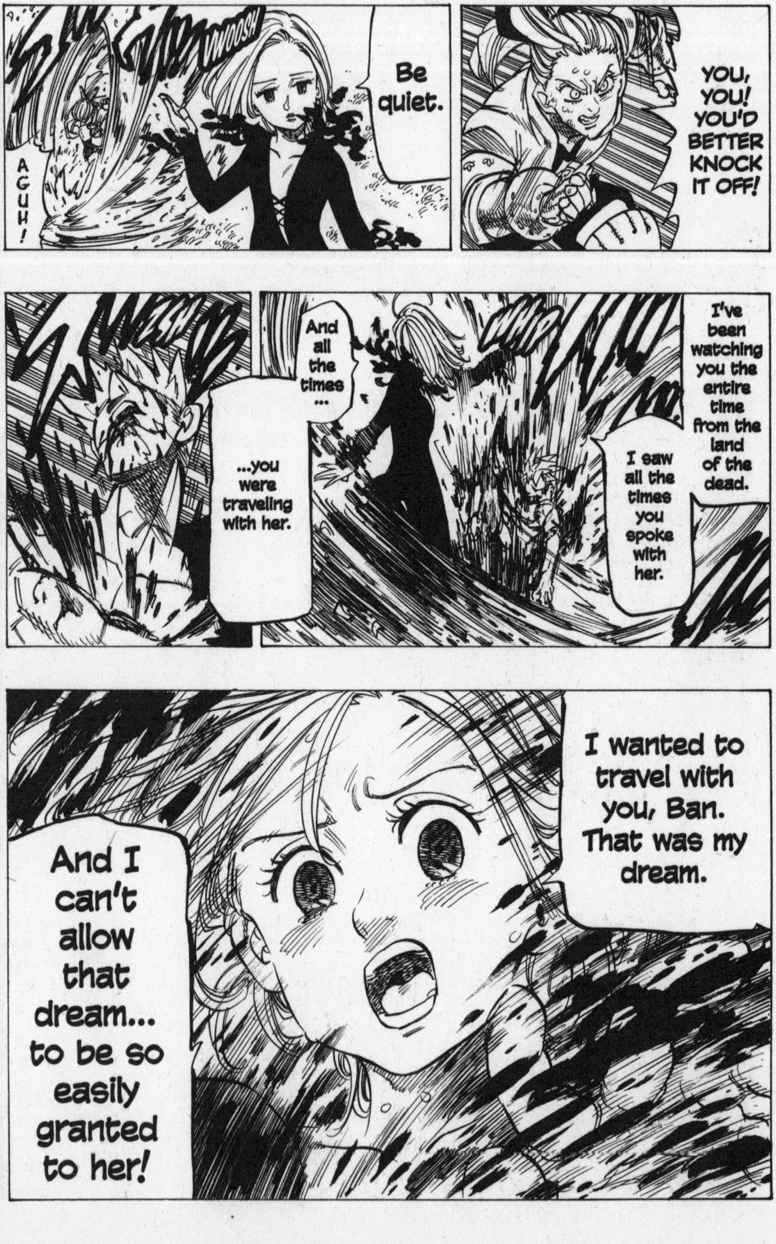
YOU, YOU! YOU'D BETTER KNOCK IT OFF!
Be quiet.
VWOOSH
AGUH!
I've been watching you the entire time from the land of the dead.
I saw all the times you spoke with her.
And all the times...
...you were traveling with her.
I wanted to travel with you, Ban. That was my dream.
And I can't allow that dream... to be so easily granted to her!

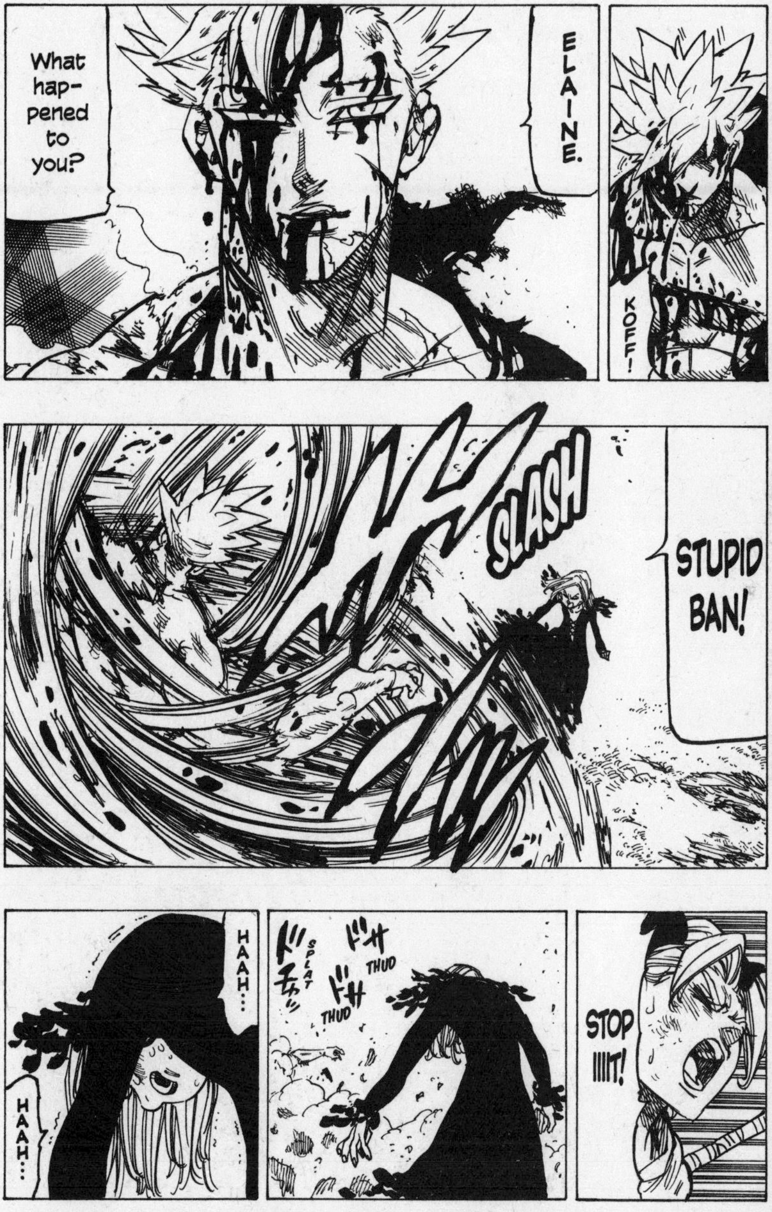
KOFF!
ELAINE.
What hap-pened to you?
STUPID BAN!
SLASH
STOP IIIIIT!
ドサ
THUD
ドチャッ
SPLAT
ドサ
THUD
HAAH...
HAAH...

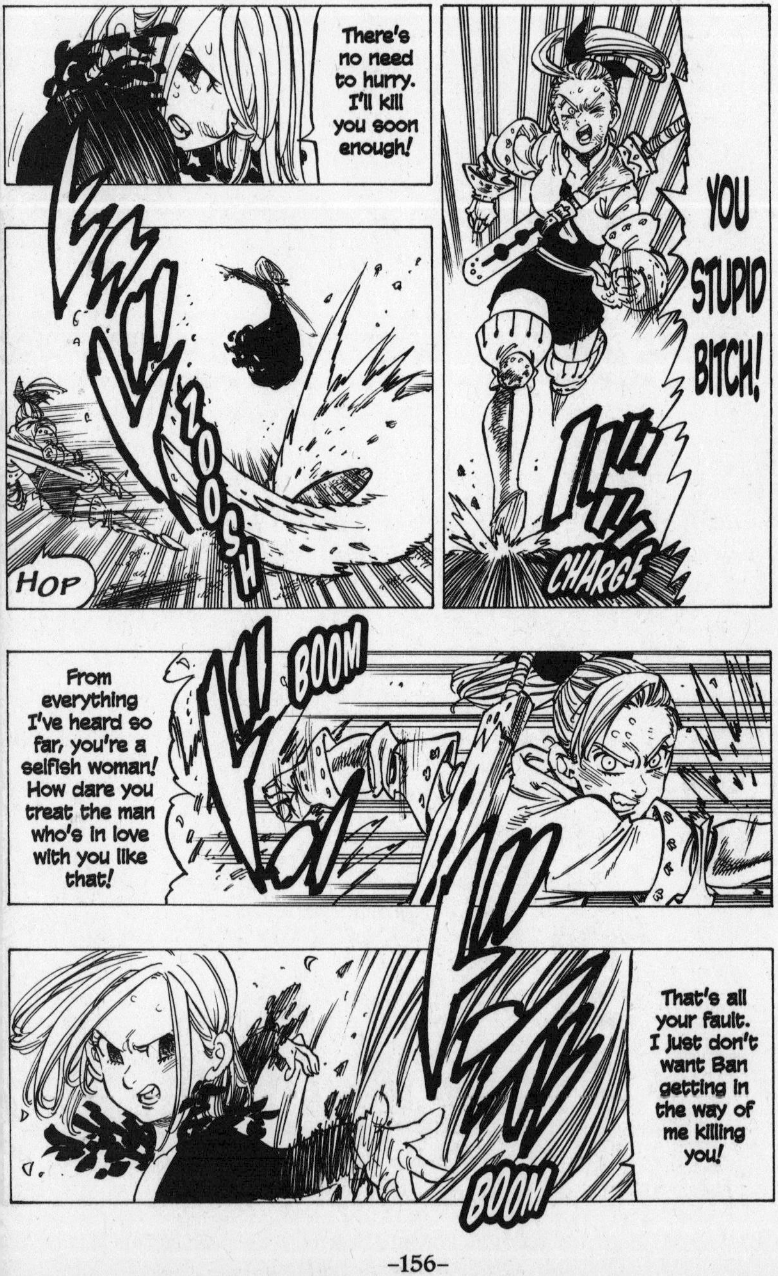

YOU STUPID BITCH!
CHARGE
There's no need to hurry. I'll kill you soon enough!
ZOOSH
HOP
BOOM
From everything I've heard so far, you're a selfish woman! How dare you treat the man who's in love with you like that!
That's all your fault. I just don't want Ban getting in the way of me killing you!
BOOM

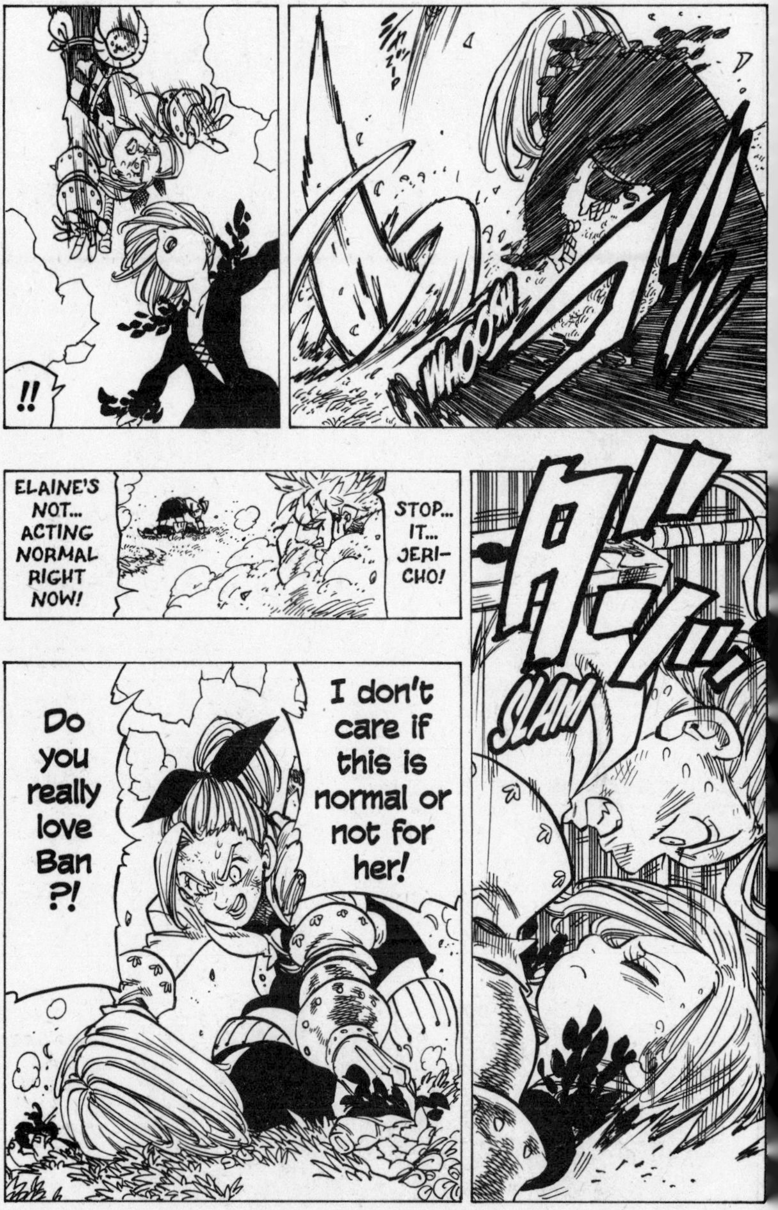
ZIP
WHOOSH
!!
SLAM
STOP... IT... JERI-CHO!
ELAINE'S NOT... ACTING NORMAL RIGHT NOW!
I don't care if this is normal or not for her!
Do you really love Ban?!

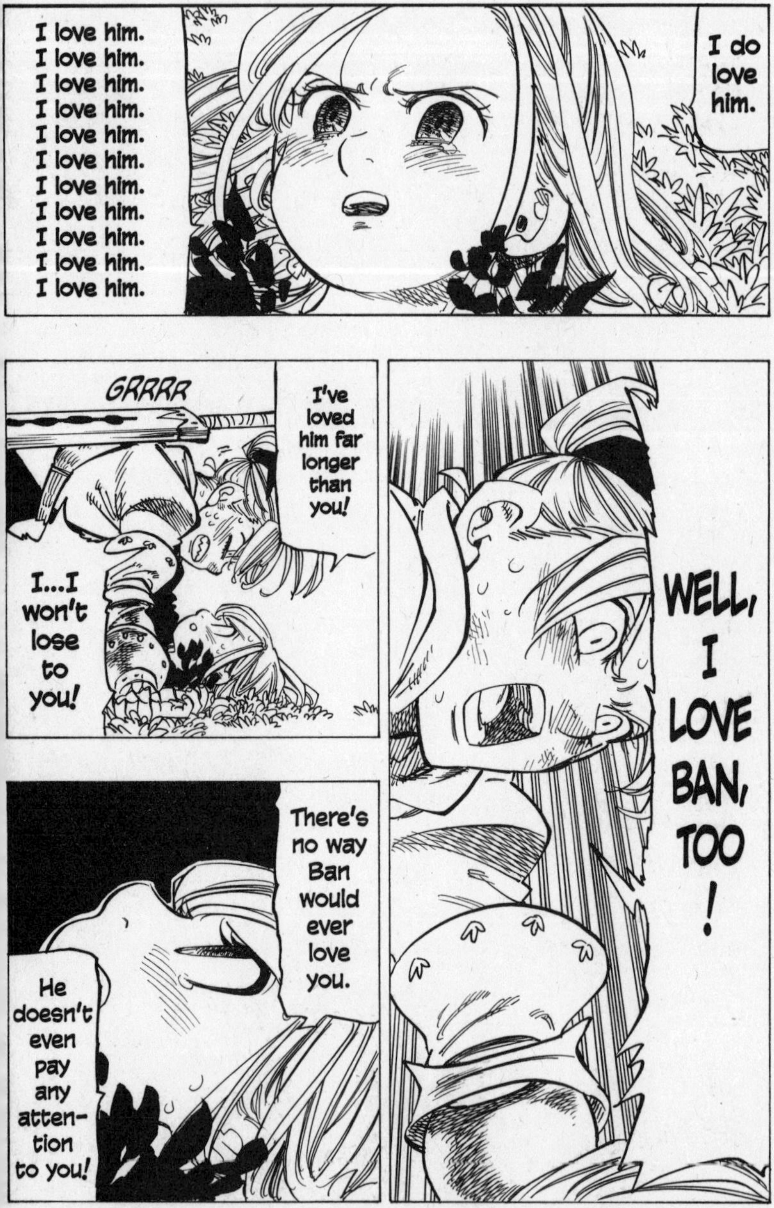
I do love him.
I love him. I love him. I love him. I love him. I love him. I love him. I love him. I love him. I love him. I love him. I love him.
WELL, I LOVE BAN, TOO!
GRRRR
I've loved him far longer than you!
I...I won't lose to you!
There's no way Ban would ever love you.
He doesn't even pay any attention to you!

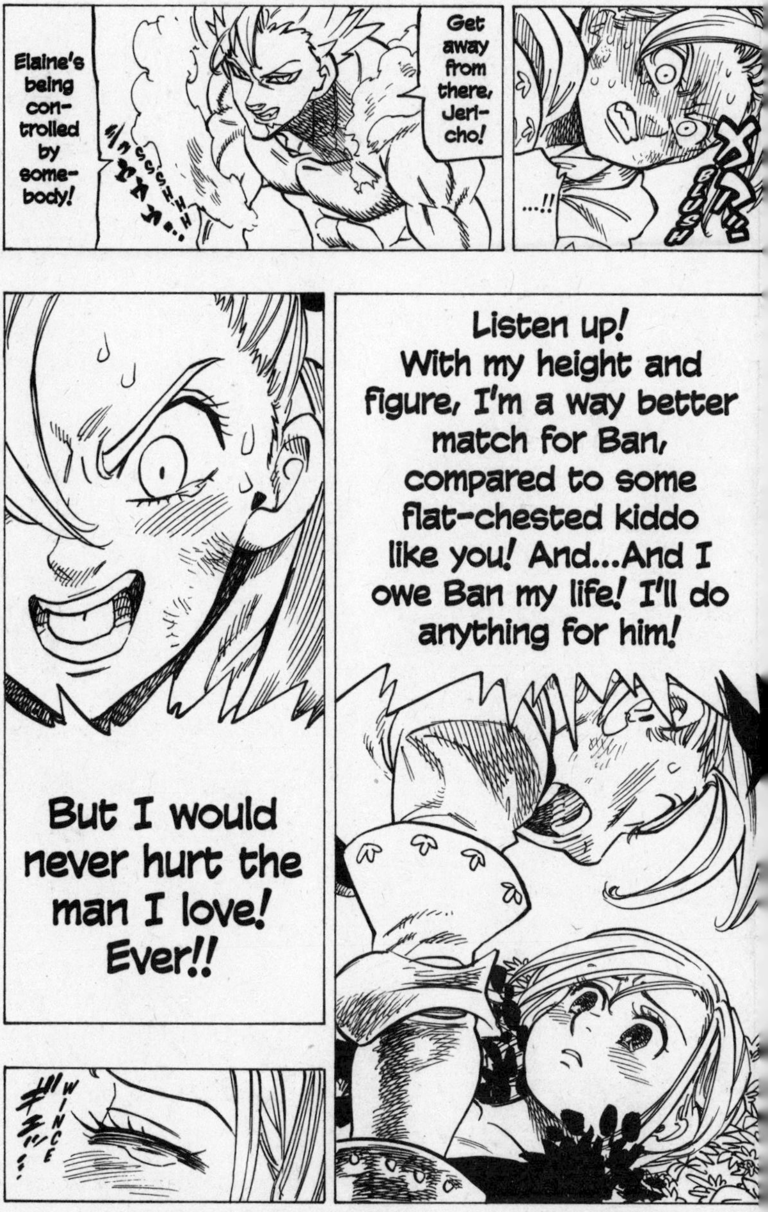
...!!
BLUSH
Get away from there, Jeri-cho!
Elaine's being con-trolled by some-body!
SSSHHH
Listen up! With my height and figure, I'm a way better match for Ban, compared to some flat-chested kiddo like you! And...And I owe Ban my life! I'll do anything for him!
But I would never hurt the man I love! Ever!!
WINCE

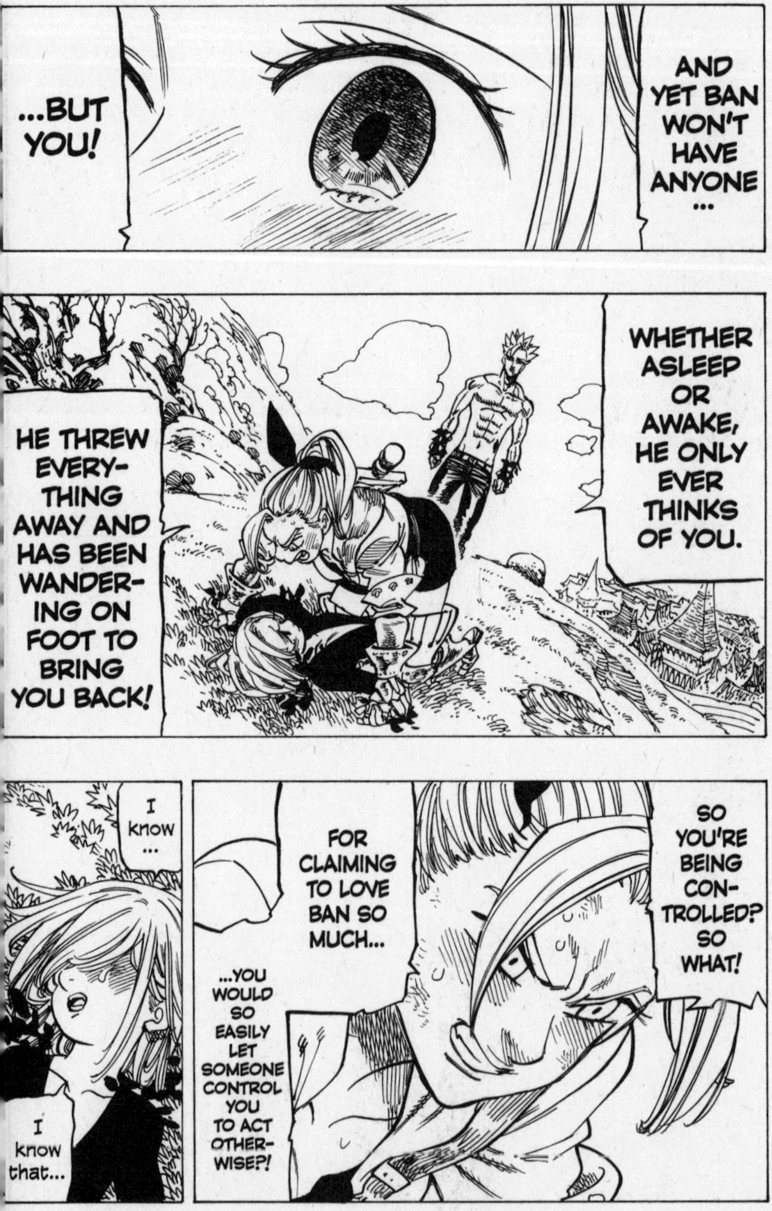
AND YET BAN WON'T HAVE ANYONE ...
...BUT YOU!
WHETHER ASLEEP OR AWAKE, HE ONLY EVER THINKS OF YOU.
HE THREW EVERY-THING AWAY AND HAS BEEN WANDER-ING ON FOOT TO BRING YOU BACK!
SO YOU'RE BEING CON-TROLLED? SO WHAT!
FOR CLAIMING TO LOVE BAN SO MUCH...
...YOU WOULD SO EASILY LET SOMEONE CONTROL YOU TO ACT OTHER-WISE?!
I know ...
I know that...

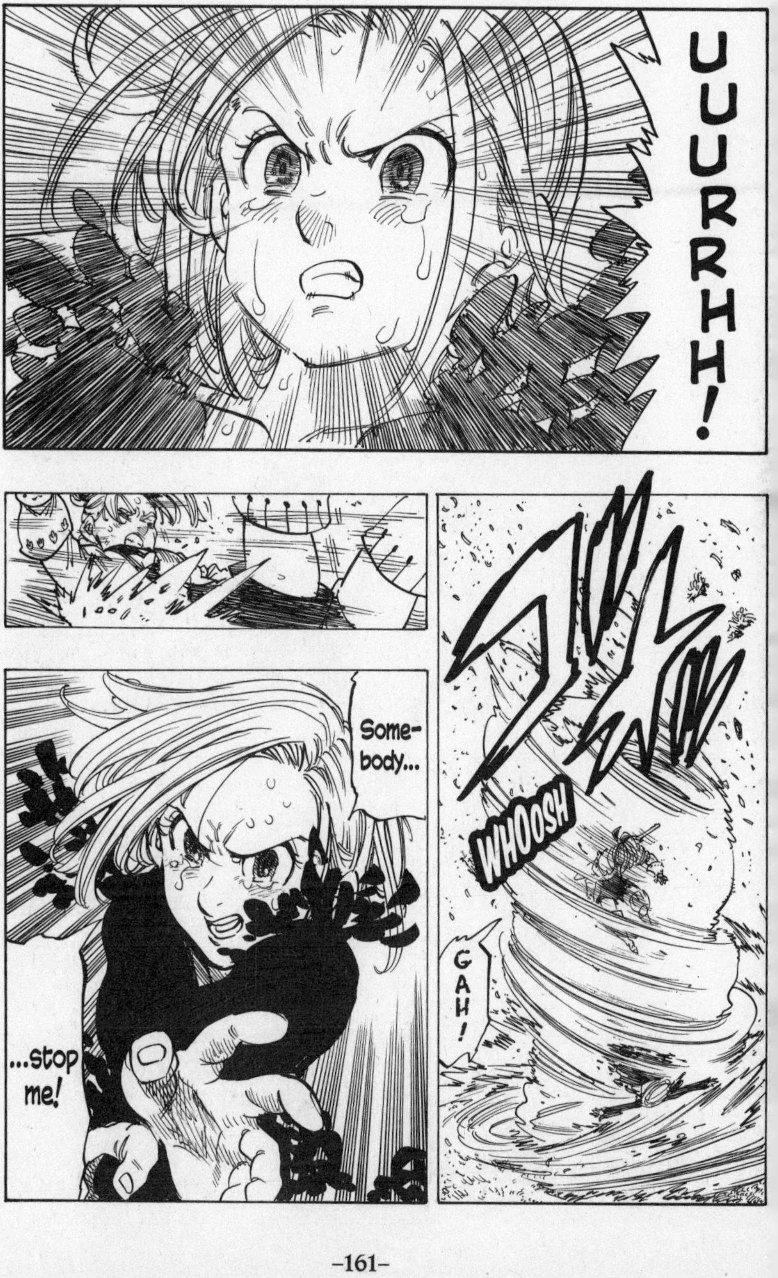
UUURRHH!
WHOOSH
GAH!
Some-body...
...stop me!

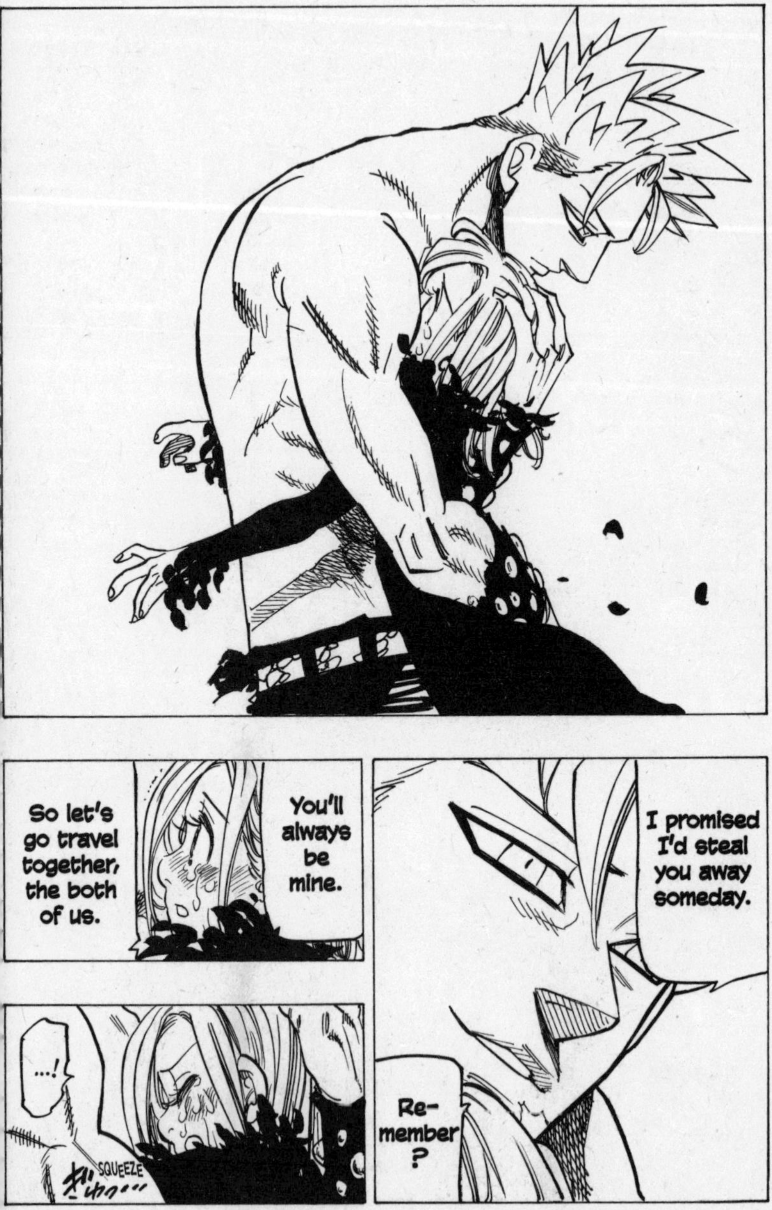
I promised I'd steal you away someday.
Re-member?
You'll always be mine.
So let's go travel together, the both of us.
...!
SQUEEZE

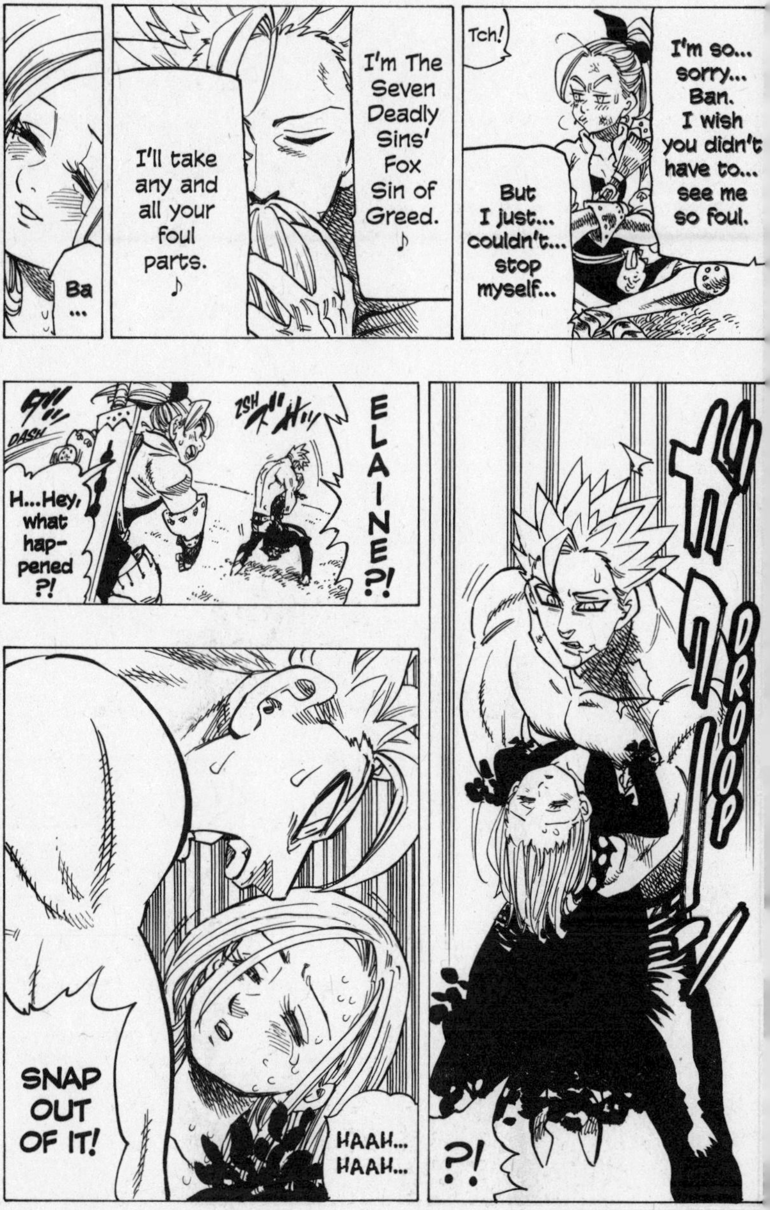
I'm so... sorry... Ban. I wish you didn't have to... see me so foul.
Tch!
But I just... couldn't... stop myself...
I'm The Seven Deadly Sins' Fox Sin of Greed. ♪
I'll take any and all your foul parts. ♪
Ba...
DROOP
?!
ELAINE?!
ZSH
H...Hey, what happened?!
DASH
HAAH... HAAH...
SNAP OUT OF IT!

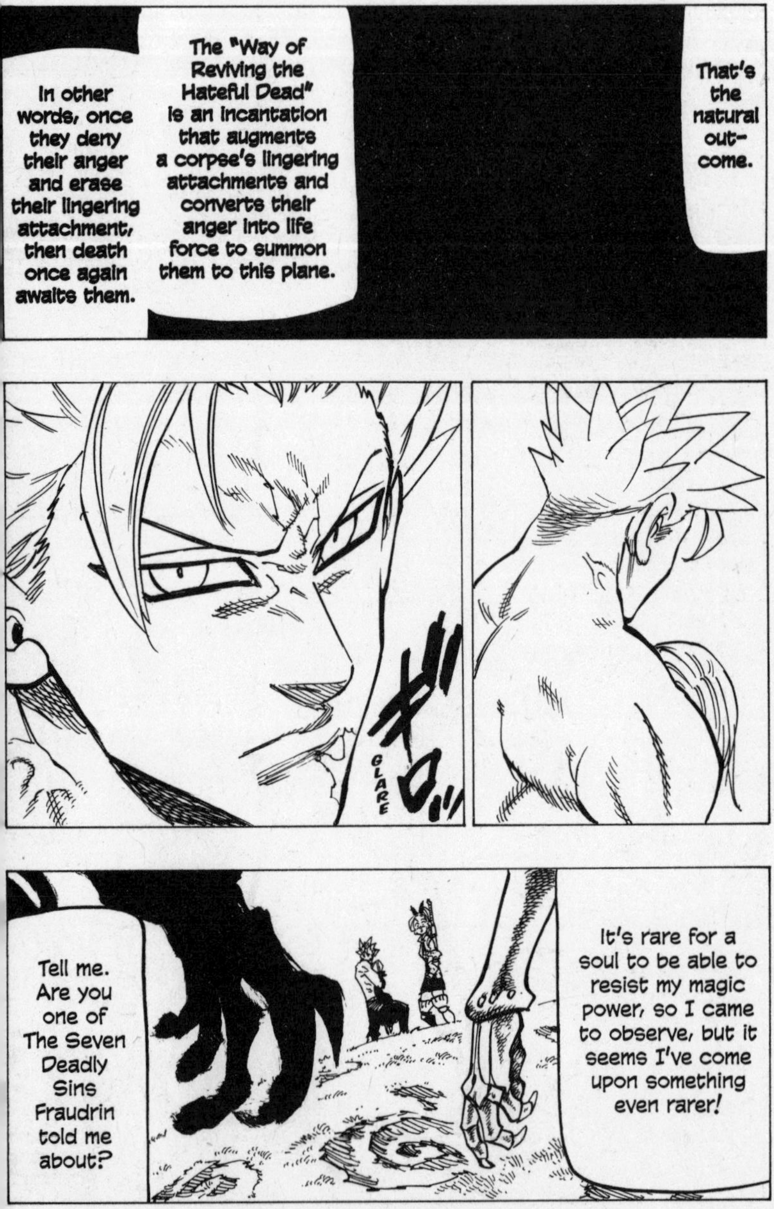
That's the natural out-come.
The "Way of Reviving the Hateful Dead" is an incantation that augments a corpse's lingering attachments and converts their anger into life force to summon them to this plane.
In other words, once they deny their anger and erase their lingering attachment, then death once again awaits them.
GLARE
It's rare for a soul to be able to resist my magic power, so I came to observe, but it seems I've come upon something even rarer!
Tell me. Are you one of The Seven Deadly Sins Fraudrin told me about?

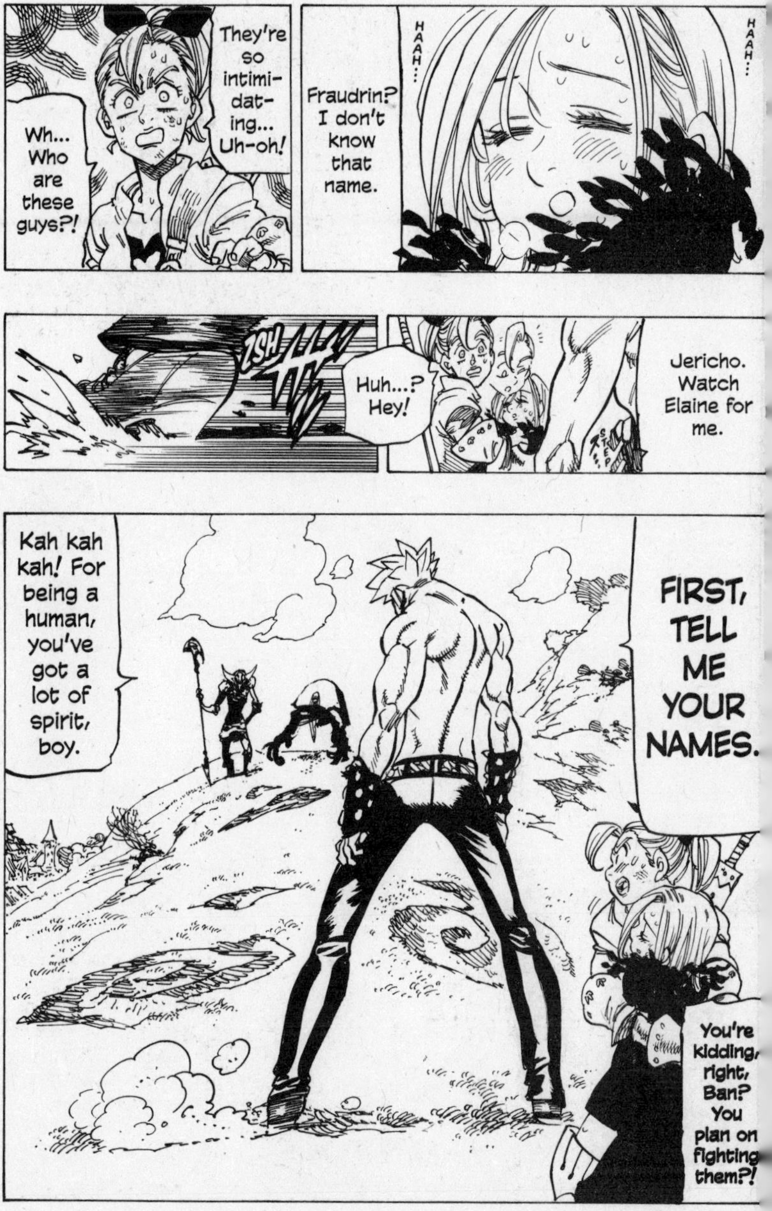
HAAH...
HAAH...
Fraudrin? I don't know that name.
They're so intimi-dat-ing... Uh-oh!
Wh... Who are these guys?!
Jericho. Watch Elaine for me.
STEP
Huh...? Hey!
ZSH
FIRST, TELL ME YOUR NAMES.
Kah kah kah! For being a human, you've got a lot of spirit, boy.
You're kidding, right, Ban? You plan on fighting them?!

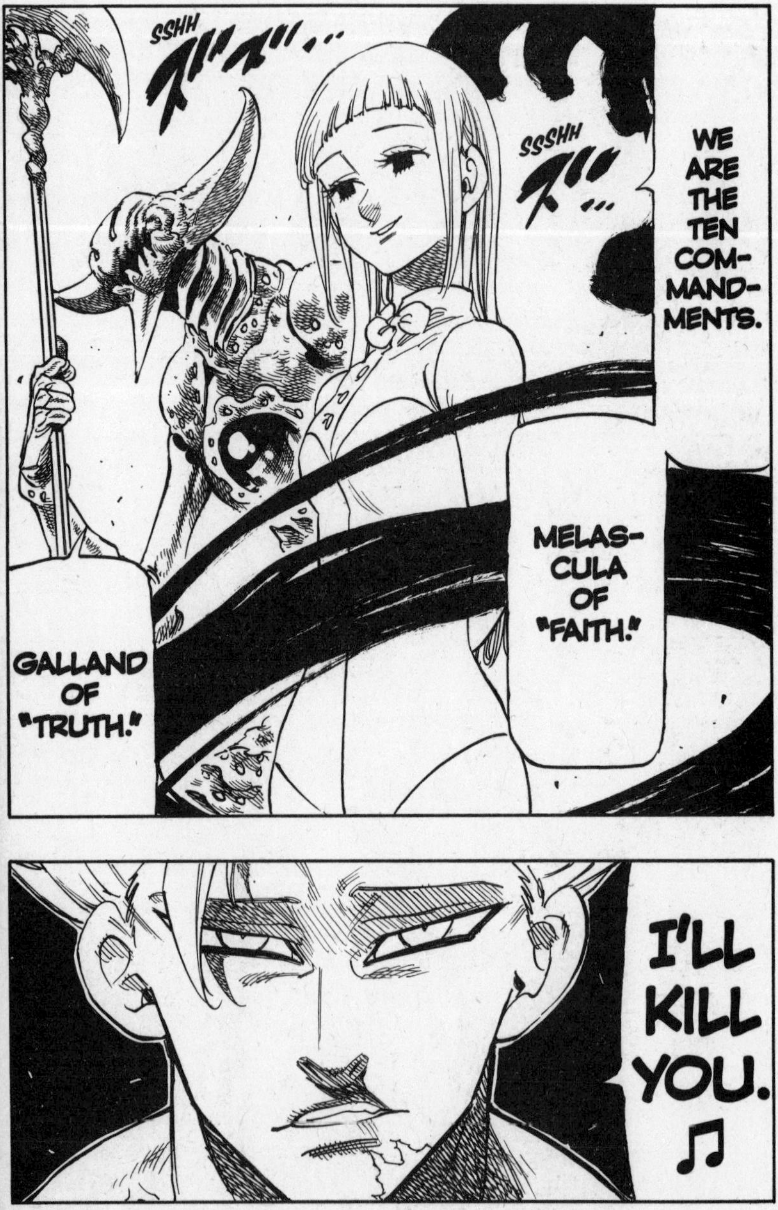
WE ARE THE TEN COMMANDMENTS.
SSSHH
MELASCULA OF "FAITH."
SSHH
GALLAND OF "TRUTH."
I'LL KILL YOU. ♫

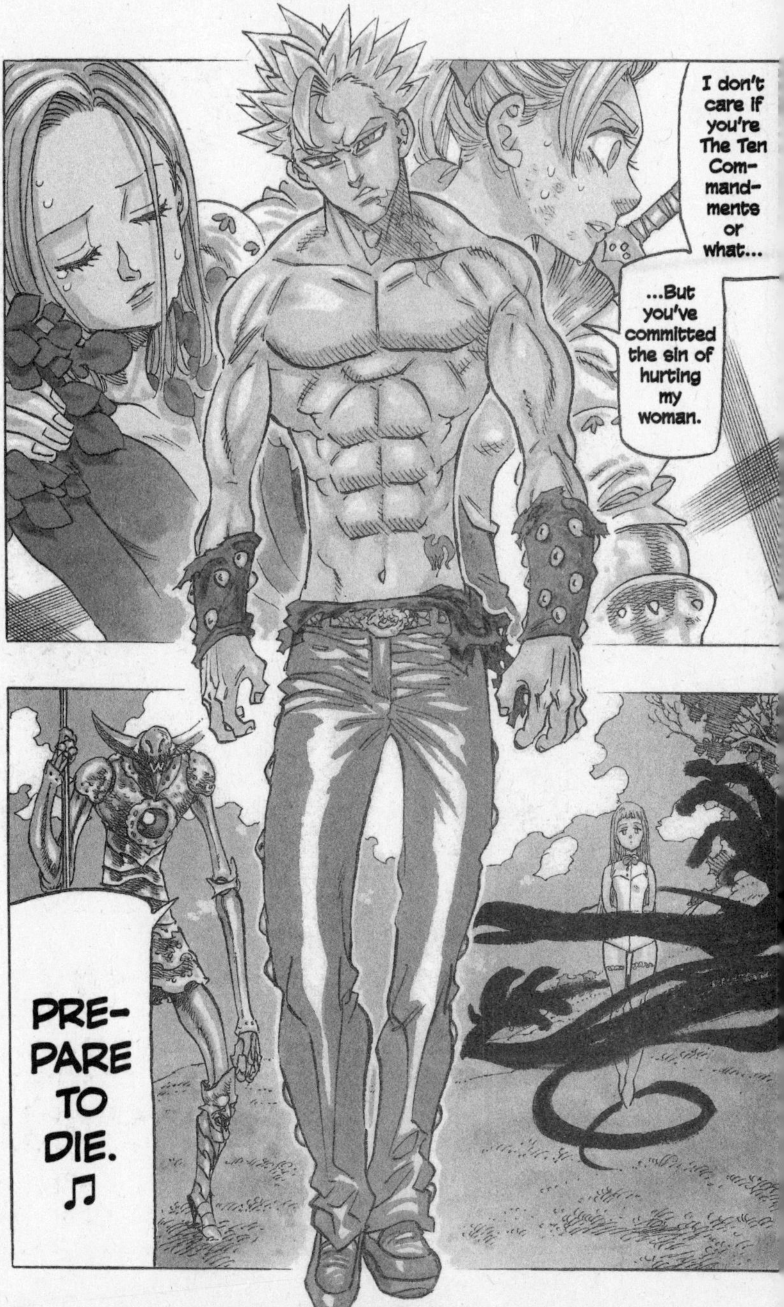
I don't care if you're The Ten Commandments or what...
...But you've committed the sin of hurting my woman.
PREPARE TO DIE. ♫

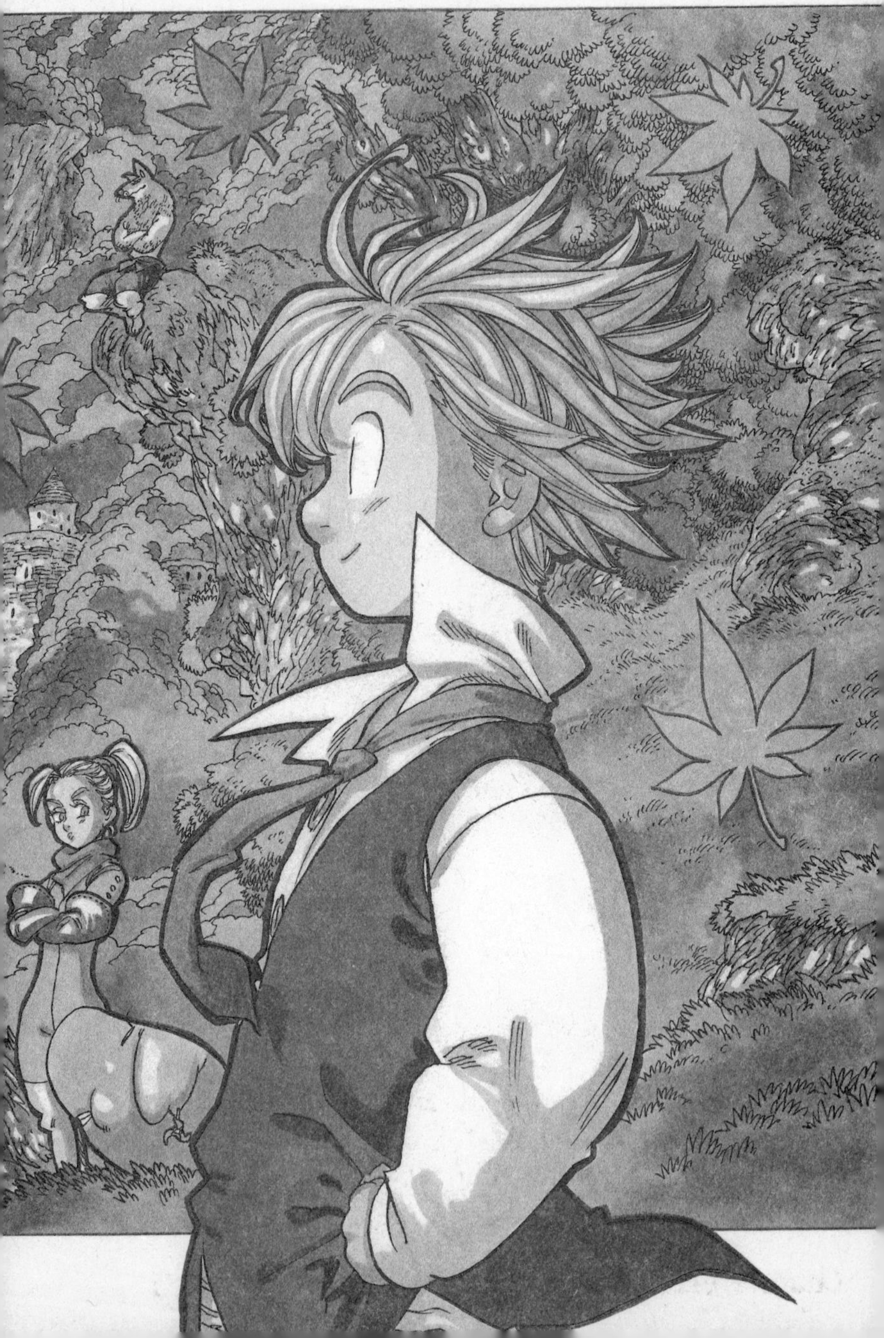

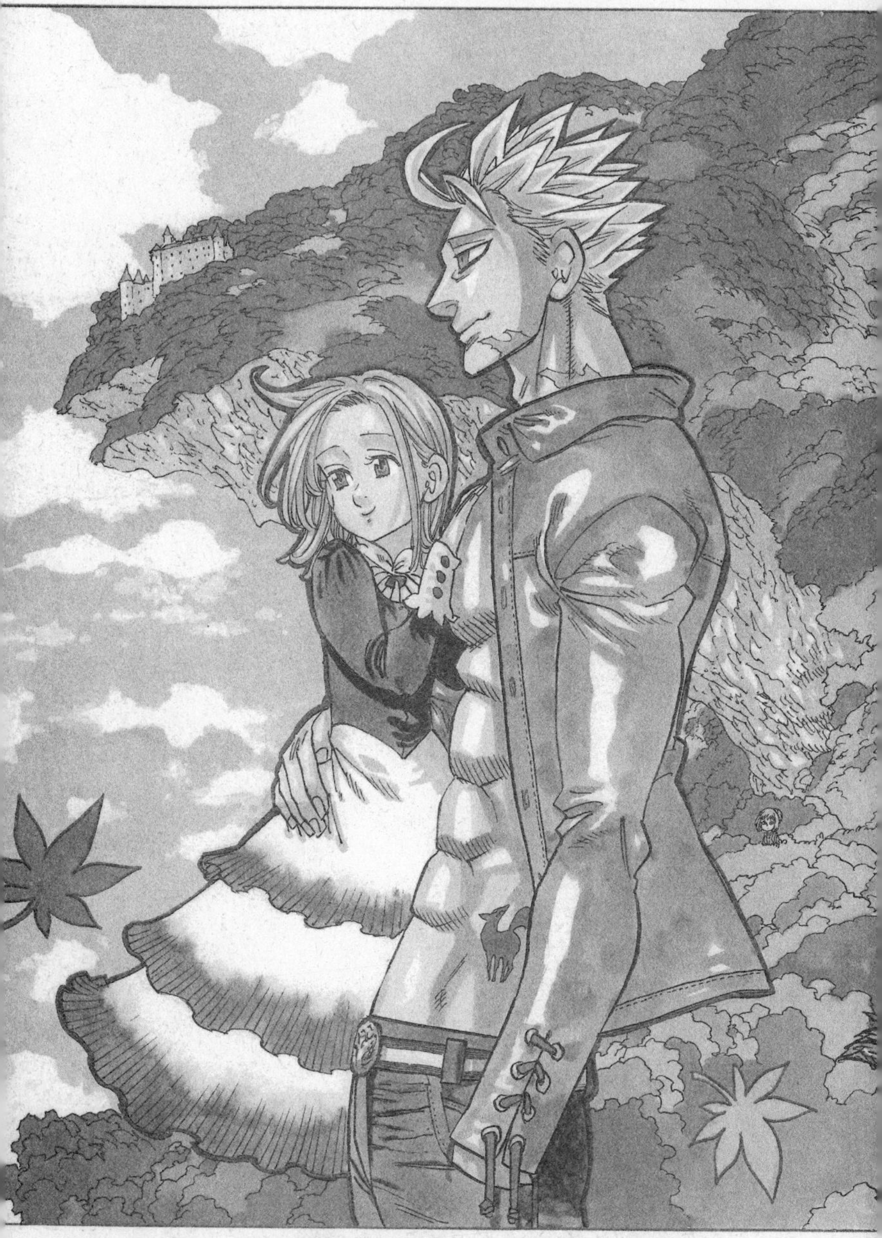

Chapter 144 - That Man Walks the Way of Greed

# Bonus Story - That Day Long Ago

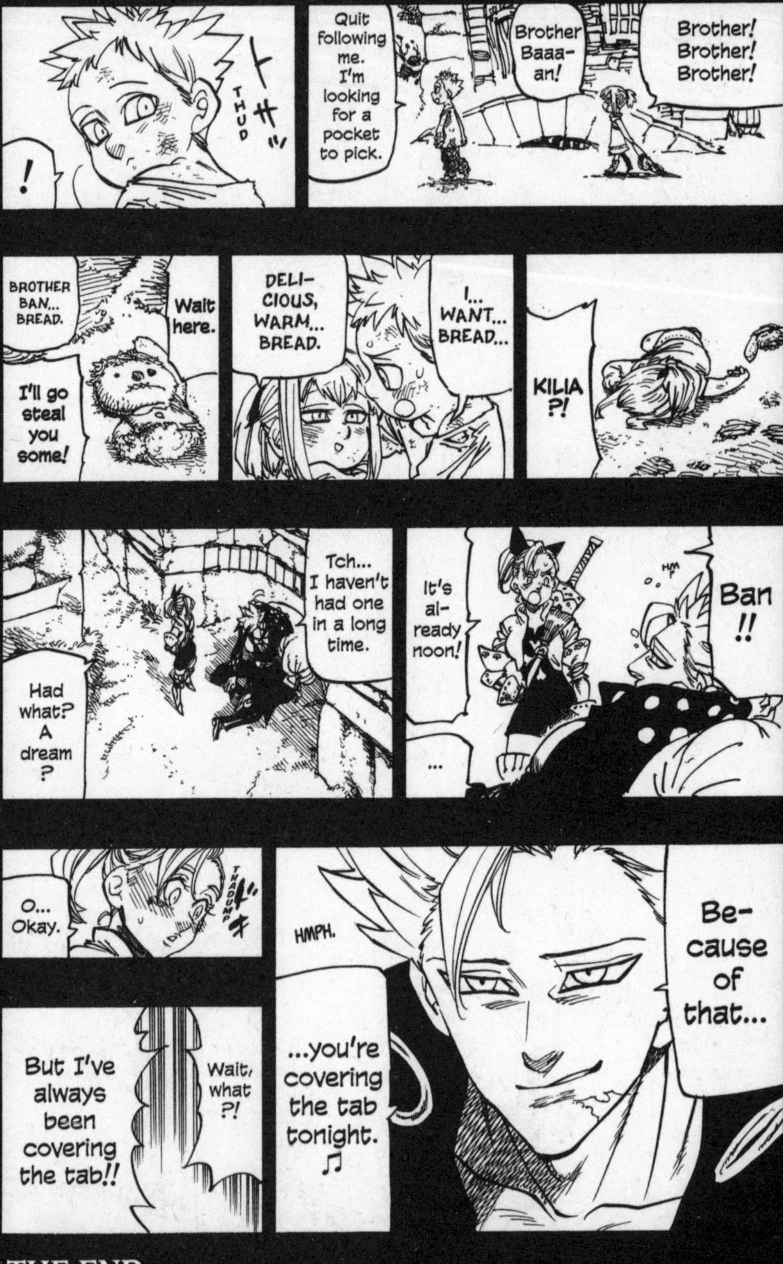
Brother! Brother! Brother!
Brother Baaa-an!
Quit following me. I'm looking for a pocket to pick.
THUD
!
KILIA?!
I... WANT... BREAD...
DELICIOUS, WARM... BREAD.
BROTHER BAN... BREAD.
Wait here.
I'll go steal you some!
Ban!!
HM?
It's already noon!
...
Tch... I haven't had one in a long time.
Had what? A dream?
Because of that...
HMPH.
...you're covering the tab tonight. ♫
O... Okay.
THADUMP
Wait, what?!
But I've always been covering the tab!!

THE END

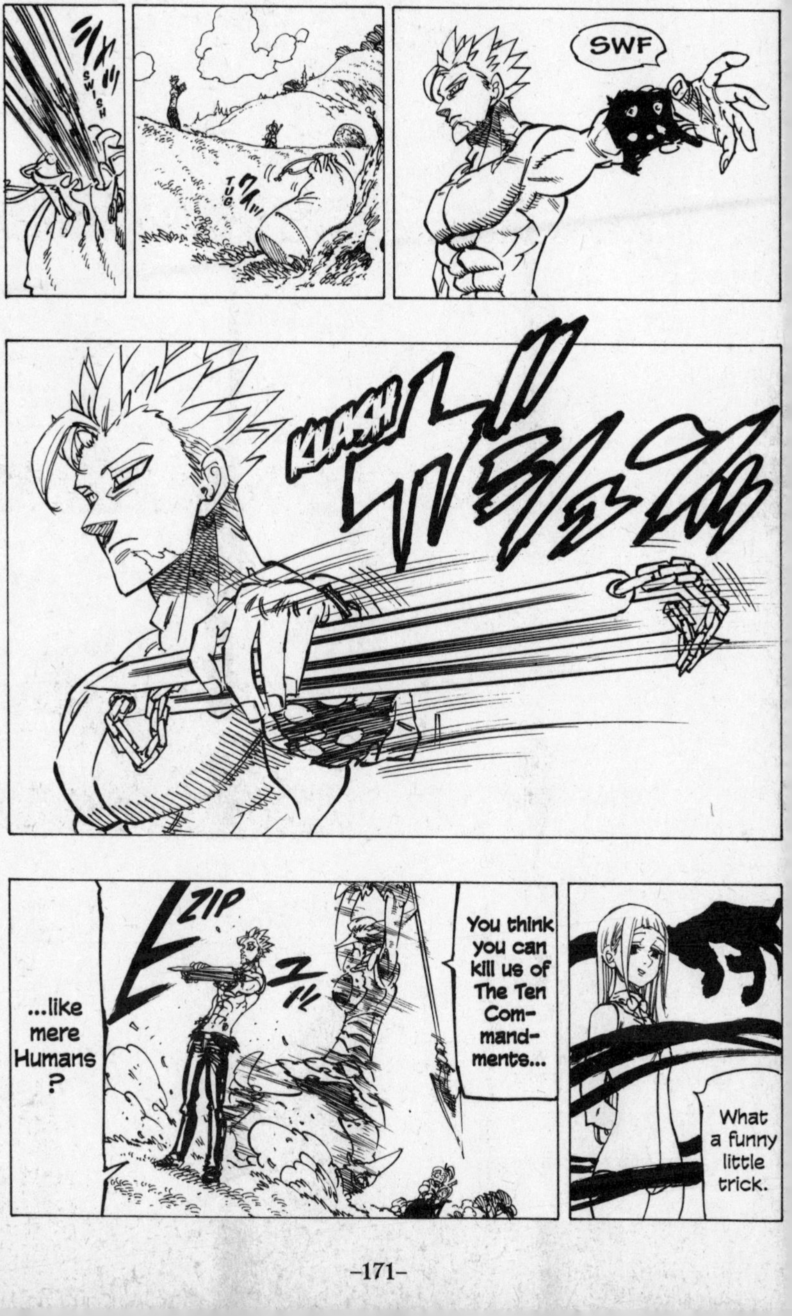
SWF
TUG
SWISH
KLASH
What a funny little trick.
You think you can kill us of The Ten Commandments...
ZIP
...like mere Humans?

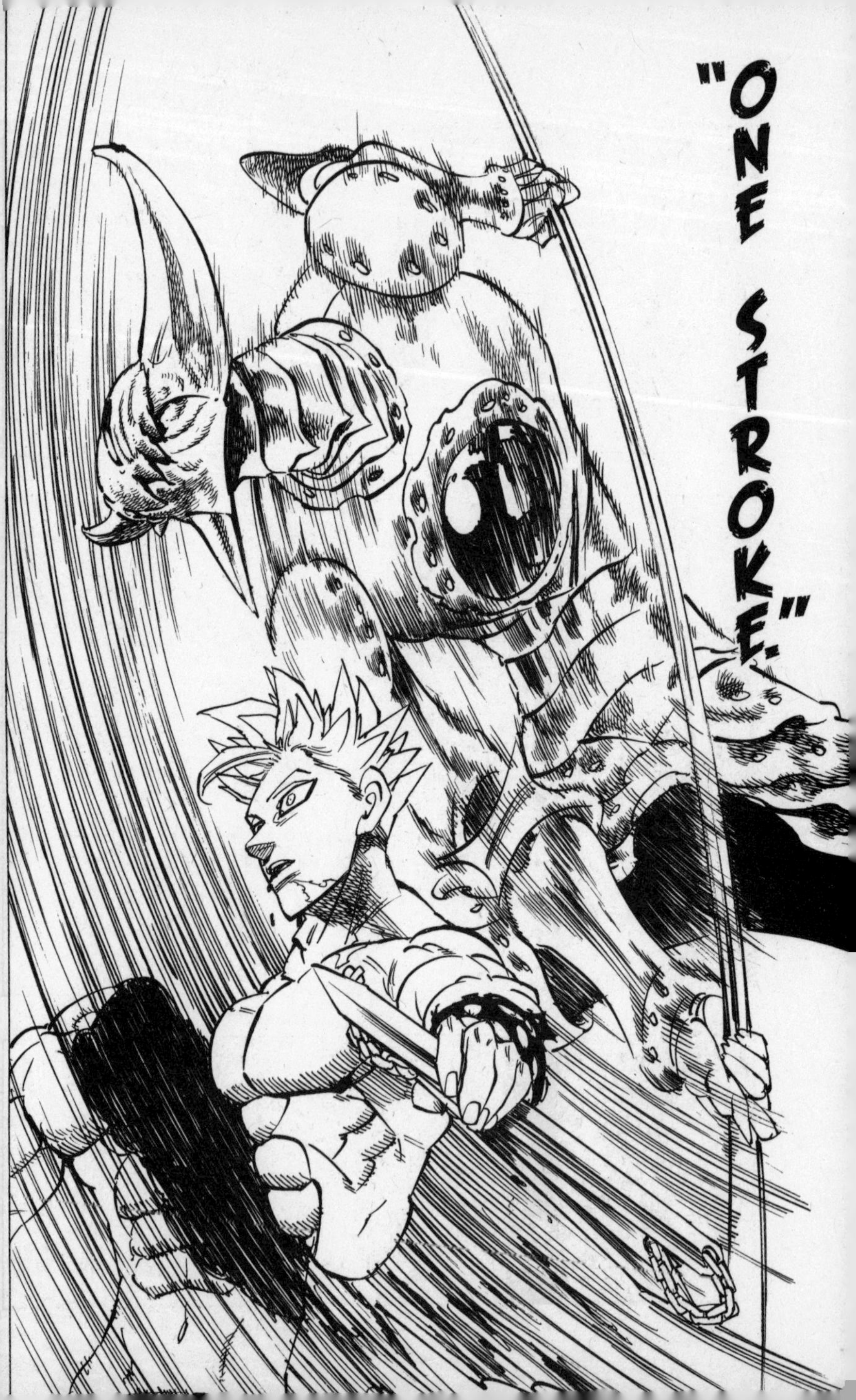
"ONE STROKE"

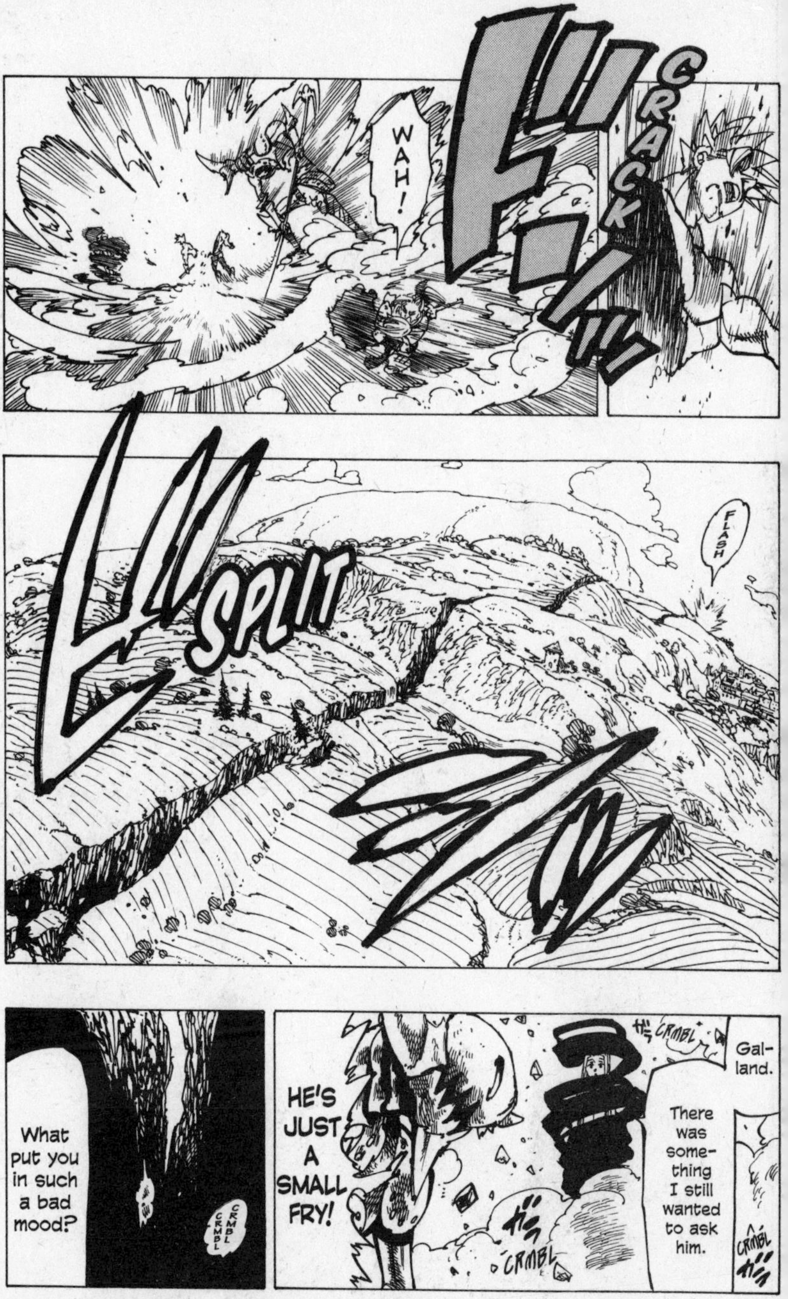
CRACK
WAH!
FLASH
SPLIT
Galland.
There was something I still wanted to ask him.
CRMBL
CRMBL
HE'S JUST A SMALL FRY!
CRMBL
What put you in such a bad mood?
CRMBL CRMBL

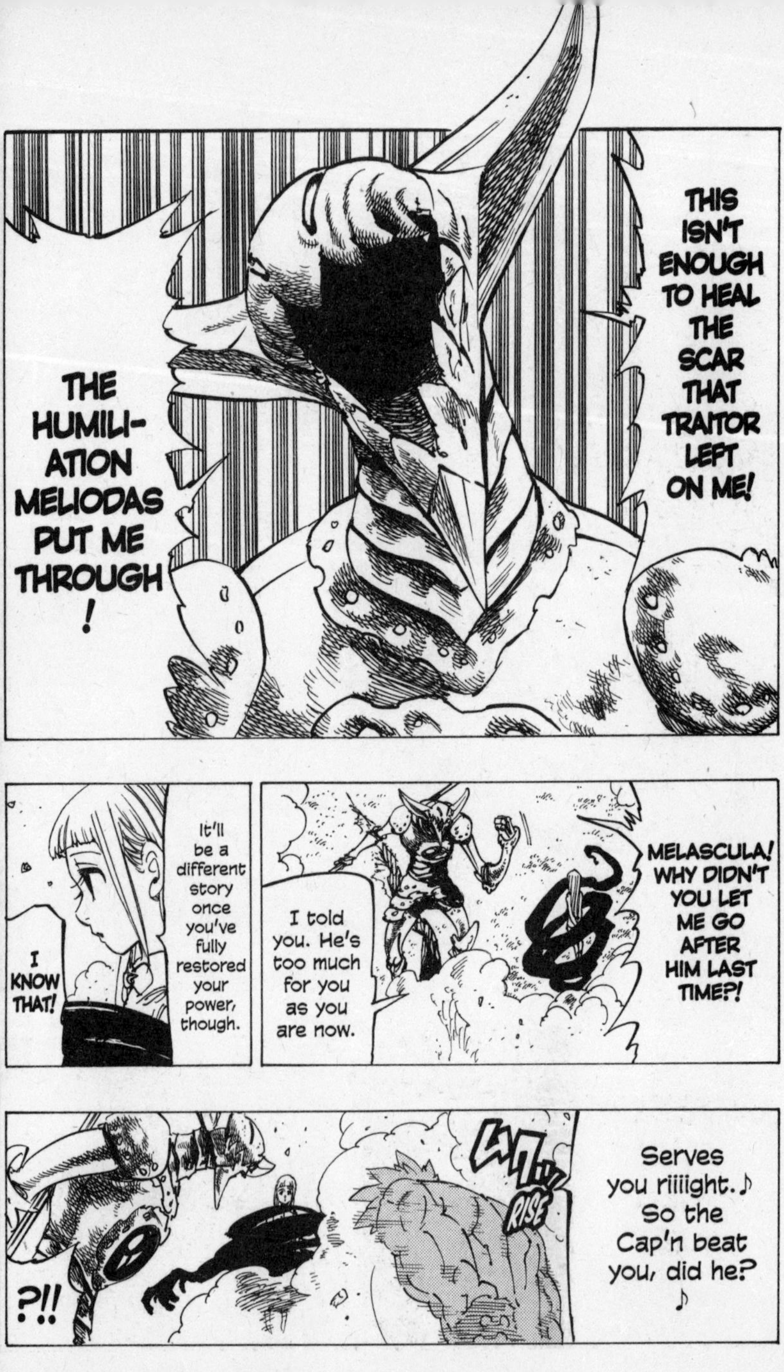
THIS ISN'T ENOUGH TO HEAL THE SCAR THAT TRAITOR LEFT ON ME!
THE HUMILIATION MELIODAS PUT ME THROUGH!
MELASCULA! WHY DIDN'T YOU LET ME GO AFTER HIM LAST TIME?!
I told you. He's too much for you as you are now.
It'll be a different story once you've fully restored your power, though.
I KNOW THAT!
Serves you riiiight.♪ So the Cap'n beat you, did he? ♪
RISE
?!!

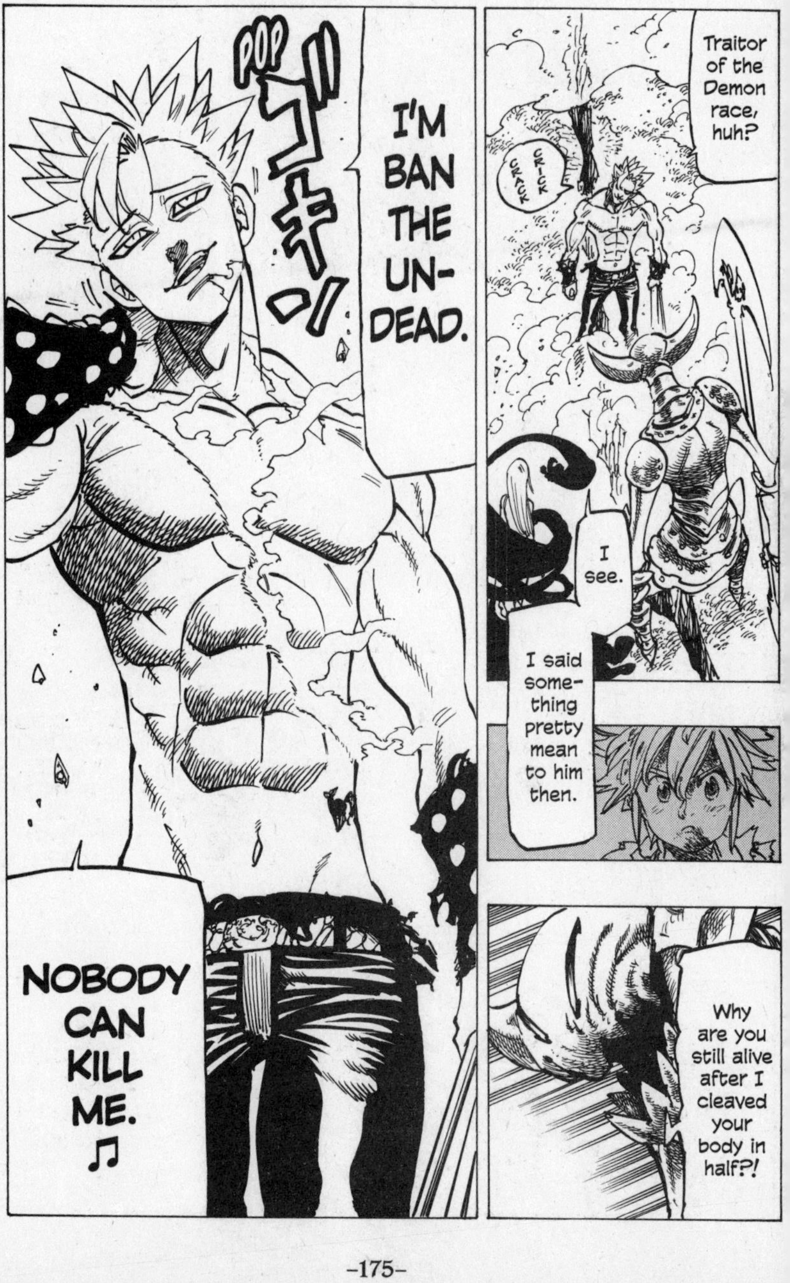
Traitor of the Demon race, huh?
CRICK CRACK
I see.
I said something pretty mean to him then.
Why are you still alive after I cleaved your body in half?!
POP
ゴキッ
I'M BAN THE UN-DEAD.
NOBODY CAN KILL ME. ♫

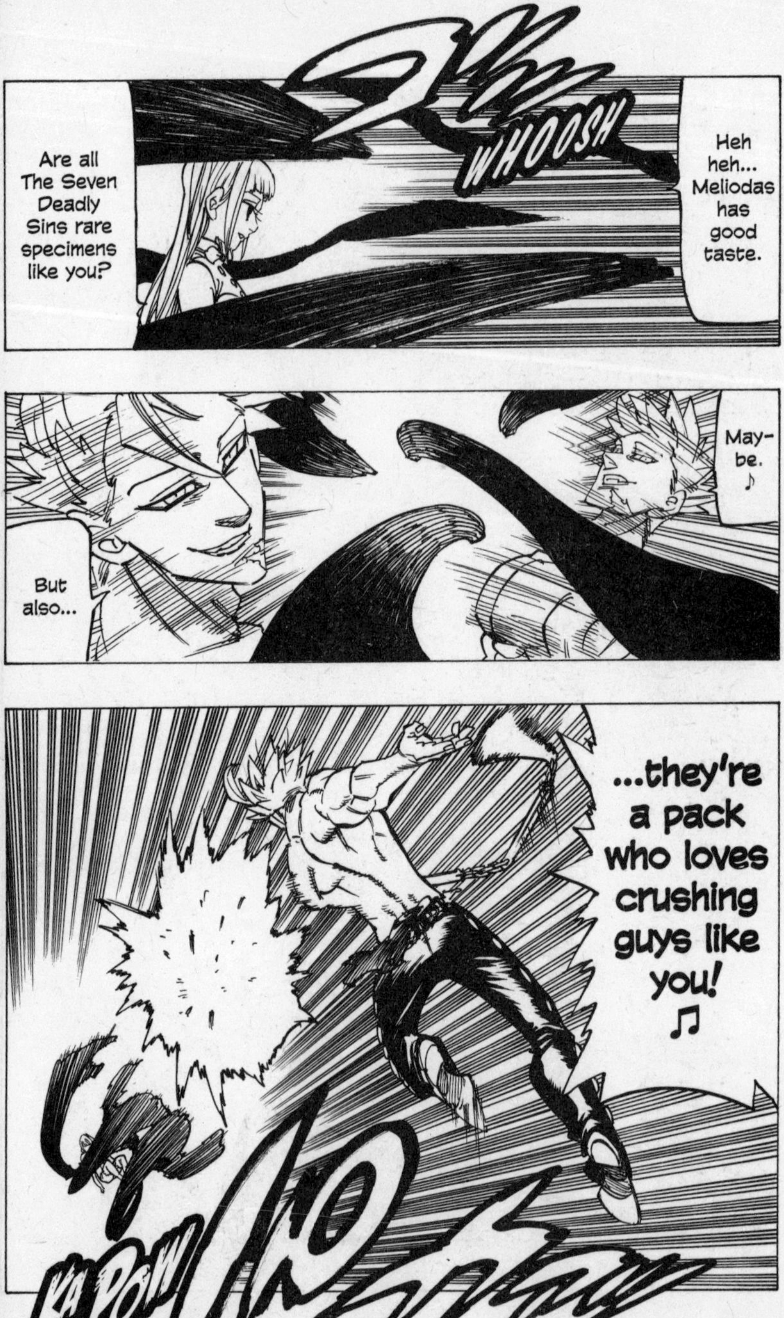
Heh heh... Meliodas has good taste.
WHOOSH
Are all The Seven Deadly Sins rare specimens like you?
May-be. ♪
But also...
...they're a pack who loves crushing guys like you! ♫
KA POW

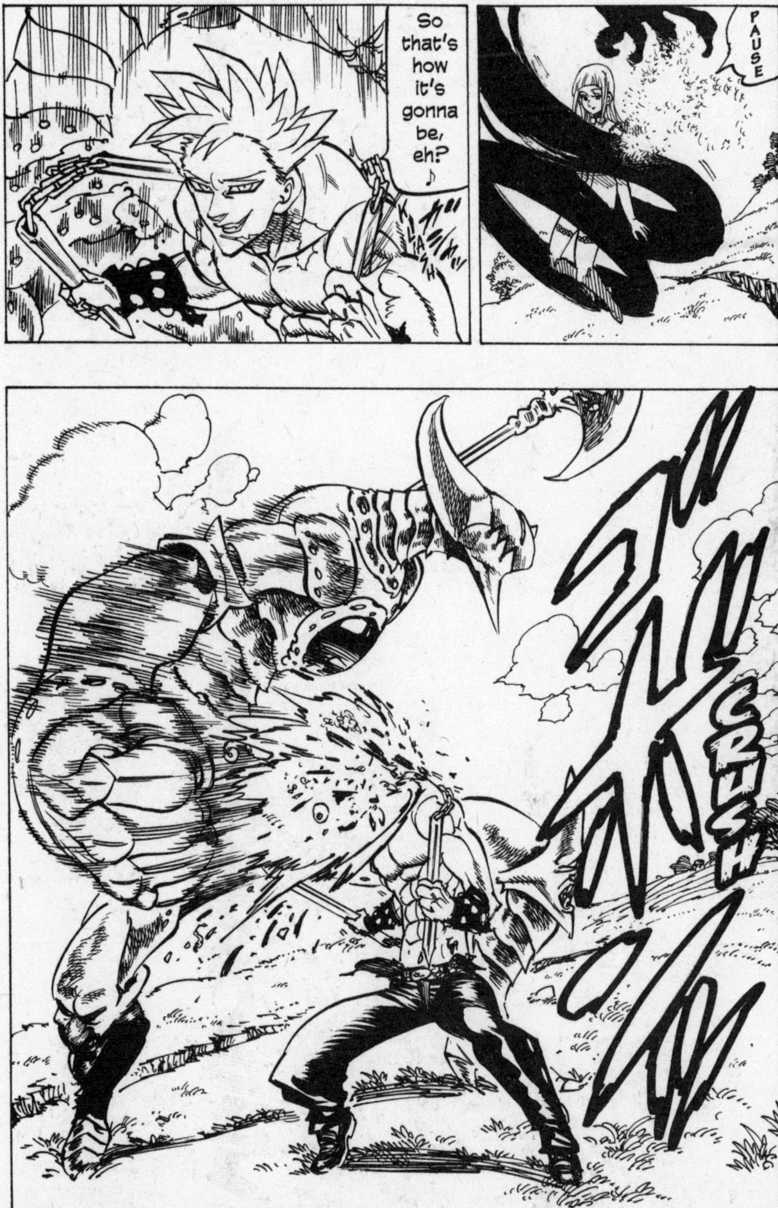
PAUSE
So that's how it's gonna be, eh? ♪
KLASH
CRUSH

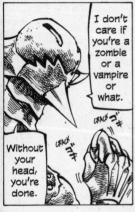

BOOM
THUD
ROLL
WHUMP
I don't care if you're a zombie or a vampire or what.
CRACK
CRACK
Without your head, you're done.
RISE
WHAT?!
I've never seen a human come back to life after having his head destroyed! Is that his magic power?!
Magic vanishes the moment its wielder perishes. In other words, this is just a characteristic of his very makeup.
SSSHHH
He must be harboring another magic power.

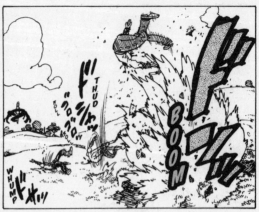

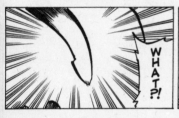

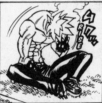

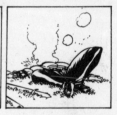

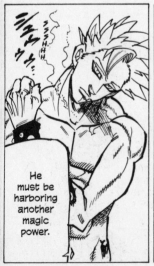

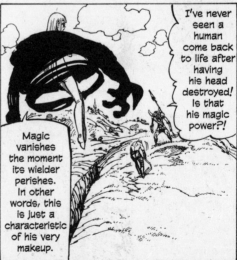

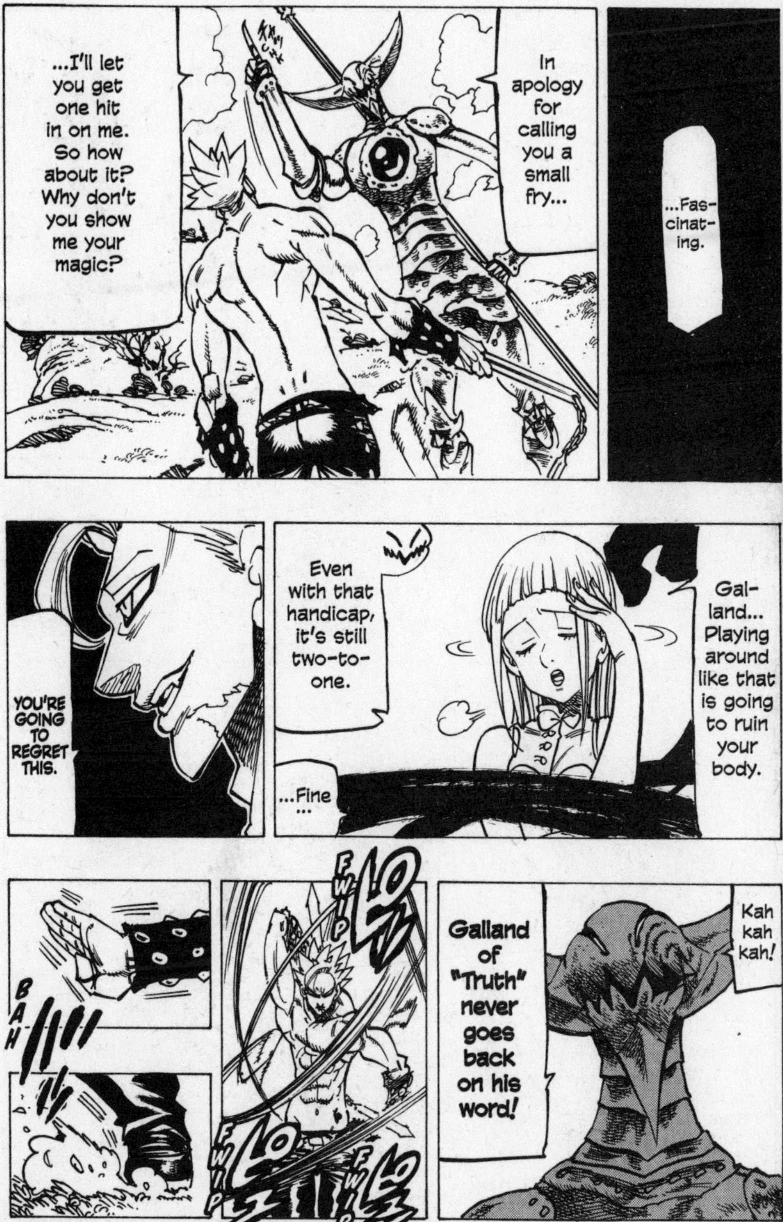
...Fascinating.
In apology for calling you a small fry...
...I'll let you get one hit in on me. So how about it? Why don't you show me your magic?
Galland... Playing around like that is going to ruin your body.
Even with that handicap, it's still two-to-one.
...Fine...
YOU'RE GOING TO REGRET THIS.
Kah kah kah!
Galland of "Truth" never goes back on his word!
FWIP
FWIP
FWIP
BAH

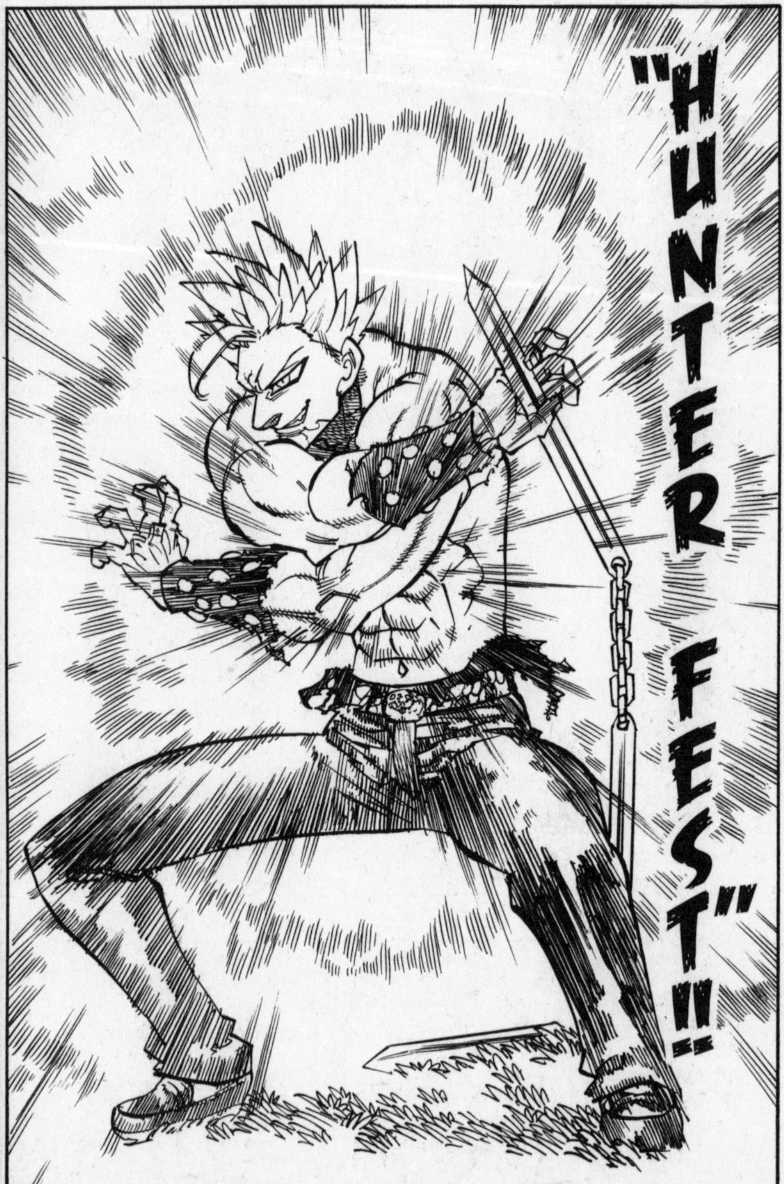
"HUNTER FEST"!!

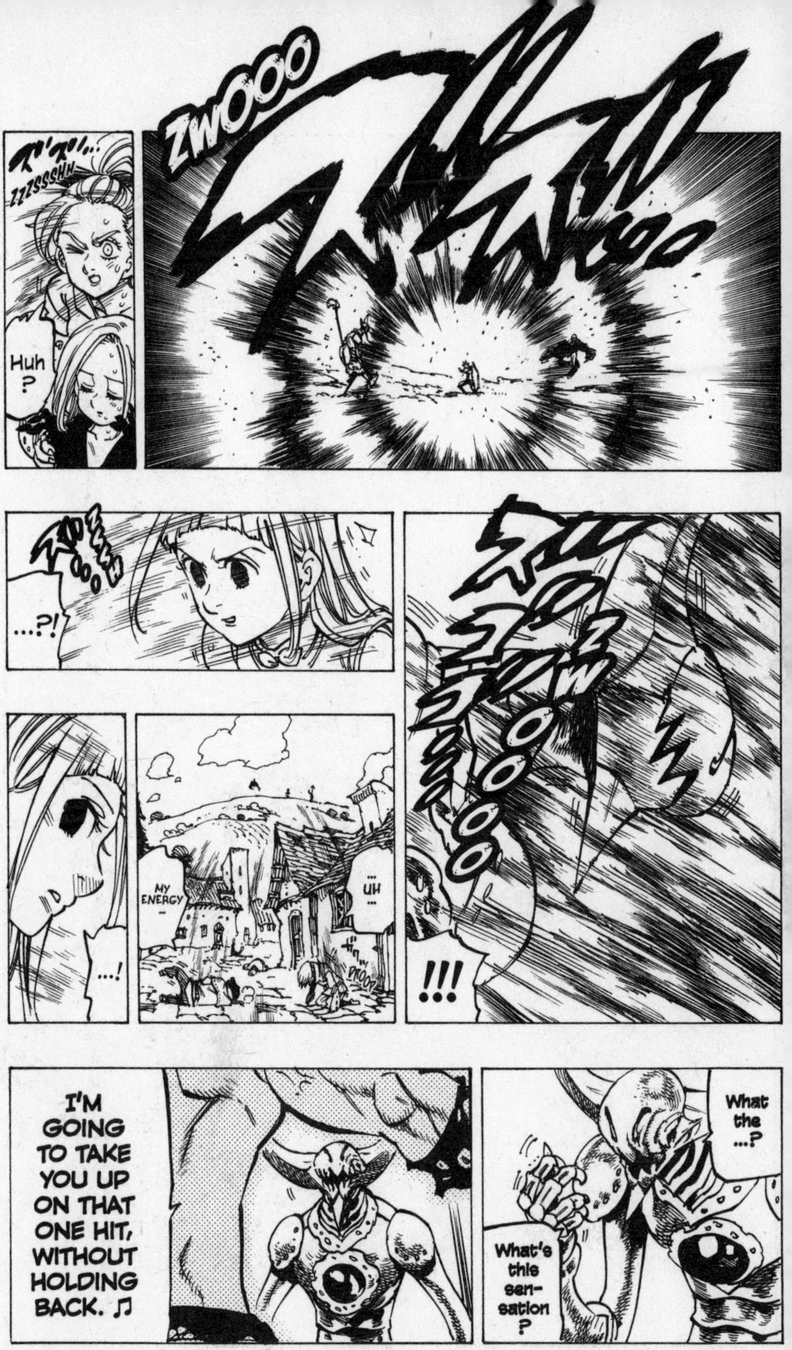
ZWOOO
ZZZSSSHH
Huh ?
!!!
...?!
...UH...
MY ENERGY...
DROOP
...!
What the ...?
What's this sen-sation ?
I'M GOING TO TAKE YOU UP ON THAT ONE HIT, WITHOUT HOLDING BACK. ♫

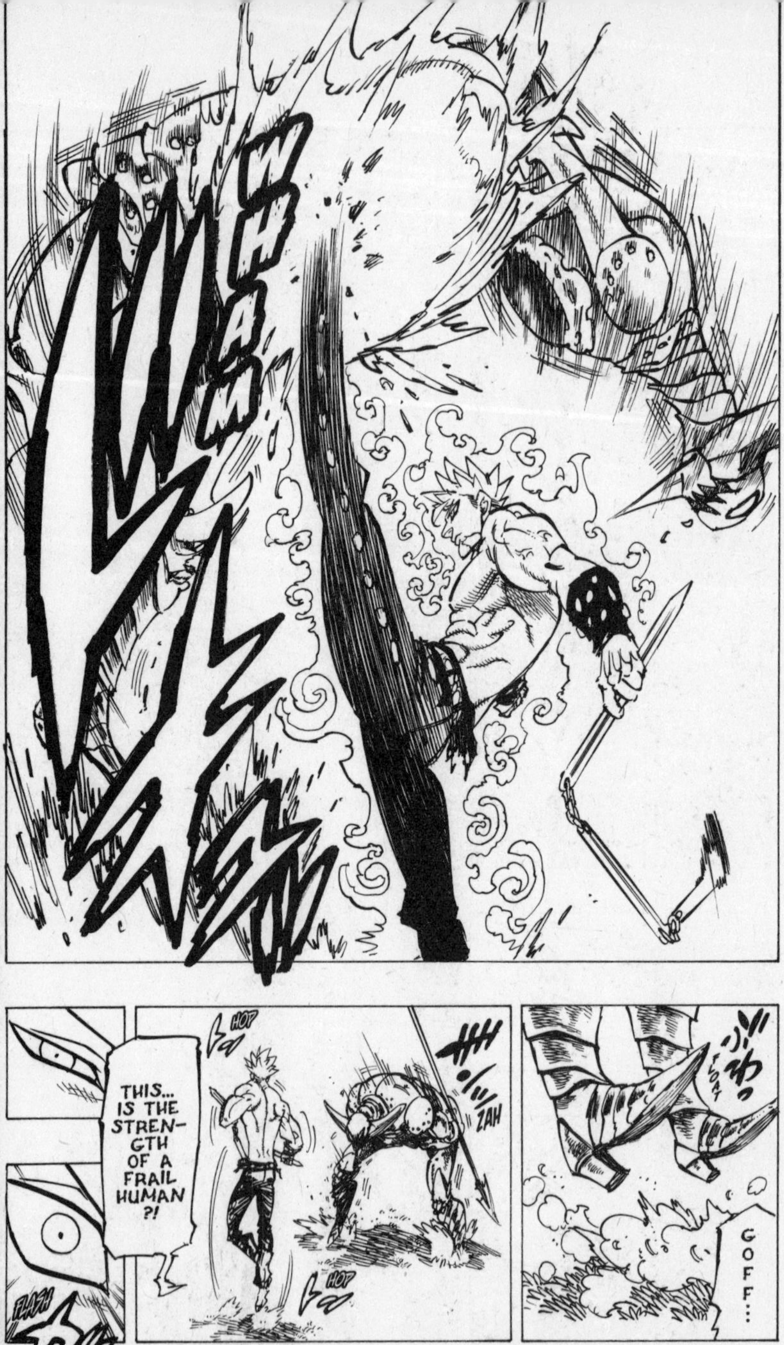
WHAAM
ふわっ
FLOAT
GOFF...
HOP
ZAH
HOP
THIS... IS THE STRENGTH OF A FRAIL HUMAN?!
FLASH

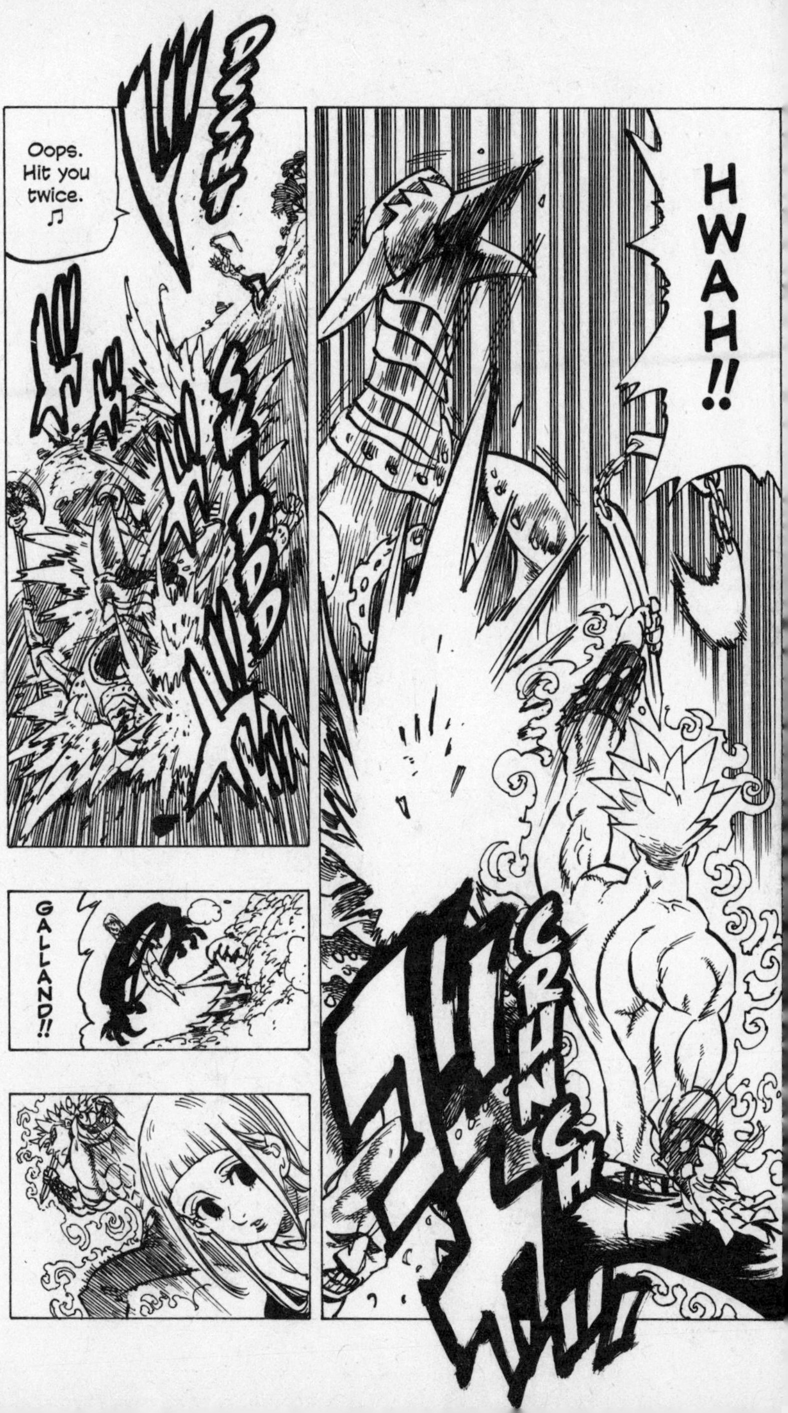
HWAH!!
CRUNCH
Oops. Hit you twice. ♫
GALLAND!!

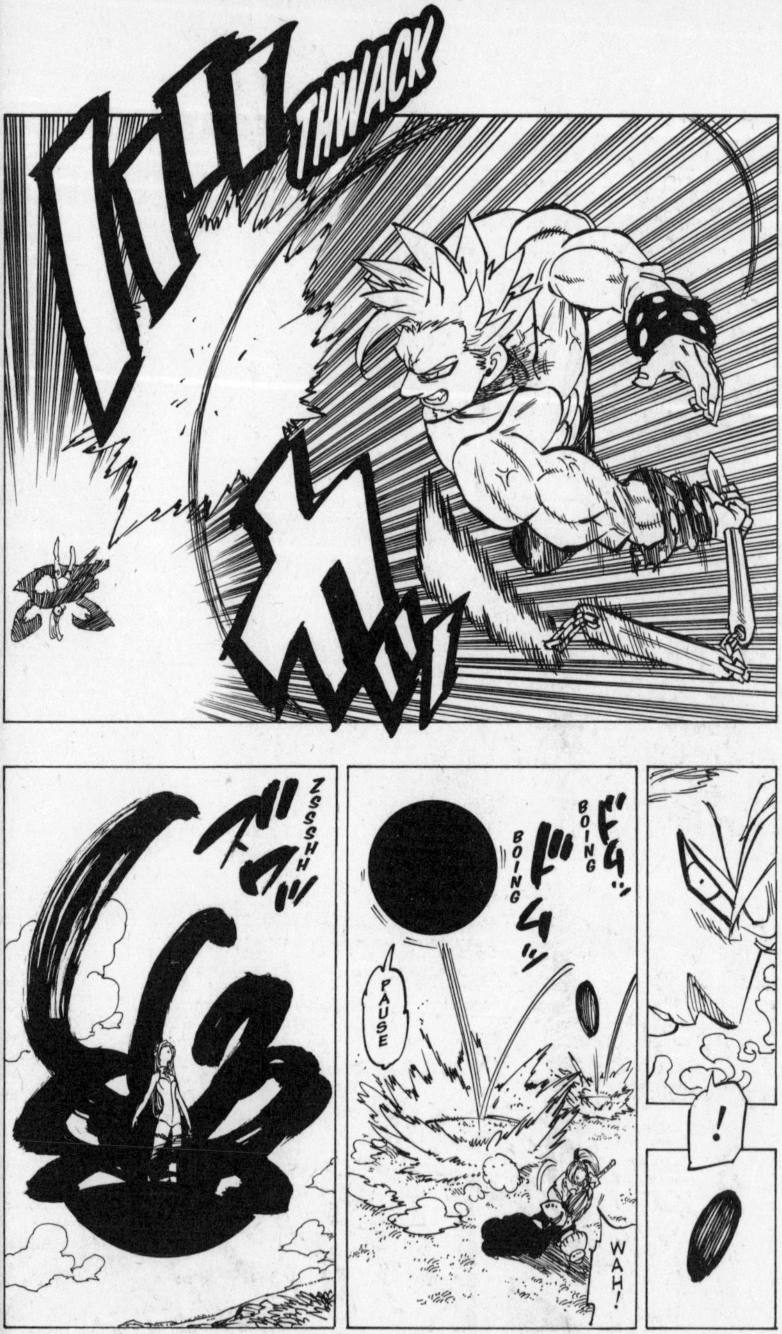
THWACK
!
BOING
BOING
PAUSE
WAH!
ZSSHH

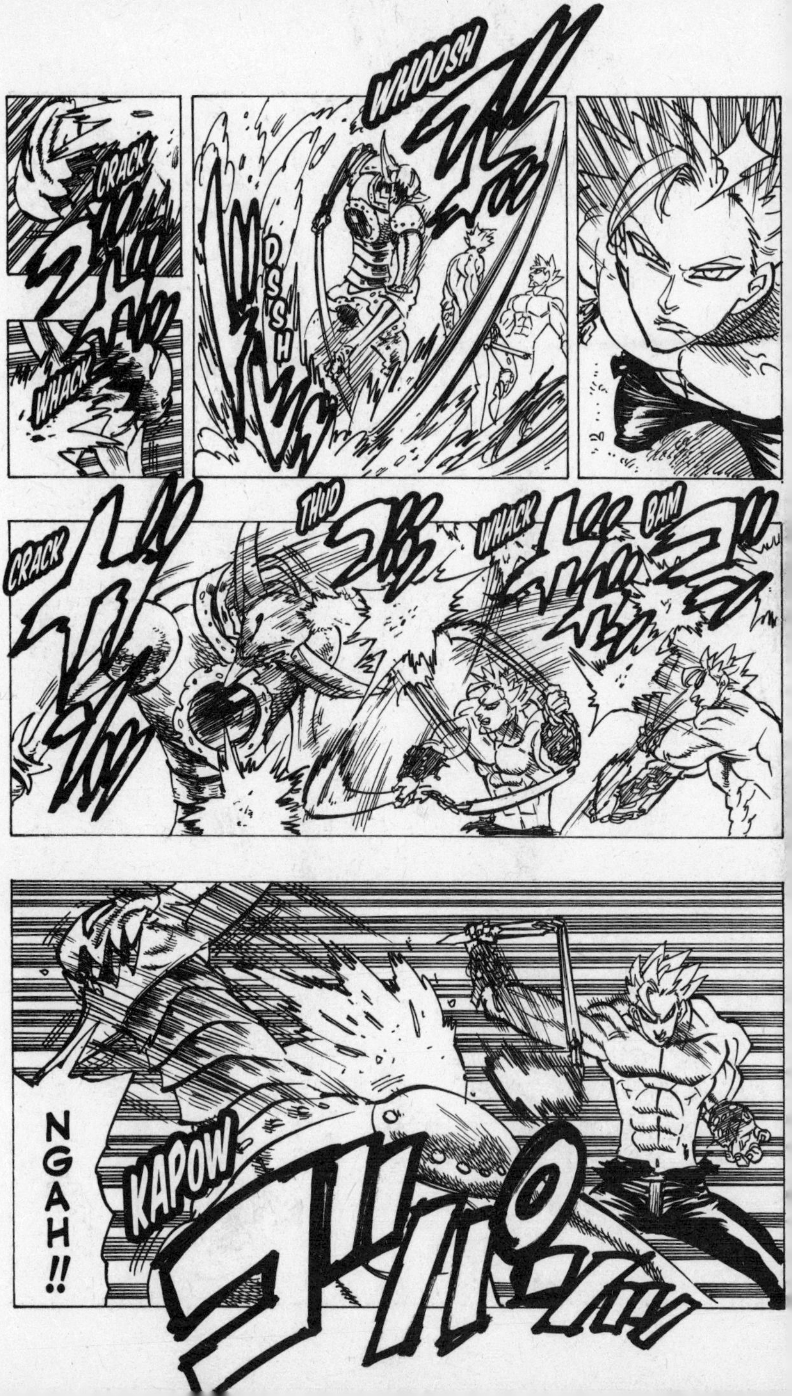
WHOOSH
DSSH
CRACK
WHACK
BAM
WHACK
THUD
CRACK
KAPOW
NGAH!!

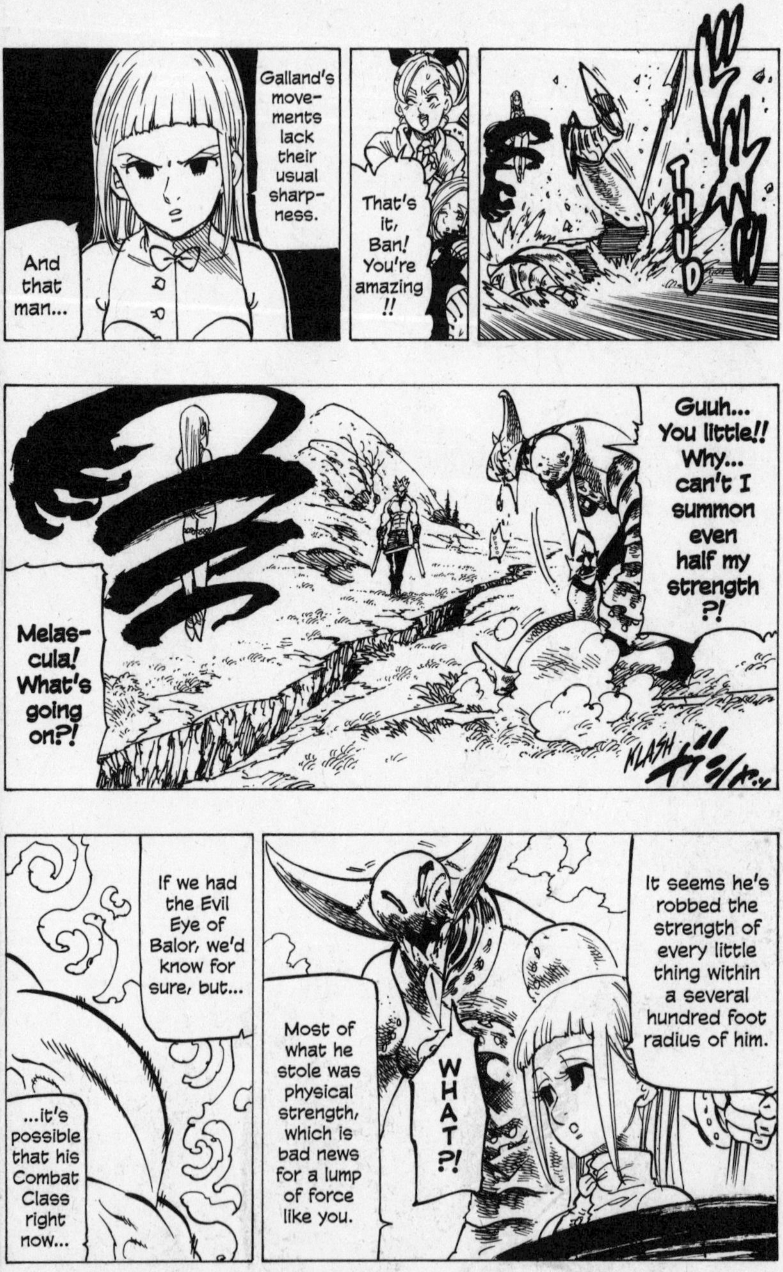
THUD
That's it, Ban! You're amazing!!
Galland's movements lack their usual sharpness.
And that man...
Guuh... You little!! Why... can't I summon even half my strength?!
KLASH
Melascula! What's going on?!
It seems he's robbed the strength of every little thing within a several hundred foot radius of him.
WHAT?!
Most of what he stole was physical strength, which is bad news for a lump of force like you.
If we had the Evil Eye of Balor, we'd know for sure, but...
...it's possible that his Combat Class right now...

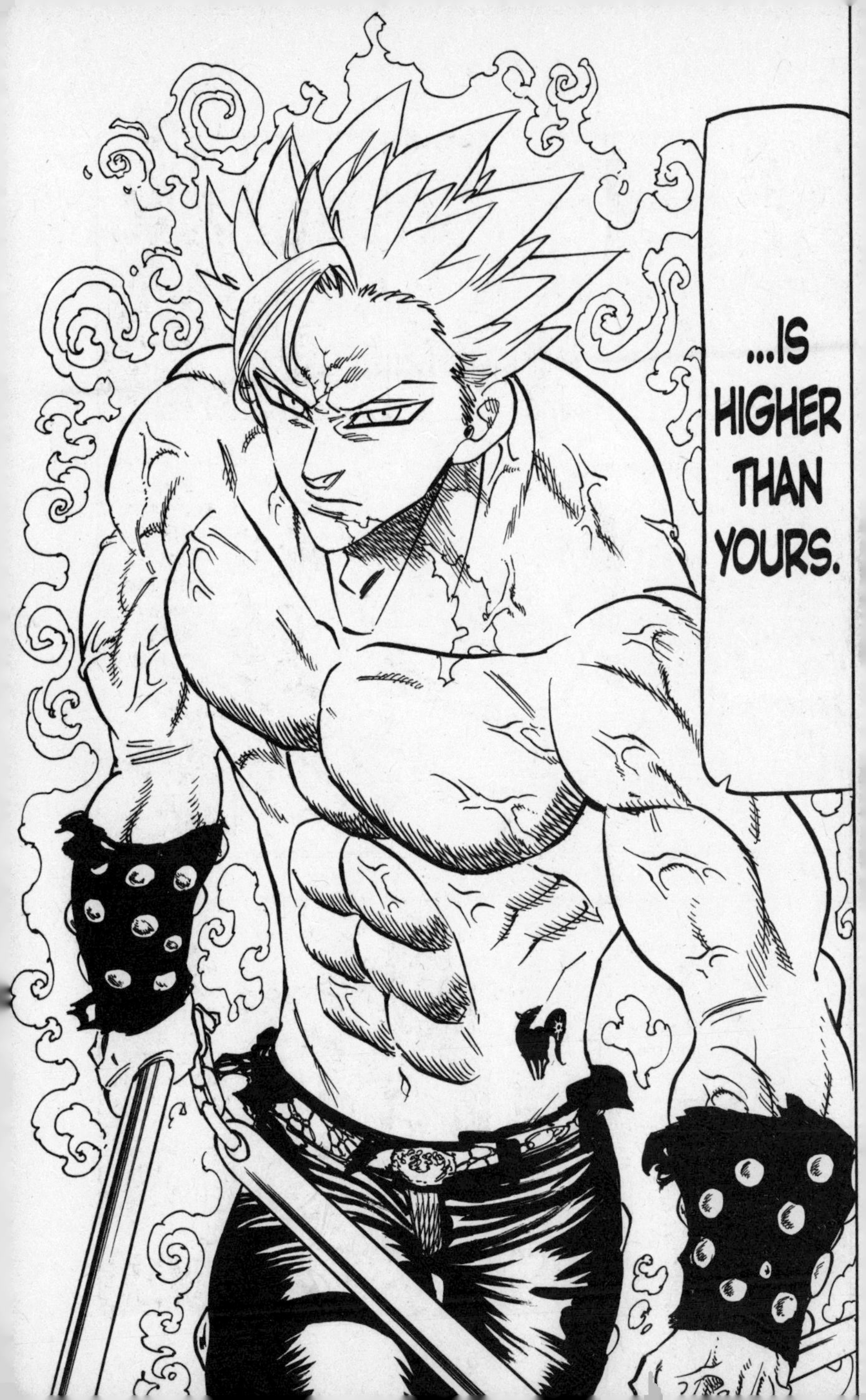
...IS HIGHER THAN YOURS.

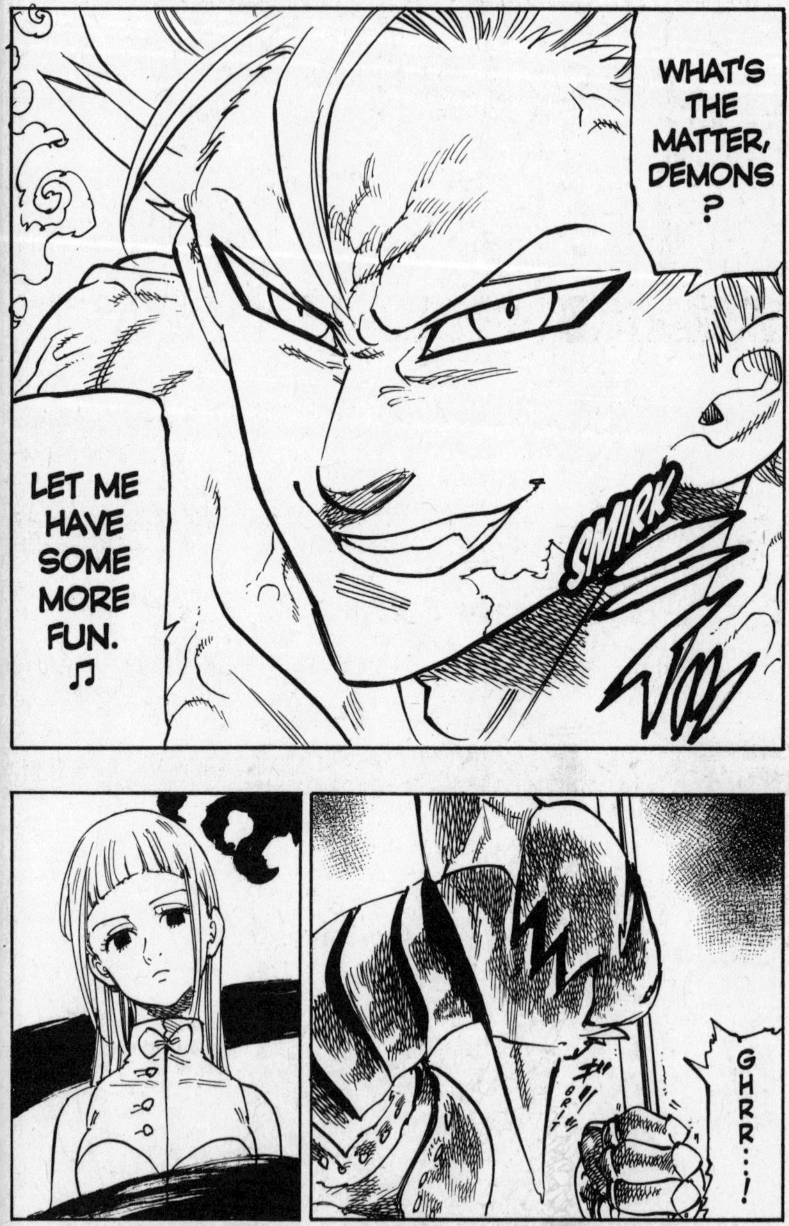
WHAT'S THE MATTER, DEMONS?
SMIRK
LET ME HAVE SOME MORE FUN. ♫
GRIT
GHRR...!

# Bonus Story - Elaine's Melancholy

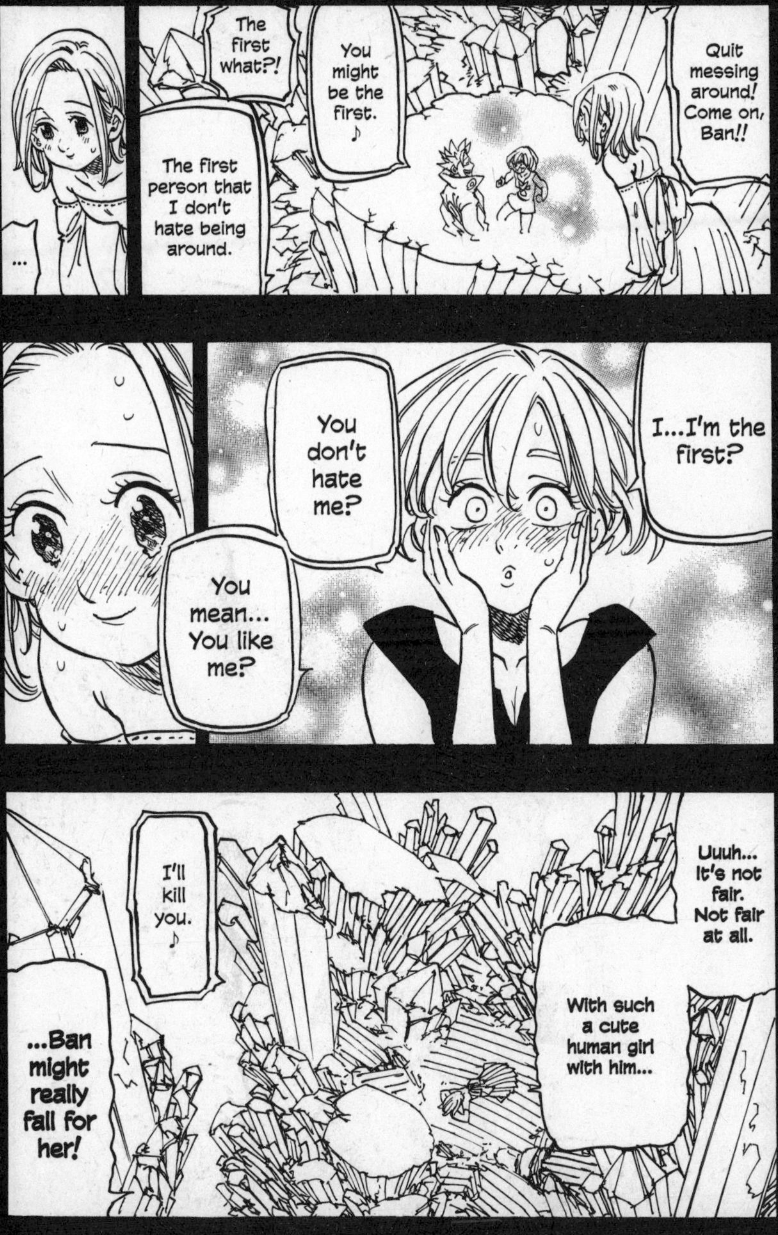

Quit messing around! Come on, Ban!!
You might be the first. ♪
The first what?!
The first person that I don't hate being around.
...
I...I'm the first?
You don't hate me?
You mean... You like me?
Uuuh... It's not fair. Not fair at all.
With such a cute human girl with him...
I'll kill you. ♪
...Ban might really fall for her!


THE END

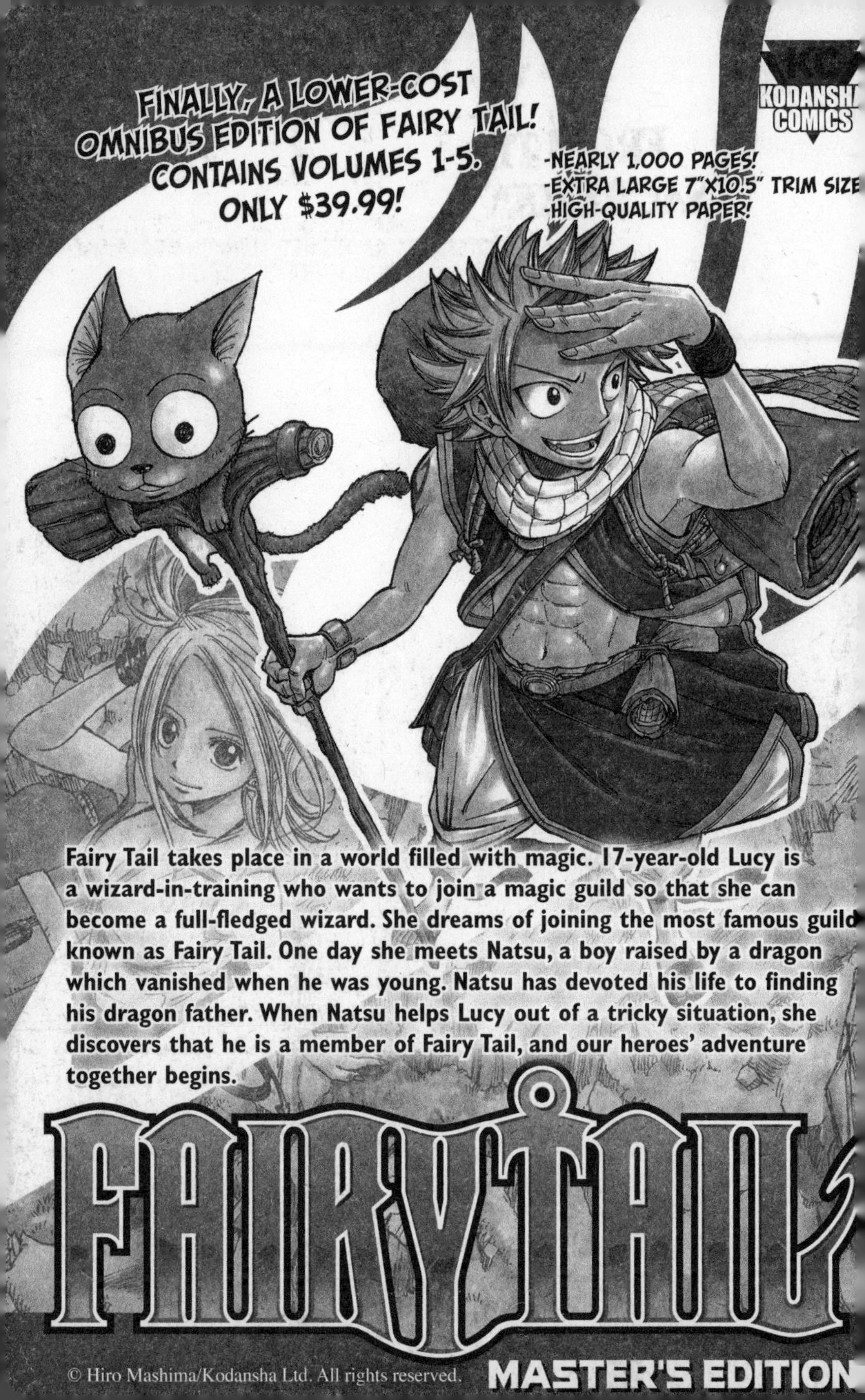
KODANSHA COMICS
FINALLY, A LOWER-COST OMNIBUS EDITION OF FAIRY TAIL! CONTAINS VOLUMES 1-5. ONLY $39.99!
-NEARLY 1,000 PAGES!
-EXTRA LARGE 7"X10.5" TRIM SIZE
-HIGH-QUALITY PAPER!
Fairy Tail takes place in a world filled with magic. 17-year-old Lucy is a wizard-in-training who wants to join a magic guild so that she can become a full-fledged wizard. She dreams of joining the most famous guild known as Fairy Tail. One day she meets Natsu, a boy raised by a dragon which vanished when he was young. Natsu has devoted his life to finding his dragon father. When Natsu helps Lucy out of a tricky situation, she discovers that he is a member of Fairy Tail, and our heroes' adventure together begins.
FAIRY TAIL
© Hiro Mashima/Kodansha Ltd. All rights reserved.
MASTER'S EDITION

*The Seven Deadly Sins* volume 18 is a work of fiction. Names, characters, places, and incidents are the products of the author's imagination or are used fictitiously. Any resemblance to actual events, locales, or persons, living or dead, is entirely coincidental.

A Kodansha Comics Trade Paperback Original.



Published in the United States by Kodansha Comics, an imprint of Kodansha USA Publishing, LLC, New York.

Publication rights for this English edition arranged through Kodansha Ltd., Tokyo.

First published in Japan in 2015 by Kodansha Ltd., Tokyo.

ISBN 978-1-63236-348-0

Printed in the United States of America.

www.kodanshacomics.com

9 8 7 6 5 4 3 2 1

Translation: Christine Dashiell
Lettering: James Dashiell
Editing: Lauren Scanlan
Kodansha Comics edition cover design: Phil Balsman